The Practical Writer's Guide

with Additional Readings

Susan X Day
University of Illinois at Urbana-Champaign

Elizabeth McMahan
Illinois State University

Robert Funk
Eastern Illinois University

Allyn and Bacon
Boston London Toronto Sydney Tokyo Singapore

Vice President: Eben Ludlow
Editorial Assistant: Liz Egan
Marketing Director: Jeff Lasser
Marketing Manager: Lisa Kimball
Editorial-Production Administrator: Annette Joseph
Editorial-Production Service: Saxon House Productions
Text Designer: Denise Hoffman
Composition Buyer: Linda Cox
Manufacturing Buyer: Megan Cochran
Cover Administrator: Linda Knowles
Cover Designer: Studio Nine

Copyright © 1997 by Allyn & Bacon
A Viacom Company
160 Gould Street
Needham Heights, MA 02194

Parts One, Two, and Three, and Appendixes on Special Skills are also published
under the title *The Practical Writer's Guide,* by Susan X Day, Elizabeth McMahan,
and Robert Funk, copyright © 1997 by Allyn & Bacon.

Library of Congress Cataloging-in-Publication Data

Day, Susan.
    The practical writer's guide with additional readings / Susan
X Day, Elizabeth McMahan, Robert Funk.
        p.   cm.
    Includes bibliographical references and index.
    ISBN 0–205–17389–6
    1. English language—Rhetoric.   2. College readers.   I. McMahan,
Elizabeth.   II. Funk, Robert.   III. Title.
PE1408.D372   1996
808´.0427—dc20   96–1201
                                                                       CIP

Printed in the United States of America
10   9   8   7   6   5   4   3   2   1   01   00   99   98   97   96

PERMISSION ACKNOWLEDGMENTS:
Page 46. Ana Maria Corona. "Coming to America, to Clean," from *Harper's Magazine,* April 1993,
pp. 33–34.
Page 59. Andy Rathbone. "Quitting, Exiting, and Returning to DOS," from *Windows for Dummies,* p. 67.
Copyright © 1992 by IDG Books Worldwide, Inc., Foster City, CA.

Permission acknowledgments continue on page 545, which constitutes a continuation of the copyright page.

Dedication

With warm appreciation to Eben Ludlow,
whose wit and charm kept us happily on track.

Contents in Brief

Detailed Contents

Part Three

A Handbook for Improving Your Writing   227

Chapter 14   An A to Z Guide to Revising and Editing   **314**

Preface

This is an all-in-one text designed to teach writing in freshman composition classes. We aim to help students gain the verbal and critical thinking skills that will make them eligible for good positions following graduation. These days prospective employees who can express themselves clearly and correctly are highly valued, even sought after, by employers.

The Practical Writer's Guide with Additional Readings is intended not only for college-age students but also for older, nontraditional, returning students. We expect our readers to represent diverse cultures and various levels of academic ability. We have tried in every way possible to make our explanations nonthreatening, easily understandable, and interesting to read. We have written in the same plain, clear, and precise language that we teach others to use.

We emphasize the process approach to writing but do not lose sight of the hard fact that writers are judged by the product they turn out. We believe that clarity is necessary and correctness counts.

Since research shows that students can learn a great deal from each other, our assignments regularly contain suggestions for group work. This experience of being involved in group dynamics also serves as practical preparation for the workplace where a large portion of the writing gets done in groups and in consultation with others.

Part One: Understanding the Process

The first section of the rhetoric explains the writing process, admitting its complexities but clarifying it through step by step instructions. The emphasis here is on audience, thesis, and purpose.

Part Two: Developing and Organizing Your Writing

Because we are convinced that good organization is essential to good writing, we provide more help to students in learning this skill than is available in other rhetorics and handbooks. Each chapter in this section covers in detail the process of composing an essay in one of seven different rhetorical patterns. Each chapter guides students through the following stages:

- thinking critically about the pattern;
- considering purpose and audience;
- organizing the material;
- writing the introduction;
- writing the conclusion;
- achieving coherence; and
- revising using a handy checklist.

The specific critical thinking abilities needed for each type of rhetorical pattern and each organizational skill are put into practice in the writing assignments. Three sample essays in each chapter (two by students, one by a professional author) demonstrate how writers employ each organizational strategy. The student essays, written by our returning adult students, are authentic in content and competence.

Part Three: A Writer's Handbook

A concise yet complete handbook provides guidance for improving drafts and achieving correctness. We include chapters on writing paragraphs, improving sentences, choosing words wisely, as well as a brief review of grammar. The handbook also includes "An A to Z Guide to Revising and Editing," which makes finding the advice for rewriting as easy as using a dictionary; and a "Glossary of Usage," which supplies current information on matters of diction.

Appendixes on Special Skills

This section offers valuable advice not always found in freshman composition texts but essential, we think, in enabling many students to succeed. It includes:

- Appendix A—Writing with a Word Processor
- Appendix B—Studying in College
- Appendix C—Writing to Find a Job

Part Four: Additional Readings

In *The Practical Writer's Guide with Additional Readings,* Part Four provides 26 essays for further study, arranged according to the rhetorical patterns covered in Chapters 3 through 8. These readings include headnotes but are offered without apparatus to increase their flexibility. They provide added reading practice for students who need it; they can also be used to stimulate class discussion and to prompt ideas for writing.

Thus, the material in this text is geared toward helping students to acquire the thinking and writing skills necessary to complete their college education and then to qualify for and succeed in a desirable job. In addition to this practical intent, we also hope to help students enrich their lives through the pleasure and the confidence that come from gaining facility with language.

Acknowledgments

Many people have helped us in preparing this text. We are indebted to Jean Brunsdale of the Illinois State University library, who graciously supplied information for our chapter on researched writing. We owe major thanks to the excellent editors and staff at Allyn and Bacon, including our editor, Eben Ludlow, editorial assistant Liz Egan, and senior production administrator Annette Joseph. Our thanks also go to Sydney Baily-Gould of Saxon House Productions, who saw our book through the production process.

We would also like to acknowledge the following reviewers: William B. Lalicker, West Chester University of Pennsylvania; Bill H. Lamb, Johnson County Community College; Ann C. (Tina) McGaughey, Austin Community College; and Carol Wershoven, Palm Beach Community College.

Susan X Day

Elizabeth McMahan

Robert Funk

Part One

Writing Well: Understanding the Process

The first two chapters of this book examine how writers go about writing—from finding a topic through writing a draft, revising and reworking it, and getting it ready to turn over to a reader. In Chapter 1, we ask you to think about what makes for good writing and to realize how important it is to understand the purpose of and the audience for any writing assignment. We also encourage you to examine your current writing habits and attitudes in preparation for improving and developing your skills as a writer. Chapter 2 gives you a guided tour through the important stages of writing—commonly called the *writing process*—and presents you with strategies to help you move more efficiently and effectively through this process.

1

Chapter One

Writing for Your Readers

This book is your guide to communicating effectively through standard written American English. The ability to write well is one of the most useful skills you can develop, one that is highly valued by prospective employers. Columnist William Raspberry notes that "Proper use of the language is routinely accepted as a mark of intelligence, the first basis on which we are judged by those whose judgments matter." You will increase your chances of a successful career if you can express yourself clearly and convincingly in writing.

If you would like to consider a more immediate need, you will have a hard time getting through college if you are not able to write. Take a look at Figure 1.1 to see how important good writing becomes in fulfilling assignments in college courses. You cannot hope to get into law school or medical school without a firm command of standard English. And if you plan to enter engineering, teaching, social work, or any other business or professional calling, you will have to write—memos, letters, reports, recommendations, summaries, directions, analyses. As business consultant Ann Lavine points out, "Recent research shows a strong correlation between writing abilities and promotions. Simply put, the ability to write well is crucial to one's career."

The truth is that being successful includes being able to write. This book will help you learn to write well. We have tried to make the process as painless as possible, but writing is seldom easy because it requires effort. We struggle and sigh and squint and swear; we chew our nails, twiddle our thumbs, furrow our brows, even gnash our teeth—but eventually we write. And you can, too. Writing is a skill that anyone willing to work at it can learn.

FIGURE 1.1

Excerpts from College Writing Assignments (at Illinois State University)

Political Science 105

An "excellent" summary meets all of the criteria for accuracy, comprehensiveness, and balance. It should read smoothly from beginning to end, with appropriate transitions between ideas. The sentence structure should be clear and varied (for ease of reading), without vagueness or ambiguity and free from grammatical errors.

Health and Safety 171

In order to earn credit for this project you must attend the demonstration on fire prevention and submit a one- or two-page report of your observation. Your writing skills will be given special emphasis in the grading of the report.

Communications 110

I cannot stipulate how many pages this paper should be in length. I am more interested in the content, in how you express your ideas, in how seriously you take this project, and I will expect proper punctuation, spelling, grammar, etc.

History 121

Remember: Your paper should be grammatically correct and should contain no spelling errors. Being literate counts in life, and it counts in this class.

What Is Good Writing, Anyway?

What people consider to be good writing today would not necessarily have been admired a hundred years ago, when great stock was put in measured rhythms, stylistic flourishes, and ornamental words. Tastes change in language, just as in dress, though not as frequently or dramatically. Good writing today, especially in the workplace, is plain and straightforward by comparison. People are busy and, unless they're reading for pleasure, need to get precise information quickly. Clear communication is the goal of the writing instruction you will find in this book.

Prewriting: The Thinking Process

The writing process begins long before you put pen to paper (or fingers to keyboard), and it does not end when you have completed the first draft. You will probably work through at least four stages—preparing, drafting, revising, and editing—before you complete your finished product. Do not attempt to rush the process. Your subconscious mind might do some creating for you during the times when you are not actively concentrating on what you intend to write. But start your thinking early enough to give your ideas time to germinate and grow.

In order to get the process going, you need to mull over three matters:

1. *Your purpose:* Why are you writing?
2. *Your readers:* For whom are you writing?
3. *Your topic:* What are you going to write about?

These questions are equally important, and your answer to one will affect your responses to the others. The actual writing process does not occur in an orderly sequence of steps. Writers loop back and forth through the various stages. For instance, you cannot separate purpose, audience, and topic; they are integral parts of the composing process. But in order to discuss these concepts, we need to consider them one by one. (Choosing a Topic is discussed in Chapter 2.)

Determining Your Purpose

Your purpose affects your whole approach to writing: how you begin, whether you state or imply your main idea, what specific details you choose, how you arrange the material, how you conclude, as well as what words you select for each sentence. You must give thought to your purpose as you begin the planning stage.

Ask yourself why you are exerting so much energy on this piece of writing. It may honestly be because your teacher or boss told you to, but that is not a useful answer. Think beyond your immediate goal. Consider the reason that makes the writing worth doing. What do you hope to accomplish?

Your aim may occasionally be self-expression, as in a diary or a journal. More often, however, you will write for other people and for some definite purpose—usually *to inform, to entertain,* or *to persuade.* If, for instance, you decide to write to the library directors on your campus to complain because the building closes at five o'clock on Saturdays, you may write simply to vent your outrage. Possibly you would write *to inform* them of the number of people who are inconvenienced. You could also write *to entertain* them with an account of your faltering social life during which Saturday night stretches before you vacant and lonely without the solace of scholarship and the joys of browsing through books and bibliographies. Probably, though, you would write *to persuade* people that the library should remain open on Saturday nights for the benefit of students with jobs, families, and academic overloads. Obviously, with each change of purpose virtually everything about your letter would also change—style, tone, content. So, as you can see, you need to keep your purpose firmly in mind as you plan and write.

Considering Your Audience: Discourse Communities

You cannot easily determine why you are writing without also determining *who* is going to read what you write. Your audience may be just one person—the head librarian, or perhaps your boss, your history professor, your senator. Or you may want to reach a wider audience—your city council; your composition class; the readership of a publication such as your local newspaper, *Time* magazine, or *Rolling Stone.*

These larger audiences are called *discourse communities*—groups of people with a common bond of similar interests and shared knowledge. Your composition class, for instance, forms a discourse community, as does the special interest group you chat with on the internet or the people you write memos to and reports with at work—not to mention the folks you socialize with in the evenings or worship with in church. The *discourse* (the ideas, information, and opinions expressed) will change considerably from group to group. Even the kinds of words you choose may change from group to group. If you use the term *discourse community* in your composition classroom, you can expect to be understood, but if you use that same phrase at your workplace, the response may well be, "Say *what?*"

Try to bring your readers into focus in your mind as you consider your purpose and plan your approach. Think about, for instance, how much your readers already know about your topic. Listen to a rural relative of ours explaining how to get to the family reunion: "Just follow the hard road down to where Snively's cow barn used to stand before the fire; then turn off onto the gravel track and go a piece until you get to the top of the second big rise after the creek. Look for Rabbithash's old pickup." All eighty-six first cousins find these directions perfectly clear, but anyone from farther away than Clay City is going to have some difficulty getting there before the potato salad goes funny.

When you want to include second-cousins-once-removed and even complete strangers in your audience, you should try to write out directions that don't rely on so much in-group information (such as where Snively's barn *used* to be). And—if your topic is technical—you need also to consider what level of difficulty your readers are willing to accept in order to learn more.

Suppose you are writing on the safety of Prozac in treating depression. If you choose as your audience the readers of a professional journal for psychotherapists, your verbal tactics will be quite different from those you would use for the readers of *Harper's* or *Esquire*—and still more different for the readers of *Woman's Day* or *Newsweek*. The vocabulary you choose will change, as well as sentence length and the need to define technical terms. Perhaps the number of examples needed for clarity will vary with each audience. You will also need to work harder on a catchy opening if you are writing not for psychotherapists who need your information but for people who are reading mainly for pleasure with enlightenment as an added bonus. (See Fig. 1.2.)

The following paragraph was written by a college student as advice for her peers. Rewrite the passage for each of the audiences listed, making any changes that might be appropriate.

WRITING
EXERCISE

1.1

1. A junior high school class
2. The teacher of a junior high school class

> Once you've firmly implanted in your mind the fact that you are definitely going to quit smoking, you must start observing the situations in which you smoke, and try to eliminate these situations. For example, go down to the cafeteria to eat lunch later than usual so you won't have time to light up before returning to class. Chew a stick of gum or your fingernails. Just don't light up. That would defeat all your effort, and remember, you don't need or want cigarettes anymore! A good idea is to put aside the money you would normally spend for cigarettes and go out and celebrate after you've accomplished your goal.

Seeing Yourself as a Writer

To be a competent, confident writer, you need to start thinking of yourself as a writer. One of the best methods for developing this self-image is to examine your own writing behavior. You will discover that you have already acquired a number of habits and attitudes about writing. Becoming aware of these practices

FIGURE 1.2

Audience Analysis Checklist

In order to increase your abilities in evaluating your audience, ask yourself the following questions about your readers during the process of planning your writing.

1. How much will they already know about my topic?
2. Will they respond emotionally to my topic? Will I need to be especially careful not to offend them? If so, how?
3. Will they be interested in my topic? If not, how can I get them interested?
4. Will they be in agreement with me? Opposed? Neutral?
5. How well educated are they likely to be?
6. Do they fall into any particular age group?
7. Is it important to consider their race, sex, marital status, possible parenthood, or religion?
8. Do they identify with any political groups (Democrats, Republicans, libertarians, independents, socialists)?
9. Are they members of any public interest group (Right to Life, Common Cause, National Organization for Women, Sierra Club, National Rifle Association, etc.)?
10. How do they make their living? Are they rich, poor, middle class?

and perspectives will make it easier for you to improve. Thinking about your own habits will also allow you to see how the writing process works.

Of course, no two writers go through exactly the same process as they compose; in fact, your own approach probably varies from task to task depending on the writing situation. Nonetheless, examining the procedures you follow may reveal valuable insights about the nature of writing. The following assignment will help you to explore your own writing experiences and confirm what you already know about the process of writing.

Writing Assignment: Your Writing Profile

Develop a profile of yourself as a writer. In response to the following suggestions, describe how you go about writing, and analyze your strengths and weaknesses.

1. In the first part of your writing profile, give an account of the procedures you normally go through in your writing; draw examples from a recent school or workplace writing experience. Think about the following questions.

The Mechanics of Your Writing

What conditions are necessary for you to write? (Quiet, music, food, equipment—what?) Do you work on a word processor or typewriter, or do you write your drafts by hand? What materials (paper, pens, etc.) do you use? Are your initial drafts messy? Do you cross out and correct as you go, or do you just write as quickly as you can? Do you leave big margins and space between lines? Do you pause a lot as you write? Do you change your procedures for later drafts? If you use a word processor, do you compose on the computer, or do you write out a draft and then type it in before revising? Do you revise at the terminal, or do you print out a hard copy and make changes on that? Do you use a spell-checker or a style-checker?

Your Mental State

Do you plunge right into a writing assignment? Or do you put it off? Do you get anxious or suffer from writer's block? If so, how do you deal with it? Do you write a paper the night before the due date or spread the writing out? Do you subdivide a paper into parts, write it all at once, or what? Do you outline your ideas before writing, or do you write a draft first and then rearrange? Do you discuss your ideas with anyone before you write? How many drafts do you usually go through? Do you leave time between drafts to let your thoughts incubate? Do you spend a lot of time rewriting and editing? What kinds of changes do you usually make when you rewrite? Do you show your drafts to classmates or co-workers and discuss them?

Your Writing Preferences

Do you like to write? How often do you write? What kind of writing is the easiest for you to do? The hardest? What is the most important piece of writing you have completed? Has most of your writing been done in or outside of school? Was there a time when your feelings about writing changed? What happened? Do you like to choose your own topics or have them assigned? Do you like to have specific requirements (such as word length, purpose and audience, deadlines)? How much time do you usually put into a paper, memo, or report?

2. In the second part of your profile, analyze your strengths and weaknesses as a writer. Consider these questions:

In the past, what have you been praised for or criticized for as a writer? How easy is it for you to come up with good writing ideas? Do you have trouble finding enough to say? Can you organize your ideas easily? Do you write clear, grammatical sentences? Do you have trouble with punctuation or spelling? What features of your writing do you think you need to work on? Is your writing process efficient and productive? Do you work through several stages in completing a paper? In order to improve your writing process, what would you work on most?

These questions are just suggestions. Use them to guide you to the information that you need to consider in evaluating yourself as a writer. As you work on the assignments in this course, think about which habits help you write and which habits you would like to change.

Benefiting from Collaboration

A great deal of writing in the workplace is done collaboratively—that is, with two or more people working together to produce a summary, a report, or an evaluation. In fact, seldom would an employee complete an extensive piece of writing without consulting a superior or reviewing the ideas with other employees to be sure everyone agrees on the content and that nothing important has been omitted.

This textbook is an example of collaborative writing by three authors. We meet to plan the focus of the text, determine its organization, divide the material, and—most important—to give and take ideas for developing the chapters. After producing first drafts, we revise and edit each other's work—adding headings and examples, suggesting word changes, revising sentences, rearranging ideas. When we get stuck at any stage of the writing process, we can call or send electronic mail to a coauthor asking for help.

If your instructor approves of peer collaboration, you and your classmates can help each other both in and outside of class—sharing ideas while planning what to write, offering advice about organizing ideas, evaluating each other's drafts, and pointing out problems in grammar and punctuation in the final draft. Having the help of classmates, friends, or co-workers makes the tough job of writing far less stressful and also improves the final product.

Chapter Two

Planning What to Say

Perhaps the most difficult stage in the writing process involves deciding what to say. If we could always write just to please ourselves, composing would be an entertainment. But seldom do we enjoy such latitude. Usually we write for a specific audience and are restricted by topic and length, as well as by the time available to do the job. The chief engineer wants a three-page report on the drilling core samples from the Gulfport well—today. The principal requires lesson plans of specified length and content—submitted a week in advance. Your history professor allows only fifty minutes to complete four essay questions. Letters to the editor are often limited to 350 words. Essays in composition classes can seldom be much longer than 700 words and may have to be even shorter if written in class. You need to learn to match your efforts to various constraints like these, and the planning stage is the best place to do so.

Thinking Before Writing

All the pondering, speculating, collecting, reflecting, judging, and sorting that goes on during the planning process seldom gets done in an orderly, step-by-step fashion. Often the stages are interchangeable or concurrent. Some people begin by brainstorming an outline; others start writing straight off and keep rewriting until they are satisfied with the final draft. As you gain experience as a writer, you will discover what process works best for you.

Choosing a Topic

In most everyday circumstances, your topic is decided for you. Your employer requests a memo or report; you need to write for information or request some type of action; you feel compelled to express yourself on a given issue. You have more latitude when your history professor asks for a paper on the Great Depression and leaves the specifics up to you, or when we require you to practice certain types of writing in this textbook but let you decide on the content.

Naturally, you are going to have a difficult time thinking of something to say on a subject that holds no interest for you. If allowed to select your own topic, try to choose what writing specialist Janice Lauer calls "an area of dissonance" in your life—an area that causes a genuine problem for you, emotionally or otherwise, a problem that needs solving or at least a thorough thinking through. Automatically you are motivated to explore the topic, and your own experience in the matter should provide useful material to support your main point. If you are divorced, you can write with authority about the effects of divorce on the immediate family. From thinking over your difficulties, you may have gained insights that will allow you to discuss specific problems in marriage and perhaps to pose solutions. Or, if a member of your family is jobless, you can probably offer valid observations about the effects—both psychological and economic—of unemployment on a person. Given a free choice of subjects for writing, select one that compels your interest. Given some requirements, try to find an aspect that is personally engaging.

Narrowing the Topic

Suppose you have been asked to write a paper on a topic you have been studying in class, such as the Great Depression. You could probably dash one off on the subject in general just by repeating what you have learned so far. But it would probably be an essay that only a loved one would willingly read. You will earn a wider audience (and a better grade) if you focus on some aspect of the Depression and cover that in detail. You need to find an approach—a central idea—and find facts and illustrations to develop this main idea, called a *thesis*.

A first step is to think of the various approaches to the topic that may exist. Let's say that your local newspaper is running a series of articles about the horrors of day care, and you are steamed up by the one-sided nature of the series. You want to write a letter to the editor emphasizing the positive side of sending children to day care. You think that day care can free women to fulfill their career goals, can provide employment and experience for young workers, can help the children themselves develop, and can relieve the parental stress that sometimes leads to child abuse. But your newspaper has a 350-word limit on letters, and if you covered all your points you would probably sound too general to be persuasive. So you choose just one point to develop, considering what is most likely to persuade your audience, such as:

> Good day-care centers allow children to learn to share with others, to build immunity to diseases, to develop communication skills, to become self-sufficient, and to respect their mothers.

This way, you focus on one aspect of the topic and have room to provide some convincing examples and details. You could keep your longer list of thoughts about day care on file, in case you ever want to write a lengthy article or essay on the subject.

The next process we discuss, *invention,* will assist you in finding a focus and in discovering supporting material.

Exploring Your Material: Invention

Some people find ideas easily, while others sit staring at a blank screen or chewing their nails in misery. In case you have difficulty, here are eight techniques to help you manage the thinking process that produces thesis statements and material to use in the first draft. Some of these techniques overlap, but one or two of them should prove helpful to you as a writer.

Keeping a Journal

Many professional writers keep journals or notebooks in which they jot down impressions, responses, descriptions, the germs of ideas—anything that might be used in developing a finished piece of writing. If you decide to keep a journal in which you record more than brief notes, try to make the entries involve you in thinking, preferably in analysis. Instead of merely recording "I went to a movie tonight," take the time, instead, to examine your response to it. How did you feel when you saw it? Why did you feel this way? What events or characters in the movie provoked this response?

Other examples: if you are having difficulty in a course this semester, try to describe how you feel about the problem. Why do you feel that way? What can you do about it? Or perhaps you learned a new word today. Look it up and record its dictionary definitions. What did it mean in the context in which you encountered it? Write a few sentences in which you use the word yourself.

When you have interesting material that you decide not to use in a writing project, keep the extra in your journal for possible future use. The same goes for ideas about subjects or approaches on which you did not follow up: they may be valuable inspirations later.

Try a Reading Journal

Keeping a reading journal that reflects your responses to school assignments will not only generate ideas for your own writing but will help you remember the assignments much more clearly. The more ways in which you process material, the better you remember it, and writing as well as reading about something makes it stick. You might choose one of the following categories as the focus of your journal:[1]

1. This reminds me of . . .
   If your reading makes you remember an experience of your own, record the association.
2. Dear Author:
   Write a letter to an author agreeing or disagreeing with one of his or her statements or points of view.
3. Sounding off!
   If something in your reading makes you angry, take it out on your journal.
4. Help!
   If you have difficulty understanding part of the reading, try to write a summary or outline of that section to clarify the meaning.
5. Today you said . . .
   Discuss something your instructor talked about in class that you have further thoughts on.
6. Let me try—.
   If you are impressed by a technique used in the reading (like vivid description, great dialogue, effective humor or satire), try to imitate that writing in a paragraph of your own.
7. What a wonderful/terrible essay!
   Explain why you admire or dislike an essay.
8. Why this title?
   Discuss the significance of the title or the headings—how they relate to the work, what clues they provide to the meaning.
9. How the author works.
   Discuss the effectiveness of some element of the reading: its organization, transitions, tone, appeal to audience, point of view.

---

[1]Thanks to our colleague Janet Youga for providing these suggestions for journal writing.

10. Beginnings and endings:
    After reading the first paragraph, explain what interests you and what
    you expect of the reading. After you finish reading, explain whether
    or not your expectations were fulfilled.

Posing a Problem

As philosopher John Dewey observed, "Thinking is a problem-solving activity." We mentioned earlier the possibility of working out a problem in your personal life by exploring an area of dissonance or conflict. Some people find they can generate ideas for writing on almost any topic by first thinking of a problem related to the topic. The solution to that problem then provides the material for the paper. "How can our country prevent another Great Depression?" is a question that could easily lead to material for an essay.

Brainstorming

The process of brainstorming involves jotting down every idea that comes to mind as you are thinking about a problem related to your topic. One of our students, Grace Pennington, wanted to write about the donating of body organs because her brother needed a kidney transplant. She asked herself: What could be a problem with donating body organs? Her brainstorming went like this:

> Donor banks— How do
> they work?
> Expense?
> How is donating done??
> Laws concerning it?
> Technical aspects?
> Who donates? Why?
> ~~Expense~~
> Why doesn't <u>everybody</u>?

With that last question Pennington discovered her problem: the need to change the attitudes of people emotionally unable or unwilling to consider donating organs.

Pennington then directed her thinking toward solving the problem of how to change people's attitudes. What arguments could she use? More brainstorming followed:

<u>Why</u> are people opposed?

    religious attitudes — body
      sacred — "temple
Don't know how of God"
to go about it??

(forms available in Drivers Bureau Licensing in Illinois)
    Self-concepts tied in w/
      physical body
    (mutilation) - afraid they
~~How do you go about it??~~ might not be <u>truly</u>
      dead??

— Argue that saving another's
  life is more valuable
  than false vanity

    in conclusion
— Argue that we should try
  to overcome our emotional
  ~~attachment to our bodies~~
  opposition to donating organs
  so that others may live!

procrastination — people put
  off making decision?
  (But that may be
    emotionally caused!)

(and some may enjoy fuller
  lives)
Think of suffering alleviated,
lives saved —
  Cite <u>examples</u> —
  (my brother,) blind, heart
    disease victims —
    children

How to get people to change?
— Counter religious argument:
  once <u>dead</u>, body not
  sacred anymore —
  "dust unto dust"

— Get more <u>real</u> examples (maybe
  from article on donating)

— Counter mutilation idea:
  once body is <u>dead</u>, the
  Self ceases to exist —
  or goes elsewhere
Eyes of corpse closed! (exterior not noticeably
  damaged by removing
  organs anyway)
  (clothing covers incisions)

Eventually, Pennington went to the library and located articles providing statistics on the need for donors and citing heartwarming examples of real people whose lives had been saved or enriched by organ transplants. She used these touching examples as a means of countering the negative emotional response—fear of donating—with a positive one—joy of giving.

Asking Questions

If presenting yourself with a problem to solve seems only to complicate the problems you already have, you might want to try instead the journalistic method of gathering information. Reporters collect data for news stories by asking *who?*, *what?*, *when?*, *where?*, *how?*, and *why?* All these questions may not be relevant to your essay topic, so try asking yourself variations like these:

What makes it important?
What are the consequences of it?
What can be done about it?
What changes need to be made?
What point can I make about it?
How does it affect people?
How is it managed?
Where does it have the most impact?
Where should changes be brought about?
Why am I interested in it?
Why are other people interested in it?
Who is most interested in this topic?
Who has some power in this area?
Who is my audience?

After you have jotted down all your answers, go over the list and try to come up with a thesis, a one-sentence statement of the point you want to make about your topic.

Freewriting

Freewriting means just what it sounds like: you write with complete freedom, not bothering about correctness or style or punctuation or anything else. You just record whatever comes to your mind as you think about the topic. Usually, you set a timer and try to write for five or ten minutes straight, without stopping. Reel sentences out of your mind as you think about the topic and record them rapidly, like this:

> The Great Depression of the 1930s. My grandparents' time, I think of listening to my parents talk about how my grandparents talk about the Depression, hearing my grandparents at Thanksgiving worrying about my uncle changing careers. Mom says they can't stand the idea of someone giving up a good job to go back to school because the Depression still controls their thinking, they will always be more security conscious than their kids will be. Wonder if she's right. They don't like the idea of my choice of a history major without a teaching minor—not enough jobs there. That goes along with Mom's idea. Also they never want to owe any money, save until they can buy their new car with cash instead of payments, feel they really own it—that may be related.

After you have finished one round of freewriting, reread your musings and underline any ideas worth developing. In our example, the writer is pretty clearly working toward a focus on how living through the Great Depression altered people's outlooks forever. After rereading, do another round of freewriting focusing on that one idea. When you finish, again underline the ideas that strike you as worth keeping. Then do more freewriting on those that seem promising. When you have generated enough material to start a paper, you can devise a thesis and draw some supporting evidence from your pages of freewriting.

Interviewing

The freewriter above can now use another invention technique: she can talk to her grandparents and parents about the topic of how the Great Depression changed people's outlooks. These informants can probably come up with plenty of convincing material. If she can find other survivors of the Depression, she can collect further data.

Almost any subject can be profitably developed by talking to people with special knowledge on the topic. Ask if your ideas make sense to them; see what information they can add. Write down every notion that you collect, whether or not it seems important. You can eliminate any items that prove irrelevant, and you may end up altering your intended focus to fit the information you have gathered.

Scanning and Reading

You may find it helpful to survey what approaches other writers have taken to the general topic. If you look up the Great Depression in *Funk & Wagnalls*

New Encyclopedia (1986), you'll be referred to the encyclopedia's section on Business Cycles. Here, the Great Depression is viewed as an extreme example of an economic cycle that naturally occurs in industrialized capitalist countries. The entry explains what efforts were made to recover from the Depression and what safeguards were later built into the U.S. economy to try to prevent such a disaster from happening again. You will also be referred to the section on Photography, where you'll find that during the Depression, a group of photographers were funded by the U.S. Farm Security Administration to take pictures representing the effects of the catastrophe on everyday people. These photographers, including Walker Evans and Dorothea Lange, became famous, and their pictures became classics. There are several other references in the encyclopedia—like *unemployment* and *money*—so you can see that very different topics could be developed starting from the general subject of the Great Depression.

You can also scan the titles of articles on a topic to get a sense of possible approaches. Lists of titles are available under the alphabetized subjects in the *Readers' Guide to Periodical Literature*. Breakdowns of subjects into smaller, more specific topics can be found in the *Library of Congress Subject Headings* (LCSH), an index every library holds. Volumes that deal more specifically with a certain field will provide more leads: for example, the *Encyclopedia of American History* (Harper and Row) would help with the Great Depression topic.

You are very likely to find an angle that is personally appealing if you make use of the research tools available, even if you are not writing a research paper.

Incubating

Many writing specialists are convinced that your subconscious mind can work for you if given a chance. Start the planning process early to allow for periods during which you are not consciously thinking about your topic. Let the ideas incubate. You may achieve a breakthrough when a valuable insight matures in your subconscious mind and suddenly surfaces. You can learn to make use of your sleeping mind by thinking about your topic right before falling asleep, inviting your unconscious to go to work on it.

Outlining and Mapping

Eventually, you must decide on an order for all the material you have collected. Go over all your scribblings again. For a composition in writing class, you need three or four supporting points for your main idea or thesis and some details, examples, or explanations to develop each supporting point. Look for patterns of similarity; then group related scribblings together and give them a label.

This is the plan or map that Grace Pennington developed for her organ donor essay:

<u>Thesis</u>:   People must be encouraged to understand and change negative emotional attitudes toward donating vital organs for transplants.

<u>Introduction</u>:   Discuss people's present unwillingness to face the issue. Explain their thinking.

<u>Body</u>:   Counter mutilation fear
                                          ↓
                              Counter religious objections
                                          ↓
                Stress need for transplants (my brother, statistics from article)
                                          ↓
                  Cite life-giving results (case studies from articles)

<u>Conclusion</u>: Plead for readers to become donors

From this plan, Pennington was able to write a six-paragraph essay. If her teacher had requested a formal outline, she would need to format the plan with roman numerals for main points and capital letters beside supporting details. Here is one section of her plan done in outline form:

II. Counter mutilation fears.
  A. Once body is dead, the "self" leaves or disappears—no self-consciousness.
  B. The exterior is not visibly marred by removing organs.
    1. Eyes are closed at funeral.
    2. Clothing covers incisions at funeral.

Think through the order in which you wish to present your supporting points. If there is no chronology (time order) involved or there are no steps that belong in a certain order, begin with a fairly important and interesting point to get your readers' attention. Grace Pennington chose the most ghastly point to deal with first. Just end with your strongest point to leave your audience feeling that you have said something worthwhile. Pennington's plan moves from negative to positive, with the upbeat examples coming last.

Probably you will change a few things as you do the actual writing—think up better details, leave out unconvincing or redundant ones, or perhaps even add a new supporting point. But with a basic map or outline, you can press on to write your first draft.

Composing the First Draft: The Writing Stage

In order to understand thoroughly the process of putting an essay together, you need to study the remaining chapters in this book. But before you do so, here is a bit of general advice about the best way to get through the actual writing process.

Writing expert Sondra Perl reports that weak writers go over and over each sentence as they try to get through a first draft. By struggling for the right word and the perfect sentence at this stage, they lose momentum and have difficulty maintaining a flow of ideas. Certainly choosing the exact word and crafting effective sentences are both crucial to writing well—but not necessarily during the rough draft. If you have trouble putting words on paper, try to get through the first draft as rapidly as possible. Do your rewriting later. If you are already a fluent writer, you can revise extensively even during the first draft.

Beginning and expert writers alike often benefit from putting off the introduction, since that part is so difficult to write. You can make do with a clunky opening sentence (maybe just the thesis sentence), knowing that you can come back and write an effective opening during the revising stage.

As you write your draft following your plan, always keep a spare piece of paper alongside you. Sometimes as you work on the body, you may have an inspiration about how to end the whole thing, and the spare paper can catch these stray ideas better than you can remember them until you get to the place where they belong. Writers often think of just-right words or phrases they want to use somewhere else in the essay, and these can be jotted on the spare page as they come to mind. Do not trust your busy memory to retrieve these gems later! Even when you compose on the computer, you need a pen and pad at your elbow to record useful fleeting thoughts.

Consider Your Writing Habits

You might give some thought to your surroundings before you begin to write. Where do you do your best writing? At a desk? Lounging in bed? In an easy chair? Stretched out on your stomach on the floor? What do you write with most comfortably? Pen? Pencil? Keyboard? Do you write most effectively with music blaring? In total silence? With the TV on? In one long session or in short sessions with breaks in between? When is the best time of day—or night—for you to write? Some people work best early in the morning; others don't come truly alive till evening. Try to do your writing when you know you are at your liveliest.

Naturally, you will be unable to choose your perfect writing situation when asked to write in class or at work. But pay attention to the situation whenever you have a particularly good writing experience. Record your observations in your journal. Given the opportunity, try to select surroundings that suit your writing habits.

Observing the Process: Sample Student Paper in Progress

Let's look at a section of a paper in progress by our student Linda Samuel. The essay concerns seasonal affective disorder, and this part comes just after the introduction.

The pineal gland is located in the cerebrum and in the past was often referred to as the "third eye" because like an eye it includes a miniature cornea, lens, and retina. One of the major functions of the pineal gland is to scan for and register the amount of darkness through light receptors in the eye and once located, it secretes a hormone called melatonin, which in turn produces narcotic-like effects that prepare us for our nightly drowse. The pineal gland is present in most vertebrates except for crocodiles, anteaters, sloths, and armadillos.

In humans, melatonin levels usually increase after an hour or so of darkness and begin dropping again after six to eight hours. This hormone is produced in response to the lack of direct sunlight on the retina of the eye, which slows our reaction time and produces fatigue. This biochemical response is perfectly normal because in reality, it prepares us for sleep at night. However, negative effects are produced because of the overproduction of melatonin due to prolonged darkness which causes lethargy, loss of enthusiasm, and loss of sex drive. Many people sleep 17 percent more in winter than in summer and gain ten to fifteen pounds more. Others experience depression, resulting in seasonal affective disorder or SAD.

The essay goes on to describe synthetic sunlight therapy for people who suffer from SAD. Later we'll let you see how Samuel revised this passage.

Rewriting the Rough Draft: The Revising Stage

Take care in budgeting your time to allow your rough draft to "cool off" before you begin revising. You will be better able to detect faulty sentences, ill-chosen phrases, and lapses in thinking if you give your brain time to rest after that first feverish burst of creative activity. You need to be at the height of your powers when you rewrite.

Getting Feedback: Peer Revision

You will usually have a chance to enlist a partner—a peer, a friend, a classmate—to help you with revision. Someone else can often see places where you *thought* you were being clear but were actually filling in details in your head, not on the page. If there are parts that you are not satisfied with, ask your helper to pay attention to those and see whether they are all right or, if not, suggest what needs to be done. If you read your paper aloud to someone, it will help you catch any careless repetition of words. Your listener can tell you whether or not what you have said is entirely clear and convincing.

When *you* are the one reading someone else's work to help improve it, remember to ask from the start what questions the writer wants answered. Most people want to make sure their points are clear and consistent. But the writer you are working with may know already that the spelling needs to be checked and may ask you to ignore those errors as you read. In the workplace, most of the writing you do will be passed around, with various writers adding their sections and making suggestions about yours. In this situation, you need to keep checking for consistency—for example, you do not want one part of the document requesting prepaid orders and another part promising to send out bills.

Everyone who acts as an informal editor should keep in mind that writing feels very personal, even when it is a list of materials for a construction project. Writers are easily insulted or wounded by criticism that is phrased in an insensitive way. If you say, "This list of materials is too disorganized," you are likely to make the writer feel that he or she is the one that's disorganized. A suggestion such as, "If we organize this list into categories like *handtools, machinery,* and *building supplies,* the contractor will be able to evaluate it faster," gives the writer a specific direction for revision without suggesting personal inadequacy. On the other hand, do not pass something by as fine when you see flaws, just to save feelings. You can figure out a way to express your criticisms kindly.

Revising from the Top Down

Looking at someone else's writing has the fringe benefit of helping you to look critically at your own. Most important of all, be positive that your whole piece makes sense. Look back to the basic elements of audience and purpose. Ask yourself if these factors are considered in what you have written. See whether your main point is clear after one reading of the opening paragraph. Then make sure that the supporting material logically and fully confirms the thesis.

At this point, you may realize that you need to rethink the paper in a big way. Perhaps you see that one of your supporting points should actually be the thesis of the paper, meaning that you need to scrap much of what you have done and go back to the invention stage with a new main idea. Less drastically, you may see that one of your supporting points wanders off on a side trip with only a passing relationship to your thesis, and only some minor cutting is necessary.

Once you are convinced that the paper as a whole is acceptable, look at the parts and their connections. If you have not yet achieved an effective introduction or a forceful conclusion, you must now apply yourself to that task. Look at the connections between ideas. Will your readers see exactly how each part is related to the next one? Are the supporting paragraphs in the most effective order, or do they need to be moved around?

Finally, drag out your dictionary and thesaurus to be sure that every word you have used is precisely the right one and is correctly spelled. Read the sentences to see whether repetitive or clumsy structure hurts the style. Choose a section and count words per sentence: if the sentences are all close to the same length, revise for variety. These matters will be taken up more completely in Chapters 10, 11, and 12 of this text. For now, we are just giving you an overview of this complicated process.

Using Checklists

In Chapters 3 through 9, we offer detailed advice on various methods of writing. You will also find checklists to help you revise and improve each paper you write. These checklists work well for peer editing if your instructor wants you to help one another during this important stage. You can also use the lists to guide your revision process if you have to work alone.

Observing the Process: Sample Student Paper in Progress, Revised

Here is the same section of Linda Samuel's essay that we included earlier in first draft form. This is the revised version she produced after close scrutiny of her work and discussion with a partner.

> The pineal gland, located in the cerebrum, functions as a photoreceptor organ. This means that it scans for and registers the amount of darkness in our environment through its connection with light receptors in our eyes. When it senses a period of darkness, the pineal gland secretes a hormone called melatonin, which produces narcotic-like effects.
>
> On spring, summer, and fall evenings, melatonin levels usually increase after an hour or so of darkness and begin dropping again after six to eight hours. Lack of direct sunlight on the retina of the eye stimulates melatonin production, which slows our reaction time and produces fatigue. This biochemical response is perfectly normal: it prepares us for sleep at night. However, during the winter in a northern climate, we are likely to get an overdose of melatonin due to prolonged daytime darkness. Such an overdose causes lethargy, loss of enthusiasm, and diminished sex drive. Many people sleep 17 percent more in winter than in summer and gain ten to fifteen pounds. They may also experience winter depression, or seasonal affective disorder (SAD).

List the changes you can find between the first draft and the revised draft of the partial essay on seasonal affective disorder. Speculate on the writer's reasons for making each change.

DISCUSSION
EXERCISE

2.1

Setting a Revision Agenda

A major skill needed by every writer is realistic time management. Obviously, you need space between getting an assignment, letting it incubate, doing invention exercises, outlining or mapping, writing the rough draft, and revising the cooled-off copy. If you wisely decide to enlist the aid of a partner, or if your composition class requires peer revision, you need to have a draft ready for your peer reader well before you hand in the final draft. You may want to prepare specific questions for your reader to consider when reading your essay. When you revise from the top down, you may need time to go back to the invention and drafting stages. Clearly, you need to look at your calendar and, from assignment to final draft, spread out your work through the days you have available. Recognize that "I work best under pressure" is merely a rationalization for procrastinating.

Revising on a Word Processor

Since computer programs have virtually eliminated the need for retyping, revision has become an easier task. In the days of the typewriter, just realizing that the paragraphs would be slightly more effective if presented in a different order rarely made students roll new paper into the machine and start over. Now, you merely need to use your word processor's block-and-move commands to make such a change. You can even block-and-move just to *see* whether a different order is better, with no commitment and little lost time.

The computer also adapts to the nonlinear workings of our minds during the writing process. In typing on a word processor, you will often think of a new detail or a whole sentence that belongs in an earlier section, and you can easily move the cursor back to that point and add the material with a click of your mouse. Or if you think of a great conclusion halfway through the draft, you can go ahead and type it and insert the rest of the draft ahead of it. On the sentence level, you can go back and change a word, move a phrase, add to a series, or just tinker with the words until you're satisfied.

Are there any disadvantages to writing on a computer? There may be. Early versions of your essay are lost as you revise. In most cases, this loss is no problem, but if you make big changes, you need to stop and print out old drafts as you go. They may contain work that can later be retrieved and used elsewhere. We encourage you to print your rough draft even when you know it is due for major revision.

In addition, certain problems are easier to see on a printed copy than on the computer screen. For example, you see more paragraphs at a time on the page. On the screen, you may not have noticed that your transitional phrases at the beginning of several paragraphs are exactly the same, or that the paragraph lengths are wildly unbalanced. You may also be aware that when you revise sentences on the screen (rather than on paper), you are much more likely to neglect to erase the old version or at least a part of it, leaving you with a sentence like this:

Writers at any level of skill can benefit from are helped by mere practice.

In this case, the writer decided that "can benefit from" sounded better than "are helped by" but forgot to take out the first phrase. Such errors must be caught during human proofreading, since the computer's spell-checker will pass them over.

A final caution about writing on computers: nowadays, instructors expect a much cleaner, neater, and more correct final copy than they have in the past. Some allow for tidy corrections done in ink, but others insist on a new printing when you find an error. Your instructor can be righteously indignant over a misspelling that should have been flagged by the spell-checker, assigning the error to your laziness or haste. Moreover, a reader can tell whether you *only* used the spell-checker, because many errors (such as *to* instead of *too*) must be found by a human proofreader.

Polishing the Final Draft: The Editing Stage

During the editing stage, you review your paper one last time and correct any errors. You must look only at the words themselves and at the punctuation: pay no attention this time to meaning.

To catch spelling errors, some people read backward—from the bottom of the page toward the top, from right to left—in order to avoid getting distracted by the content. We have a friend who cuts a thin rectangular slit (about two inches long and half an inch wide) in the middle of a three-by-five-inch notecard. By passing the card slowly across each line, he forces himself to look at no more than two or three words at a time. Use whatever system works for you, but *do* proofread.

Careless errors can be funny and Freudian, like this one from a student discussing changes in fashion during the 1920s: "Ladies' skirts finally rose so high that the pubic was shocked." But careless errors are usually witless and annoying, such as repeating a word needlessly (*and and*) or leaving off an *s* and producing a nonstandard construction: "The record were lost." Such mistakes do nothing to encourage admiration for the brilliance of your observations—no matter how keen or well stated. So, watch the little things, too. Do not write *probable* if you mean *probably,* or *use to* for *used to,* or *then* for *than.* Check possessives to be sure the apostrophes are there—or not there in the case of *its.*

As author Jessica Mitford cautions, "Failure to proofread is like preparing a magnificent dinner and forgetting to set the table, so that the wretched guests have to scramble for food as best they can." Be polite—proofread. Your grade may depend on it.

Trying Out the Process: Writing an Essay

In this chapter, you saw examples of writers working on the topics of organ donorship, the Great Depression, and seasonal affective disorder. Now it's time for you to try out the process of developing a topic and writing an essay yourself. The rest of this textbook will give you much more detailed advice about stages discussed only briefly here, so no one expects you to produce a perfect draft. But just as your swimming teacher eventually asks you to jump in, so do we.

Begin with an area of dissonance in your life, a starting place we mentioned near the beginning of this chapter. Think of something that causes a problem for you morally, emotionally, intellectually, or practically. Perhaps a good friend asked you to keep a secret about how he has done something you really disapprove of. Or maybe your child is threatening to go live with your ex-spouse. If you don't feel comfortable writing about such personal dilemmas, there are plenty of other choices. For example, what to do about a problem at your workplace may serve as a starting point, or what type of floor covering to choose for your kitchen, or where to go on a vacation that will please four wildly different family members.

Go through the process of narrowing the topic, exploring the material (using one or more of the eight techniques we describe), outlining or mapping, composing a first draft, revising, and editing. Keep all your materials as you go along, in case your instructor wants to see them (or in case you can rejuvenate some of the ideas for future papers). You may also want to keep a running journal about your own process: What did you expect from each step, and what did you get? Which part seemed most difficult? Which was easiest? At what point did you feel most and least confident about your essay? What would you do differently if you had to do it all over again? These notes will help you analyze your own individual writing process. You will be able to see how your writing changes as you work through this book.

Part Two

Developing and Organizing Your Writing

We now turn to the written work as a whole—the essay, report, memo, personal memoir, research project—whatever you will eventually let other people read. Part Two, which includes Chapters 3 through 9, gives you help with strategies for developing what you have to say into an easily readable form.

We begin with some basic cornerstones of composing: description, narration, process, example, and definition. Although seldom used as the sole means of development, these *modes* (as they are often called) are basic in expressing ideas. Next, we ask you to focus, one at a time, on specific patterns of development: classification and division, comparison and contrast, cause and effect, and persuasion. In each case, your finished essay will probably be a blend of several methods of development, but if you practice each one separately, you will have them all readily available in your mind when you need them. Look at this as practice comparable to scales and drills on the piano—you will never play them at a recital, but they contribute to your expert performance nonetheless.

As you begin to write longer essays, remember to schedule your time generously. You can revise with greater objectivity and renewed vigor if you and your writing have a little time to cool off. Ideally, too, you can get valuable advice from a trusted friend or classmate who will read your essay carefully and answer the questions on our revision checklists. Don't forget to leave time for editing and proofreading the final draft, both on the computer and on the hard copy.

Chapter Three

Description, Narration, and Process

In this chapter you will practice using description combined with the two chronological patterns of development, narration, and process.

Description

No matter what you have to say, accurate and evocative description will help you say it better. Descriptive detail adds liveliness, interest, and feeling to your writing—but it is not just a frill for special occasions. It is an integral part of all writing, for without description your reader may become lost in generality and abstraction. Imagine trying to tell someone how to find your apartment, how to take over one of your jobs, or why you are upset, using only abstract and general terms. You would not even attempt it. Your first impulse, in real life, would be to describe specific, concrete details: "My apartment is practically in the parking lot of Schooner's Supper Club"; "First, check in with Juan, the service manager, and get a computer printout of the day's appointments from him"; "The door handle broke off my Pinto again this morning." You must make use of your descriptive skills in all your writing, whether you are informing, persuading, entertaining, or simply expressing yourself.

Find the descriptive details in the following passage, which is the opening of an essay titled "Under the Influence: Paying the Price of My Father's Booze" by Scott Russell Sanders. Point out words and phrases that bring forth mental pictures.

EXERCISE

3.1

My father drank. He drank as a gut-punched boxer gasps for breath, as a starving dog gobbles food—compulsively, secretly, in pain and trembling. I use the past tense not because he ever quit drinking but because he quit living. That is how the story ends for my father, age sixty-four, heart bursting, body cooling, slumped and forsaken on the linoleum of my brother's trailer. The story continues for my brother, my sister, my mother, and me, and will continue as long as memory holds.

How briefly can you summarize this passage without sensory detail? How effective is that summary?

Technical Description

When you are writing at work or when you are writing instructions, you will need to produce accurate technical descriptions. You need to set down clearly and objectively the details your readers will need to identify whatever it is you are describing. Here, for example, is a technical description from a drafting textbook:

> *Drawing paper* in the better grades contains a high percentage of rag stock, is tough and durable, and has a smooth, fine-grained, hard surface that will withstand frequent erasures. It is used primarily for precise graphical solutions and preliminary design layouts made with a sharp, hard pencil (3H to 6H). The drawing is not intended for reproduction.
>
> —B. Leighton Wellman, *Introduction to Graphical Analysis and Design*

This concise description covers what good drawing paper is, what its uses are, and what its uses are not. Notice that although the passage contains fifteen descriptive adjectives (almost 28 percent of the words), none of them is intended to be connotative, to arouse emotion. The writer of this description may have a deep appreciation for fine paper, but you would never know that from this passage.

WRITING
EXERCISE

3.2

Write a short, technical description of a material or tool that you know well. Be sure to choose something minimal enough to describe in 50 to 100 words. Keep your feelings about the subject out of the description. Use the drawing paper description as an example.

Imaginative Description

In contrast to technical description, imaginative description creates not only visual or other sensory images but also ideas or emotions about the image.

Thus, you will use more connotative language and will select only those details that reinforce the idea or feeling you want to convey. Here is a descriptive paragraph by novelist Kaatje Hurlbut about a small statue of Eve in her grandmother's living room.

> Sometimes I only considered Eve herself because of her loveliness. When the room was dim she gleamed in the shadowy corner; but when the sun came into the room in the morning she dazzled until she seemed to be made of light pressed into hardness. And the cleanness of her was cleaner than anything I could think of: cleaner than my grandmother's kid gloves; cleaner than witch hazel on a white handkerchief.

Notice that Hurlbut chooses descriptive details that give you an image of the child's fascination with the statue as well as the statue's luminous appearance.

Following is an excerpt from a student essay about an accident on a construction site. The writer uses descriptive details to set the scene.

> My fitter and partner Ed and I were assigned to fit and weld six six-inch valves to a twelve-inch diameter header, which was approximately twenty feet long and weighed thousands of pounds. This header was located in a long narrow hallway about five feet wide. We had lifted the header up onto a set of pipe stands so that we could weld on the valves. The hallway, besides being narrow, was also very busy as it was used by many others in performing their jobs. Other pipefitters were working on part of the same system at the other end of the hallway. They were welding and grinding to install valves on the header, much the same as we were doing. Their and our work would alternate between the ear-piercing scream of the grinders and the blinding flash of intense light produced by the welding arc. Some boilermakers were working on a tank in the bay in front of us. Their work calls for enormous amounts of sledge hammering and the use of large heating torches to shape the parts of the tank. When we work in close proximity to them, it's like having a bucket over our heads with someone banging on it with a hammer. The boilermakers also weld and grind in their work, so we have all of the light, noise, smoke, and dust of those operations along with the teeth-jarring sound of the sledge hammers. Besides the other fitters and boilermakers, a small crew of two carpenters and a laborer worked in the bay next to us building a scaffold. The clap of their hammers and the screech of their circular saw, not to mention the sawdust, add to the general state of confusion. You can imagine the concert which

the light, smoke, heat, dust, and sound make; it is almost like something out of a science fiction movie. In this environment it is difficult to think, let alone communicate.

—Jesse Hunter

1. List phrases of technical description in Hunter's writing. List phrases of imaginative description. What ideas and feelings does Hunter convey in this passage? What would you expect to happen in the rest of the essay?

2. Write a paragraph or two describing a typical scene at your workplace. Consider using words that involve sound, sight, movement, and emotion.

The most imaginative descriptive writing you will likely do will be expressive—that is, you will describe your thoughts and feelings. Be sensitive to all the words available to convey emotional states. Choose the most specific one. If you write, "I felt terrible," question yourself closely. Be more accurate. That vague sentence could mean anything from "I was humiliated" to "I had a stomachache" to "Guilt overwhelmed me." Say which it was. Consider also the gradations and fine distinctions among feelings you can express. Are you restless, bored, exhausted, or dead? Impressed, surprised, stunned, astounded, or shocked?

A student writer describes her feelings about her favorite old shoes in the following excerpt.

Something about an old pair of beat-up, ragamuffin tennies has an inherent appeal. The mud stains, the frayed nylon, the holes, the scuffed leather—all these add to the shoes' attractiveness. This attractiveness is more than just the comfortable feel of shoes that have been well broken in. It is a warm familiarity, a feeling akin to the love you have for friends who have seen you through your worst and best times. This feeling is often so strong that you stand up to your parents in order to save your tennies from the jaws of the garbage truck.

I believe that this strong emotional tie to a favorite pair of tennies comes not only from familiarity and a peculiar aesthetic pleasure in their ragged appearance but, more powerfully, from the situations that these shoes have seen you through. After all, you rarely grow so attached to a pair of black pumps or dress shoes because you usually wear them only to church and formal events. But those tattered tennis shoes have been with you in your everyday life, where your highest joys and your bitterest pains come to pass. The events you've lived through and the lessons you've learned are symbolized by your dusty old tennies.

—Brenda Stalcup

Write a paragraph or two about some article of clothing or household item that you would have a hard time throwing away even if it were worn out. Be sure to describe your feelings, give concrete details, and explain why you feel the way you do.

WRITING
EXERCISE

3.4

SAMPLE OF STUDENT DESCRIPTIVE WRITING

In the examples so far, we have seen descriptive writing used to identify a material, to convey an idea about an object, to set a scene, and to communicate a feeling. The complete, unified student essay below uses description to achieve all of these purposes.

Last Visit

The curtains were closed. They made light and dust into a fog that played with some leftover tobacco smell. The stuff tricked me into thinking it was pipe smoke, just for a minute, until I remembered no one had smoked a pipe there for months. Just like no one had worn the soft felt hats hanging on the rack, no one had used the pipe cleaners lying on the desk, and no one had slept in the flannel pajamas lying lifelessly across the twin bed. I was the first in months to look at the pictures on my grandpa's dresser through that smoky haze of sunlight. I had seen them before when I came into grandpa's room to steal some candy he had hidden to save my teeth or to look at his jars full of pennies; the pictures looked strange and solemn now.

Until I stepped on a crumpled paper on grandpa's floor and jumped at the loudness of the rustle, I hadn't noticed how silent the room was. When I walked to his bed over the hardwood floor, my steps echoed. My eyes ran over a hundred different familiar things: the earth-colored hats, the massive typewriter that sat like a lead weight on his desk, rows of brown leather shoes and ancient

1

2

pipe-cleaner animals I made him to trade for the candy. They looked so soft and dear in the strange light that I almost forgot they were just things that didn't mean much when he wore them or used them.

3   Everything was different, and his room looked like a dream or a church or a shrine full of treasures that look soft through the clouds of incense. Nothing really moves in those places; real people only pass through to feel time stop, to feel outside their real world. I wanted to stay and nap on the bed like I did when Grandpa was gone to work, but his bedroom didn't feel like it belonged to the real world anymore either; it felt like a place to stop and remember but not to stay and disturb. I sat on his bed and hugged his old pajamas; they smelled like a forgotten teddy bear pulled from an attic. I lay my head on his pillow and watched the dust roll through the sunlight.

4   It rolled down and rested on grandpa's bedside table and onto his alarm clock. It was the old type, made of yellow metal with bells on the top. The haze made it look like an ancient relic. I could remember the sound of its tick in my head, but I never heard it ring; Grandpa was always up cooking bacon in his pajamas long before I dressed for grade school. I wanted to wind it and hear it again, maybe even set it to ring. But it didn't seem like I should change it or anything else there. When it was Grandpa's it had always been my favorite room, but everything that was warm and messy and comfortable was frozen into a frame like a picture.

5   I wanted to stay; still I felt like I had been playing somewhere where playing is forbidden. I took a last look at the pictures and hats and wondered who would clear the room; I wondered who would take the penny jars. My feet clacked over the hardwood on my way out into the sounds of bacon snapping and the conversation of my mom and grandma in the kitchen. When I pulled shut the door of the room, I felt the weight of the old alarm clock swinging in my coat pocket.

—Kathleen McNeal

Idea for Descriptive Writing

Write a three- or four-paragraph essay describing a solitary experience you once had—for example, being alone with nature, doing something alone for the first time, catching some private time, being alone in a crowd, being unexpectedly alone, having to do something by yourself. Try to convey, as McNeal does, the dominant feeling of the experience, whether it was positive, negative, or tedious.

Narration

If you have had the pleasure of knowing a good storyteller or the agony of knowing a terrible one, you already understand a lot about narration. A poor narrator can make you yawn during an account of being kidnapped at gunpoint. In contrast, a great narrator can make you smother your laughter so as not to miss the next detail of her problems with her kitchen carpeting. The difference between the two storytellers does not come from one having more inherently interesting subjects than the other; the difference lies in the narrator's style and selection of detail. As you write your narrative, keep in mind the image of someone you know who tells particularly good anecdotes, and try to imitate those good qualities.

When to Use a Narrative Pattern

You see narration in its pure form whenever you read fiction. But that is not the only appropriate place for it. Every pattern of development is likely to include sections of narration. For instance, a paper in which you attempt to persuade college students not to procrastinate will probably include somewhere a story of your own grim experience with procrastination, and in that story you should exercise all the narrative skills you are about to learn. At work, if you must write a letter to your customers explaining why the new catalogs are so late, you may find yourself narrating a series of events, from last-minute changes in prices to the printer's pneumonia.

Narration ties ideas to real, sensory, day-to-day experience: it binds the abstract to the concrete. That is why narration helps make all kinds of writing more interesting and meaningful. Writing down stories from your life can be one of the most significant things you can do for people born after you: consider how Anne Frank's diary has touched millions of people and has made them treasure a free society. If you have writing that was passed down from your own ancestors, you appreciate how much your relatives value knowing about those earlier lives.

Although your personal stories are probably not appropriate for the types of writing you do at school and work, writing them down can build skills that will serve whenever you need to write a clear narrative explanation.

How to Organize Narration

Not too many things can go wrong with straight chronological organization. Getting events out of order is possible, but not likely. More likely people will digress, or wander off the main track, as you have noticed poor storytellers do. No one wants to hear details about the syllabus of your college philosophy course, when the main point of the story has to do with the unusual way you disposed of the textbook when the class was over.

Thinking Critically About Narration: Selection of Details

Sometimes, a certain kind of digression—a *flashback*—is exactly what you want. A jump into the past can reinforce a mood, explain a character's motivation, or give background necessary for the reader's understanding of the event. How do you decide whether material out of sequence is an important flashback or a tiresome digression? Keep your goal firmly in mind. Ask yourself how much the proposed addition contributes to that goal, and give it space in direct proportion to its contribution. Kathleen McNeal, in the essay earlier in this chapter (p. 35), flashes back to her grandfather's daily life just enough to give us some insight into his character. Notice, though, that the writer does not tell us how Grandpa died or what he did for a living, facts that are unimportant to the focus—her own reactions to his empty room. This process of choosing details to include and exclude is called *selection,* and a good storyteller does it all the time, both consciously and unconsciously.

Remember that as you respond to our writing suggestions here, your goals do not always have to involve heavy revelations about the Meaning of Life or Human Nature. Your goal can be to tell an amusing, entertaining, exciting, unusual, or puzzling story; this kind of story can have a worthwhile point too. Just keep in mind that when you are describing a peaceful stroll on a perfect fall day, you may choose to ignore the squished squirrel you saw in the gutter.

Writing the Rough Draft

Once you know your goal and what details you are going to include in order to get there, your next step is writing a rough draft of the paper. And that means you will have to decide where to divide paragraphs. We admit that this is hard to do when you are writing a chronological sequence, because events and details seem to run together.

One hint is to look for breaks in the time sequence and try dividing paragraphs at each break. For instance, if your narrative concerns the problem of moving to a new apartment on Monday, discovering many cockroaches and no hot water on Tuesday, and fighting with the landlord and moving out on Wednesday, you might try dividing the paragraphs so you have one for Monday, one for Tuesday, and one for Wednesday.

Your action will not often divide itself tidily into Monday, Tuesday, Wednesday, or morning, afternoon, evening. If you do not have clear and even time breaks, look for other kinds of breaks. In narrative writing, sometimes the focus will shift from description of environment to description of character, from incident to incident, from a character's inner thoughts to that character's outward action, from one character to another, from main story to flashback and back again, or from background material to action. These shifts of focus are possible places to divide paragraphs. Remember that a traditional paragraph within the body of an essay runs about 100 words long, so do not divide too often. In a technical memo or report, you divide paragraphs (or sections) much more frequently.

SAMPLE OF STUDENT NARRATIVE WRITING

The student essay that follows and McNeal's "Last Visit," earlier in the chapter, are good examples of narrative writing. The questions after the next essay will focus your attention on the strategies used. You may also refer to these essays as you study narrative introductions, conclusions, and transitions.

Running Home

The pitch was perfect, low and outside. I swung the bat as hard as I could. The sound the bat made when it contacted the ball was as loud as thunder. I started running as if my shorts were on fire. I didn't hear anything except the sounds of my labored breathing and my cleats chewing into the loose dirt. 1

The player in center field had almost reached the ball when I rounded second base. In my mind he was too late; I had already made the decision to run all the way to home plate. I shifted into high gear. I could feel every muscle straining. I was running as fast as I ever have—or ever will again. 2

The silence was broken when I touched third base. All of a sudden, I was aware of an amazing amount of noise. Everyone was yelling, cheering me on, jumping up and down like little kids. Then I heard someone scream at me to hit 3 the deck, which meant for me to slide. I leapt off my feet in midstride, pushing my body into a head-first slide. I stretched my arms out and extended my body as long as I could. I was trying to grab just a tiny piece of the rubber mat lying in the dirt, commonly referred to as home plate.

4   I never saw the umpire stretch both arms out to his side and yell, "SAFE!" I never heard the whoops and squeals of joy by my teammates. I never heard the roar in the bleachers. All I heard was a disturbing grinding noise that sent a chill up my spine. Immediately after hitting the plate, I was overcome with excruciating pain radiating from my left knee. I grabbed my knee and started rolling around on the ground. I screamed, "Ouch, darn, that hurts"—or some similar phrase.

5   The doctor put my leg back down on the examining table and said, "You have torn a radial cartilage and strained, or torn, a ligament." Dr. Wright had looked at me only for a minute or two, but she knew what was causing my pain. She scheduled me for an operation on Friday. Four days after my big game-winning home run, I underwent knee surgery.

6   During my rehabilitation therapy I was taught several exercises that, as far as I could tell, had only one purpose—causing me great pain. All I had to do was lie flat on my back. Then, while keeping my leg straight, I was supposed to lift my leg six inches off the floor. It sounds very simple and easy, but I couldn't accomplish this small task for quite some time. My muscles would shake, and sweat would pour off of me. I would grit my teeth, grunt and groan, but my leg wouldn't budge an inch. During my recovery, I couldn't do many things, so I had plenty of time for thinking.

7   One of the things I thought about was how much I resembled my grandfather. My grandfather was a very big man, and really strong, but he moved slowly, had a slight limp, and made funny noises in the process of standing up and sitting down. I thought it was quite humorous and made fun of him. "Just you wait," he would warn. "One of these days you'll be old too."

8   I came to the startling conclusion that my grandfather was right. I would get old. I just didn't think it would happen so soon. When I was young, I broke several bones in different accidents. I never really thought much about these injuries, because I always healed quickly, and I have no long-term side effects. Now that I'm edging ever closer to my thirtieth year, I don't seem to heal as fast. I'm sore for a day or two after going water skiing. My joints make cracking noises when I get out of bed in the morning, and sometimes when I get into bed at night.

Sometimes my knee is a little stiff, so I walk with a limp. Sometimes, I even grunt and groan when standing or sitting. I guess for the next fifty years, I'll have to slide into home plate feet first.

—Matthew D. Kraft

EXERCISE

3.5

1. Choose from each student narrative in this section one paragraph that seems to have especially vivid details. Note the details and tell what sense they appeal to: sight, hearing, taste, touch, smell.

2. Try to summarize each writer's goal.

3. How does each writer limit the time frame—that is, keep the story from expanding to an unmanageable size?

4. Identify each writer's flashbacks or digressions (if any) and tell what (if anything) these contribute to the goal of the essay.

5. Find in each essay events that are condensed and summarized rather than told in detail. Why do you think the writer chose to condense?

6. Note how paragraphs are divided in each paper. Identify the principles each writer used in choosing where to start new paragraphs.

How to Introduce a Narrative Essay

The introduction to a narrative essay is usually quite different from introductions to other common types of papers, in which stating your thesis is important. In narrative essay introductions, your best plan is to barely hint at your main point, focusing instead on preparing your reader psychologically for what is to come. Most good narratives move *inductively;* that is, they move through specific incidents and details leading to a main point at the end. The exception is a narrative written to explain or inform, in which you *do* want to state the main idea up front: "We at XYZ know that you look forward to your new catalog each February. Let us explain why your XYZ catalog was a month late this year."

For personal essays like Kraft's and McNeal's, a more subtle touch is appropriate. Notice that both writers let the readers join the action as it is happening, and we fill in the necessary background as we go. McNeal does not begin with her grandfather's death, and Kraft leaves out all early innings of the baseball game. The readers must build the context for themselves, which involves them directly with the narrative.

Inexperienced writers almost always need to cut the flab off narrative introductions. A poor storyteller would start "Running Home" (p. 39) something like this:

> I was always a person who took his youth and health for granted. Because I was so cocky, I would take physical risks that put me in danger, just for the sake of scoring a point or even for a thrill. However, two years ago I had an experience playing baseball that made me revise my ideas about being invulnerable. Our baseball team, the Rat's Kisses, was playing our rivals, the Beich's Bananas. . . .

This introduction offers lots of background in a boring way and practically slaps you with the main point of the narrative. All of it is unnecessary, as we can see from reading "Running Home."

Because openings are so difficult to write, though, we suggest that you go ahead and put down whatever you can bring yourself to write, boring or not. Then cut and revise later after you have finished the rough draft. Be sure to check the first sentence or two to see whether they should be left off completely.

WRITING
EXERCISE

3.6

1. Pretend that you are going to write a narrative about a childhood incident. As an introduction, you have decided to describe briefly your own childhood character. Write the introduction in two different ways:
   A. As though the main goal of your story is to be light and amusing.
   B. As though the main purpose of the story is serious.
   Be ready to point out the changes you made to alter the mood.

2. Pretend that your boss has asked you to write a memo explaining what brought about a mistake you made at work. You intend to write a narrative about what happened. Write the first two or three sentences of your memo.

How to Conclude a Narrative Essay

You may want to come right out and tell the reader your conclusions. "Running Home" does this clearly (see p. 39). Notice how the conclusion continues the mood of the paper by ending with a humorous look at the writer's own faulty thinking.

"Last Visit" relies on understatement for its conclusion (see p. 35). It does not come right out and say, "I bid a final goodbye to my grandfather and took a reminder of his life to become a part of my own." This point comes across from concrete images: the shutting door and the weight of the clock in the writer's pocket as she leaves. Several details in the closing paragraph echo earlier details, giving the paper a satisfying feeling of completeness.

The same advice goes for conclusions as for introductions: do not overstate. Do not express your main point the same way in both the introduction and the conclusion, and do not repeat it over and over in the conclusion. Even in business writing, one concise sentence of summary or request for action is better than a lengthy rehash.

Write a closing sentence or two for the memo you began in Writing Exercise 3.6, item 2 (see p. 42).

WRITING EXERCISE

3.7

How to Hold a Narrative Together

Since a narrative organization is basically chronological, the transitional words you use will usually refer to time: *then, after, when, during, meanwhile, later, earlier, before.* Their main purpose is to make time relationships between events clear. In a narrative, such transitions will probably come naturally, but there is one you have to watch out for: *and then.* In conversation, we usually join events in a story by saying, "Then . . . and then . . . and then." In writing, the repetition of this transition seems childlike. It's better to have too few transitional terms than too many. When the time sequence is clear and straightforward, your readers can follow a narrative with no trouble.

Guidelines for Exchanging Papers

If you do exchange papers for revision suggestions (see Fig. 3.1), here are some guidelines to follow as you write out your responses:

1. Be polite. Adopt the role of helper rather than critic.
2. Make your comments constructive. If you intend to complain about something, try to offer a suggestion for improvement. If you can't think of such a suggestion, you might phrase your feelings as a question like, "Does this sound right to you?"

FIGURE 3.1

*Checklist for
Revising a
Narrative
Essay*

Here is a handy checklist to refer to as you work to improve a rough draft written in the narrative pattern. You may want to exchange papers with another student and answer these questions about each other's rough draft.

1. Is the main goal clear but not too bluntly stated?

2. Does the paper focus on events within reasonable time limits? How long is the period covered?

3. Do any digressions or flashbacks serve a purpose?

4. Are the verbs correct? Past tense for past events ("I sneezed"), past perfect tense for past events that occurred even earlier than those in past tense ("I had sneezed"), and present tense for the thoughts and events happening now ("I sneeze") or happening both in the past and continuing in the present ("I sneeze when I eat chocolate," "I am sneezing a lot these days").

5. Does every paragraph contain specific details that appeal to the reader's senses and help build the desired response?

6. Are the body paragraphs divided according to a reasoned principle, not according to whim? What is the principle? Do most paragraphs contain more than two sentences?

7. Does the tone in the introduction, body, and conclusion either stay consistent or shift for a reason (not changing accidentally)?

8. Is there dialogue that reflects character when appropriate? Is the dialogue punctuated correctly? (See Quotation Marks in "An A to Z Guide to Revision and Editing," Chapter 14, for help with punctuation.)

9. Are the introduction and conclusion free from unnecessary padding?

10. Does the conclusion tie in with the introduction?

3. Try to help the author meet his or her own goals. Do not try to make the paper over to suit what *your* goals might be, if it were yours. Do not put words in the author's mouth.

4. Do not rush the job. A series of short, choppy answers, unexplained, will not help your partner. Put in the same amount of concentration as you hope your own partner will put into your paper.

Ideas for Narrative Writing

As you choose your subject for narrative writing, be sure to identify what your purpose is and who you are writing for. For instance, the first suggestion below is "I learned _____ the hard way." A student choosing this one might think to herself, "I'm going to write about how I learned the difference between love and infatuation the hard way. My purpose is to clarify the distinction for other teenagers who might make the same mistakes I did."

If the student has not given the nature of her audience some thought, she might unconsciously address several different ones. Her paper might sound partly like an academic definition, partly like a midnight chat in the dorm, and partly like a sappy country-western song. The parts would not hang together.

1. I learned _____ the hard way.
2. I really liked my _____, but I lost it.
3. Describe a misunderstanding you had when you were younger of the world or of language, and tell how the misunderstanding was corrected.
4. Narrate a situation in which you fortunately or mistakenly followed someone else's judgment rather than your own; or narrate a situation in which you trusted your own judgment over someone else's.
5. Narrate an experience that led you to a new realization about yourself (or about someone else).
6. Tell the story of a tough ethical decision you once had to make and its consequences.
7. Write an account of your initiation into some element of the adult world—for example, violence, hypocrisy, racism, sexism, sexuality, etiquette, obligation, self-sacrifice.
8. Read "Coming to America, To Clean," the narrative reprinted in the next section of this chapter. Interview someone about their immigration experience, and edit the interview into a narrative essay.
9. *Possible collaborative essay*: Do some research into the historical beginnings of the school you are attending. Write "The Story of College X," a narrative that will be mailed out with your school's informational material to prospective students and their parents.

COMING TO AMERICA, TO CLEAN

Ana Maria Corona

Ana Maria Corona collected interviews in Spanish with illegal domestic workers in California. She translated and edited these workers' stories, making a collection called "Like a Flower in the Dust: What They Really Think While They Wax Your Floor," which was printed in the San Diego Reader *in 1993. The narrative we reprint here appeared in* Harper's *magazine and was narrated by a Mexican housekeeper, Antonia.*

1   I grew up in a *pueblito* in Sinaloa, in the countryside not far from Rosamorada. I was happy enough, but my friends always talked about getting married or leaving town and going someplace more exciting. My friends told me I was too pretty to stay there, that I should go where I would be appreciated by real men, have a fine life. Even my uncle told me I should go out into the world, not stay there. "Like a flower in the dust," he said. But how was I to make my way?

2   There was one way. Go to the border and find work as a maid in a foreign household. Every year some of the girls would catch the bus to Tijuana or Ciudad Juárez and try to get jobs on the other side of the frontier. Some came back to visit with nice clothes and money. Some never came back.

3   My cousin Blanca was the one who first made the decision to go to Tijuana. She was pretty wild, but even she wouldn't travel alone, so she asked me to go with her. Her argument was that if we didn't leave when we were young, we would be trapped. Our families wanted us to stay, because they didn't want to lose us as workers and producers of more workers. She said, "If we are going to clean house, we might as well get paid for it." I thought about it and realized she was right. I begged my uncle to loan me money to go to Tijuana. I had a little money of my own, and we could stay with Blanca's aunt in Tijuana. He gave me the money but made me promise not to tell my mother he had given it to me. I left without saying good-bye to her; I just left a letter. Blanca and I caught a ride to Rosamorada and bought tickets to Tijuana. We were two very excited girls, giggling but scared half to death. I'll never forget stepping off the bus into that huge station full of men looking us over and *coyotes* offering us rides to Los Angeles. I was very excited and glad that I had come.

4   Blanca found us both jobs in homes in San Diego in less than a month—with the help of our aunt and a thousand of her friends, of course. That's how it works: it's all word of mouth. Young girls move on or get married or make enough money

to go back home, so they give word to their friends and the news passes around. There's a huge network of relatives, friends, inquiries, lost phone messages, old women carrying tales.

Once Blanca and I had jobs, we had to find a way to get across the border to claim them. Our future *patrones* were not willing to smuggle us across in their cars, which would have been the safest way for us. We would have to report to work through our own efforts.   5

We had heard the usual terrible stories of difficult crossings through dangerous terrain, of people being betrayed and sold, of people being robbed and raped and killed. But we were lucky. We met an excellent *coyote* named Javier, who said he could take us across as easily as we could cross a street downtown. He wanted $300 apiece, which my uncle said was a high price but fair enough if Javi was as good as he said. Blanca's aunt loaned her the fee and mine would be paid by my *patrones* when Javi delivered me. In return, I would work the first month for them without pay. This had all been arranged through the network of calls and whispers and customs.   6

On the night we were to go, I was terrified. If Blanca hadn't been going with me, I wouldn't have left the house. We met Javi at La Dichosa, a large open-air taco stand in lower Libertad. I was nervous and scared, and couldn't eat a thing. There were eight of us—five men in their twenties and another girl, the fiancée of one of the men. We waited in La Dichosa, everyone nervous, until after midnight. Finally a big red-and-black taxi came, and we all got in.   7

At first we seemed to be just driving around. Nobody was talking except Javi and the taxi driver. We were driving without headlights and we stopped several times while Javi and the driver stared across into the dark and said things that made no sense to me. Then we entered a short alley that led to a fence. I looked at it, wondering if I could climb it. Javi got out, walked over to the fence, and just opened it up like a door.   8

The fence had been neatly cut and hooked on nails so that the cuts could not be seen from the other side. Javi motioned us out of the taxi and through the opening in the fence. He told us, very casually, to walk behind him and keep quiet. But if he said "Drop," we were to fall flat on the ground, and if he said "Back," we should run back to the fence, where the taxi driver would be waiting to open it for us. But there was no need. We walked across the weeds like we were strolling through a park. When we reached the highway a van pulled over, Javi opened the door, and we jumped in and drove off. Javi smiled at me and said, "See? You could have worn your high heels." I realized that we were in the United States, and that I was an outlaw.   9

When we got to the parking lot where I was to meet my new *patrones*, Javi walked me over to a huge blue Cadillac. The people in the car looked like good people to me, a middle-aged couple that you could tell had been married a long time by the way they sat.   10

11   Javi took money from the man, counted it, then told me, "Get in, go with them. They just bought you for a month, a year, who knows how long." I got in the backseat of the Cadillac, and the lady turned around and smiled at me. She said, *"Bienvenidos."* She kept on talking to me, but I couldn't understand her. I felt like I'd jumped off a bridge and was washing down the river. It was two weeks before Christmas. I had just turned sixteen.

Process: Making Steps Clear

Like narration, process writing has an order set by time. Just as there are poor narrators and great narrators, some people have a knack for explaining a process clearly and painlessly, while others could not be trusted to tell you how to get out of a telephone booth.

When to Use a Process Pattern

You make use of process writing whenever you follow written directions, whether you are putting together a three-speed bicycle or hanging wallpaper. The most common form of process writing is a list of directions for how to do something. Process writing can also describe how something works: how a cigarette lighter lights, how yeast makes bread rise, or how seeing-eye dogs are trained.

You have seen the victims of bad process writing—kids who grimly pedal everywhere in first gear, homeowners who keep a bottle of Elmer's Glue in each room to fix the walls as they unpeel. In the face of such confusion there is still hope. You are about to learn to write clear, step-by-step prose, a valuable skill to possess in the workplace.

Identifying your intended audience is crucial to good process writing. A microcomputer manufacturer would write wholly different set-up instructions for computer engineers than for brand-new micro owners. Be sure to ask yourself questions about your audience: Who are they? What do they already know about this process? What background and definitions do they need? What will make this process easy for them to understand?

How to Organize a Process Paper

To write a process paper, you should make sure that all the different things are in there. First, an introduction is written. Next, the body of the paper is developed fully in several paragraphs. Near the opening of the paper, terms should be well defined. The conclusion does not have to be very long—just long enough to tie it all up.

Before you give up, read on. The paragraph you just read is a sample of some truly miserable process writing. Jot down a list of five problems you see in it. Your list is likely to fit in with the following advice about how to do the job right.

First, process writing involves a sequence of time and action, and that sequence is easiest to follow if it is in order. Do not jump around, as our sample does by telling you what to put in the opening *after* it brings up the body paragraphs. The importance of order makes it absolutely necessary to write a scratch outline for process papers. This outline can be a numbered list of steps. You have to write the steps in the order that they should or do occur, which may not be the same order in which they happen to flit through your mind.

When you have an outline, you can go back and fill in the details about each step no matter when you think of them. (Writing on a computer gives you similar flexibility.) Be sure not to skip any steps, accidentally sabotaging your reader. Computer manuals are so frequently guilty of such omissions that a series of manuals "for dummies" are hot sellers at the bookstore. (We have reprinted a section from *Windows for Dummies* at the end of this chapter.) Of course, computer users are not actually dummies—they have just been undermined by very poor process writing.

A Sample Sentence Outline

One way to be quite sure that your ideas are in order is to prepare a sentence outline. This type of outline differs from an informal list of topics and subtopics because it requires that you put each paragraph idea and supporting idea into a complete sentence. What's the use? The process will prevent you from jotting down a word or phrase like "Advantages" or "Imp. of materials" without really thinking about what you are going to say about those topics. Here is a sentence outline devised by a student who has an almost foolproof system for housecleaning.

    I. <u>Thesis</u>: After eighteen years of practice, my spouse and I have a great system for cleaning our house without ruining our lives, and this system can help you, too.

   II. Set aside a realistic time for your cleaning.

      A. When you begin your program of systematic cleaning, check and record how long it takes you to do a task, so you won't underestimate it in your schedule.

       1. The bathroom floor, though small, usually takes longer to clean than you might think.

       2. In contrast, mopping a well-swept kitchen floor doesn't take very long.

   B. Decide when to do your housework, keeping in mind how it fits into the rest of your life.

       1. Don't sabotage yourself by choosing a time when you are usually tired or stressed out (like directly after work on Monday).

       2. Choose a time when you can listen to some entertainment at a volume loud enough to be heard throughout one whole floor; be sure to consider the neighbors' schedules, too.

          a. We clean during our soap opera, since we don't need to see the screen.

          b. You might listen to books on tape or your favorite operas.

III. Be sure that all your cleaning materials are ready before you start.

   A. Keep all your products together stored in your work bucket so you don't have to round them up from odd places.

   B. When you notice a product is running low, put it on the grocery list immediately, and put the replacement in the bucket (not under the sink, on the basement steps, or in other weird locations).

   C. Buy good quality cleaning tools.

       1. We struggled with a cheap kitchen mop for a year before springing for one twice as expensive and three times as easy to use.

       2. A specialized duster for cleaning cobwebs off ceilings is preferable to a clumsy improvised tool for the same purpose.

IV. Clean each room systematically.

   A. Pick up and put away clutter from the whole room, and move the light furniture out before you start cleaning.

   B. Know what products and tools you will need for each room, and take those in with you (instead of running back and forth to fetch them).

   C. Clean from top to bottom.

       1. Fallout from cleaning the ceiling and counters should land on the kitchen floor before, not after, you clean the floor.

       2. Window cleaner from doing the mirrors will drift down onto sinks and fixtures, so the mirrors need to be cleaned first.

V. Build a good reward into your system to keep you motivated.

    A. The only time we go out to lunch together is after cleaning the house.

    B. You might take a nap in your clean bedroom when you're done.

    C. Entertain friends the same evening in your spotless house.

VI. <u>Closing</u>: Put the money you haven't spent on a cleaning service in a jar and plan a vacation.

Thinking Critically About Process Writing: The Challenge of Comprehensiveness

The biggest challenge in process writing is to think through the process carefully, keeping your readers in mind, so that you are able to explain each step fully. One weakness that you probably noted about our bad opening paragraph was lack of explanation. Here are five tips for explaining a process fully.

1. *Define Terms.* When you use a word that is unfamiliar to most of your readers, or use a common word in an unusual way, you should let your readers know what you mean. For example, in describing how to adjust a sewing machine stitch, you might advise the reader, "Check the tension of the bobbin thread." If your audience includes only people who sew, there is no problem—but if not, both the terms *tension* and *bobbin* need defining.

2. *Be Specific.* In writing, you must learn to make yourself clear without all those gestures and grimaces you use in conversation. If you are *telling* someone face to face how to wire a fuse box, you can say, "Strip the insulation off a short piece of the wire," demonstrate by holding your thumb and index finger about an inch apart, and the instruction is understood. But in writing, you have to change that "short piece" to "one inch," because when your reader is gaping at a twenty-foot length of wire, a "short piece" could reasonably be anything from half an inch to three feet—and you do not want to be responsible for three feet of stripped wire exposed in someone's basement.

3. *Include Reasons.* You could probably prevent someone from stripping three feet of wire if you explain that the stripped wire is used to make a little hook that fits snugly under a screw in the fuse box to form an electrical connection. Knowing the reason for stripping the wire could help the reader do it right. So *tell not only what to do, but why.* The same rule applies to a descriptive process paper—the kind in which you describe a process without asking your reader to do anything but understand it. For instance, you may write, "The carburetor mixes gas and air," but it would be better to write, "The carburetor mixes gas and air to make the most highly combustible combination possible, so it can be easily ignited by the spark plugs." Telling why the carburetor mixes gas and air makes the process more intelligible and meaningful.

4. *Include Don'ts.* If there happens to be a common (or uncommon but disastrous) mistake that people can make in performing the process you are describing, you had better warn your readers. Tell *why* it is a mistake, too (remember tip 3). For instance, "Do not stick your fingers in the fuse box unless you have pulled out the main fuse" is handy advice. You may even go on to explain, "or you are likely to electrocute yourself by touching live wires" to emphasize your point. Sometimes, as you can see, the *don'ts* are as important as the *dos*.

5. *Mention Pitfalls.* People could follow your yogurt recipe meticulously and still end up with a batch that just will not yog (thicken). It would be a great comfort to these people if you mention that this problem might occur if the starter or culture used was old or if the cow the milk came from was given penicillin, which kills the bacteria that make yogurt thicken. Whenever things are likely to go wrong despite your careful directions, let your readers know about it. You may help save their sanity.

Finding a Subject

Your best prospect in finding a subject is to describe a process that you happen to know more about than most people do. Do you know how to paste up a page for a newspaper? Do you have a foolproof method of washing the dog? Are you especially good at analyzing poetry, building picture frames, playing backgammon, or writing letters home for money? Do you happen to know why the sky is sometimes red at night? Make a list of your skills and interests. Surely you will find a process that will instruct or entertain your readers, or maybe even do both.

Concerning more practical experience, you may decide to explain a process you perform at work, such as leaving directions for a substitute worker. Or detail a process that occurs at your workplace; for example, "How a Printing Press Works" or "How Responsibilities Are Divided at XYZ Corporation."

Facing the Blank Page

The paragraphs in your essay will probably be divided by steps and substeps in the process. Your decisions about paragraph division can be based on the suggestions we made in the previous section on narratives (see pp. 38–39). Or your essay may be a presentation of several alternative methods of performing an activity, like one student essay advising small children "How to Get Rid of Your Peas." Its paragraph topics are:

> Feed them to the dog under the table
> Hide them under other food on your plate
> Put them in your mouth, but quickly transfer them to your napkin

When you are doing process writing in a technical or business setting, you often use visual elements to separate the steps or sections. It's traditional to use bullets (symbols like ● or ◆) or numbers before each entry and to insert white space between the entries.

The most difficult task in process writing, as in so many areas of life, is to do it with grace, wit, and charm. Even very practical how-to books, like cookbooks, bicycle repair manuals, and textbooks, are sometimes happily endowed with these qualities.

Using the informal *you* to refer to the reader helps your style sound smooth. We use *you* in this textbook to address you, our readers. We could make a more formal tone by substituting "the writer" or "one" for you: "The paragraphs in a writer's essay will probably be divided by steps." Alternatively, we could avoid the *yous* by writing in passive voice: "The paragraphs in an essay will probably be divided by steps." Always ask your instructor or your supervisor at work whether to use the informal *you* or whether to be more formal. Whichever you choose, be consistent throughout your writing.

SAMPLES OF STUDENT PROCESS WRITING

The student writer of this first process paper focuses on recommending a system she has developed for putting together items that require assembly.

Some Assembly Necessary

"Oh, no!" cried my friends upon opening the brand new Jeopardy game we   1
intended to play on Christmas. As three pairs of hands quickly passed the box
my way, I heard a chorus of "You do it, Georgia!" and "Georgia actually likes this
stuff." I knew what was coming: yes, the box held several bags of plastic parts

to be assembled into home Jeopardy screens. As my friends know, I enjoy the challenge of putting together "easy-to-assemble" objects. I have assembled countless toys and games, a handsome kitchen island, a router mount and guide, a workbench, and most of the bookshelves and cabinets in our household—all without going crazy. I've enjoyed the admiration and gratitude of my friends and neighbors. If you'd like to develop this skill, I can give you some advice. My most important pointers have to do with how to approach the task, before you ever fit Tab A into Slot B.

2   Many would-be assemblers fail by plunging hastily and blindly into the project. My system involves a Zen style, starting with frame of mind. First, concentrate on staying calm and gathering your strength. Rid the area of innocent bystanders. Whining children and impulsive adult helpers need to be distracted so you can concentrate. I suggested on Christmas that my friends play a round of Trivial Pursuit while I put the Jeopardy game together. Next, fix yourself a refreshing hot or cold drink, making the occasion more casual than compelling. Put all thoughts of hurry out of your mind, and think instead about relishing the process rather than the product.

3   With this mental state, get an overview of the project before you. I look at all the stuff provided in an idle, detached way, fondling the parts as a curious lab chimp might. Don't force yourself to understand how each piece functions at this point: much of your comprehension will grow naturally as you follow the directions, so there's no point to frustrating yourself now. Glance at all the paperwork included in the kit to see what types of information you have there. My kitchen island kit was fairly typical, including a list of parts, an instruction sheet, a diagram of the completed piece, and some close-up diagrams of certain parts of the island. Pay attention to the diagram of the final product, so you can visualize what you're aiming at.

4   Now you're ready to prepare for action. Clear a space for your work. I cleared just half the dining room table to put together the Jeopardy game, but I used the whole backyard for the kitchen island, which arrived in three large crates. Crowding impairs your serenity. If you have a parts list, check the parts against the list to make sure you have everything. This checking will also familiarize you with the terms you'll need to know. Our Jeopardy game included twelve very similar plastic pieces: only close examination showed that six of them were "contestant display frames" and six were "host Q & A frames," to be

snapped together sandwich-style. Read lightly through the directions now to get a general idea of the order of the steps and to find out what tools of your own you need to collect. I always like to have a few bowls on hand to dump small parts into, as well as some masking tape so I can stick little washers, clips, and nuts to my work surface. Otherwise, these tiny pieces tend to disappear into the carpet or grass and to roll under the furniture, creating irritating setbacks and spoiling your meditative mood.

Finally, you are prepared to follow the directions. No doubt things will go   5
wrong, but errors will be fewer and less fatal than if you had gone straight to work with no pre-assembly stages. I sometimes even think that my system might be successfully applied to almost any of life's challenges.

—Georgia Metesky

The next sample of process writing is more technical. We have excerpted the first two paragraphs of a student paper explaining "How an Airplane Flies."

To many people, the idea of an airplane weighing several tons and being   1
able to fly seems magical, even though airplanes have been around since the beginning of this century. But the basic principles that keep a plane in the air can be explained in simple, easy-to-understand terms and related to common experience.

The parts of an airplane most important to flight are the wings. The wings   2
are pitched, or angled, so that the front or leading edge of the wing is slightly higher than the rear or trailing edge. As the plane moves forward, the pitch of the wings forces quantities of air to pass under the wing, while little air passes over it. The greater amount of air under the wing has a higher pressure than the air over the wing. If the speed of the plane is great enough and the pressure under the wing sufficiently high, then the pressure will push the wing, and consequently the plane, upward. You can see this principle for yourself when you are riding in a car. Put your hand out the side window with your palm facing down. If you tilt the front edge of your hand upward, the pressure from the wind will force your hand to move upward, pulling your arm up with it.

—James M. Kotte

1. What is the tone of "Some Assembly Necessary"? What audience would most enjoy the essay?

2. How do you know that Metesky has sufficient knowledge about her subject to give advice to others?

3. What principle does Metesky use to divide the paragraphs?

4. What warnings and pitfalls does Metesky include in the process of assembly?

5. Who is an appropriate audience for the Kotte piece? How much knowledge do readers need to understand it? In what way is it different from Metesky's essay?

How to Introduce a Process Paper

By the time your readers finish your first paragraph, they should know exactly what process you are about to describe. To open a "how-to" process paper, you may want to reassure your readers by giving your credentials—telling them why they should listen to *you* on this particular subject. You also might mention what the advantages would be of knowing how to do the particular activity. One student wrote this clear, straightforward introduction:

> Sand crafting is a Native American art form that I decided to learn several years ago because I like to make unusual gifts for my friends and family. Sand crafting takes a lot of concentration and patience, but it is a relaxing and immensely satisfying creative outlet. It is a very personal art form, because no two scenes or pictures are ever the same. Sand crafting can be used to make candles, pictures, planters, aquariums, or terrariums.
>
> —Sharon Tallon

Write an introductory paragraph for a process paper on one of the following topics: How to Make Whole Wheat Bread, How Batteries Work, How to Interview for a Job, How to Make Your Sweetheart (or Spouse's) Parents Approve of You, How to Train a Dog to Sit, How to Take Care of Your Computer.

How to Conclude a Process Paper

A really impressive closing can be hard to come by, but we have here a few ideas that may help. You can mention related or complementary processes that your reader might be interested in. Or you can get specific about the advantages of knowing the process. Be sure that you are not just repeating the introduction, though. The sand crafting essay explains a simple project and then concludes this way:

> This candle project is an excellent one to enable the novice sand crafter to learn some basic skills and to become comfortable working with the materials. It is a first step in making individually designed scenes using a traditional art form.
>
> —Sharon Tallon

Or you can give your readers a few cheery words of encouragement.

In a strictly utilitarian how-to piece, you do not really need a closing. Your reader will be satisfied just to know what steps to follow.

---

1. Identify the closing strategies of "Some Assembly Necessary" (p. 53). Write an alternative conclusion for that essay.

2. Write a conclusion for the introduction you wrote in Exercise 3.9 (p. 56).

WRITING EXERCISE

3.10

How to Hold a Process Paper Together

Because your process writing is most likely chronological, your transitions will refer to time, just like the narrative transitions we listed. It is common to number steps with written numbers (first, second, third) or, in technical writing, with numerals (1., 2., 3.). Instead of numbering, you may prefer to make up labels for the different steps you describe. Metesky could have labeled parts of her paper: Adjust Your Mental State, Survey the Scene, Prepare for Action. These labels can be inserted as headings or subheadings like the ones used in this text. Headings make your writing easier to read and can also be used to emphasize your main points.

FIGURE 3.2

Checklist for Revising a Process Essay

Check your rough draft for these elements of a good process theme (or exchange papers with someone else; refer to the "Guidelines for Exchanging Papers" on pages 43 and 45).

1. Does the introduction make clear what process is being explained? Does it list necessary materials and working conditions?
2. Are all the steps or stages of the process included and in order?
3. Are terms defined? Are there any words that need further explanation?
4. Is each step explained fully?
5. Does the paper give reasons for the steps or stages?
6. If necessary, does the paper include *don'ts* and warnings about possible dangers?
7. Is the informal *you* used or avoided consistently?

Ideas for Process Writing

Be sure to identify your audience when you choose a topic. Ask yourself the questions in Figure 1.2 (on p. 8) before you start writing.

1. How to train an animal (choose a specific animal—dog, parrot, turtle, cat, and so on).

2. How to get rid of the blues. You might focus on recovering from a specific depressing event or situation, like being unemployed, rejected for a promotion, or divorced.

3. How to perform a certain task you do at work. You might pretend you are writing a training manual for new workers.

4. How to solve a specific kind of problem.

5. Think of some established process that could use improvement (a procedure at your workplace, for example). Describe how a preferable substitute system would work.

6. How to clean a carburetor, change a light switch, build a successful campfire, or do any small task at which you consider yourself an expert.

7. *Possible collaborative essay:* How to get rid of a bad habit. Choose only one habit to discuss (for instance, nail biting, smoking, or interrupting others).

A PUBLISHED ESSAY ILLUSTRATING PROCESS

QUITTING, EXITING, AND RETURNING TO DOS

Andy Rathbone

This piece is excerpted from Windows for Dummies, *one of the "for Dummies" series of computer books, which are "guaranteed to appeal to even the most reluctant computer phobic." If you are one of these, you should know that DOS is the Disk Operating System. windows is software that runs a group of programs, like spreadsheets and word processors.*

When you're ready to throw in the computing towel and head for greener pastures, you need to stop, or quit, any programs you've been using. The terms *quit, exit,* and *return to DOS* mean pretty much the same thing: making the current program on your screen stop running so you can go away and do something a little more rewarding. 1

Luckily, exiting Windows programs is fairly easy because all of them use the same special exit command. You hold down the Alt key (either one of them, if you have two) and press the key labeled F4. (The F4 key is a *function key;* function keys are either in one row along the top of your keyboard or in two rows along its leftmost edge.) 2

Don't quit a program by just flicking off your computer's power switch. Doing so can foul up your computer's innards. Instead, you must leave the program responsibly so that it has time to perform its housekeeping chores before it shuts down. 3

When you press Alt + F4, the program asks whether you want to save any changes you've made to the file. Normally, you click on the button that says something like "Yes, by all means save the work I've spent the last three hours trying to create." (If you've muffed things up horribly, click on the No button. Windows disregards any work you've done and lets you start over from scratch.) 4

If, by some broad stretch of your fingers, you press Alt + F4 by accident, click on the button that says Cancel, and the program pretends that you never tried to leave it. You can continue as if nothing happened. 5

Chapter Four

Exemplification and Definition

In this chapter you will study two ways to develop your ideas and make your meaning clearer by giving examples and defining terms. Both methods of development will help guarantee that your readers won't ask, "What do you mean by that?"

Examples and Illustrations

Examples appear in almost all writing—and for good reason. There's no quicker and easier way to say what you mean than by giving examples. You say Danforth is an irresponsible lout? Give some examples of his behavior: he's two months behind in his rent; he's always asking co-workers to cover for him (and never says thanks); he calls all the women "honey" and all the men "bozo." You claim there's more to do in Charleston on weekends than go to the bars? Give some examples. Adverbs ending in *-ly* can be placed almost anywhere in a sentence? Please illustrate.

 ### Thinking Critically About Examples: How to Use Them

Examples and illustrations are valuable for a number of reasons. They help make writing livelier and more interesting. But primarily, they give readers something to grab on to mentally. Examples will help you in your writing in these situations: (1) when you want to explain an idea, (2) when you need to clarify a concept, and (3) when you have to support a claim or judgment.

Explaining an Idea

Many ideas are abstract and general. Examples force us to write in specific terms. They also give the reader something concrete to relate to. Look below at the first of two versions of a paragraph explaining why the author envies people "who accept old age as a series of challenges":

> For such persons, every new infirmity is an enemy to be outwitted, an obstacle to be overcome by force of will. They enjoy each little victory over themselves, and sometimes they win a major success.

This brief passage leaves a lot of questions unanswered. How could old people outwit an enemy or have a major success? What obstacles could they possibly overcome? What are "victories over themselves"? Read the same passage as it appears in Malcolm Cowley's essay "The View from 80"—now with examples.

> For such persons, every new infirmity is an enemy to be outwitted, an obstacle to be overcome by force of will. They enjoy each little victory over themselves, and sometimes they win a major success. Renoir was one of them. He continued painting, and magnificently, for years after he was crippled by arthritis; the brush had to be strapped to his arm. "You don't need your hand to paint," he said. Goya was another of the unvanquished. At 72 he retired as an official painter of the Spanish court and decided to work only for himself. His later years were those of the famous "black paintings" in which he let his imagination run free (and also of the lithographs, then a new technique). At 78 he escaped a reign of terror in Spain by fleeing to Bordeaux. He was deaf and his eyes were failing; in order to work he had to wear several pairs of spectacles, one over another, and then use a magnifying glass; but he was producing splendid work in a totally new style. At 80 he drew an ancient man propped on two sticks, with a mass of white hair and beard hiding his face and with the inscription "I am still learning."

The examples not only explain Cowley's ideas; they also provide colorful details that engage our interest and keep us reading.

Clarifying a Concept

The second valuable use of examples, a close cousin of the first, is to clarify a concept. This next passage proves conclusively that few people would ever understand linguistics without examples.

> In an elaborated [communication] code, the speaker and listener are acting parts in which they must improvise. Their standing with each other is such that

neither can take much for granted about the other. Intentions and purposes have to be brought into the open and defined. What the speaker will say is hard to predict, because it is not about commonplaces but about something more or less unique. He is wearing not a comic nor a tragic mask but his own face, and that is harder to put into words. An example would be that of a man told to do something by his boss and having to explain why it is impossible for him to comply.

—Dwight Bolinger, *Aspects of Language*

We found this explanation abstract and fuzzy until the end of the paragraph, where the concrete example gave us the flash of recognition we needed to understand the concept. In fact, we think that we would not have been puzzled at all if the writer had slipped the example in earlier.

Supporting a Claim or Judgment

When you are trying to prove a point, you need examples to support your opinion. In the following excerpt, a guest editorialist offers two examples to support his claims about the effects of video violence on children.

By failing to put safeguards and controls on entertainment for children, America has the dubious honor of being the largest exporter of video violence for children around the world. In February of last year, two 10-year-old boys lured a 2-year-old named James Bulger away from a shopping center in Bootle, England, and bludgeoned him to death with an assortment of sticks and stones from a nearby rock quarry. Tried as adults, the two youngsters admitted that their evil actions were inspired by an incredibly violent movie they saw entitled *Child's Play 3*.

Last month, another child was lost to copycat violence abroad. While frolicking with her playmates in the first big snowfall of the year, 5-year-old Silje Marie Redergard was brutally attacked and left to freeze to death in the otherwise peaceful town of Trondheim, Norway. Incredibly, her assailants were three little boys, ages 5 and 6, who were considered to be her friends. All four children were fans of the cartoon shows *Teenage Mutant Ninja Turtles* and *Mighty Morphin Power Rangers,* which center on likeable characters who pummel their opponents with fists and weapons.

—Raymond K. K. Ho, "How Many Children Must We Bury?"

While these examples do not form an airtight argument—there could well be other reasons for the children's violent behavior—they do lend some credibility to the author's theory. As a writer, you should believe your examples are honest when you use them to support a debatable point.

Types of Examples

An example may consist of a single word, a phrase, a list, a sentence or two, a whole paragraph or more, or a brief anecdote or story. Examples can also be general or specific. In our previous samples, Malcolm Cowley and Raymond K. K. Ho refer to actual people and incidents, which they describe with specific relevant detail. Dwight Bolinger, on the other hand, keeps his generic example to a single sentence. Part of your job as a writer is to select the kinds of examples that fit your audience and purpose.

You can also use counterexamples—instances that explain or support a point through contrast. Suppose you are writing a paper on the qualities you need to do your job successfully, and you want to illustrate the importance of being on time. You could use an example that shows what happens when you are not on time, like this:

> When I'm late for work, things never seem to go right. I usually go to work at 8:00 A.M., but one time I called in sick and told one of my co-workers that I'd be in later in the day. She said, "O.K." But when I got there at noon, I had so much work to do that I thought I would never catch up. They seemed to have saved everything up and left it for me to do. I mean, things that should have been typed and sent out by ten were still there.

You can see that this counterexample makes the writer's point clear and interesting, just as a regular example would. (For more on contrast, see Chapter 6.)

How to Organize an Essay of Example

Once you have a topic and a central idea, the essay of example is an easy one to write. It can follow the simple

Paragraph 1: Introduction
Paragraph 2: Example 1
Paragraph 3: Example 2
Paragraph 4: Example 3
Paragraph 5: Conclusion

pattern that you are probably familiar with. Even in its fancier forms, this one is hardly a brainteaser. Coming up with engrossing examples will be your biggest challenge.

Within the body of a simple example essay, each example will be developed in a paragraph of its own, with the introductory or concluding paragraph (or both) making a general statement that ties the examples together, thus:

1. *Introduction with thesis:* Finding the perfect apartment in Bloomington is impossible.
2. *My first apartment:* perfectly located but infested with roaches, spiders, and waterbugs.
3. *My second apartment:* beautiful and bugless, but four miles from work and a $170-a-month heating bill in winter.
4. *My third apartment:* inexpensive, bugless, and close to work. Has two tiny windows and wallpaper that looks like paneling, but I think I'll stay.
5. *Conclusion:* When apartment hunting in Bloomington, do not look for the perfect place; look for one with faults you can tolerate.

Each of these body paragraphs could be fully developed with appropriately horrifying details.

A variation on this simple pattern would be suitable when you have two or three minor examples and one big convincing illustration of your thesis. For instance, in a paper about the impact of your father's alcoholism, you might mention the job he lost and the school events he missed; but you would probably devote the bulk of your paper to the automobile accident that put him in the hospital for five months, especially since that was the event that finally caused him to quit drinking.

The order of your examples is something else to think about. The apartment outline above is arranged according to time, like a narrative or process paper. But if time is not important to your topic, you may consider arranging your examples in a *progressive* order, from the least to the most compelling. Putting the strongest example last will create a forceful final impression.

Although you will sometimes need to use transitional terms like *for example, as an illustration, in one case,* and *for instance,* many times the introduction to this type of essay clearly indicates that the readers should expect a series of examples, and there is no need to remind them repeatedly of that fact. In such a case, you need transitional expressions only when you want to include a paragraph that is *not* an example.

SAMPLE OF STUDENT ESSAY OF EXAMPLE WRITING

The following student essay is representative of the pattern we have been describing. Notice that the writer here omits obvious transitional terms at the beginnings of paragraphs, assuming that the reader will quickly grasp that each paragraph describes one humorous scene.

Look Around First

Have you ever noticed that when people think that no one is around, they do some of the strangest things? What makes the scene funny is that when people realize they are being watched, they try to make it seem as though they are not acting ridiculous. 1

One experience you can surely relate to is stopping at a red light and looking to see the clean-cut businessman in the next car lip-synching to the "easy listening" tunes on the radio. He starts out slowly, but by the time the light is green, he looks as though he's trying out for <u>The Music Man</u> as his head begins bobbing and his body swaying to the sound. What makes me laugh is that after being caught in this act, he tries to make it seem as though he's inspecting his forty-dollar hairstyle in the rearview mirror, meanwhile glancing nervously at you through the corner of his eye. 2

"Fire engine! Fire engine! Say it! Fire engine!" cried my father. I stood in amazement wondering if I dare look into the other room for fear of seeing my father going wild over a passing vehicle or teaching the dog how to speak. I peeked around the corner to sigh in relief, finding him yelling at a "Family Feud" game show. I watched as he kicked his feet, screamed, and pointed furiously at the innocent contestant who could not hear him. Moments passed, and then he heard me laughing from behind while he went through these childish antics. He turned around with a look of embarrassment as his face began to redden. He looked away, muttering small phrases under his breath such as "how stupid," "show's no good," and "just turning the station" while slowly sinking into his chair like a turtle going into its shell. It made me want to put a mirror between him and the television to show him the real definition of <u>silly.</u> 3

Just the other day, as I was making my way to my room at the end of the hall, I heard music accompanied by a continuous thud coming from one of the 4 other rooms. I knocked but was unanswered as I stood there, curious about what the noise could be. Slowly I opened the door and to my amazement I found my sister dancing around the room looking like the latest thing from "MTV," bouncing, hopping, and writhing wildly. Swinging her arms, she went into a spin, only to stop halfway, freeze, and glare at me. Quickly she began trying to reach the center of her back as though she had a terrible itch that caused her to hop around the room. She blurted a few mumbled words, only to have me interrupt her and say, "Nice song, huh?"

5   As you can see, people can do some pretty strange things, and the highlight always comes when they're caught. So when you're doing something nutty and you think no one is watching, don't be too surprised when you look around to find someone laughing at you.

—Nick Boyer

How to Revise an Essay of Example

Consider the questions in the following checklist (Fig. 4.1) when you are working your rough draft into a polished essay. Exchange papers with another partner or two to get additional opinions on each question.

FIGURE 4.1

Checklist for Revising an Essay of Example

1. Is each example truly representative?

2. Does the thesis, whether stated or implied, make some point to which all the examples relate?

3. Does each example support, clarify, or explain the thesis?

4. Is each example detailed enough to serve its purpose?

5. Would a counterexample help improve a point?

6. Is the order of the examples effective?

7. Do transitions appear when the reader needs a guide to what to expect next? Are any transitions repetitive or too obvious?

Ideas for Example Writing

1. Brainstorm with a group of classmates about the meaning of the following quotations. Then choose one and use examples to explain it:

"Love is what happens to a man and woman who don't know each other." (W. Somerset Maugham)

"Insanity is hereditary; you get it from your children." (Sam Levinson)

"Fashions are induced epidemics." (George Bernard Shaw)

"It is not enough to succeed. Others must fail." (Gore Vidal)

2. Explain your relationship with one of your parents or children by giving three examples.

3. Explain/defend/disprove one of these generalizations:

Marriage involves a lot more conflict than I anticipated.

A word processor makes revising a lot easier.

Time is more important than money.

Most people are poor listeners.

Customers expect different behavior from female clerks than from male clerks.

If you don't like any of these generalizations, devise one of your own.

4. Discuss with your classmates some superstitions that you or members of your family or community have held. Frequently, these superstitions have to do with success or bad luck in sports, performances, weather, or work. Do the superstitions have any validity? How did they develop? Write an essay of example about the role that superstition plays in your life or the life of someone you know.

5. Many areas of our lives and studies are guided by rules or principles. Your household probably has ground rules; scientific experimentation follows principles; your school has course requirements; even your love relationships have certain mandates. Use examples to explain and describe the rules or principles guiding one area of your life.

6. Explain and give examples of three or four healthy ways of dealing with painful situations. If you are not sure what to write about, discuss this topic with some classmates and solicit ideas from friends and relatives.

IN GROUPS, WE SHRINK FROM LONER'S HEROICS

Carol Tavris

In the following essay, which appeared in the Los Angeles Times *(1991), a social psychologist uses examples to explain the nature of groups and the problem of "diffused responsibility."*

1   The ghost of Kitty Genovese would sympathize with Rodney King. Genovese, you may remember, is the symbol of bystander apathy in America. Screaming for help, she was stabbed repeatedly and killed in front of her New York apartment, and not one of the 38 neighbors who heard her, including those who came to their window to watch, even called for help.

2   One of the things we find appalling in the videotape of King's assault is the image of at least 11 police officers watching four of their colleagues administer the savage beating and doing nothing to intervene. Whatever is the matter with them, we wonder.

3   Something happens to individuals when they collect in a group. They think and act differently than they would on their own. Most people, if they observe some disaster or danger on their own—a woman being stabbed, a pedestrian slammed by a hit-and-run driver—will at least call for help; many will even risk their own safety to intervene. But if they are in a group observing the same danger, they hold back. The reason is not necessarily that they are lazy, cowardly or have 50 other personality deficiencies; it has more to do with the nature of groups than the nature of individuals.

4   In one experiment in behavioral psychology, students were seated in a room, either alone or in groups of three, as a staged emergency occurred: Smoke began pouring through the vents. Students who were on their own usually hesitated a minute, got up, checked the vents and then went out to report what certainly seemed like fire. But the students who were sitting in groups of three did not move. They sat there for six minutes, with smoke so thick they could barely see, rubbing their eyes and coughing.

5   In another experiment, psychologists staged a situation in which people overheard a loud crash, a scream and a woman in pain, moaning that her ankle was broken. Seventy percent of those who were alone when the "accident" occurred went to her aid, compared with only 40% of those who heard her in the presence of another person.

6   For victims, obviously, there is no safety in numbers. Why? One reason is that if other people aren't doing anything, the individual assumes that nothing needs to

be done. In the smoke-filled room study, the students in groups said they thought that the smoke was caused by "steam pipes," "truth gas" or "leaks in the air conditioning"; not one said what the students on their own did: "I thought it was on fire." In the lady-in-distress study, some of those who failed to offer help said, "I didn't want to embarrass her."

Often, observers think nothing needs to be done because someone else has already taken care of it, and the more observers there are, the less likely any one person is to call for help. In Albuquerque, N.M., 30 people watched for an hour and a half as a building burned to the ground before they realized that no one had called the fire department. Psychologists call this process "diffusion of responsibility" or "social loafing": The more people in a group, the lazier each individual in it becomes.   7

But there was no mistaking what those officers were doing to Rodney King. There was no way for those observers to discount the severity of the beating King was getting. What kept them silent?   8

One explanation, of course, is that they approved. They may have identified with the abusers, vicariously participating in a beating they rationalized as justified. The widespread racism in the Los Angeles Police Department and the unprovoked abuse of black people is now undeniable. A friend who runs a trucking company told me recently that one of her drivers, a 50-year-old black man, is routinely pulled over by Los Angeles cops for the flimsiest of reasons "and made to lie down on the street like a dog." None of her white drivers has been treated this way.   9

Or the observers may have hated what was happening and been caught in the oldest of human dilemmas: Do the moral thing and be disliked, humiliated, embarrassed and rejected. Our nation, for all its celebration of the Lone Ranger and the independent pioneer, does not really value the individual—at least not when the person is behaving individually and standing up to the group. (We like dissenters, but only when they are dissenting in Russia or China.) Again and again, countless studies have shown that people will go along rather than risk the embarrassment of being disobedient, rude or disloyal.   10

And so the banality of evil is once again confirmed. Most people do not behave badly because they are inherently bad. They behave badly because they aren't paying attention, or they leave it to Harry, or they don't want to rock the boat, or they don't want to embarrass themselves or others if they're wrong.   11

Every time the news reports another story of a group that has behaved mindlessly, violently and stupidly, including the inevitable members who are just "going along," many people shake their heads in shock and anger at the failings of "human nature." But the findings of behavioral research can direct us instead to appreciate the conditions under which individuals in groups will behave morally or not. Once we know the conditions, we can begin to prescribe antidotes. By understanding the impulse to diffuse responsibility, perhaps as individuals we will be   12 more likely to act. By understanding the social pressures that reward group-think, loyalty and obedience, we can foster those that reward whistle-blowing and moral courage. And, as a society, we can reinforce the belief that they also sin who only stand and watch.

Definition

When Barney thinks he can leave work at 4:30 P.M., go to the central post office and mail a package, run to the bank for some cash, pick up a frozen pizza at the grocery, stop at the liquor store for some wine, and be ready for his dinner guests at 6:00, we might describe him as "not very intelligent." On the other hand, the same fellow may be the author of three books on plate tectonics, a scientist whom we admire for his "intelligence." What do we mean? The answer to this question is a matter of definition—an extremely difficult one, when you think about it.

Thinking Critically About Definitions: When to Use Them

A good definition can be reassuring or troubling: it can simplify your thinking and ease your mind, or it can shake up your long-held views and little-considered opinions. Either way, definition concerns meaning and therefore has a place in every method of writing. Making your terms clear is a responsibility you take on whenever you use language. Definitions will help you to do the following.

1. *Clear up unfamiliar terms.* You should define any word that you think your intended audience won't know. The special vocabulary of certain vocations, hobbies, and social groups usually needs definition. Labeling someone an "oralist" can be quite misleading if your readers know nothing of education for the deaf.

2. *Explain an abstraction or concept.* An abstraction—like intelligence or compassion or prejudice—is an idea that cannot be directly observed. Its meaning has to be understood indirectly from observable evidence. Even if you are quite sure that your readers know the general meaning of a word like love, you want to be sure that their idea is the same as your own. Otherwise, serious misunderstandings can occur. You might write, for instance, "We all need more love in our lives." Unless you go on to define what kinds of love you have in mind, your readers could let their imaginations run wild and think you are promoting

free love—and maybe you are. But if you are, then you certainly need to make it clear that's what you mean by "love."

3. *Provide an interpretation of a controversial term.* Before you launch into a discussion of "family values" or "affirmative action" or "the right to life," you want to be sure that your readers know how you are using this phrase. A productive exchange of views depends on a clear understanding of key words and phrases. If you are trying to convince people to accept your meaning, you have an even greater stake in defining controversial terms.

4. *Investigate the nature or essential qualities of a word or phrase.* Sometimes you want to define a term not just to promote clarity but as a challenge in itself. Perhaps you would like to explore what the word *friend* means to you or share your appreciation of zydeco music or detective fiction with others. Both are admirable goals for writing a definition.

How to Present a Definition

If you are defining a word because it is a specialized term, something quite brief will usually do. A quick definition can be handled by adding a word or two in parentheses after the term, like this:

> If you want the yogurt to yog (thicken), start with a fresh culture.

> Miscommunication occurs when reader and writer do not share the same idea about a word's denotation (direct meaning) or connotation (emotional associations).

If there is no apt synonym, you can try the traditional three-part definition, which goes like this: (1) the *term* to be defined, (2) the *class* to which it belongs, and (3) *specific differences* to distinguish it from other members of its class. This procedure may sound dry and academic, but it produces efficient one-sentence definitions:

Term	*Class*	*Specific Differences*
A friend	is a person	whom you know, like, and trust.
Intelligence	is the capacity	to acquire and apply knowledge.
A smooch	is a kiss	of casual affection.

You can leave these single-sentence definitions as they are, or you can expand the third part. Abstract, controversial, or ambiguous words often require more than one sentence of definition. You can extend the definition by enumerating specific differences in several ways. Look at this student's expanded definition of her understanding of *smooch,* and consider how her techniques could be applied to other definitions.

> A smooch is a quick kiss. The lips of two people press together for a short time, just a second. The eyes close briefly while the closed lips protrude and touch the other set of lips. Smooching is not limited to members of opposite sexes, for you can smooch with anyone. It is considered a sign of affection, not an expression of deep feeling; or like a warm smile, it's a gesture of pleasant emotion. A smooch is a casual kiss that can be done anywhere and still be considered proper. A person mostly smooches with relatives and friends. More intimate kissing is for lovers, although they occasionally smooch, too. For instance, a husband and wife may smooch before they go to work in the morning. They save their passionate kissing for later.
>
> —Mary McMurray

Extending a Definition

When you want to provide a longer, more detailed explanation that thoroughly defines a word or phrase, you can develop it with all or any of these techniques:

1. *Give descriptive details.* In the smooch definition, the writer describes the process in detail in the first three sentences. To expand the one-sentence definition of *friend,* you could list specific qualities that you think a friend must possess (loyalty, sensitivity, a sense of humor) and provide descriptive illustrations. To give a better idea of Barney's *intelligence,* you might mention his large vocabulary, his quick wit, his ability to program a VCR.

2. *Exemplify and narrate.* The smooch paragraph gives examples of who might smooch and when. To define *friend* you might tell the story of how your best friend Stan stayed with your children so that you could go to a party. Or, to illustrate *intelligence,* you could give examples of the time Barney diagnosed the problem with your computer or explained what causes earthquakes in a way that you could understand.

3. *Compare.* A smooch, says our writer, is "like a warm smile." In a similar way, you might say that "A friend is a safe port in a storm" or "a cross between a therapist and a pet who can cook"—and then elaborate. If you want to clarify what *egotists* are, you could say that they are like misers, keeping love and admiration, instead of money, all for themselves, and both are lonely, insecure, and neurotic. This kind of comparison is effective when your reader is better acquainted with the comparable term (*misers*) than with the one you are defining (*egotists*).

4. *Contrast.* Since a good definition will make clear the difference between the term you are explaining and other words with similar meanings, you might show the distinction between *friends, acquaintances,* and *buddies.* Or you could say how being *intelligent* is different from being *creative* and *clever.* In the paragraph example on page 72, a smooch is contrasted with an intimate kiss.

Using an apt combination of these four techniques, you can write anything from a paragraph to an entire essay of definition.

SAMPLE OF STUDENT EXTENDED DEFINITION WRITING

The student essay that follows uses examples and makes distinctions to define a popular colloquial expression.

Give Me a Break!

The slang expression "give me a break" is familiar to most Americans. Not many, however, stop to think about all of its different meanings. It is used in a variety of contexts, although never in a formal situation. Generally, a "break" is a rest or respite from something. For example, workers often take a break for lunch or coffee to give themselves a chance to rest in the middle of the workday. This concept carries over into the phrase "give me a break," as the speaker asks for a rest or respite from something that somebody else has said or done. 1

"I wish my boss would give me a break. There's no way that I will ever finish these projects in time!" In this case, the speaker is using "give me a break" as a plea for mercy. The person in this scenario feels overworked and overloaded. He wants his boss to take away some of the work, so he asks for a rest from it. The phrase can also be used in this context when asking someone to refrain from doing something annoying. A mother, for example, might say to her boisterous child, "Give me a break! You've been whooping like a lunatic all morning! Can't you play more quietly?" Like the overworked employee, the mother is asking for a respite from something that bothers her. 2

People also use the "give me a break" phrase when they want to contradict a remark. One of the most common examples of this use is in reaction to a com- 3 pliment. For instance, a man may say to his wife or girlfriend, "Your hair looks really great," to which she replies, "Oh, give me a break. It's a mop, and I'm thinking of cutting it all off." Although not accepting the compliment very gracefully, the wife or girlfriend is trying to be modest by asking for a rest from the man's flattery. Or perhaps she is just letting him know that she doesn't take his praise seriously. Another example of saying "Give me a break" to contradict might occur when someone makes a remark like "A woman's place is in the home" or "We ought to send all those immigrants back where they came from." A person might well respond to such remarks with "Give me a break! You're living in the Dark Ages." In this instance the phrase is being used to ask for a rest from some ridiculous and bigoted views.

4   The final use of "give me a break" is for expressing disbelief. For instance, a college student says to her roommate, "Guess what? My psychology teacher canceled the test today and gave everybody twenty bonus points!" The roommate might counter with "Give me a break! Only in your dreams!" She would, in effect, be saying, "That could never happen. Let me have a break from your teasing."

5   Whatever way people use this expression, it's clear that a lot of them think they deserve a break today—and not at McDonald's.

—Teri Schmidt

Introductions, Conclusions, and Transitions

As you have seen, definitions come in all sizes and serve many different purposes. How you introduce, conclude, and tie together a definition is so dependent on its function and length that we cannot give you an easy formula. Of course, a synonym or a one-sentence definition does not need an introduction or conclusion.

If you are writing an extended definition, you may want to state the need for the definition in the opening. For example, "Before we can identify the best living jazz musicians, we must agree on a definition of *jazz*." Or your thesis statement can be a traditional three-part, one-sentence definition that you proceed to expand. If you are going to clarify a little-known, misused, or slang term, you may provoke curiosity by using the term at the beginning:

When my friend Rusty comes over, I put my Oriental rugs in the hall closet and lock the closet door. Rusty's a klutz.

One student began an essay that gave her personal definition of *boredom* in this way:

> For me, boredom usually sets in during a three-day holiday weekend. This break comes over Labor Day just after school has started, and everyone but me treks home by bus, car, or train to spend the holiday feasting with relatives while I halfheartedly ponder how I'll spend my hours alone. The fact of being cooped up at college on this long weekend hits me when I see the last suitcase or overnight bag sail into the elevator going "down."
>
> —Cindy Reynolds

You should also tailor the transitions and conclusions to your length and purpose. You can borrow closing and transitional strategies from other patterns of development, especially narration (pp. 42–43), process (p. 57), classification and division (pp. 91–93), and comparison and contrast (pp. 109–112).

How to Revise a Definition

Answer the questions in the following checklist (Fig. 4.2) about your own or a classmate's essay to see if your definitions are clear and effective.

Ideas for Definition Writing

Short Prewriting Practice

1. Write one-sentence, three-part definitions for the following: *magazine, flower, cream, anthropology, infancy, rap music.*

2. Develop one of the definitions you just wrote for number 1 into a one-hundred word paragraph. Use one or more of the four strategies listed on pages 72–73.

3. Write a paragraph that defines a slang term.

4. Think of a subject that you know more about than the general reader probably does. Choose a term from that subject and define it. Examples:

Subject	*Term*
journalism	lead, kicker, justified
cooking	boil, simmer, scald
basketball	transition game, zone defense, pick
cinematography	dissolve, tracking shot, voiceover

FIGURE 4.2

*Checklist for
Revising
Definitions*

1. Does the essay avoid using *is when* and *is where* in sentences of definition? These phrases are not only inaccurate but awkward, as in these examples:

   (avoid) Risible is when you laugh a lot.

   (avoid) Geometry is where you do math to measure lines and shapes.

2. Are there any circular definitions—that is, definitions in which the specific difference basically repeats the term? For example:

   (avoid) Organized crime is done by criminals in an organization.

   (avoid) A dietician is a person who studies diets.

3. Are the differentiating characteristics stated precisely? Phrases like *kind of small* can mislead a reader whose idea of *small* differs from yours.

4. Does the writer keep common ground with the audience in mind? Be sure that your definition is phrased in terms your readers know. For example, you would not offer the following definition to anyone but a group familiar with computer science.

   A compiler is a kind of master program that translates source code into object code.

Read your definitions to some classmates who don't know much about the subject, and ask them if they understand your definitions.

5. Write a paragraph defining a term mainly by means of contrast with another similar term or terms. For example: *shyness* and *reticence, ignorance* and *stupidity, religious* and *spiritual, anxious* and *eager, tragic* and *sad, patriotism* and *chauvinism.*

Longer Paper Ideas

1. Define a slang term (like *diss* or *homeboy*) or a saying (like "nothing to write home about," "put the moves on," "not playing with a full deck") by giving examples of its uses and applications.

2. Write an essay in which you clear up the definition of some commonly misunderstood concept: *femininity, masculinity, freedom, love, intelligence, progress, happiness.*

3. With several classmates, go to a store that has a large collection of greeting cards and review the text of the cards designed for wives, husbands, mothers, or fathers. Putting together the ideas you find, write an essay defining a wife, husband, mother, or father as viewed by the greeting card industry.

4. Write an essay defining your idea of what it means to be an "understanding" person: an understanding man, an understanding woman, an understanding boss, an understanding teacher.

5. For an audience of people from another culture, define *situation comedy, fast food, soap opera, human potential movement, aroma therapy,* or another term that labels a cultural phenomenon.

6. Discuss a controversial term with a group of fellow students. Then write an extended definition that summarizes the various views of your peers about this term. Examples: *date rape, family values, political correctness, safe sex, assisted suicide, sexual harassment, resident alien, jury nullification, recovered memory, gay rights.*

7. Write an essay in which you redefine some abstract quality, such as *laziness, impatience, stubbornness,* or *procrastination.* Take a quality that is usually viewed negatively, such as *evasiveness* or *cowardice* or *boredom,* and turn it into a favorable attribute.

A PUBLISHED ESSAY ILLUSTRATING DEFINITION

AIDS: A REAL MAN'S DISEASE

Michael S. Kimmel and Martin P. Levine

In this article, written in 1991 and reprinted from the Los Angeles Times, *two sociologists argue that the definition of what it means to be a "real man" is at the heart of the AIDS crisis.*

As the AIDS epidemic begins its second decade, it's time to face some unpleasant realities: AIDS is the No. 1 health problem for men in the United States; it is the leading cause of death of men aged 33 to 45; it has killed more American men than were lost in the Vietnam War.   1

No other disease that was not biologically sex-linked (like hemophilia) has ever been so associated with one gender. And yet virtually no one talks about AIDS as a men's disease. Americans generally think of it as a "gay disease," or a "drug   2 addict" disease; some people even refuse to see it as a disease, arguing that it is "divine retribution" for "deviant behavior."

3   This dehumanizing has a lot to do with the fact that compassion and support for AIDS patients continue to be in relatively short supply among Americans. Perhaps by looking at AIDS as a "men's disease" we can put it in a more humane perspective.

4   In our society, the capacity for high-risk behavior is a prominent measure of masculinity. Men get AIDS by engaging in specific high-risk behaviors, activities that ignore potential health risks for more immediate pleasures.

5   As sociologists have long understood, stigmatized gender often leads to exaggerated forms of gender-specific behavior. Thus, those whose masculinity is least secure are precisely those most likely to follow hyper-masculine behavioral codes as well as hold fast to traditional definitions of masculinity. In social science research, hyper-masculinity as a compensation for stigmatized gender identity has been used to explain the propensity for authoritarianism and racism, homophobia, anti-Semitism, juvenile crime and gang activities.

6   Gay men and IV drug users can be seen in this light, although for different reasons. The traditional view of gay men is that they are not "real men." Most of the stereotypes revolve around effeminacy, weakness, passivity. But after the Stonewall riots in 1969, in which gay men fought back against the police raiding a gay bar, and the subsequent birth of the Gay Liberation Movement, a new gay masculinity emerged in major cities. The "clone," as he was called, dressed in hyper-masculine garb (flannel shirts, blue jeans) with short hair (not at all androgynous) and mustache; he was athletic, highly muscular. In short the clone looked much more like a "real man" than most straight men.

7   And the clones—who composed roughly one-third of all gay men living in the major urban gay enclaves in the mid-1970s—enacted a hyper-masculine sexuality in steamy back rooms, gay bars and bathhouses where sex was plentiful, anonymous and very hot. No unnecessary foreplay, romance or post-coital awkwardness. Sex without attachment.

8   One might say that, given the norms of masculinity (men are always supposed to want sex, seek sex and be ready for sex), for a time, gay men were the only men in our culture who were getting as much sex as they wanted.

9   Predictably, high levels of sexual activity led to high levels of sexually transmitted diseases among clones. But no one could have predicted AIDS.

10   Among IV drug users, we see a different pattern, but with some similar outcomes when seen from a gender perspective. The majority of IV drug users are African American and Latino, two groups for whom the traditional avenues of successful manhood are blocked by poverty and racism. More than half of the black men between 18 and 25 in our cities are unemployed, which means that they are structurally prevented from demonstrating masculinity as breadwinners.

The drug culture offers alternatives. Dealing drugs can provide an income to support a family as well as the opportunity for manly risk and adventure. The community of drug users can confirm gender identity; the sharing of needles is a demonstration of that solidarity. And the ever-present risk of death by overdose takes hyper-masculine bravado to the limit.   11

By now, most men have heard about "safer sex," the best way (short of abstinence) to reduce one's risk for contracting AIDS by sexual contact: have fewer partners, avoid certain practices, use condoms, take the responsibility for safe behavior. In short, safer-sex programs encourage men to stop having sex like men. To men, you see, "safe sex" is an oxymoron. That which is sexy is not safe; that which is safe is not sexy. Sex is about danger, risk, excitement; safety is about comfort, softness, security.   12

Seen this way, it is not surprising to find in some research that one-fourth of urban gay men report that they have not changed their unsafe sexual behaviors. What is astonishing is that slightly more than three-fourths have changed, are practicing safer sex.   13

What heterosexual men could learn from the gay community's response to AIDS is how to eroticize responsibility—something that women have been trying to teach men for decades. And straight men could also learn a thing or two about caring for one another in illness, supporting one another in grief, and maintaining a resilience in the face of a devastating disease and the callous indifference of society.   14

In short, we must enlarge the definition of what it means to be a real man.   15

Meanwhile, AIDS is spreading, and every day there are more men who need our compassion and support. They did not contract the disease intentionally; they do not deserve blame. We must stand with them because they are our brothers. We are linked to them not through sexual orientation (although we may be) or by drug-related behavior (although we may be) but by our gender, by our masculinity.   16

They are not "perverts" or "deviants" who have strayed from the norms of masculinity. They are, if anything, over-conformists to destructive norms of male behavior. Like all real men, they have taken risks. And until daring has been eliminated from the rhetoric of masculinity, men will die as a result of risk-taking. In war. In sex. In driving fast and drunk. In shooting drugs and sharing needles.   17

Men with AIDS are real men, and when one dies, a bit of all men dies as well. Until we change what it means to be a real man, every man will die a little bit every day.   18

Chapter Five

Classification and Division

In the next three chapters we will describe several methods of thinking about and organizing material—classification and division, comparison and contrast, and cause and effect. You will discover that you already use these thought patterns in your everyday reasoning processes. You classify tasks, analyze problems, compare products, and employ cause and effect reasoning when you decide on any course of action.

In these chapters we provide a number of handy templates (patterns or guides) that illustrate plans for ordering material. Bear in mind that these patterns are designed only as guides, useful as you develop skill in organizing. Feel free to depart from them whenever you can think of an arrangement that better suits your subject and purpose. As you gain experience, you will find that you no longer need to rely on these patterns. But practicing them should help store organizing strategies in your brain for future use.

Understanding Classification and Division

The processes called *classification* and *division* are like the words *effect* and *affect:* most people have a hard time keeping them straight because they overlap in meaning. By the same token, you may well be doing division while you are busy classifying. But basically the distinction between the two terms boils down to this: In classification, you take *several* elements and sort them into a few groups; in division, you take *one* element (or entity) and separate it into its component parts. If your subject is single mothers and you find yourself thinking about four different kinds of single moms, you are classifying. If instead you start thinking about four problems faced by a typical single mother, you are dividing.

The reason we discuss the two processes together here is that they are similar in some important ways. First, both are based on the logical process of division, and second, both are written using the same kind of organizational tactics.

Thinking Critically About Classification and Division

These processes help to stave off confusion and chaos in either your reader's mind or your own. Both types of organization impose or reveal order, and order makes things much more understandable and can be quite reassuring. The kind of order you impose depends on who you are and what your purpose is. If you are working on a political campaign, you are likely to classify people into Republican and Democrat or conservative and liberal; if you are a literary snob, you are likely to classify people into those who read Milton and those who read Harlequin romances; if you are a parent, you are likely to classify small children into obnoxious brats, barely tolerable youngsters, and your own perfect offspring.

When you divide a subject, you make it easier to understand by revealing and explaining its makeup. Describing a process, speculating on cause and effect, arguing a point, and interpreting literature—all require division and analysis. In fact, almost everything you write involves dividing your ideas into smaller, more manageable parts. The division pattern we discuss first is all-purpose. In other sections of this chapter we go into more specific ways of subdividing a topic.

Division is always a part of effective problem solving. Consider this topic: Why is it so hard to study? Rack your brains to think of the component parts of your difficulty in studying. You may come up with several fairly fixable contributing factors, such as: (1) I have not bought the textbook, (2) the light bulb in my desk lamp has been burned out for three months, and (3) I turn on the TV as soon as I get home every day. Then all you have to do is borrow a book, change the bulb, leave off the television, and think up three more rationalizations. Eventually you may get to the heart of the problem, and you will owe it all to your powers of analysis and division.

Analyzing Your Subject

After you select a subject, you need to exercise your critical thinking skills to find a logical basis for division. You must take care here, or your results could be a disaster. Heed these warnings.

1. *Know the Difference Between Useful and Useless Bases of Division.*

Classifying history teachers into those who wear black socks and those who wear dark blue socks is useless. The grouping is not significant because it has nothing to do with teaching. But classifying history teachers into those who use a lecture-and-question format and those who rely more on open discussion could be significant, as well as useful to a prospective history student, because it may reveal the teachers' philosophies and attitudes toward their subject and their students.

2. *The Division Should Cover All the Times and Parts You Claim It Covers.*

If, for instance, you know of several history teachers who are not strictly either lecture-and-question or discussion types, you cannot pretend they do not exist just to make your classification tidy. At least mention exceptions, even if you do not give them as much space as you give the major divisions.

3. *The Bases of Division Should Not Shift, and the Divisions Should Have Parallel Rank.*

This sounds like gobbledygook, but if you can find the faults in these outlines, you already understand parallel rank.

Types of Aardvarks	*Types of Recorded Music*
1. The fuzzy aardvark	1. Classical
2. The hairless aardvark	2. Easy listening
3. The three-toed aardvark	3. The Rolling Stones
4. The striped aardvark	4. Heavy metal
5. The friendly aardvark	5. Rap

In the aardvark outline, the basis of division shifts: the first four types are divided according to physical characteristics, whereas the last type is defined by personality. You can see the worry this causes. Can a hairless aardvark be friendly? Are fuzzy aardvarks ill-tempered? How much hair does a friendly aardvark have? Can striped aardvarks ever be hairless?

The music outline displays a problem in rank. Although the Rolling Stones do represent a type distinct from classical, easy listening, heavy metal, and rap, the category is not parallel to the others—it's too small. Number 3 should be rock 'n' roll or hard rock (with the Stones used as an example).

4. *Ask Yourself Whether You Can Handle the Subject and Its Divisions in the Number of Words You Want.*

Entire books have been written on heroes and their qualities and the types that exist. If you want only a 750-word paper, maybe you should consider "Types of Heroes on Popular TV Shows" or "Barney Fife's Heroic Qualities." Or, if you have decided to analyze American transcendentalism and you list twelve characteristics to develop in a 500-word essay, you will be wise to write instead about the appeal of *Sesame Street*. Whenever you discover that you will be able to devote fewer than fifty words to each type or section of your topic, that is nature's way of telling you

- to change topics,
- to consolidate groups, or
- to select the most important divisions to develop fully, mentioning the less important ones only briefly.

Considering Audience and Purpose

Before you begin writing, be sure that you can think of someone who would like to read what you are about to write. Many classification or division essays are informative, so try to think of someone or some group who would appreciate the information. Consider also *why* you are writing—some reason other than the obvious fact that it was assigned. Are you planning to inform your readers, amuse your readers, or perhaps influence your readers' thinking? You could analyze a cigarette ad, for example, to convince teenage smokers that they are being manipulated by advertising even though they may not be aware of the subtle pressure.

Think of an appropriate audience and purpose for each of the following classification and division subjects, and discuss your choices with classmates.

1. Types of bosses or supervisors
2. Types of mutual funds
3. Reasons for workaholism
4. Methods of insect control in gardening

DISCUSSION
EXERCISE

5.1

How to Organize Classification and Division Writing

You should end up with a list of classes (if you are classifying) or a list of entities, components, factors, or plain old parts (if you are dividing). From here on in, we will call these divisions "parts" to simplify matters. These parts will be the main divisions of your paper. In a short essay, you will probably write a paragraph on each part. For example, a fairly brief essay on "Irritating Argumentative Techniques" could include one paragraph on the "Yes, But . . . " Interruption, one paragraph on Pernicious Premises, one paragraph on Endless Evasion, and one paragraph on Stony Silence. Of course, if you get turned loose without a word limit, you could write a much longer paper using the same plan and, by including more examples and material, write several paragraphs on each category.

Devising a Plan

Ideally, your subject will divide naturally into parallel, meaningful categories, and these categories will slip conveniently into well-developed paragraphs of roughly equal length. Ideally. In reality, that seldom happens. You may discover (after you have your categories all nicely set up) that you need to reorganize them. For example, consider this informal preliminary plan for an analysis.

The Contents of My Closet

1. Items that do belong there: clothing I wear a lot
2. Items that do not belong there.
   A. Clothing I wear seldom or never
      —Because it's not mine
      —Because I forgot I had it
      —Because it's my donkey costume from my 4th grade Christmas pageant
      —Because I hate it
   B. Miscellaneous
      —Nonperishable items:
         boardless Monopoly game
         broken Veg-O-Matic
         K-Tel record rack
         sunblock lotion bottle

——Perishable items:

> forgotten sack lunches
>
> orange in raincoat pocket
>
> box of fused coughdrops
>
> fermented Fig Newtons

In a case like this, it would be a mistake to restrict your discussion of section 2 to the length of the first category, and equally ineffective to expand section 1 (which is quite bland) just to make it as long as section 2. A good strategy might involve focusing on those items that do not belong in your closet. You could then mention in your introduction that although your closet does contain some clothing that you actually wear, you're going to devote the body of your paper to examining clutter that doesn't belong there.

Arranging Your Ideas

After you have decided how you are going to develop your paragraphs, consider how to arrange them. The order in which you first thought of the categories may not be necessarily the best. Your items might lend themselves to chronological order (according to time). The types of recorded music classification, for example, are ordered roughly according to date of composition—from earliest to most recent. The parts of a machine or a process may be divided spatially—top to bottom, left to right, inside to outside. A classification of types of people, like gamblers, may be arranged numerically—from the group with the fewest members to the group with the most. Consider arranging by degree, too: least important to most important, simple to complex, mildly irritating to totally repulsive. When you organize classifications, it is traditional (except in business writing) to put the strongest category last for emphasis.

SAMPLES OF STUDENT CLASSIFICATION AND DIVISION WRITING

The following papers were written by students enrolled in the College of Continuing Education at Illinois State University.

What's Your Style?

While it's not mandatory to have lived with two husbands and five house-mates to analyze different styles of housekeeping, the experience makes the diagnosis easier. Many disagreements could be avoided if everyone followed the 1 same housekeeping practices. Instead, the people I have known have followed widely varying housekeeping habits. But for purposes of discussion, their behaviors can be classified into three categories—each with its own different behavior.

2   Perfectionists, like my first husband, seem to find the everyday, mundane tasks of life to be of crucial importance. These people waste hours in an effort to keep everything firmly in its place and achieve that never-lived-in look. Their world must be perfectly ordered: every can, label facing forward, in its permanent place on the pantry shelf; each towel, precisely folded with edges inward, in its own spot in the bathroom closet; the scissors, points facing to the left, in the exact center of the middle desk drawer.

3   These perfectionists are the most difficult to live with because frustration is their faithful companion. Whenever their sense of orderliness is disturbed by a spoon facing the wrong way in the silverware drawer, they heave a huge sigh of disappointment and cast their eyes heavenward as if hoping for divine assistance. Since these people can seldom adapt to any other way of living, the noncompliant housemate will prudently choose to adapt to the perfectionist—or divorce him after fifteen years of disagreement, as I did.

4   The second type, the aspiring neatniks, find housekeeping almost as troublesome as the perfectionists do—but for different reasons. These people cherish the look of a perfectly organized, spotlessly kept household, but they bitterly resent the time sacrificed to achieving the results. I belong to this category and will spend hours absorbed in a good book with a cup of coffee in hand and my faithful dog curled up beside me.

5   People like me suffer mild pangs of guilt about the messy kitchen and the cluttered coffee table, but the guilt is never strong enough to make us put down the book and swing into action. We pause sometimes in our reading and tell ourselves that if we got up and vacuumed the dog hair off the sofa, a new supply would appear by evening. If we suffered through cleaning the oven, tonight's casserole would surely run over. If we straightened and dusted the coffee table, the cat, without fail, would choose that spot for a nap. We learn to cohabit with nagging guilt.

6   Casual slobs, the third type, are undoubtedly the most content housekeepers—because they hardly keep house at all. Their world is in total disarray, but they never even notice. Piles of dirty clothing at the foot of the bed, dust and clutter on the tabletops, stacks of dirty dishes in the sink, towels all wrinkled in the

dryer—this is life as it should be for them. Only when slobs run out of clean clothes will they pick up the piles and do the laundry. Only when the last dish is dirty will they think about washing a few.

Trying to reform casual slobs is a thankless task. Since they never see the mess, they require constant nagging. Many housemates get tired of nagging and simply clean up after their resident slob. That option is not really satisfactory for aspiring neatniks since mild guilt is easier to deal with than smoldering resentment. It goes without saying that perfectionists should move out before becoming homicidal. The only possible solution to living with slobs is to devise a twelve-step program for improving their household habits—and hope they can stick with it.   7

Perhaps a certain stress level makes life interesting. Since Murphy's Law guarantees that two similar types rarely share a household, various housekeeping styles assure a certain amount of stress. These differences may even help maintain the necessary tension to keep personal relationships healthy—to keep tedium and boredom at bay.   8

—Sheralyn Thomas

Macho Lights

"Camel. Where a man belongs." At least that is what the advertiser would like us to believe. The advertisement features a rugged-looking individual leaning against his dusty jeep, taking a cigarette break from his strenuous work. The advertiser is trying to get us to buy Camel Lights by showing us that Lights are not cigarettes for sissies—even the most macho of men smoke them.   1

The picture in the ad focuses on a man who has been, for some unexplained reason, digging in a substantial pile of rocks. He is dressed in work clothes—soiled, worn khaki pants, a thick black leather belt, and a shirt with the sleeves rolled up to his bulging biceps and the buttons open to expose his muscular chest. His face is weatherbeaten—no doubt from working in this harsh climate—and his hair is tousled. This man is no cream puff who constantly worries about his appearance. No, indeed. He has enough confidence and determination to be what he wants to be and, we are led to believe, smoke the cigarette that suits him.   2

The man is smoking a Camel Light while leaning against his vehicle. He does not drive a Porshe or a Corvette like some spoiled rich kid might. This man drives   3 a jeep. What other automobile has a more rugged image than the work-horse of World War II? This jeep is not for weekend recreation, either. Its dirty, battered condition makes it obvious that the man uses his four-wheel drive vehicle for tough jobs, like digging rocks. This is not the kind of transportation that might be seen in a parking garage in the city. No, sir. This guy has jockeyed the jeep right up to the top of the pile of rocks that he is digging in—and there it sits, this testimonial to toughness.

4   The harsh natural setting also emphasizes the man's ruggedness. The rocks that the jeep is resting on are heavy, jagged boulders. Only a bulldozer could actually move stones that size, but this man is up to the job. The scene is a desert, obviously hot, dry, gritty. Hard physical labor done under those conditions would exhaust the average individual, but not this man: he smokes Camel Lights.

5   The brand name and slogan are printed in bold, black type; no wimpy italics here. Neither does the advertiser fool around with catchy jingles or clever sayings. The slogan is blunt and to the point: "Camel Lights. Low tar. Camel taste." The information is straightforward and lean, the way every real man should be.

6   The most telling part of the ad, though, appears in the lower left-hand corner of the page. A small white box contains this message: "Warning: The Surgeon General Has Determined That Cigarette Smoking Is Dangerous To Your Health." Cigarette smoking can lead to killer diseases such as lung cancer, heart attacks, and tuberculosis. Only a truly fearless man would flirt with death so casually. The final line sums up the message:

"Camel. Where a MAN belongs."

—Bob Petkoff

DISCUSSION
EXERCISE

5.2

1. Identify each student paper as either mainly classification or mainly division—or a fairly equal combination of both.

2. Make a brief outline of just the main points in the body of each paper.

3. Can you identify the principle used by each writer to order the paragraphs—that is, why is the first item placed first, and so forth?

4. Can you think of any other way to organize the material in each essay?

5. Find the transitions between the body paragraphs in Thomas's sample paper and explain how each one works.

Drafting Classification and Division Writing

As a rule, an essay will have three parts: the introduction, the body, and the conclusion. The body is the longest, most detailed part—the one that most puts your organizational skills to task—so we suggest that you deal with it first. Then, after you are warmed up, you can tackle a lively introduction, a stirring conclusion, and helpful transitions to hold it all together. We follow this same plan in ordering our advice in these chapters—body, then introduction, conclusion, transitions, and revisions.

How to Introduce Classification and Division Writing

When working on your first draft, you need not spend a lot of time trying to come up with a compelling opening paragraph. Eventually, you should produce a compelling one, but unless a good opening springs immediately to mind, postpone the introduction for now and get going on the first paragraph of the body of your paper. Think about your introduction during idle moments during the day, and let your unconscious mind work for you while you sleep. If by the time your paper is finished you still have no introduction, you may find that a deadline looming does wonders to focus the mind. Here are a few strategies that may prove useful in beginning classification and division papers.

Set a Historical Context

Somewhere in the opening you need to let your readers know just what you are classifying or dividing. Sometimes you can slip neatly into your topic by placing it in a historical context—either past history ("In the 1950s few people criticized the nutritional value of the American diet. Now . . .") or personal history ("When I was a teenager, I lived on pizza and potato chips and never thought I could turn into a health food enthusiast. But now . . .").

Pose a Problem

Simply presenting the problem to be discussed may set an appropriate context for some topics: "Affluent city dwellers are faced with the dilemma of choosing what kind of housing to live in—a rented apartment, a mortgaged condominium, or a single-family house." Then you present information on these options in the body of your paper.

State Your Purpose

Another opening strategy you may try is to state the purpose or value of your classification or division: "As a child, I was the victim of baby-sitting blues until I learned to classify the behavior of my sitters and cope with each type differently."

Use Narration

If your subject is suitable, you can set the whole paper, including the introduction, in a narrative context, as our student Sharon Sacchi did in an essay titled "Drunks." Here is her opening paragraph:

> It was about 1:00 A.M. when I finally got out of my apartment and headed for what I anticipated to be a fabulous party. When I arrived I discovered—to my eternal regret—that the thirsty crowd had already sloshed down the entire evening's ration of beer. By hanging around, cold sober, and conversing with a bunch of intoxicated people, I discovered several distinct types: the obnoxious drunk, the dizzy drunk, the denying drunk, and the depressed drunk.

To List (or Not to List) Your Divisions

You can mention the divisions in your introduction, as Sharon does above, or you could stop where she has put the colon and reveal the types in following paragraphs. Listing them at the beginning tends to defuse the surprise. If your purpose is to entertain, you probably should allow your readers to discover your clever categories as you introduce each one.

But if you are writing an extremely long piece—a term paper, a business report, a thesis or dissertation, for instance—you should consider announcing your divisions at the beginning. Similarly, even in a short paper, if you are discussing complex material—or material that for you may be simple but for your audience may be complex—you would certainly want to state the divisions at the beginning to make your points easier to follow.

Practice writing introductions using these subjects. Decide on an audience and a purpose for each one before you begin writing.

Qualities of a Perfect Picnic

Types of Advertising Appeals

Problems of Rearing Children with Attention Deficit Disorder (ADD)

How to Conclude Classification and Division Writing

Closing your essay in much the same way you opened it is familiar but dreary advice. Your readers will think you cannot come up with anything more inspired. Following are some tactics that work particularly well for division or classification essays.

Advise the Readers

Try to think of a way that your readers can put your division or classification to use, such as, "If you recognize the third type of teacher in your classes next fall, drop the course immediately and save yourself headaches, heartaches, and grade points." Here is the conclusion to the paper on drunks in which the writer points out some benefits of staying sober at a party.

> As a result of this experience, I have come to the conclusion that going to parties can be enlightening if you happen to be sober. Examining a party environment without the interference of alcohol can give you a clear view of what alcohol does to various people. You are then better able to recognize the ones who would be safe to talk to and distinguish them from the ones you need to avoid at all costs.
>
> —Sharon Sacchi

Look into the Future

Ask yourself, "What are the long-term implications of what I've said here? Will this classification or division hold true in the future? Why or why not?" The answers might provide you with a meaningful conclusion.

As researchers continue to study ADD, we can look forward to more exact pinpointing of how this disorder evolves and who exactly is a sufferer. Nevertheless, parents of ADD children will need special training and an extra degree of patience for years to come.

Point Out Exceptions

Indicate areas in which your division or classification may be partial or incomplete, such as:

I realize that several other factors, which I have not had space to analyze here, cause women to feel insecure about their appearance, but I am confident that the fashion industry is the main culprit.

This disclaimer makes you sound fair and reasonable but still insists on the importance of the points you did cover in the essay. Be careful, though, not to give the exceptions so much emphasis that you undercut the convincingness of your whole paper.

Focus on the Categories

You might point out underlying similarities among the parts—that all bores are basically insecure, for example. When writing to entertain, you could conclude, as this student did, by admitting that the types depicted are perhaps entirely subjective.

My wife told me that she has noticed a pattern to my classification of drivers. Speed demons are those people driving faster than I do. Turtles are the ones driving slower than I do. The safe drivers seem to be the people who are driving the same way I do. I'm not sure, but I think she might be on to something here.

WRITING
EXERCISE   Write practice closings for the topics in Writing Exercise 5.3, page 91.

5.4

How to Hold Together Classification and Division Writing

The basic function of transitions in a classification or division paper is to remind your readers of the relation between the parts or categories as you bring them up, paragraph by paragraph. The transitional words and phrases you use depend on what principle you chose for ordering the paragraphs.

According to Time

If you order your parts chronologically, you can use the "first, . . . second, . . . third, . . ." method. Here are the first sentences of three body paragraphs of such a paper.

> The first thing I noticed when Arnold asked me to dance was his suggestive leer.

> As we twirled around the floor, he revealed his second annoying characteristic—wandering hands.

> Before the dance was half over, I discovered his third disquieting mannerism—heavy breathing in my ear.

> The music stopped, and his strongest quality—his persistence—became obvious as I tried in vain to escape.

Other useful chronological transitions are phrases such as, "The *next* quality encountered . . ."; "*Later,* another problem emerges . . ."; and "*Finally,* the solution may be. . . ."

According to Degree

If you have organized the material according to degree or importance, the transitions can be references to the degrees, such as, "The *most urgent* question is . . ."; "The *least* convincing part of the film is . . ."; "An *even more* specious argument is . . ."; "The *simplest* (or most complex or most dangerous or least alarming or most appealing) requirement in the health care plan is . . ."

Just one more bit of advice: never use the tired phrase *last but not least* as a transition.

Revising Classification and Division Writing

The first four items on the following checklist (Fig. 5.1) concern possible problems that occur in the planning stage—what composition specialists call *global* features (important characteristics that can determine the success or failure of your writing). So allow time for a complete overhaul of your first draft in case you discover a need for extensive rewriting.

If possible, arrange for a literate, caring friend to read your paper and respond to the questions on the list. Or trade papers with a classmate and help

FIGURE 5.1

Checklist for Revising Classification and Division Writing

1. Is the subject limited enough for the length of the paper? Consider these examples:

Too Broad	Improved
parenting	problems of single fathers
cars	safety features on new American cars
sex	sex in women's magazine cosmetics ads

2. Is the topic of the paper apparent in the introduction?

3. Do any of the parts overlap, shift in basis of division, or lack parallelism of rank as discussed on page 82?

4. Is the classification or the division based on sufficient evidence or knowledge?

5. Is each of the divisions (or parts or types) discussed fully enough?

6. Are the transitions effective when moving from one type to the next?

7. If subgroupings are used, are they clearly distinguished from the main groupings?

8. Does the introduction capture your interest? Does the conclusion leave you satisfied, rather than let down?

9. Is either the opening or the closing more formal or informal than the body of the paper?

10. Are *analysis* and *category* spelled correctly?

each other. This *peer editing* can be quite effective if both parties take the task seriously enough to read carefully and respond thoughtfully and honestly.

 ## Ideas for Using Classification and Division in Writing

Short Prewriting Practice

1. *Classification.* In outline form, classify the cartoons in the Sunday funny papers. Then do it again, using a different form of classification.

2. *Classification.* Write a paragraph using an extrovert (or introvert) you know as a specific example of the general type.

3. *Division.* In a small group, exchange jokes with other students, and discuss the elements that make the jokes funny.

Longer Paper Ideas

Before you begin to write on one of these subjects, be sure that you can write a sentence telling *why* you are making the classification or the division (your purpose) and *who* might be interested in reading it (your audience).

1. *Classification and Division.* What types of TV shows are the most popular this season? Explain why you think each type is popular.

2. *Division.* Contemplate a magazine advertisement, a TV ad, or an ad campaign (like Taster's Choice coffee ads or Camel cigarettes' Joe Cool ads). What gender and age group is it designed to appeal to? What emotions and thoughts does it try to make the viewer feel?

3. *Division.* Choose one of your heroes, and analyze what qualities make this person seem admirable.

4. *Classification.* If you have ever been a salesperson, waitress, or waiter, how would you classify your customers?

5. *Classification.* Here are some more subjects that can be classified into types: neighborhoods, dreams, courage, happiness, freedom, intelligence, marriages, laughter, suicide, prisons, tennis players, drinkers, pet owners, jokes, passions, bike riders.

6. *Division.* Describe the qualities of the ideal pet, housemate, dinner date, novel, Saturday afternoon, parent, or child.

THE PLOT AGAINST PEOPLE

Russell Baker

1   Inanimate objects are classified scientifically into three major categories—those that don't work, those that break down, and those that get lost.

2   The goal of all inanimate objects is to resist people and ultimately destroy them, and the three major classifications are based on the method each object uses to achieve its purpose. As a general rule, any object capable of breaking down at the moment when it is most needed will do so. The automobile is typical of this category.

3   With the cunning typical of its breed, the automobile never breaks down while entering a filling station with a large staff of idle mechanics. It waits until it reaches a downtown intersection in the middle of the rush hour, or until it is fully loaded with family and luggage on the Ohio turnpike.

4   Thus it creates maximum misery, inconvenience, frustration, and irritability among its human cargo, thereby reducing its owner's life span.

5   Washing machines, garbage disposals, lawn mowers, light bulbs, automatic laundry dryers, water pipes, furnaces, electrical fuses, television tubes, hose nozzles, tape recorders, slide projectors—all are in league with the automobile to take their turn at breaking down whenever life threatens to flow smoothly for their human enemies.

6   Many inanimate objects, of course, find it extremely difficult to break down. Pliers, for example, and gloves and keys are almost totally incapable of breaking down. Therefore, they have had to evolve a different technique for resisting people.

7   They get lost. Science has still not solved the mystery of how they do it, and nobody has ever caught one of them in the act of getting lost. The most plausible theory is that they have developed a secret method of locomotion which they are able to conceal the instant a human eye falls upon them.

8   It is not uncommon for a pair of pliers to climb all the way from the cellar to the attic in its single-minded determination to raise its owner's blood pressure. Keys have been known to burrow three feet under mattresses. Women's purses, despite their great weight, frequently travel through six or seven rooms to find hiding space under a couch.

9   Scientists have been struck by the fact that things that break down virtually never get lost, while things that get lost hardly ever break down.

10   A furnace, for example, will invariably break down at the depth of the first winter cold wave, but it will never get lost. A woman's purse, which after all does have

some inherent capacity for breaking down, hardly ever does; it almost invariably chooses to get lost.

Not everyone agrees, however, that this indicates a conciliatory attitude among inanimate objects. Many say it merely proves that furnaces, gloves, and pliers are incredibly stupid.   11

The third class of objects—those that don't work—is the most curious of all. These include such objects as barometers, car clocks, cigarette lighters, flashlights, and toy-train locomotives. It is inaccurate, of course, to say that they never work. They work once, usually for the first few hours after being brought home, and then quit. Thereafter, they never work again.   12

In fact, it is widely assumed that they are built for the purpose of not working. Some people have reached advanced ages without ever seeing some of these objects—barometers, for example—in working order.   13

Science is utterly baffled by the entire category. There are many theories about it. The most interesting holds that the things that don't work have attained the highest state possible for an inanimate object, the state to which things that break down and things that get lost can still only aspire.   14

They have truly defeated us by conditioning us never to expect anything of them, and in return they have given us the only peace we receive from inanimate society. We do not expect a barometer to work, an electric locomotive to run, a cigarette lighter to light, or a flashlight to illuminate, and when they don't, it does not raise our blood pressure.   15

We cannot attain that peace with furnaces and keys and cars and women's purses as long as we demand that they work for their keep.   16

Chapter Six

Comparison
and Contrast

When you think of who you are and then think of who you would like to be, you are practicing a common (though, in this example, perhaps painful) type of comparison and contrast. If you are well on the way to achieving your goals, the process is mostly *comparison* since, in one sense of the word, comparison refers to discovering similarities, whereas *contrast* refers to discovering differences. But any time you contrast two things you are making a comparison; thus the word *comparison* is commonly used to refer to both processes.

 ## Thinking Critically About Comparison and Contrast Writing

Comparison is one kind of analysis. Probably you do it every time you make a choice between two things—two movies, restaurants, shampoos, or artificial sweeteners. Logical comparison is the intelligent alternative to simple strategies like flipping coins.

Compare Reasonably Similar Things

Whenever you reveal and explain similarities and differences, you should be considering *comparable* items—that is, items having some basic similarity. You would not, for instance, choose to compare a banana and a clock. You might reasonably compare a banana and a mango, though, or a clock and a wristwatch, if you can think of some worthwhile reason for doing so.

Compare When Making Decisions

You probably already use comparison and contrast in making decisions and solving problems. Often you perform the process in your head without consciously making a comparison. But if you are faced with a major decision (whether or not to change jobs) or a genuine problem (how to save enough money for next year's tuition), you may find it helpful to record and organize your thinking on paper.

Compare to Solve a Problem

Consider this cheerful prospect: You have just been offered a promotion to become a manager at your workplace. Before making your decision, you would do well to spend some time considering the advantages and the disadvantages. One strategy would be to write down in two separate columns the advantages and disadvantages of accepting.

Pros	*Cons*
higher salary	more hours at work
more prestige	less time with family
possible chance of further promotion	no chance of future promotion, if answer is no
nicer office	greater stress
personal secretary	more paper work
chance for creative leadership	many more meetings

The length of each list should not be the deciding factor. Consider instead the quality of your possible gains and losses. A person with drive and ambition would probably choose the promotion but a person with staunch family values might well decline. The important point is to think through your options and weigh them well. Putting your thoughts on paper will help you make rational decisions.

Considering Purpose and Audience

If you are going to write an essay developed largely through comparison and contrast, you should have a purpose for doing so. Here are several possible reasons for making comparisons:

1. *To convince your readers that one item is superior to another* or simply that you prefer it (choosing one contracting firm over another)

2. *To explain something your readers probably do* not *know about* by comparing it with something they probably *do* know about (using a new word processing program compared to using an old, familiar program)
3. *To show how two seemingly similar things, places, or people are really different* in important ways (trail bikes compared with regular bicycles)
4. *To show how two seemingly different things, places, or people are really similar* in important ways (operation of a CD player compared with the operation of a tape player)
5. *To compare the past with the present*—or vice versa (life before parenthood compared with life as a parent)

It is important to keep in mind your readers. Consider who would benefit or get pleasure from reading your comparison and contrast writing. If you cannot think of anyone, maybe you had better switch subjects. Here are possible audiences for each of the above examples:

1. Contracting firm A versus firm B

   Audience: Someone building or remodeling a house

2. New word processing program versus old one

   Audience: Staff who must convert to the new program, or personnel responsible for choosing a word processing program

3. Trail bikes versus regular bicycles

   Audience: Members of a cycling club

4. CD player versus tape player

   Audience: Someone owning a tape player who has just purchased a CD player

5. Child-free lifestyle versus parenthood

   Audience: People who are considering parenthood

Remember that when you are done, your reader should respond with an "Aha!" and not a "So what?" Brilliant organization will help bring the desired response.

EXERCISE

6.1

Think back over the last few days, and list occasions when you used comparison and contrast thinking. For instance, did you choose one product over another? Did you justify a choice you made? Did you teach someone something new? Did you set priorities for your daily activities? On your list, note the pros and cons that helped make up your mind.

How to Organize Comparison and Contrast Writing

Writers organize comparison/contrast essays in a number of ways. Here we discuss two of the most useful methods. The one you choose depends on your subject and your purpose—as well as on how much time you have to write.

Keep in mind that these patterns can be expanded to allow for comparison of more than two elements. We focus on two-part plans, because in college, two-part comparison and contrast topics are common writing assignments. Also, as you practice these methods of organization, it makes sense to start with the simplest forms.

The Easy *Block* Plan

If you are answering an essay examination question that asks for a comparison or contrast and your time is limited, you should use a simple method of organization—the *block pattern*. You discuss the main points of the first part of your comparison, make a transition, and then discuss the same points *in the same order* for the contrasting part.

Imagine that, as a discussion question on a history exam, you have been asked to compare puritan beliefs with transcendentalist beliefs in nineteenth-century American society. You would want to discuss first the important aspects of puritanism; then, with a clear transition, discuss the important aspects of transcendentalism. If you outlined your response, it might look something like this:

I.   Brief intro
II. Puritan beliefs
   A. Human nature corrupt
   B. God is sovereign ruler
   C. Doctrine enforces conformity
III. Transcendental beliefs
   A. Human nature perfectible
   B. God is in nature and in each person
   C. Doctrine encourages self-reliance
IV. Brief conclusion

This plan is also well suited for before-and-after or then-and-now types of comparisons or contrasts.

The Precise *Point-by-Point* Pattern

If you are not writing under pressure and have plenty of time to think about what you want to say and how to present the ideas, you should consider using the *point-by-point* organization. This method requires solid critical thinking because first you need to classify the material. That is, you mull over your ideas until you come up with several characteristics or categories that will cover the specific details of your comparison. Your hard work will produce its reward, though, in a sharp highlighting of the differences or similarities.

For example, if you were given a take-home examination asking you to discuss the major differences between puritanism and transcendentalism in America, you could adopt a more complex arrangement of ideas than the one recommended for writing in class. You could focus directly on the major ways the creeds differ:

I. Attitude toward human nature
   A. Puritanism—human nature corrupt
      —"In Adam's Fall we sinned all"
      —Doctrine of Original Sin
   B. Transcendentalism—human nature basically good
      —Rejects idea of "the Fall"
      —Declares human nature perfectible

II. Attitude toward God and salvation
   A. Puritans—God is sovereign
      —Human purpose to glorify God
      —Bible sole authority on morality and religion
      —People saved by divine election, not good works
   B. Transcendentalists—God is everywhere
      —God exists in nature and within each person
      —God found by "intuition" and study of nature

III. Attitude toward society
   A. Puritanism enforces conformity
      —Little tolerance for beliefs of others
      —People need to oversee behavior of neighbors
   B. Transcendentalism encourages self-reliance
      —Rejects traditional authority
      —People should follow own consciences

This outline would produce a complete and orderly response to a take-home essay exam question—or, for that matter, a good informative essay setting forth two conflicting ideologies.

SAMPLES OF STUDENT COMPARISON AND CONTRAST WRITING

Life BC and Life AC

In my experience there was a life-before-children (BC), and there is now a life-after-children (AC). These lives are strikingly different. My husband and I have made numerous changes and quite a few sacrifices in order to accommodate the addition of two daughters to our family.   1

In 1987, BC, we lived in a pretty, seven-year-old, bilevel brick house with lots of room: three bedrooms, one and a half baths, kitchen, living room, family room, and two-car attached garage with an electric door opener. The carpets throughout were cream-colored, and the living room couch was covered in pale blue silk. The house, located on a busy street, was no more than five minutes from anywhere we wanted to go, including our favorite grocery store. True, we did not need such a large house, but the extra space made it possible for each of us to have plenty of privacy.   2

Sleeping late on the weekends was another luxury we enjoyed, BC. My husband and I belonged to a mixed bowling league, BC, and had great fun while getting good exercise. Although we both worked, I often found time, BC, to relax in my favorite easy chair and do fancy cross-stitching. I took great pride in my artistic creations and was able to give them as presents, much valued by family and friends. Almost every weekend, we would have friends over for dinner, as we both liked to cook. And every Friday evening we dined out—not necessarily at a fancy restaurant, but that was one night when nobody needed to plan dinner—and if there was a good movie in town, we would go.   3

In 1988, AC, came the big life changes—along with our first baby, an adorable little girl. After we decided to have children, I wanted to stay home with them to enjoy their accomplishments and watch them grow, instead of dropping them off at a sitter's every workday. But without my salary, we needed to cut expenses. The best way to save money was to reduce our mortgage payments. So, we moved to a trashed, twenty-year-old ranch house with far less room than we   4 were used to: three tiny bedrooms, one bathroom, a kitchen, living room (no family room), and a huge detached garage—with no electric door opener, but a door too heavy for me to lift. This house, located at least twenty minutes from anywhere we wanted to go, was in such bad shape that we gutted it before moving in, replacing everything but the walls and roof. We did all the work ourselves to save money and were exhausted by the time we finished, but at least the place was livable.

5   The other major changes in our lives were not the result of conscious decisions but simply came about as a result of parenthood. By 1990, AC, we had two lovely daughters, and no leisure time. Sleeping late on the weekends was a luxury that we missed immediately. The baby never understood that we were used to getting up AFTER the sunrise. Cross-stitching is now a thing of the past, along with our bowling league. In fact, all of those friends who used to come over for dinner seem to have vanished. We have new friends, people who also have children and whose lives are similarly hectic, but we have little time to entertain. The privacy we used to enjoy, the intimate evenings spent together, just the two of us—gone as well. We do still have a few hours alone after the girls are in bed, but most evenings we have trouble holding our eyes open until we drop into bed ourselves.

6   Our lives have changed in many ways since our precious children were born, but I would not have it any other way.

—Kristi Kull

Four Eyes

1   Among people with less than perfect eyesight, there exists a longstanding, sometimes heated argument between those who prefer to wear glasses and those who favor contact lenses. Both glasses and contacts are essential in improving the vision of millions of people. But setting aside these benefits, I want to argue that glasses are in several ways superior to those tiny bowl-shaped discs inserted into your eyes.

2   Glasses begin to show their advantages from the very moment the alarm wakes you. As you lift your head from your feather pillow, wiping the sleep from your eyes, the contact lens wearer will greet the new day as one great blur. Your impaired vision will continue to trouble you as you dodge fuzzy objects while struggling to find the place where your lenses are stored. Take the beginning of

the same day for the glasses wearer. The alarm wakes you; you lift your head from your comfortable pillow, rub the sleep from your eyes, and reach for your custom-fitted glasses. Instantly the world is crisp and clear. You walk toward the bathroom in confidence, knowing you will not stub your toe on invisible obstacles. Those first few moments of the day are critical, for they can set the mood for the remainder of your waking hours. You can either choose a bleak beginning, fogged in by blurred surroundings, or you can select a bright new day free from floundering. Only glasses can provide this positive outlook for the vision impaired.

Another way in which glasses make life easier than contacts for the wearer involves their care. Maintaining a pair of glasses requires a minimum of upkeep. To keep them sparkling clean, all you need is tap water and a soft cloth. It need not even be a fancy cloth—a worn-out T-shirt or holey handkerchief works just fine. But with contact lenses the maintenance is time-consuming and costly. You need to clean them daily in an expensive solution, then store them in a disinfecting solution (also expensive). Before putting the lenses in your eyes, you must rinse off those chemicals in a saline bath. After wearing them a week, your lenses need to be soaked in an enzymatic solution (incredibly costly) to remove the protein build-up secreted from your eyes. With the time and money you save by wearing glasses, you can enjoy the finer things which make living worthwhile.

For many people, another reason for preferring glasses to contacts is summed up by Olivia Dukakis, who wisely observes in <u>Steel Magnolias</u>, "The difference between us and the animals is our ability to accessorize." Just so. The person who wears glasses may select a variety of styles and colors to suit the occasion or complement the costume. With contact lenses, though, the wearer is hard pressed to create an image. Even a person of rich imagination and rare creativity is left with no possibility for flair or originality, having only two tiny, totally transparent lenses to work with.

The final reason why glasses are preferable to contact lenses is, for me, the most persuasive, for it is based on human vanity. Each and every one of us faces the unpleasant prospect of aging—the old biological clock, constantly ticking. Most of us struggle to keep a youthful appearance as long as possible. But if you choose to wear contacts, you will find yourself squinting a lot more than if you wore glasses. It's a known fact. And, of course, one result of squinting is the formation of those unsightly crow's feet around the eyes. Squinting adds undue stress to the delicate tissues. By wearing glasses, you can retard those wrinkles and retain that youthful glow for years longer.

6   Considering all these factors, you will surely agree that if you need to improve your vision, the choice between glasses and contact lenses is an easy one. Next time you find yourself at your local Lens Crafters, demand the very best for your eyes. Cast your lot on the sensible side: insist on glasses.

—David A. Dean

WRITING AND
DISCUSSION
EXERCISE

6.2

1. "Life BC and Life AC" is written following a *block* pattern of organization. Using the same material, make an outline for a paper following the *point-by-point* pattern. Were there any specific details that you had to omit after devising your points of contrast?

2. Is the conclusion of Kull's essay convincing? Why or why not?

3. "Four Eyes" is written following a *point-by-point* pattern of organization. Using the same material, make an outline for a paper following the *block* pattern. Do you think the essay would be as effective if written this way? Why?

4. Can you identify the tone of "Four Eyes"? What changes might you make if you were rewriting the paper in a serious tone?

5. State what you take to be the purpose and audience for each paper.

6. Examine the transitions between paragraphs in both essays. How do they help guide the readers?

How to Introduce Comparison and Contrast Writing

Like the classification and division introduction, the opening paragraph of your comparison essay should disclose the subject and set it within context. Recall the purposes suggested earlier for using comparison and contrast:

1. showing one element to be superior to another;
2. explaining the unfamiliar through the familiar;
3. showing differences between similar elements;
4. showing similarities between different elements; and
5. comparing the past and the present.

You may want to begin by stating one of these purposes in the introduction of your paper.

For instance, if you intend to convince your readers of the superiority of one item over another, you might begin your essay by stating briefly the terms of the controversy you are resolving: "Some people claim that fuzzy aardvarks are splendid pets because of their docile temperaments and cuddly bodies. Others say that fuzzy aardvarks are dull and placid; these people endorse the passionate, excitable hairless aardvark as a perfect pet." Then, of course, you would go on to compare the two kinds of aardvarks and prove which is actually in your opinion the superior pet. The sample student paper on page 104 titled "Four Eyes" begins with this type of introduction.

Here is an example of an introduction to a student paper ("The New Theater") explaining the unfamiliar through the familiar.

> New styles of play production have caused theater architects to redesign the stage. Theater-in-the-round, also called an arena stage, is quite intimate because the audience closely surrounds the playing area. The traditional proscenium arch theater, on the other hand, is usually much larger and seats the whole audience in front of the acting area, looking into a boxlike stage. Although any theatergoer can easily see the variations between the two stages, the required differences in production techniques are less apparent but quite important for an effective performance.
>
> —Lynn Cooper

Lynn then goes on to discuss those differences in production techniques.

The following paragraph introduces an essay focusing on the differences between two similar events—two concerts given by Elton John.

> Time changes everything, or so we are told. Over a period of time our looks, opinions, and viewpoints often change. When I was a teenager, I was a rabid fan of Elton John. I idolized Captain Fantastic when I saw him perform at McCormick Place in June 1976. Still a devoted admirer, I more recently attended another concert and was surprised by the differences in the two performances.
>
> —Debbie Brown

Using the block pattern, Debbie in the body of her paper describes her response to the first concert; then, she describes her response to the second concert, concluding with a summary of her changed impressions.

For an illustration of an introduction to an essay comparing past to present (or before-and-after), see the opening paragraph of the sample essay "Life BC and Life AC" on page 103.

Revealing (or Not Revealing) Your Main Points

Once more, if your essay is long, or if the material is difficult to understand, you may want to indicate in the introduction how you have organized the ideas. For example, the last sentence in the opening paragraph of "The New Theater" (p. 107) could include the main points to be covered, like this:

> Although any theatergoer can easily see the variations between the two stages, the required differences in scenic design, lighting design, and acting techniques are not as apparent but are nonetheless quite important for an effective performance.

When you set up the terms of your comparison this way, your readers will know what to expect and will follow your point more easily, even if the material is complex.

If, however, your subject is not difficult, you may decide to develop your material inductively (see p. 145), saving the statement of your main idea until the end.

DISCUSSION
EXERCISE

6.3

1. Analyze the writer's techniques in the following opening paragraph of a student essay. Consider (a) the introduction of subject, (b) how the context is set, (c) the statement or suggestion of purpose, and (d) the mentioning of basic similarities, differences, or both, in the comparison.

   Aldous Huxley's <u>Brave New World</u> and George Orwell's <u>1984</u> are two of the most compelling novels concerning mankind's self-inflicted destruction by technological advances. Both set in what was then the future, the plots illustrate technology and its misuses resulting in evil, not good. The ultimate evil is the damage to human character. Each novel relies on the elimination of human emotion as necessary in achieving absolute power for the government. Huxley creates 16,000 identical twins through the use of biological technology; Orwell presents a society brainwashed through the use of mechanical technology.

   —Carla Barrows

2. Find an introduction to a comparison/contrast article in a magazine or newspaper and analyze the introductory techniques listed in number 1.

How to Conclude Comparison and Contrast Writing

Your closing should briefly tie your subjects and your purpose together without repeating what you have already said in the introduction or in the body of the paper. To accomplish this feat, you can try again the tactics we suggested for classification and division papers: advise the readers or look into the future. Reviewing these strategies often brings to mind something reasonable you can say in closing, like, "So do not let anyone sell you a hairless aardvark unless you want to spend the rest of your life at the mercy of your pet's whims." Both of the sample student papers in this chapter close with the writers' evaluations of their topics.

If your paper has focused on personal experience, you can close by offering your own opinion, as Debbie Brown (p. 107) does in her contrast of two Elton John concerts.

> As his third encore, he sang "Your Song." I stood on that hillside, tears streaming down my face, once again listening to my favorite singer performing my favorite song. By now my initial disappointment at discovering that Captain Fantastic had turned into Reg Dwight was totally gone. Teenage idolizing had changed to respect. Yes, time changes many things—but not everything.

The first sentence of Debbie's introduction was this: "Time changes everything, or so we are told." Notice how neatly she echoes that line in her final sentence, giving her essay a satisfying closure.

Avoiding Common Pitfalls

Let us warn you about two ways of concluding that seem quite tempting at two o'clock in the morning but usually weaken the paper. First, summarizing similarities and differences in concluding a short paper, of say 500 to 800 words, is not a good idea. If you have written the paper well, any intelligent reader will be able to remember your main points. And if you have not written well, a clear conclusion cannot make up for the muddle in the middle.

Second, the temptation to apologize may seem appropriate after you have presented a strong case for the superiority of one item over the other. You get to the conclusion and panic, so you apologize repeatedly ("Well, this is just my opinion; others might feel differently," and so on). This tactic undercuts the purpose of your paper. If you express a strong opinion and support it in the body of the essay, do not back off in the conclusion. Look again to see how forcefully the conclusion of the sample student paper titled "Four Eyes" (p. 104) reinforces the writer's certainty that he is right.

1. Write possible introductions and conclusions for comparison/contrast essays about the following subjects:
   a. nuclear energy versus solar energy
   b. strict parents versus permissive parents
   c. a "pal" boss versus an "authority" boss
   d. full-time school versus part-time school
   e. taking a shower versus taking a bath

2. Analyze the student writer's tactics in the conclusion of Barrows's essay (begun on p. 108) comparing two cautionary novels.

> The fact that both novels give a pessimistic outlook on the future may also be a reason society takes their message seriously. Neither novel offers any hope for humankind. The characters in <u>Brave New World</u> and <u>1984</u> are unable to change or make any improvements. But then, if the novels had ended happily, no one would have taken them as a warning. They could simply have been considered entertaining but fanciful stories.

3. Find a comparison/contrast conclusion in a magazine or newspaper and analyze the writer's tactics.

How to Hold Together Comparison and Contrast Writing

Transitions are particularly important in making comparisons because you must keep your readers straight at all times about which element you are discussing.

The block pattern, the easiest to organize, requires the fewest major transitions. If, for instance, you are comparing puritan and transcendental beliefs, you only need one major transition between the two parts of your comparison:

> Transcendentalism, <u>on the other hand</u>, departed in several major ways from puritan doctrines.

> Transcendentalism, <u>in contrast</u>, offered a much less restrictive system of beliefs.

> <u>Although</u> the puritans worshiped a distant, often angry god, the transcendentalists believed God was within all.

You may occasionally want to use a brief transitional paragraph in moving from one element to the other, as Brown (p. 107) does in her comparison of two musical performances.

> Over the years, I still enjoyed Elton John's music. Every once in a while, I would recall that concert and wonder what it would be like to see Captain Fantastic in action again. In September 1988 I was to find out.

The point-by-point pattern, which sets up a sharper contrast, calls for more transitions, as you will be shifting from one element to another throughout the paper. If you are showing how two subjects are similar, try not to overuse the term *similarly.* Consider using these terms as well—*also, likewise, in the same way, in a similar manner.*

When you are focusing on differences, you may employ a lot of comparative (*better, more, fancier*) and superlative (*best, most, fanciest*) forms of adjectives and adverbs to show the relationships between your subjects. Between paragraphs, and sometimes even within paragraphs, you will occasionally need to use some of the common transitional terms that indicate contrast: *but, still, on the other hand, on the contrary, nevertheless, contrary to, however, nonetheless, conversely, yet, although, granted that, in contrast, neither.* Notice how the following sample paragraph, beginning with a transition from the previous paragraph, shifts midway, using another transition to present the second element of the contrast.

> *Another* major difference between the two characters lies in their level of self-confidence. George, who is defensive about the slightest criticism, always expects disaster and frequently finds it. When he borrows his parents' car, it gets trashed in the mall parking lot. After he gets engaged, he knows at once that he's picked a woman who will make his life miserable. Kramer, *on the other hand,* overflows with self-confidence, most apparent in the way he bursts into Jerry's apartment. Almost every week he comes up with some hairbrained idea that he thinks will make him a millionaire. And despite his crazy schemes, he somehow avoids the unfortunate consequences that plague the more cautious George.

Remember that you achieve *continuity* (the smooth flow of ideas) partly through the use of transitional words, but, as we mentioned earlier, it also helps to present your contrasts in the same order each time. If you begin with George and then consider Kramer, continue that arrangement throughout each point of the contrast.

Before you revise your paper, you should review the checklist (Fig. 6.1).

 ## Ideas for Comparison and Contrast Writing

Short Prewriting Practice

1. Find a magazine (like *Esquire*) that is primarily written for men and one (like *Cosmopolitan*) that is aimed at women. Brainstorm two lists of paired details (about the nature of the articles, illustrations, advertising, etc.) in these publications. Then write down or discuss with several classmates three or four different thesis statements a writer might choose from if writing a comparison of the magazines.

FIGURE 6.1

Checklist for Revising Comparison and Contrast Writing

Here are some basic points to check as you work to improve your rough draft (or a classmate's).

1. Do the elements being compared have a logical basis for comparison?

2. Is the subject too big to handle in the number of words available? For instance, "good and evil" or "men and women" have a logical basis for comparison, but a writer will run into problems trying to compare them in 700 words.

3. Is the purpose for comparing the elements clear? What is it?

4. Is the organizational pattern the best one? Why?

5. Are the points given similar treatment? That is, if *A*'s durability is discussed, is *B*'s durability (or lack of it) also discussed?

6. Are comparable details taken up in the same order for each element?

7. Does the essay include all the pertinent points of comparison or contrast and eliminate points that were irrelevant to the purpose?

2. Make up three writing topics (like comparing a typewriter and a computer; buying versus leasing a new car; keeping a cat indoors versus outdoors) that would be suitable for a brief paper of 500 to 700 words. Exchange topics with another student and write comments for each other in response to these questions:

    a. Which would be the most interesting?

    b. Which would be the most boring?

    c. Which would be the most difficult to write?

    d. Which might be too broad or too narrow?

    e. What special problems might come up in the writing?

3. Read the sample student papers in this chapter (pp. 103–106), and write an outline of the major points of each paper. Write the paper's thesis at the top of each outline.

Longer Paper Ideas

1. Discuss one or more illusions that are presented as reality on television and compare the illusion to the reality as you know it. Write for an audience who might be taken in by the illusion. Soap operas offer a rich source here.

2. Compare and/or contrast any of the following: the work of two painters or sculptors; two novels (or two poems) by the same writer; two CD's by the same musicians; two organizations or groups you belong to. Be sure to identify an audience before you begin who will be interested in or informed by your essay.

3. Compare how you perceived some person, place, or activity as a child with how you perceive the same thing today.

4. Write about a situation in which you expected one thing and got another—in other words, in which the expectation and the reality were different. Many times these occurrences are "firsts": your first day at kindergarten; your first teenage crush; your first wedding; your first day on the job; your first health food restaurant.

5. Write an essay suggested by any of the topics mentioned in the first two prewriting assignments above.

Remember to select an appropriate audience before writing on any of these topics. That audience can, of course, be your classmates in this or another course.

A PUBLISHED ESSAY ILLUSTRATING COMPARISON AND CONTRAST WRITING

WOMEN AND MEN*

Scott Russell Sanders

1   The first men, besides my father, I remember seeing were black convicts and white guards, in the cottonfield across the road from our farm on the outskirts of Memphis. I must have been three or four. The prisoners wore dingy gray-and-black zebra suits, heavy as canvas, sodden with sweat. Hatless, stooped, they chopped weeds in the fierce heat, row after row, breathing the acrid dust of boll-weevil poison. The overseers wore dazzling white shirts and broad shadowy hats. The oiled barrels of their shotguns flashed in the sunlight. Their faces in memory are utterly blank. Of course those men, white and black, have become for me an emblem of racial hatred. But they have also come to stand for the twin poles of my early vision of manhood—the brute toiling animal and the boss.

2   When I was a boy, the men I knew labored with their bodies. They were marginal farmers, just scraping by, or welders, steelworkers, carpenters; they swept floors, dug ditches, mined coal, or drove trucks, their forearms ropy with muscle; they trained horses, stoked furnaces, built tires, stood on assembly lines wrestling parts onto cars and refrigerators. They got up before light, worked all day long whatever the weather, and when they came home at night they looked as though somebody had been whipping them. In the evenings and on weekends they worked on their own places, tilling gardens that were lumpy with clay, fixing broken-down cars, hammering on houses that were always too drafty, too leaky, too small.

3   The bodies of the men I knew were twisted and maimed in ways visible and invisible. The nails of their hands were black and split, the hands tattooed with scars. Some had lost fingers. Heavy lifting had given many of them finicky backs and guts weak from hernias. Racing against conveyor belts had given them ulcers. Their ankles and knees ached from years of standing on concrete. Anyone who had worked for long around machines was hard of hearing. They squinted, and the skin of their faces was creased like the leather of old work gloves. There were times, studying them, when I dreaded growing up. Most of them coughed, from dust or cigarettes, and most of them drank cheap wine or whiskey, so their eyes looked bloodshot and bruised. The fathers of my friends always seemed older than the mothers. Men wore out sooner. Only women lived into old age.

4   As a boy I also knew another sort of men, who did not sweat and break down like mules. They were soldiers, and so far as I could tell they scarcely worked at all. During my early school years we lived on a military base, an arsenal in Ohio, and every day I saw GIs in the guardshacks, on the stoops of barracks, at the wheels of olive drab Chevrolets. The chief fact of their lives was boredom. Long after I left the

*An excerpt from "The Men We Carry in Our Minds."

Arsenal I came to recognize the sour smell the soldiers gave off as that of souls in limbo. They were all waiting—for wars, for transfers, for leaves, for promotions, for the end of their hitch—like so many braves waiting for the hunt to begin. Unlike the warriors of older tribes, however, they would have no say about when the battle would start or how it would be waged. Their waiting was broken only when they practiced for war. They fired guns at targets, drove tanks across the churned-up fields of the military reservation, set off bombs in the wrecks of old fighter planes. I knew this was all play. But I also felt certain that when the hour for killing arrived, they would kill. When the real shooting started, many of them would die. This was what soldiers were *for,* just as a hammer was for driving nails.

Warriors and toilers: those seemed, in my boyhood vision, to be the chief des-   5
tinies for men. They weren't the only destinies, as I learned from having a few male teachers, from reading books, and from watching television. But the men on televi-sion—the politicians, the astronauts, the generals, the savvy lawyers, the philosophical doctors, the bosses who gave orders to both soldiers and laborers—seemed as removed and unreal to me as the figures in tapestries. I could no more imagine growing up to become one of these cool, potent creatures than I could imagine becoming a prince.

A nearer and more hopeful example was that of my father, who had escaped   6
from a red-dirt farm to a tire factory, and from the assembly line to the front office. Eventually he dressed in a white shirt and tie. He carried himself as if he had been born to work with his mind. But his body, remembering the earlier years of slogging work, began to give out on him in his fifties, and it quit on him entirely before he turned sixty-five. Even such a partial escape from man's fate as he had accomplished did not seem possible for most of the boys I knew. They joined the Army, stood in line for jobs in the smoky plants, helped build highways. They were bound to work as their fathers had worked, killing themselves or preparing to kill others.

A scholarship enabled me not only to attend college, a rare enough feat in my   7
circle, but even to study in a university meant for the children of the rich. Here I met for the first time young men who had assumed from birth that they would lead lives of comfort and power. And for the first time I met women who told me that men were guilty of having kept all the joys and privileges of the earth for themselves. I was baffled. What privileges? What joys? I thought about the maimed, dismal lives of most of the men back home. What had they stolen from their wives and daugh-ters? The right to go five days a week, twelve months a year, for thirty or forty years to a steel mill or a coal mine? The right to drop bombs and die in war? The right to feel every leak in the roof, every gap in the fence, every cough in the engine, as a wound they must mend? The right to feel, when the lay-off comes or the plant shuts down, not only afraid but ashamed?

I was slow to understand the deep grievances of women. This was because, as   8
a boy, I had envied them. Before college, the only people I had ever known who were interested in art or music or literature, the only ones who read books, the only ones who ever seemed to enjoy a sense of ease and grace were the mothers and

daughters. Like the menfolk, they fretted about money, they scrimped and made-do. But, when the pay stopped coming in, they were not the ones who had failed. Nor did they have to go to war, and that seemed to me a blessed fact. By comparison with the narrow, ironclad days of fathers, there was an expansiveness, I thought, in the days of mothers. They went to see neighbors, to shop in town, to run errands at school, at the library, at church. No doubt, had I looked harder at their lives, I would have envied them less. It was not my fate to become a woman, so it was easier for me to see the graces. Few of them held jobs outside the home, and those who did filled thankless roles as clerks and waitresses. I didn't see, then, what a prison a house could be, since houses seemed to me brighter, handsomer places than any factory. I did not realize—because such things were never spoken of—how often women suffered from men's bullying. I did learn about the wretchedness of abandoned wives, single mothers, widows; but I also learned about the wretchedness of lone men. Even then I could see how exhausting it was for a mother to cater all day to the needs of young children. But if I had been asked, as a boy, to choose between tending a baby and tending a machine, I think I would have chosen the baby. (Having now tended both, I know I would choose the baby.)

9   So I was baffled when the women at college accused me and my sex of having cornered the world's pleasures. I think something like my bafflement has been felt by other boys (and by girls as well) who grew up in dirt-poor farm country, in mining country, in black ghettos, in Hispanic barrios, in the shadows of factories, in Third World nations—any place where the fate of men is as grim and bleak as the fate of women. Toilers and warriors. I realize now how ancient these identities are, how deep the tug they exert on men, the undertow of a thousand generations. The miseries I saw, as a boy, in the lives of nearly all men I continue to see in the lives of many—the body-breaking toil, the tedium, the call to be tough, the humiliating powerlessness, the battle for a living and for territory.

10   When the women I met at college thought about the joys and privileges of men, they did not carry in their minds the sort of men I had known in my childhood. They thought of their fathers, who were bankers, physicians, architects, stockbrokers, the big wheels of the big cities. These fathers rode the train to work or drove cars that cost more than any of my childhood houses. They were attended from morning to night by female helpers, wives and nurses and secretaries. They were never laid off, never short of cash at month's end, never lined up for welfare. These fathers made decisions that mattered. They ran the world.

11   The daughters of such men wanted to share in this power, this glory. So did I. They yearned for a say over their future, for jobs worthy of their abilities, for the right to live at peace, unmolested, whole. Yes, I thought, yes yes. The difference between me and these daughters was that they saw me, because of my sex, as destined from birth to become like their fathers, and therefore as an enemy to their desires. But I knew better. I wasn't an enemy, in fact or in feeling. I was an ally. If I had known, then, how to tell them so, would they have believed me? Would they now?

Chapter Seven

Cause-and-Effect Analysis

Most people believe that things happen for reasons. Furthermore, most people cannot help trying to figure out those reasons. If you planted tomatoes last summer and got a luscious crop, and you plant tomatoes this summer and get none, you are not likely to just shrug your shoulders and say, "Well, whaddaya know, those tomatoes didn't grow this year," and go calmly about your business. No, you are much more likely to say, "Now, how come those dumb tomatoes didn't grow?" and try to figure out the causes for their failure.

People with good sense think about the effects or consequences of happenings, too. For instance, if it has not rained in three weeks, and you keep putting off hosing down the tomato patch, you have to consider the effects of your procrastination.

Most of us do go around every day blithely analyzing causes and effects as though everything makes sense. Whether or not it does is debatable, but we shouldn't let that stop us from analyzing.

Thinking Critically About Causes and Effects

When engaged in cause-and-effect analysis, you may want to concentrate on either causes or effects, especially if your thinking will lead to writing. For instance, you could follow the line of inquiry illustrated in the professional writing sample at the end of this chapter and begin by briefly stating or implying the problem (wife beating), and then focus on a possible cause or causes in the body of the essay (in this case, society's glorification of masculine aggression). Or you could state the problem and focus on the effects (on the wife's self-esteem, on children in the household, on costs to society). Of course, if you have no word limit, you could examine both causes and effects in a single essay. But if space or time is limited, concentrate on one or the other.

Avoid Tempting Logical Errors

As you think about the topic, be careful not to oversimplify the relationship between cause and effect. Consider this statement, for example:

> It has been proved that most cocaine addicts smoked marijuana in their youth. Therefore, smoking marijuana causes cocaine addiction.

All you have to do is change the causal factor to see the faulty logic involved.

> It has been proved that most cocaine addicts chewed gum in their youth. Therefore, chewing gum causes cocaine addiction.

To avoid this error (called the *post hoc, ergo propter hoc* fallacy, meaning "after this, therefore because of this"), never assume that if event *Y* happened after event *X*, then *X* must be the cause of *Y*.

A closely related problem is the *concurrence fallacy*, which goes like this:

> All teenagers who like rap music have little interest in school and often wear nose rings. Therefore, rap music causes school dropouts and wearing nose rings.

The error in thinking here involves assuming that just because *X* and *Y* happen at the same time, *X* is a cause of *Y* or *Y* is a cause of *X*.

Whenever you make a *generalization* (a broad statement), be sure you have enough evidence to support what you claim. Be especially careful not to state an opinion as fact. For instance, suppose you write

> Nose rings are barbaric and revolting.

The statement suggests that everyone finds nose rings barbaric and revolting, a generalization that would be hard to prove—especially if you consulted the people wearing them. Qualify your observation to make it less sweeping:

Many people find nose rings barbaric and revolting.

As a rule, avoid general observations involving *all, none, everything, nobody,* and *always.* Instead, try *some, many, sometimes,* and *often.*

Considering Purpose and Audience

Unless you are writing a personal essay to entertain, your purpose in cause-and-effect writing will often be to persuade. You may be discussing the causes or effects of some social problem, trying to convince readers to work for change—or perhaps just to see the problem from your point of view. For instance, you might focus on the lack of concern for individual responsibility in our society as encouraging adults to see themselves as victims.

Or, you may have an informative purpose in cause-and-effect writing if you choose a topic like "How do shock treatments work on the brain?" or "What causes forests to die?" Or, you may be combining an informative with a persuasive purpose if you discuss an issue like "What effect does Head Start have on families?"

Whatever audience you choose to address in persuasive writing, your aim is to bring your readers into agreement with you. If you are writing on a controversial issue—like condom distribution, homosexual marriage, or welfare—adopt a reasonable tone. Never sneer. Never make fun of people who hold an opposing opinion—these are the very people you are trying to reach. You want to win them over, not offend them. Respect your readers; let them see that your analysis of the issue poses no threat to them.

You need not be as touchy about your audience if your purpose is simply to inform. But then, you won't be tempted to rant and rave when all you're trying to do is present information as clearly and interestingly as possible. You will, however, need to consider how much your readers already know about your topic in deciding how much background information to provide, what terms need defining, and what kind of examples to include.

How to Organize
a Cause-and-Effect Analysis

For the body of your essay you have several kinds of organization to choose from. The first two are essentially the same.

Single-Cause/Many-Effects

With this pattern, you can bring up the cause in the introduction, write a paragraph about each effect, and establish a conclusion at the end. Here's a diagram to show you how easy it is.

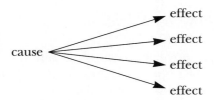

Here's a rough outline for a single-cause/many-effects paper.

I. After ten years as a housewife, I went back to college. (cause)
II. Negative effects
    A. My husband feels intimidated.
    B. The children's clothes don't get ironed.
    C. I no longer have time for my own reading.
III. Positive effects
    A. Husband is learning to deal with our children.
    B. Kids are learning to deal with their father.
    C. I am learning to deal with myself.
IV. Conclusion.

The writer wants to emphasize the positive effects, so she puts them last. Effects can also be arranged by topic instead of by the positive-negative method. You might arrange the effect paragraphs from most obvious to most subtle, from least important to earthshaking, or from local to national to worldwide to galactic. Like most elements of writing, the arrangement is likely to be better if you think about it than if you don't.

Many-Causes/Single-Effect

The second kind of organization is similar to the first, only flip-flopped. You begin with the effect and try to explain the causes.

Again, you have to think about the order of the paragraphs. In this pattern, too, you can present the single item (the effect) in the introduction and devote a paragraph to each cause in the body.

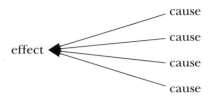

Here's an outline arranging material for a paper speculating on many possible causes of a single effect.

    I. What makes your engine overheat? (effect)
   II. Reduced circulation of coolant caused by a slipping fan belt or a damaged water pump.
 III. Increased internal friction heat caused by too heavy motor oil.
 IV. Retained hot exhaust gases caused by clogged exhaust system.
   V. Conclusion.

In that outline, any one of the causes could be the culprit, but in the following outline, all the causes contribute to the final effect.

    I. Why I flunked philosophy 101. (effect)
   II. I am not a good reader, especially of abstract material, and the textbook confused me.
 III. I am not a skilled writer and couldn't express the complicated ideas asked for on exams.
 IV. I was intimidated by the class discussion, so didn't ask questions that might have helped.
   V. The class met at 8 A.M.—I often slept through it.
 VI. Conclusion.

The above outline is arranged from the most understandable causes (poor reading and writing skills) to the least defensible (missing class).

Causal Chain

This kind of organization doesn't diagram neatly because the causes and effects are linked together, like a chain. But a narrative or chronological framework works well. Begin with a cause and trace how that cause leads to an effect, which starts another cause, which then leads to another effect, and so on in a series. Here's an example.

cause: You drink alcohol.

effect: Alcohol turns off your antidiuretic hormone, ADH,

cause: which causes your cells to absorb water.

effect: Your body passes liquid you drink right through,

cause: which causes little of it to be absorbed,

effect: which is why you go to the bathroom so often while drinking alcohol.

effect: Your cells slowly dry up, including brain cells,

cause: as you continue to drink.

effect: In the morning you have a hangover: a headache, dry mouth, and furry teeth, all caused by thirsty cells.

Single-Cause/Single-Effect

This cause/effect pattern is the easiest but also the least common. It isn't used much because most things just don't happen that way. Things usually have more than one cause and more than one effect. But sometimes a single-cause/single-effect pattern does apply to personal changes or decisions: one event can cause a dramatic shift in your life or outlook. Again, a chronological narrative pattern will serve nicely to show how the cause produced the effect. Here's a passage, related by a World War II submarine commander, that illustrates how a single event caused him to change his attitude toward war.

I think I can date the beginning of my conversion—for that, as you will see, is what it really is—to a precise event during the war. I had torpedoed an Italian merchant ship in the Mediterranean. She sank in less than three minutes, but they managed to get a lifeboat away. I surfaced to see if I could discover some information about my target. There were five men in the boat. Two of them were horribly injured, and one in particular, a lad of about nineteen, had had the side of his face blown away. We gave them what medical aid we could spare—and then a German plane came down at us and we had to dive in a hurry. Even during the depth-charging that followed, the face of that boy haunted me. It was no good telling myself that this was one of the inevitable accidents of war: this was something I personally had done to a young man on the threshold of life, the only life he would ever have. It was *my* act in firing that torpedo that had done it. The beastliness of war began to obsess me, and from that time on I could never fire a torpedo without feeling quite sick.

—Edward Young, *The Fifth Passenger*

SAMPLES OF STUDENT CAUSE-AND-EFFECT WRITING

Effects of the Remote Control

Do you own a little black oblong box? You know, the one that controls your TV. This seemingly innocent device comes with your new TV set and changes the behavior of an otherwise normal household. You begin to wonder after a few weeks, who really is in control here?

1

The first person the remote control takes over is the man of the house. He plops down in his easy chair after a hard day's work. He puts his feet up and zap! turns on the TV with his handy little black box. He is just getting good and comfortable when his wife comes in the living room to discuss the day's happenings. As she is telling him about the washer making a funny sound, the brownish goo dripping out of the car, and the two-weeks overdue electric bill that she just found, he presses a button on his black box and turns the volume up, drowning her out. Next, the kids come bounding in full of stories about their adventures outside. One push, the volume goes up still further, and he is now oblivious to anything going on in the house.

2

A related effect of the remote control is the couch potato syndrome, which also afflicts Dad. Once sitting down with the remote in his hand, he becomes a helpless being. The remote is holding him down, cementing him to his chair. He asks his son to fetch him a beer. He has his daughter pull down the shades. He yells at his wife to answer the phone. He becomes almost paralyzed by that little black box.

3

A missing remote means a code blue alarm at our house. No couch is left unturned. No one can leave until the box is found. Everyone is detained and searched; everyone is forced to look frantically. We fan out into the bedrooms in desperation, into the kitchen, even the bathroom. Then, at last! It's found—under an easy chair. Everyone sighs with relief.

4

5   Clearly, the person who holds the remote holds the power. It controls not only what appears on the screen but the sound also. With a mere flick of a button, the set goes on, off, the channel changes. I luck out one evening, get the remote, and tune in <u>Frasier</u>. My husband comes in, picks up the remote, and switches it to a basketball game. He says he just wants to watch it for a minute to see what the score is. I wait five minutes. The game is still on. He gets a phone call and has to leave the room. I grab the remote, turn it back to <u>Frasier</u>. He returns, looks for the remote, and sees it firmly clutched in my hand. He smiles at me; I smile back. I am in control now. It's a truce, until next time. . . .

6   If you have one of these devilish devices, get smart and get rid of it before your loved ones become addicted. Stash it in the freezer, drop it in the bathtub, or encourage the dog to bury it in the yard. No small object should have this much control over the behavior of a family.

—Dorothy Armstrong

Shades of Horror

1   In the salon my co-workers refer to me as the color expert. I don't remember when this title was officially given to me, but somehow I went from just being good at coloring hair—to being the expert. I enjoy this distinction; I like the authority. But sooner or later, the inevitable happens—the big mistake. I'm not talking about the little problem you can smooth over by saying something like, "No, honestly, it isn't brassy—just a warm gold." The <u>big</u> <u>one</u> is much more drastic than that. My professional nightmare happened on a typical Saturday morning. The day was overbooked; my time was at a premium. Little did I know, the elements that led up to this horror had started several months ago.

2   The chain of events began when a regular client requested a slight change in hair color. She wanted to brighten up her dark brunette shade with a slight red tone. I thought this was an excellent idea. I simply adjusted her regular formula by adding a small amount of deep auburn tint to the mixture and subtracting the same amount of brown. This variation achieved only a slight reddish highlight to the hair. She seemed pleased, however. She left the shop smiling.

3   On her next visit five weeks later this customer told me how much she and her husband liked the red hint and asked if we could add some more. I personally think you can never have too much red, so naturally I said, "Great, no problem." This time I formulated the color with almost equal parts of the dark auburn and

the deep brown. The results were again quite satisfactory to both of us. I explained to her how difficult it is to get red tones to show through such a dark shade of hair color. I told her that because the red tones are the hardest to get into the hair and the hardest to get out, fine tuning is needed to achieve just the right shade. Once more, she left the shop smiling.

The client's next visit to the shop a month later was for a permanent wave.   4
I used the same procedure and the same chemicals as I had in the past when she needed a light curl. During our chat, while I wrapped her perm, she told me she had liked the last color so much that she wanted to get even more daring by adding still more red to her hair. As she was leaving, I confirmed her scheduled color appointment for the following week. Without my knowledge, the wheels had already been set in motion for the disaster that was to come.

The day of doom arrived, appearing to be just another typical Saturday. I   5
ran behind schedule most of the morning. By the time my color client arrived, I was already slightly frazzled. As she had suggested, I mixed her color formula to achieve an even more noticeable red hue. In fact, I used the dark auburn shade completely. I innocently applied the color, and while the tint was processing, went on about my business. My color customer was a well-known regular client, and at this point, several of my co-workers stopped to ask me, "Are you changing her color?" Unconcerned at this point, I told them "Yes," but didn't bother to give any details.

The feeling of panic did not hit until I was shampooing the tint out of her   6
hair. Then, my stomach did a few moves that would have made a gymnastics coach proud. I knew at once this situation was not one I was going to gloss over with a few insincere phrases. My shampooing had uncovered the most unnatural, the most shocking, the most horrifying shade of purple I had ever seen! This was the big one. Bluffing was out of the question, so I calmly said to the client, "I think we have a little bit too much red. In fact, it's rather violet." You would think that statement would have sent her straight into hysterics, but she just as calmly asked, "Can we fix it?" I replied, "Of course! No problem."

As soon as I saw the color, I realized that the sequence of events leading   7
to this purple head of hair resulted from an unfortunate miscalculation. The first two times I had added the red, there was already a strong base of brown pigment in the hair shaft, resulting in a combination of the new color that I was adding and the old color that was already there. The red, layered over the brown, didn't show through too much. But over the span of several months, the dark

brown had been both cut down and finally stripped out by her recent perm. Consequently, when I applied the straight dark auburn that day—bingo! bright purple hair.

8   Since I knew the reasons for this unfortunate color, the solution was simple. I merely applied her original deep brunette formula right on top of the purple. Tah-dah! Beautiful red-brown hair. I would never be able to duplicate it again, of course, but it was the perfect shade—the one we had wanted all along. She left the shop smiling. However, as a result of this color crisis, my former pride in being the resident "expert" has dwindled considerably. I now just hope for no unsettling surprises.

—Bethany Cottrell

DISCUSSION
AND WRITING
EXERCISE

7.1

1. Identify the organizational pattern of "Effects of the Remote Control."
2. What specific details does Armstrong use to make the essay believable and interesting?
3. Describe the opening and closing tactics used by Armstrong in "Effects of the Remote Control." Can you suggest alternatives?
4. How has Cottrell organized "Shades of Horror"?
5. Describe how the transitions between paragraphs are handled in Cottrell's essay.
6. In her opening and closing paragraphs, Cottrell uses several sentence fragments. What is the effect?
7. Three times in the essay, Cottrell repeats the same sentence, "She left the shop smiling." Can you explain why she employed the deliberate repetition?
8. For practice, write *many-cause/single-effect* and *single-cause/many-effect* outlines for these subjects: nervousness before exams or speeches, a shortened work week, student cheating, depression.

How to Introduce a Cause-and-Effect Analysis

Since curiosity about causes and effects seems to be practically built into people, you shouldn't have too much trouble writing an appropriately seductive introduction. Anything that will get your readers to ask "Why?" or "Why did you say that?" will do.

One way is to jolt them with an arresting statement of cause and effect right away. You could, for example, start the hangover paper we outlined earlier (p. 122) by saying, "When you take two aspirins with a glass of water to cure a hangover, the water probably does you more good than the aspirin."

Another way to begin a cause-and-effect paper is to make a prediction. Then proceed to show the line of reasoning that allows you to make such a prediction. For example, you might begin an essay with "If you put radial tires on your car, you will probably save twenty-five dollars on gas next winter." Your readers will want to know how radial tires save gas, and so you tell them.

How to Conclude a Cause-and-Effect Analysis

When you are trying to bring your discussion to a close, you can fall back on one of the tactics we have discussed at length elsewhere: (1) advise the reader, (2) predict the future, or (3) summarize points (use this one only as a last resort). But there are other closing strategies that suit cause-and-effect papers especially well.

Causes and effects have a tendency to branch out until the whole worlds of philosophy, science, and psychology are involved. Of course, you must control that branching-out in order to write a short paper—and to keep your sanity. But in the conclusion, you are free to suggest some of the larger areas that your subject could branch into if you let it. This leaves your reader with something extra to think about. If you're writing about agricultural chemicals getting into the grain fed to animals, you could close with a comment on the probable pollution of drinking water, as well as soil, by herbicides and pesticides. Or you could end by speculating on the grim global effects of such pollution.

A less exciting but sometimes necessary function of the conclusion is to present causes and effects you did not discuss in the paper because space was limited. If you write about only two causes of the Civil War, or only two effects of motherhood, you should probably point out in closing that you have written only about the ones you find most interesting or important or personally relevant. You may name some of the others, too. This tactic keeps you from sounding like an airhead who really thinks that there were just two causes for the Civil War.

1. Find a cause-and-effect essay in a popular news magazine (science, economics, and psychology sections are good places to look). Does the conclusion summarize the points of the essay? Why or why not?

2. Can one sentence be enough to open or close a cause-and-effect essay? What conditions might make such short paragraphs sufficient?

3. How would the opening and closing of a scientifically provable cause-and-effect paper probably be different from the opening and closing of a more personal or speculative cause-and-effect essay?

Tying a Cause-and-Effect Analysis Together

The transitional words for this kind of paper have to do with cause-and-effect relationships, just as you might have suspected. Some handy terms are *thus, therefore, then, so, consequently, accordingly, as a result,* and *hence.* If you inspect samples of cause-and-effect writing, you will also find many paragraph transitions of the plain old type: "First, . . . Second, . . . Third" or "One effect . . . Another effect . . . A final effect. . . ."

Because cause-and-effect relationships are so intricate, check over your transitions within paragraphs as well (see Fig. 7.1). Each sentence should have a clear relationship to the sentence before it. Therefore, the transitional words mentioned in the paragraph above may be needed occasionally within your paragraphs.

Ideas for Cause-and-Effect Analysis Writing

Short Prewriting Practice

1. Write one or two paragraphs in which you explain what causes some natural phenomenon. Examples: rain, dew, twinkling stars, sweat, hiccups, phases of the moon.

2. Make a list of twenty possible cause-and-effect topics with five entries under each of these headings: personal life, science/technology, social trends, politics. Each topic can be phrased as a question beginning with "Why?" or "What effect?" Compare your list with those of other students, and discuss which ones would be likely to produce good papers.

FIGURE 7.1

Checklist for Revising Cause-and-Effect Analysis

Numbers 2 through 8 concern logical errors to watch out for; see Chapter 8 for a further discussion of these fallacies.

1. If the subject is something you're trying to prove, does the factual knowledge seem sound?

2. Does the essay admit that event *X* does not necessarily cause event *Y* just because *X* happens before *Y*?

3. Does the essay assert that there is just one cause when possibly there are more?

4. In a causal chain, are any links omitted that might cause a reader to miss the connection?

5. Does the essay attribute the wrong cause to an effect?

6. Do transitional words make clear the distinctions between causes and effects?

7. In a personal paper, does the writer rationalize? That is, are generous and kind motivations (causes) given when the real ones may be less admirable?

8. Does the writer state personal prejudices as fact?

9. Are the words *affect* and *effect* used correctly? (Usually, *affect* is a verb and *effect* is a noun: "The smog *affected* me with a burning *effect* in my eyes.")

10. Are conjunctive adverbs punctuated correctly? (Many causal transitions—*thus, therefore, then, hence, consequently*—fit this category. Look up Comma Splice and Semicolon in Chapter 14 for help.)

3. In a small group, discuss major decisions in your lives. Take notes as you investigate the causes and effects of your decisions.

Longer Paper Ideas

1. Describe a past failure, and give its causes or effects (or both).

2. Explain the causes (or effects) of any drastic change of opinion, attitude, or behavior you have undergone in your life.

3. Investigate the possible causes for any opinion, prejudice, interest, or unreasonable fear about which you feel strongly.

4. Discuss the probable causes of any situation, practice, law, or custom that strikes you as unfair.

5. A close friend of your own sex tells you that she or he is homosexual. What are your reactions, and why would you have them?

A PUBLISHED ESSAY ILLUSTRATING CAUSE-AND-EFFECT ANALYSIS

WHY MEN BEAT WOMEN

Olga Silverstein and Beth Rashbaum

1   We don't know and perhaps never shall know whether O. J. Simpson killed his wife. We do know, because we heard it happening on the now-infamous phone call to 911, that last October he broke down the door of her house and hurled obscenities at her; that in 1989 he beat her—or at least pled no contest to charges of beating her; that in 1985 he broke her car windshield with a bat. We also know that Simpson is a "hero" whose "fall" has been mourned in countless media stories.

2   What we never seem to learn and desperately need to know is why a culture gives rise to a wife-batterer like Simpson and then continues to celebrate him despite chilling evidence of his violence. We're a culture that loves a hero, and has identified great athletes as perhaps the purest and most viable expression of heroism—outside of the battlefield. Aggression, power, dominance, control—that's what we think heroism is about.

3   A recent issue of *Sports Illustrated* sums it up: 14 pages of pictures and text devoted to an "in-depth" analysis of the tragedy, followed on the overleaf by a reprint of a story from 1973 about the momentous day Simpson "topped Jim Brown's single-season rushing record and broke the NFL's 2000-yard barrier."

4   There's a message here and it's not that hard to read. A "real man" is a winner. He sees the world in terms of victories and losses. If he accepts another's terms, he has lost. Winning—on the gridiron, where Simpson had his glory days; in the courtroom, where his high-priced legal team is battling for his life; and in every other competitive, male-dominated arena—means all-out pursuit of that single goal, no questions asked about the price paid.

5   To accomplish the heroic deeds we ask of them, men must shut down emotionally, lose all contact with any feeling but anger. Because we also want our heroes to come home at night as loving husbands and fathers, their only recourse is to com-

partmentalize, to confine that raw aggression to the battlefield, gridiron, courtroom or stock exchange.

Like Superman, our heroes are to return from their exploits, shedding their capes and charisma to become Clark Kent. And many women collude in the celebration of Superman; indeed, they disdain Clark Kent, fearing that "mild-mannered" means soft, gentleness means powerlessness. But women can't live with this definition of masculinity; they are dying from it in record numbers.   6

The urge to win, to overpower, to control can't be shut on and off. Wife batterers have a sense of entitlement—she's "mine," and it's nobody else's business what happens in our home. Women aren't allowed to walk out on these "heroes," as apparently Nicole Simpson tried to do. Attempting to escape puts them in the greatest jeopardy, for that's when a man's sense of power and dominance—everything that he thinks makes him a man—is most threatened.   7

Which is not to say that O. J. murdered Nicole. But we don't have to think he murdered her to deplore what we do know he did to her. And we don't even have to know that to be appalled by the degree to which this man is cut off from his own feelings. What has been billed (by his lawyer and much of the media) as a suicide note—written at what must surely have been the absolute nadir of his life, his wife dead, himself the prime suspect in her murder—is signed with his initials. Inside the O he inscribed a "smiley face."   8

We can launch another generation of heroes on an ocean of press ink about this fallen "hero"; or, we can begin thinking about how to raise good men, not heroic men, men who can own up to feelings other than anger, who know when they're sad and how to reach out for help. A "good man" would be competent, active, engaged in real relationships, empathetic enough to recognize his own feelings as well as those of others. A "good man's" ambitions are tempered by his sense of right and wrong. He would be righteous in his anger over the abuse of others, not just of himself.   9

As mothers, we may grieve to see our little boys developing the masculine traits of aggressive competitiveness, but we have been programmed to fear any kind of softness (read femininity). As young women we admire strength and power perhaps because we question our own.   10

Maybe if women were to stop cheering the winners and learn to love ourselves enough to value those qualities we assign to women—relatedness, caring, empathy— love them enough to impart them to our sons and lovers. . . . Then, maybe, men will love those attributes in themselves. Then we would have a new definition of masculinity, one that women could live with safely.   11

Chapter Eight

Persuasion

All the writing patterns in Chapters 3 through 7 can be used to persuade your readers or to argue a point. You will combine many of the patterns of development that you already know when you write a persuasive paper, but you will also need some skills that we have not yet discussed.

Thinking Critically About Persuasion

You already know when to use persuasion: when you hope to get your readers to agree with you and maybe, as a result, to take some kind of action (like giving you a refund or picketing city hall). You surely have an opinion that you believe any reasonable person should agree with. This is your chance to set forth that opinion without interruptions—which is one of the delightful advantages of the written argument over the spoken.

Many of the essays you have written so far may be persuasive. Your comparison/contrast essay may aim at demonstrating the superiority of whole wheat over white bread. Your cause-and-effect analysis may convince the reader that rap music reinforces violent attitudes toward women. Your definition may show that computer nerds are more interesting than most people think. To persuade is a common goal of writers. In this chapter, you will use all your skills at structuring your writing as you learn how to influence readers' opinions about controversial or unfamiliar issues.

Finding a Controversy

At times, all of us doubt that we have an opinion worth writing about. But we all do, and a little prewriting activity will reveal at least one. Here are some approaches to finding a persuasive topic.

1. Think of an issue about which you have recently changed your mind. For example, you may have once thought that husbands should be the bread-winners and wives should run the home; now you think a division of these re-sponsibilities is necessary. You are well enough acquainted with both sides of this issue to try to persuade others to believe as you do now.

2. Think of a conflict you have observed, experienced, or read about. For example, if you have been a waitress or waiter, you have no doubt had conflicts with customers. One way to develop a persuasive essay that stems from this con-flict is to write to restaurant customers and convince them to alter their rude or unthinking behavior.

3. Think of any subject in the context of problems that are related to it. If you pick up a book, for instance, you may think of problems like censorship, inadequate funds for libraries, the high price of textbooks, or widespread illit-eracy. A few minutes' thought about the seashell you use as a paperweight may bring forth ideas about oil spills, commercialization of national seashores, en-dangered species, and boating accidents.

Jot down all the ideas you come up with using these invention methods: whichever one you use now, you may need the extras some day when your brain refuses to storm.

Taking a Stand

As you explore possible topics for persuasive writing, focus on ideas that can be debated. In order to develop a topic persuasively, you need to view it as a controversy with at least two sides. What you know about the topic (or what you find out about it) will lead you to take a stand and defend one side. Do not exhaust your persuasive skills on a position that almost everyone already agrees with. This approach is a waste of time. For instance, you could certainly support the thesis "Children need love," but unless you handle it with great originality, developing such a claim would prove to be an empty exercise in stating the ob-vious. Neither matters of fact ("Some Jewish people follow orthodox law and some do not") nor matters of personal preference ("Van Gogh's paintings are more suitable for a living room than Dali's are") will provide worthwhile material for a persuasive paper.

DISCUSSION
EXERCISE

8.1

Examine the following list of potential topics for a persuasive paper, and identify those that are (a) fact, (b) personal preference, or (c) open for debate. Discuss ways to refine these topics and make them more suitable for persuasive writing.

1. Men make better managers than women do.
2. More than 90 percent of corporate executives in America are white males.
3. Older students are more interesting than younger students.
4. Random drug testing of college athletes is ineffectual and unnecessary.
5. People who smoke take more sick days than nonsmokers.
6. Macintosh computers are easy to learn and fun to use.
7. Distributing condoms and birth control devices to teenagers encourages promiscuity.
8. Business communications have undergone many changes in recent years.

Establishing Credibility

Everything you write is marked with your personality. Whether it's a shopping list, a letter of application, or a paper for sociology class, you inevitably convey an image of yourself in your writing. This effect is especially apparent in persuasive writing, in which personal beliefs and feelings are a necessary part of the presentation. Over two thousand years ago the Greek philosopher Aristotle recognized that an oration (a formal speech) is more forceful and effective when the audience trusts the speaker. He maintained that to be persuasive a person must project an image of being responsible, fair minded, and believable. Aristotle called this impression of credibility the appeal from *ethos*—or the ethical appeal.

Although the strongest ethical appeal comes from having a reputation for honesty and sensible thinking, an unknown writer can also convey credibility in several ways:

- by showing that you understand the issues and know a lot about the topic,
- by demonstrating fairness, and
- by avoiding errors in reasoning.

Keep in mind that you will not be able to establish your credibility completely ahead of time: it will develop from the work you do while drafting, revising, and editing your persuasive writing. But you can make some preliminary plans and decisions that will help you shape the image that you want to present to your readers.

Be Knowledgeable About the Topic

The most important means of conveying your credibility is to *be* credible. You want to show your readers that you know what you are writing about, that you understand the issues and have a wealth of evidence (examples, personal experiences, statistics, reasons) to make your case. For example, in his article "Medicine's New Frontier," about the benefits of alternative medical practices, journalist Bill Moyers begins by pointing out that he has "spent three years researching and reporting the mind-body connection and its role in healing." He also presents a series of detailed examples to show that he knows what he's writing about:

- In Boston, Jon Kabat-Zinn has taught more than 6,000 people how to control stress and pain through meditation. Three-fourths of his patients report improvement in their condition after a year.
- In Beijing, Zhaos Zang has helped women with fibrocystic breast disease using massage. The Chinese use massage to treat bodily imbalances, to release the flow of "chi"—the body's vital energy. Zang has treated 27 women, he says; 11 of them have been completely cured, and 15 more have had some relief. Western medicine currently has no cure.
- At the University of California at San Francisco, Dean Ornish has shown for the first time that coronary heart disease actually can be reversed without drugs or surgery. Ornish's patients follow a low-fat diet and an exercise regimen, plus a program to reduce stress that includes yoga, meditation, and group support. At the end of a year, 82 percent had improved blood flow to the heart and clearer arteries.

In this next example, author and scholar Sidney Hook uses his personal experience to establish his credentials for writing about voluntary euthanasia.

A few short years ago, I lay at the point of death. A congestive heart failure was treated for diagnostic purposes by an angiogram that triggered a stroke. Violent and painful hiccups, uninterrupted for several days and nights, prevented the ingestion of food. My left side and one of my vocal cords became paralyzed. Some form of pleurisy set in, and I felt I was drowning in a sea of slime.

At one point, my heart stopped beating; just as I lost consciousness, it was thumped back into action again. In one of my lucid intervals during those days of agony, I asked my physician to discontinue all life-supporting services or show me how to do it. He refused and predicted that someday I would appreciate the unwisdom of my request.

A month later, I was discharged from the hospital. In six months, I regained the use of my limbs, and although my voice still lacks its old resonance and carrying power, I no longer croak like a frog. There remain some minor disabilities and I am restricted to a rigorous, low-sodium diet. I have resumed my writing and research.

My experience can be and has been cited as an argument against honoring requests of stricken patients to be gently eased out of their pain and life. I cannot agree.

Demonstrate Fairness

In addition to showing that you are knowledgeable, you can also establish credibility by exhibiting fairness toward other points of view. You may feel so strongly about an issue that you want to attack those who disagree with you and express contempt for their opinions. But that strategy can be counterproductive, especially if you are trying to influence readers who are undecided. It can make you seem stubborn and irrational. Your ethical appeal will be stronger if you can demonstrate that you treat opposing views with respect and understanding. Observe how Bill Moyers acknowledges some of the objections to mind-body medicine and addresses these differing viewpoints with care and intelligence.

I know alternative treatments such as acupuncture, meditation, and group therapy seem like so much New Age quackery to many people. But I looked at alternative approaches that in no way reject the best that modern technology has to offer. For instance, at Commonweal, a retreat in Bolinas, California, cancer patients come for a week of counseling, massage, meditation, and conversation. But Commonweal accepts only people under the care of an oncologist or other qualified physician. In China, the doctors we interviewed were trained in Western medicine but also practiced the medicine of their ancestors.

Avoid Logical Fallacies

Besides being knowledgeable and fair, you also need to be logical. Errors in logic are called *fallacies* and are sometimes hard to detect. Even in professional writing and speechmaking, fallacies occur without arousing much objection—

but they *are* objectionable. Logical fallacies, conscious or accidental, detract from your persuasiveness when they become evident. In order to examine your thinking for fallacies, follow these four general rules.

1. *Be sure you deal directly with the issue you have introduced.*

This advice may seem overly obvious, but in reality your argument can wander before you know it. Appeals to emotion rather than reason, for example, are perfectly acceptable in persuasive writing—as long as both you and your reader recognize that your appeal is emotional, not logical—but sneaking in emotion disguised as logic is unacceptable. This fallacy happens when you use your own or your readers' already existing prejudices as logical arguments:

> As a militant feminist, Emma was doomed to disappointment in her love life.

This *premise* (the underlying idea or belief of an argument) that feminists have unhappy love lives reflects an irrational prejudice. Like many premises, it is unstated and must be brought out into the open for examination.

An emotional appeal is wrongly used when you cite either respected or scorned authorities in contexts where their authority doesn't logically apply:

> As Christ told us, we are our brothers' keepers, and a crash helmet law protects our brothers from harm.

> Passing a mandatory crash helmet law makes the specter of Big Brother a reality today.

Appealing to an abstraction is also not logical:

> Common sense tells us that idealists cannot be great leaders.

We can tell this use of the abstraction "common sense" is questionable because the opposite sounds just as persuasive:

> Common sense tells us that great leaders must be idealistic.

2. *Identify each generalization and be sure it is sound.*

Sweeping generalizations (overly broad statements) immediately weaken an argument:

> Because they don't pay attention to details, men make poor proofreaders.

> Unions have ruined this country's competitiveness.

Hasty generalizations are those made after examining too few pieces of evidence:

> My nephew's experience with steroids shows that these drugs are more beneficial than harmful.

> The book I needed on Reyes syndrome was checked out of the library. Somebody's hoarding all the research material on this topic.

Many generalizations are true but nonetheless need evidence to support them:

> Children's early years dramatically influence whether they will enjoy positive self-concepts or struggle with negative ones later in life.

3. *Be sure that your evidence is sound and related to the issue.*

For example, movie stars and athletes frequently offer testimonials in commercials. But an ex-football player isn't an expert on life insurance, and a movie star doesn't know anything more about coffee than most people do. The "evidence" these celebrities present is questionable, to say the least, and relates more to their own popularity than to the value of the products they are advertising.

Analogy is often used as supporting evidence. We take two similar situations and claim that what holds true for one holds true for the other. For instance, psychologist Naomi Weisstein, in her article "Woman as Nigger," contends that women are conditioned with a slave mentality and exploited for the economic benefit of society just as African Americans were for centuries. As this example suggests, analogies can add interest and clarity to a persuasive paper, and they often illustrate points effectively. But the conclusions you derive from an analogy are not certain. People may enjoy one movie directed by Woody Allen but not another; parents may find that what worked in raising one child doesn't work with another; coaches may discover that last year's team could win with the shotgun offense but this year's team can't.

A *false analogy* occurs when the two situations are not comparable. For example, you often hear people saying something like this:

> If we can put people on the moon, we should be able to find a cure for AIDS.

Although both of these situations involve solving a problem with scientific knowledge, the difficulties facing medical researchers are very different from those solved by space engineers.

4. *Check that your line of reasoning doesn't have any embarrassing gaps in it.*

Two common problems of cause-and-effect reasoning are illustrated in these examples:

> Of course Sheila flunked three courses. Just two months ago, she started hanging out with the rollerblade crowd.

> The Antarctic ozone layer decreased in October, about the same time that California had a huge earthquake. If the ozone layer keeps disintegrating, we can expect more big earthquakes.

The first example illustrates *post hoc reasoning* (from the Latin *post hoc, ergo propter hoc,* meaning "after this, therefore because of this"). This fallacy assumes that because one event follows another, the first is the cause of the second. But Sheila's academic decline may have nothing to do with rollerblading. The second example shows a related error in thinking—the *concurrence fallacy.* Just because two things happen at the same time does not necessarily mean that one (ozone depletion) causes the other (earthquakes).

Finally, presenting only two possible options when more exist results in the *either-or fallacy:*

> If you don't learn how to use a computer, you won't be able to get a good job.

> Overcrowded prisons have left us with two alternatives: let criminals loose on the street or make capital punishment a real threat.

The following quotations are all taken from bona fide letters-to-the-editors of various newspapers around the country. With a group of fellow students, examine these examples and see how many logical fallacies you can identify.

DISCUSSION EXERCISE

8.2

1. The only remedy against poverty is to worship God as God, honor His word and obey His doctrines, call upon Him and humble ourselves. Then He will hear and heal the land.

2. Liquor is something we can get along without to a very good advantage. The problem of rap music is a very grave one in this city, also, as it produces an attitude of disrespect in the listener. . . . Rock music is just as damaging, as it originates from undesirable heathen rituals, which should keep anyone from performing it.

3. If we want a society of people who devote their time to base and sensuous things, then pornography may be harmless. But if we want a society in which the noble side of man is encouraged and mankind itself is elevated, then I submit that pornography is surely harmful.

Considering Your Readers

Your persuasive success depends on your relationship to your audience. Consider carefully: which readers are you trying to reach in your essay? Some people will never change their minds on the subject you choose; they have decided their opinion and will stick to it no matter what. It is useless to include them when you define your audience. The appropriate audience for persuasive writing is unfamiliar with the subject, undecided, or in disagreement but still open to change.

Who are they? Well, you really have to imagine them, using your experience of people and the world. If you plan to write a persuasive letter to your local newspaper, for example, you must think about the readers of that newspaper—what ideas they probably have about your subject, what they see as important and unimportant in life. The newspaper readers in our city, we imagine, are mostly middle- and upper-middle-class, full-time workers who value security, family life, and upward mobility. Most are conservative and Republican and go to Protestant churches.

Targeting Your Audience

Such an analysis would be important to anyone trying to persuade the citizens of our city. If, for example, you were writing an editorial to convince this audience to walk, ride bicycles, and take buses to work instead of driving individual cars, you must be aware that most of your readers would be quick to dismiss certain reasons as crackpot. Thus, you might not mention that walking or biking to work would provide them with valuable time for meditation and getting in touch with themselves—at least not in those terms. Instead, you would build your case on the grounds of fewer traffic accidents, fewer exhaust fumes, more revenue to improve bus lines (due to higher ridership), and lower cost to each person.

You would limit your audience, then, not trying to appeal especially to minority segments of the newspaper's readership: the new young professionals with cosmopolitan backgrounds, the university students, or the farmers in the large rural area that the paper serves. If you happen to persuade them, that's great, but you need to aim at the majority as you understand them. (For further help in pinpointing the characteristics of your audience, review our Audience Analysis Checklist on page 8.)

You may choose to make up a more specific audience for a persuasive piece, and that will help you focus your purpose. For example, let's say you are trying to persuade people to read detective fiction. If you decide on an audience of avid readers who have never tried a mystery, your goal would be to convince them to read a few. If your audience is made up of people who already read four mysteries a week, your purpose may be to provide *them* with persuasive reasons to justify their addiction. If you are writing for literary critics, you will attempt to show that detective novels can be just as artful in form, characterization, style, and plot as other forms of fiction.

Respecting Your Readers

At no time should you suggest, in tone or content, that your readers are ignorant, unfeeling, or ridiculous. People dig in their heels and won't budge when someone challenges not only their ideas but their personal worth. Choose an audience that you can respect, and let your respect for them show, even as you ask them to change their opinions or actions.

Recognizing the Limits of Reason

Pretending that people's opinions and positions on issues are based solely on reason is naive. We also hold our views because of our fears and prejudices; we may cling to positions that are completely unreasonable because the alternatives are threatening. So if you really want to persuade someone, you first must figure out what is threatening about your opinion. The process of calming your readers' qualms involves two parts: (1) sympathetically restating their fears and giving reassurance, and (2) stating a shared assumption or agreement as a starting point for your argument.

For example, let's say you decide that you would rather study to be a court reporter than go to graduate school, as your parents want you to. Since this decision is likely to upset your parents, you might begin your announcement by using fear-reducing tactics: "I know you two think that going to graduate school is a great opportunity, one that you never had, and I realize that you're right. But I also know that you want me to use my own judgment and that what you want most is for me to be happy." How can they disagree?

How to Organize a Persuasive Paper

When writers want to persuade their readers to accept a particular interpretation of events or an opinion about an issue, their work sometimes follows a system called *classical argumentation*. This three-part method of organizing a persuasive paper makes good sense and is still useful today in planning an essay or a speech. After introducing your subject (more on that later on p. 149), you present your case (the *confirmation*), refute the opposition (the *refutation*), and concede points while reinforcing your stand (the *concession*).

Present Your Case

The first part of the body of your essay, the *confirmation,* is the longest, for in it you present evidence that supports (confirms) your thesis, paragraph by paragraph. You can develop each paragraph in a different way (see Chapter 10, pp. 229–250), but each should present one major contention or reason for your position. Whether you write from your own experience or rely on research, you should support your opinion with examples, definitions, case histories, analogies, and logical reasoning.

With a little research, you can gather even more evidence to present on your side. You can get facts and statistics, which sound much better than "I think I read somewhere that nowadays half of the couples who get married end up getting divorced." You can also support your case with

- other writers' firsthand accounts of their experiences,
- the testimony of experts in the field,
- reports of experiments,
- reports of interviews, and
- interviews.

(You do risk finding out that your opinion is partially or totally wrong, but we do not consider that a good enough reason for staying out of the library.)

DISCUSSION AND PREWRITING EXERCISE

8.3

Decide, if you can, what your opinion is on each of the following statements. In a group, discuss why you feel the way you do. Then choose one of the statements and make a list of how you could go about defending or disproving it. Look at the descriptions of reference works on pages 169–170 to discover where you could find appropriate facts, statistics, and quotations by authorities (you do not need to actually put your hands on them now). Also include in your list personal experiences and observations that support your opinion.

1. Childhood is the most wonderful part of life.
2. Sex education should begin in junior high school.
3. Journalism can best be learned by doing it rather than studying it in school. (Substitute any other vocation for journalism, if you wish.)
4. The pass/fail option in college courses encourages students to be intellectually lazy.
5. On-the-job drug testing is an invasion of workers' privacy.

Refute the Opposition

In your research, or maybe just in discussing your paper at lunch, you will find out what the major opposing views are. Choose the most popular arguments against your thesis, and devote a paragraph or so to undermining each one. In terms of classical argumentation, this is the *refutation.*

Many refutations point out problems with the opposition's logic, as do the following two examples. The first, in a student paper, points out an unfair comparison between cars of the 1950s and modern cars.

> Another common misconception about modern cars is that they are lemons, constantly being recalled. The truth is that no one was around to do the recalling in the fifties. A good example of a lemon of the fifties is the Edsel by Ford Motor Company. The Edsel was equipped with a gimmicky push-button automatic transmission that had a bad habit of going into reverse when the driver pushed DRIVE. A defect such as that would demand a total recall today, but nothing was done at the time. Today, one no longer buys cars without protection from the government and consumer agencies.
>
> —Steve Stepke

Joseph Arena, a *Newsweek* sports writer, provides a refutation that simply rejects the opposing premise in his article "A Strike for Bowling":

> Some say the reason bowling isn't covered by the print media is that the sport is a bore—just not exciting. Once you print the scores what else can you say? I don't buy that. After all, the number of people who bowl on a regular basis far exceeds the number who play tennis. I'm willing to wager that plenty of these keglers would find bowling exciting to read about, too. ABC has been televising the Professional Bowlers Association tour for the past 21 years, and the program has been known to get higher ratings than the Masters golf tournament. Doesn't this say something about the enduring appeal of the game as a spectator sport?

Other schemes for refutation involve accepting the opposing line of thought up to a certain point, but no further. The following student's refutation in her essay against curving grades is of this type:

> Teachers can come up with several arguments in favor of curving grades. Some feel that the exams they give are too difficult for grading on a regular scale. If this is the case, they should revise the exam to a more appropriate level, not curve the grades. Other teachers like to see

competitiveness among their students. But many students choke under this type of pressure. They would probably do much better if they were judged individually.

—Anne Ryan

If you want to ridicule your opponents in the refutation section, be sure that your chosen audience does not identify themselves with the opposition. If we were writing an antiracist essay, we would feel free to jeer at the excesses of the Ku Klux Klan—we would never include them in our target audience anyway. But remember our earlier advice about not alienating the very people you have chosen to persuade. Most people respond to a tone of sweet reason—especially those who were prone to disagree with you at the outset.

<table>
<tr><td>

PREWRITING
EXERCISE

8.4

</td><td>

Pretend that you are defending one of the following statements in a persuasive essay. For each, write three points that your opposition might bring up—points that you might need to refute. You may do this exercise individually or in a group of classmates.

1. Government agencies protect us from harmful additives in our food.
2. Every family should consider abolishing Christmas gift giving.
3. The government should discourage the use of private automobiles by funding cheap, efficient public transportation.
4. The food industry purposely misleads the public about the facts of nutrition.
5. A mother has the responsibility to stay home with her children until they are of school age.

</td></tr>
</table>

Concede Points but Reinforce Your Stand

Sometimes the opposing view is based on reasoning that is not illogical, ill-founded, untrue, or stupid. You can grant any valid points in the *concession*. You can also explain why these points do not sway you to the other side and remind your readers of your own position. For instance, you might write, "I agree with some critics of the custom of tipping who say that it allows the restaurant owner to get by with paying the employees a substandard salary. But I do not believe that I should deprive an individual server of a tip just because I think the principles behind the practice are exploitative."

Modify the Pattern:
The Inductive Approach

In most persuasive essays you present your thesis first and then provide reasons and evidence to support that thesis. But the reverse order can also be effective. In this approach, called *inductive organization,* you begin with specific observations and examples and arrive at a general claim or a reasonable conclusion based on this evidence. This method of presenting an argument is effective because it leads your readers into the thesis that you want them to accept (*inductive* comes from a Latin word meaning "lead into"). Notice how journalist Katha Pollitt, in her article "Being Wedded Is Not Always Bliss," uses research and statistics to lead the reader to the conclusion that wifehood is not a happy state for many women today.

Here is another set of statistics. Married women earn $626 a week for every $1,000 earned by men; single women who work full time earn $910. Wives describe themselves as less happy than do married men or single women (only single men are more dissatisfied), and they are much more likely than single women to be clinically depressed. As many as one in seven women have been raped by their husbands; two-thirds have been beaten at least once. Despite the tremendous influx of married women into the work force, men do only 6 percent more housework than they did twenty years ago, and the husbands of women who work outside the home pitch in only slightly more than the husbands of housewives. All of which helps to explain why, according to an upcoming *Women's Day* survey, only 50 percent of wives say they would marry their husbands again.

SAMPLES OF STUDENT PERSUASIVE WRITING

The following student essays illustrate the use of persuasive strategies. Examine them in preparation for writing your own persuasive essay.

Is Craft Dead?

We live in a technological society where most goods are mass produced on assembly lines by unskilled laborers. Because of the prevalence of assembly-line production, most people assume that craftsmanship, whether it be in making autos or building houses, no longer exists. It might be dead as far as the production of autos is concerned, but it is certainly not dead in the building of houses. In fact, carpenters of today are actually much better craftsmen than their counterparts of fifty years ago. Today's builders are more intelligent, possess more highly sophisticated tools, and if given the proper material, are capable of producing a much better home than those built in the past.

2   People who think older houses are better crafted usually support their view by pointing to fifty- and one-hundred-year-old homes that are still solid and assuming it is the craftsmanship that is responsible for the durability. "Homes in those days were really built well," they say. No doubt these homes were well built, but what these people have done is confuse the quality of the materials used in the homes with the quality of the craft used in building them. Since these homes have lasted for so many years, people wrongly assume that the craftsmanship was responsible. In reality, it's the quality of materials which has given these homes their long life, not the craftsmanship.

3   Homes today could be built to last just as long as those old homes if people were willing or able to pay the price. For instance, most people can no longer afford solid oak stairways, although they were once fairly common in older homes. Nor can people afford the high cost of employing a carpenter to build the stairway. Yet if someone can pay the high cost, there are still plenty of carpenters around capable of making those stairways. And not only would these carpenters know how to build them, but they would also be able to do a better job than carpenters of the past.

4   One advantage modern carpenters have which enables them to do a better job than old-time carpenters is access to much more highly sophisticated tools, tools which were unheard of even twenty years ago. Such tools as transits, power-mitre saws, laser beams, and powerplanes not only enable the modern carpenter to lay out a house better but also make more precision cuts on the lumber. Also, it is not uncommon anymore to find carpenters with college degrees and carpenters with a solid knowledge of trigonometry and calculus. This knowledge enables the carpenter to understand such matters as the amount of stress and strain pieces of lumber are able to take.

5   The problem of modern quality, then, really boils down to the problem of materials. The modern carpenter is just as capable of skillful craftsmanship as the carpenter of fifty years ago, but only if given the proper material.

—Tom Zaffiri

Non-Traditional and Proud of It

After working as a secretary for eight years and also taking evening computer courses for the last two years, I took the plunge. I am an adult learner, or a non-traditional student, as the university likes to call us. (It's a nice way of saying we're old.) I first attended college twenty years ago when I was a young and foolish seventeen-year-old. By age twenty, I had managed to go from the Dean's List to probation (too much partying and no focus, I guess). However, I had earned two years of college credit with most of my general education requirements out of the way. Since then, I got a job, got married, had two children, went back to work (different job), had two more children, took night classes, and finally quit my job. As you can see, I managed to keep busy, but I still didn't have my degree. So now I am a full-time student once again. Because I have had to justify my decision many times to myself and my family, I have monitored the situation closely and can honestly say that returning to school was the right move. Not only am I improving my status on the job market, but my family and I have learned a number of valuable, unexpected lessons along the way.

One of my first considerations about returning to school, as you can probably guess, was money. With four children ranging in age from thirteen to two, the money I brought in, if not absolutely necessary, made things more comfortable. Of course when I was working, I had to buy clothes and lunch, pay the baby sitter for a full week, and pay for my night class; but there was always some extra money. We could go out for pizza and a movie without worrying about being able to buy groceries the next week. Now, not only am I not bringing in any money, but we are paying the university $1700 a semester. Needless to say, finances are a little tight. I'm sure Kate and Kelly get tired of hearing, "Wait until I go back to work." Because of our tight finances, however, we have learned to work on a budget. We have had to set priorities and stick to them. We are trying to stay within our budget without borrowing money, but if we need to, that safety net is there. The long-term benefit—and the main reason for returning to school—will be to make more money. I was stuck in a dead-end job with no room for advancement. With my degree, I will be able to get a better job with better pay and help my daughters go to college.

Another potential problem was that my time would be less structured and my schedule more variable. When I was working from eight to five every day and taking only one class, I found it easy to focus on that class. Now I am pulled in five different directions with five different classes, and I have some trouble deciding what I should be working on. But out of necessity, I am becoming more organized and flexible. With five very different classes, I am also getting to know a lot of new and interesting people.

4   I was particularly concerned how Margaret, my four-year-old, would adapt to my variable schedule. She is kind of a worrywart and functions more comfortably with some structure. At first, she was somewhat confused about where she was going on a particular day. But now, we put her schedule on bright yellow paper, with the days of the week and where she is going each day clearly marked, and post it on the refrigerator. She knows whether it's "a Sandy-day, a home-day, or a school-day." I needn't have worried. She has adapted quite well.

5   My husband is still not accustomed to my schedule. The fall semester is half over, and he still wakes me up on Tuesday and Thursday, forgetting that I don't have classes. It is one of my small pleasures, though, to remind him that I don't have to get up on those days. Also, because my time is less structured, I am able to spend more time with my kids. I give Maggie and Molly my full attention on Tuesdays and Thursdays; Kate and Kelly tell me what is going on in their lives and what happened at school; the mornings are not as rushed; I can take Kate and Kelly to school, and they don't have to ride the bus for an hour. And on Thursdays, I can even get the garbage out before the garbage collectors come.

6   Another benefit of becoming a student is that I can set a good example for my children. This role model is especially important for Kate, who is a freshman in high school, and Kelly, who is in eighth grade. They see how much time I put into my studies. I let them know when I make a good grade and how good I feel about it. I let them read my papers, and they ask me to help them with theirs. Kate has even started to use topics for her English papers that bear a remarkable resemblance to some of the ideas that I have used in this class (English 101). I have even heard Kate telling her friend on the telephone that "Mom is a brain. She got an A+ on her history test." Their friend Stacey has asked me a lot of questions about college. She thinks it's "cool" that I'm back in school.

7   I think you can see why I'm glad that I made the decision to return to school. The benefits far outweigh the problems. Our difficulties are manageable and only temporary; they have also forced us to learn to enjoy what we have. When I'm finished, I will be able to get a better-paying job. Along the way, I have learned a lot about myself and, most important, I have grown closer to my family.

—Ellen Odum

1. Analyze "Is Craft Dead?" in light of these questions: How convincing are the writer's arguments? Can you refute any of them? What audience would most likely be swayed by the essay? What kinds of evidence does Zaffiri use to support his points?

2. How does the writer of "Non-Traditional and Proud of It" win the attention and goodwill of her audience in the introduction (if, indeed, she does)? Give some examples of her effective word choice. What patterns of development does she use? What is the tone of her writing? Does she include a refutation or concession?

DISCUSSION
EXERCISE

8.5

How to Introduce a Persuasive Paper

A well-developed persuasive essay will often turn out longer than your other essays, especially if you include research. In a paper that approaches 1,000 words, you can present two paragraphs of introductory material instead of just one. Sometimes you will need it. We have identified four introductory tasks that you can tailor to fit your paper.

Be Charming

Your first goal is to win the attention and goodwill of your readers. You can get attention by telling an intriguing or humorous story, quoting a well-phrased comment on the issue, or using any of the other clever opening devices you have learned so far. You win goodwill by avoiding pomposity and showing concern for your readers. Remember: you want to establish credibility, and you do so by showing your readers that you know and care about your topic.

Be Informative

Sometimes the issue you are discussing involves words that your readers do not know, or words that you are using in some special way (like *text* in a literary paper), or words that are easily misunderstood or controversial in meaning (like *romantic* in an art history textbook). You can define such terms in your introduction.

Your readers may need other background material. If your issue has not made the front pages, you may need to explain why there is a controversy about it, how the dispute came about, who is on what side, what the claims of each side are (in brief, of course), and why anyone should care. The following introduction, written by a student, sets the thesis in an informative context.

Coal-fired power plants annually pour about 53 million tons of sulfur and nitrogen compounds into the atmosphere, where they turn into highly corrosive acids. The resulting high-acid rain is destroying the life in hundreds of lakes and streams every year. Furthermore, one coal plant alone pours many tons of radioactive carbon-14 into the air. As world needs for energy increase, our coal supplies dwindle at an ever-increasing rate. Estimates show that the earth could be out of coal reserves as early as the year 2200. Nuclear power was once considered the gradual replacement for coal produced power. But public acceptance of nuclear power is now small because of the possibility of catastrophic accidents. Solar power is the logical alternative. According to a long-range plan for one of the large utility companies, a Solar Power Satellite (SPS) may be the most environmentally acceptable power-generating source ever proposed.

—Ted Giehl

Be Straightforward

Being coy about your thesis is usually as annoying as being evasive about anything else. It is helpful to tell your readers directly what the issue is and what you are persuading them to believe or do.

Be Organized

If your paper is long, you can tell your readers in the introduction *how* you plan to present your case. For example, "Using the evidence of personal experience and the reports of two recent experiments at major universities, I will show that people can fly if they set their minds to it." This is a *plan of proof.* The following introduction to a student essay includes one.

When I was a child, each Saturday morning the family room would become the social center of our household as my brothers, sister, and I all sat glued to the television set laughing hysterically at Moe, Curley, and Larry as they poked one another in the eye or slapped one another in the face. That was until our parents forbade us to watch <u>The Three Stooges</u> because what we viewed as funny Saturday morning often became reality at some other time during a typical sibling quarrel, when someone would get poked in the eye or slapped across the face.

As my own family situation indicates, violence on television affected children ten years ago, and I believe that today it is even more common and more influential. In this paper I will present facts, statistics, reasoning, and counterexamples to show how violence on television influences children today.

—Marianne Cullnan

---

1. In the preceding introductions, find examples of the following elements: winning attention and goodwill, defining terms, explaining the issue, and stating the thesis.

2. Find examples of introductory elements in essays from magazines and anthologies.

DISCUSSION EXERCISE

8.6

How to Conclude a Persuasive Essay

If the paper is long, you may want to repeat your major points. In fact, you may need to do so if you followed the classic three-part structure that we recommend, since the last thing you did before the closing was to concede points. Before that, you were refuting your opponents' reasoning, so it has been quite a while since your readers focused on the main ideas of your case. Sometimes it can be impressive, too, to list all your main points in a bunch; the list can seem formidable.

The following is the conclusion of an essay by Vine Deloria Jr. about the occupation of Alcatraz Island by Native Americans. The essay, titled "This Country Was a Lot Better Off When the Indians Were Running It," argues that the U.S. government, which had left the island abandoned for six and a half years, should turn the area over to the Indians to use in experimenting with new forms of society.

> By making Alcatraz an experimental Indian center operated and planned by Indian people, we would be given a chance to see what we could do toward developing answers to modern social problems. Ancient tribalism can be incorporated with modern technology in an urban setting. Perhaps we would not succeed in the effort, but the Government is spending billions every year and still the situation is rapidly growing worse. It just seems to a lot of Indians that this continent was a lot better off when we were running it.

In this conclusion, you can see the outline of Deloria's whole case: its thesis, main points, and refutation.

Once you have your readers firmly on your side, you can also call on them, if you wish, for support or action. Deloria, in the closing, could have asked the Indians in his audience to join the group occupying Alcatraz; he could have encouraged all his readers to write their representatives in Congress on behalf of the occupying group; or he could have invited people to organize and hold demonstrations to put pressure on the government. The following conclusion to an article by journalist Susan Shown Harjo, titled "Last Rites for Indian Dead," urges congressional action and a change in attitude.

> There remains a reluctance generally among collectors of Indian remains to take action of a scope that would have a quantitative impact and a healing quality. If they will not act on their own—and it is highly unlikely that they will—then Congress must act. The country must recognize that the bodies of dead American Indian people are not artifacts to be bought and sold as collector's items. It is not appropriate to store tens of thousands of our ancestors for possible future research. They are our family. They deserve to be returned to their sacred burial grounds and given a chance to rest.
>
> The plunder of our people's graves has gone on too long. Let us rebury our dead and remove this shameful past from America's future.

In deciding how to conclude your essay, consider again what your persuasive goals are. They could be

1. getting readers to think about something in a new way.
2. getting readers to agree with your opinion.
3. getting readers to agree with you and to take some overt action.

How to Hold a Persuasive Essay Together

Your transitional words and phrases should identify the logical relationships between paragraphs. Avoid sneaky transitions that cover up the lack of logic rather than reveal logical process. Phrases like "Any reasonable person would agree . . ." are suspicious. Also avoid "Undoubtedly," "Certainly," "Any fool can plainly see," and "Even a five-year-old knows . . ."—messages that attempt to prove the truth of a statement by insisting beforehand that it is true. As an overall guide, consult our list of transitional terms on page 239.

How to Revise a Persuasive Essay

The first thing you should do with your draft is attempt to read it through the eyes of your chosen audience. Putting yourself in their place, do you see anything that offends you, alienates you, or seems poorly supported? If so, change it.

The next thing you should do with your draft is to check it rigorously for logical fallacies, using the logic section early in this chapter (p. 136). Search out and destroy every error in logic, even the ones you think no one else would notice. Then ask yourself the questions in the following checklist (Fig. 8.1).

FIGURE 8.1

Checklist for Revising a Persuasive Essay

1. Have you identified an audience and analyzed it?
2. Have you got the facts straight?
3. Have you defined all unfamiliar and unusual terms?
4. Is the thesis stated clearly somewhere within the first two paragraphs?
5. Are your generalizations fair?
6. Are the authorities you refer to reliable?
7. Are there pompous statements you can humanize?
8. Are the tone and level of usage appropriate for the subject and the audience you're trying to persuade?
9. Have you tried to ease your audience's fears?
10. Did you anticipate and deal with the main arguments against your thesis?
11. Did you refrain from apologizing for having an opinion?
12. Did you avoid putting an extra *e* in *argument*?

Now ask a friend or classmate to read your essay and answer the questions above.

Ideas for Persuasive Writing

Short Prewriting Practice

1. Choose some controversial subjects in class and stage brief informal debates between students. Discuss the debaters' persuasive techniques in terms of being knowledgeable, demonstrating fairness, appealing to emotion, and appealing to logic.

2. Record the times you use persuasive strategies in the course of an average day or two.

3. Write a paragraph or two using definition or analogy to support an opinion you hold.

4. Make up a dialogue in which one person uses fear-reducing tactics to persuade someone else. Try one of these situations:

A worker would like the boss to pay more attention to hazardous working conditions.

A teenager would like her or his parents to do away with a set curfew.

A parent would like a teacher to drop a particular book from the required reading list.

A secretary would like the company to change her title to "office manager."

5. Examine the three automobile advertisements (for Toyota, Honda, and Mercury) on pages 156–158. Write a paragraph about each ad, examining its credibility. Which one does the best job of establishing credibility and targeting its audience?

6. Select and study one of these following advertisements. Write a letter to the advertiser, either criticizing or complimenting the company for its advertising strategy.

Longer Paper Ideas

1. Defend why partners in a marriage should (or should not) write their own detailed marriage contracts.

2. Write a persuasive essay in which you use your own experience and other evidence to challenge a common assumption or stereotype.

3. In our families, school, and work, we can sometimes see problems brewing that will become worse and could result in ugly consequences unless they are addressed soon. Write a letter to someone who can do something about such a problem. Persuade the person that the problem is serious and that some specific action(s) may prevent or defuse the adverse consequences. For example, you might write a letter to your supervisor at work explaining that his or her lack of planning the schedules properly is damaging employee respect and morale.

4. Defend why home schooling is (or is not) more valuable than public education.

5. Write a persuasive essay on a social or political issue about which you have changed your mind, such as: taxing social security; workfare for welfare recipients; distributing condoms in high schools; a change in workplace policy; community service instead of prison for nonviolent criminals. Explain your reasons for believing as you formerly did, and tell what reasoning caused your change of opinion. Direct your essay to someone who believes as you did before the change.

6. Most of us break laws or regulations that we consider unjust, inconvenient, or silly. Write a defense of breaking one such law (whether or not you personally break it).

7. Explain a problem that you solved, and persuade your readers that your solution was the best one.

8. Write a letter to the editor about a campus or community issue that you feel strongly about.

9. Start with a dialogue similar to the ones created by the situations in number 4 of the prewriting topics above. Then write a persuasive letter from one person in the conflict to the other.

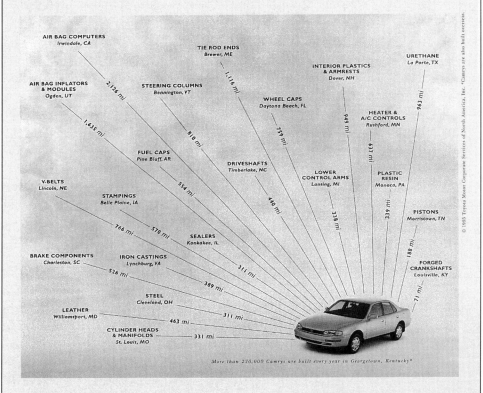

Before you buy a Camry
CHECK THE MILEAGE.

EVERY YEAR, Toyota buys thousands of parts from communities right across the country. In fact, we buy more than $5.6 billion per year in parts for both domestic and overseas production, from more than 440 U.S. suppliers. Whether it's engine blocks from Ohio, batteries from Tennessee or wiper systems from New York, our investment in local industries is paying off in the form of thousands of jobs across the United States.

INVESTING IN THE THINGS WE ALL CARE ABOUT. **TOYOTA**

For more information about Toyota in America write Toyota Motor Corporate Services, 9 West 57th Street, Suite 4900-J6, New York, NY 10019

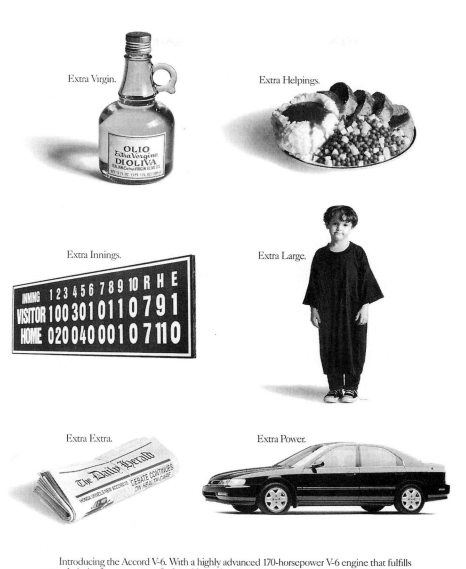

Extra Virgin.

OLIO
Extra Vergine
DI OLIVA
ITALIAN Extra VIRGIN OLIVE OIL
NET 17 FL. OZ. (1 PT. 1 FL. OZ.) 500 ml

Extra Helpings.

Extra Innings.

INNING	1	2	3	4	5	6	7	8	9	10	R	H	E
VISITOR	1	0	0	3	0	1	0	1	1	0	7	9	1
HOME	0	2	0	0	4	0	0	0	1	0	7	11	0

Extra Large.

Extra Extra.

The Daily Herald
DEBATE CONTINUES ON HEALTH CARE
HONDA UNVEILS NEW ACCORD V6

Extra Power.

Introducing the Accord V-6. With a highly advanced 170-horsepower V-6 engine that fulfills anyone's desire for more power. In fact, this car rises to a higher level in many ways. A chrome grille and wider tires add to the aggressive appearance. And the leather-trimmed interior features an 8-way power driver's seat. Because some people are never satisfied. Our engineers, for example.

The New Accord V-6 Sedan   ⊞ **HONDA**   A Car Ahead

Accord EX V-6 Sedan model shown and described.   © 1994 American Honda Motor Co., Inc.

Eat No One's Dust.

All-New Mercury Mystique With Exclusive MicronAir® Filter.

Here, quite literally, is a breath of fresh air in automotive design. The new Mercury Mystique. The only car in its class with a MicronAir filter that removes virtually all dust, pollen and other impurities from the interior.

The MicronAir filter is particularly useful should you ever find yourself following another car on a dusty road. Then again, given the performance of Mystique's available 24-valve Duratec V-6, such occasions could be rare. And with Duratec, Mystique is the only car in its class* that goes 100,000 miles between scheduled tune-ups.

The Duratec V-6 and MicronAir filter are just two of Mystique's 21 first-in-class innovations. You'll also find things like all-speed traction control, solar tint glass and a remote locking system.**

Drive the new Mystique and you'll see why we feel it's more than just a new car. It's a whole new Mercury. For more information, call 1 800 446-8888. **MERCURY**

WHO'S NOT SUPPORTING WHOM?

Robert Moog

1   Two years ago here in North Carolina, Harvey Gantt was running for the U.S. Senate against incumbent Jesse Helms. It was a heated campaign, with Helms, perhaps the most reactionary senator ever, accusing Gantt of favoring minorities, welfare cheaters, gays, and immoral musicians and artists at the expense of the moral white majority. Those of us who had Gantt bumper stickers on our cars could depend on hearing nasty remarks from some of our fellow citizens.

2   One day back then, I was filling the tank of my Toyota when another customer at the gas station came up to me and asked, "Why is it that all you Gantt people have Jap cars?" For an instant, the question made no sense to me, so I said to him, "I give up. Why is it that all us Gantt people have Jap cars?" With steam coming out of his ears, he sputtered, "Well, you're all so goddamn patriotic!" Then he turned, bolted to his shiny new Chevy, slammed the door, and varoomed off in a cloud of smoke.

3   If my mind was quicker, I could have told him why I have a "Jap" car. Since 1950 I'd been trying to buy a small, well-made car—one in which the gas mileage was good, the doors didn't leak, and the frequency-of-repair records were favorable. Such cars were simply not made in the United States. From my perspective it appeared that Detroit was so busy building land-going versions of the Queen Mary, changing model years, fighting with their unions, voting themselves obscene salaries, and making sure that their stockholders got their dividends every quarter, that they did not have time to find out what kinds of cars people like me wanted. And the automotive unions seemed to be too busy negotiating big fat wage and benefit packages for their members to worry about the unseemly number of "Monday cars" (*i.e.,* lemons) that were populating the highways of our country.

4   So I did what any good patriotic American would do. Believing in the free enterprise system and in the benefits of rigorous competition, I did the only thing that made sense—I bought a superior competitive product, one that met my needs. That, I thought, would certainly help stimulate some action in the marketing departments of the Detroit establishment. That's how progress happens in a free market. Companies that are truly customer-oriented thrive, and the less able companies—those that are burdened with inflexible or incompetent management . . . well, too bad, that's how our system works.

5   During the past two decades, millions of Americans like me have opted for Japanese cars, and Detroit is beginning to get the message. American cars being

made today are smaller, more reliable, and more fuel-efficient than the wheeled dream-boats of the '50s and '60s. Our free market system is working. In the meantime, I have my Toyota, which still gets 35 miles per gallon and runs like a top after seven years, and has cost me a total of $200 in repair bills. It's all part of our capitalist system; my car is an ongoing reminder to Detroit of what they have to do in order to get my business.

6   That's what I would have told the man with the Chevy at the gas station—if my mind had been quicker.

7   I remembered the gas station incident when I read Richard Marshall's letter in the June '92 issue of *Keyboard*. Like my Chevy-driver acquaintance, Marshall was off on a be-patriotic-and-buy-American rant. Marshall's nuggets of protectionist wisdom rang familiar: "Every time we purchase an instrument, we vote with our wallet, either to keep our neighbors employed and off welfare or to fill the bank accounts of those wonderful people who brought us Pearl Harbor. Going out of one's way to buy American is neither paranoid nor racist, as some have accused, but rather economic common sense," intoned Marshall, as if his logic were irrefutable.

8   Well, I, for one, don't buy any of this patriotism-through-purchase logic. I'll tell you why, from the perspective of a person who has been deep in the electronic musical instrument business for nearly 30 years.

9   Under the free-market system, which is certainly a cornerstone of American capitalism, producers are free to make and sell any products they choose, and consumers are free to buy any products they choose. Under this system, producers who offer desirable products at the right prices thrive, and those who don't must either improve their products' desirability or fail. This system has been the engine of genuine economic progress in our society. Under this system, the United States has become the wealthiest and most powerful nation on Earth.

10   Now, when some foreign producers enter our free market and offer more desirable products than some domestic producers, how does it suddenly become the patriotic duty of consumers to abandon their role of free-market buyer and "go out of their way" to buy American? Buying a less desirable product in order to "help keep our neighbors employed and off welfare" is not "economic common sense" at all. It's charity. It's short-term humanitarian aid, a form of middle-class welfare that subverts our cherished free-market economy and hurts our national strength in the long run.

11   So who's not being patriotic and supporting their fellow countrymen when American musicians buy Japanese instruments in ever-increasing numbers? I'll tell you who. It's us instrument builders whose instruments you're not buying, that's who! Somewhere along the line, each of us has neglected to build desirable instruments at the right price, or we've neglected to manage our businesses so they are profitable and financially sound. Many of us have faltered or failed, and in doing so we've taken a toll on our national economic vitality.

When I began studying electrical engineering at Columbia University, our 12
Dean of Students gave us a definition of an engineer: "An engineer is someone who
can do for two cents what any damn fool can do for three cents." This should be the
golden rule of engineering. But we seemed to lose sight of this wisdom as we worked
through courses in circuit theory, solid state electronics, and advanced mathemat-
ics. We were taken with how clever we were becoming, and sneered at those of our
fellow students who were majoring in mere industrial engineering. Those were the
guys who would be running the factories while we would be sitting in our air-con-
ditioned offices, designing one clever circuit after another. By the time we graduated from Columbia, we'd forgotten about our Dean's advice to be better than a
damn fool when it came to making things at the best price.

Thus, when I started Moog Music (called R. A. Moog, Inc. back then), I had 13
little understanding of how to manage manufacturing. But what's worse, I had no
understanding at all of how to manage a business. I hired several electrical engineers like me, and together we managed to build a lot of synthesizers in the 1960s.
But we wasted a lot of effort and money, and when our market became saturated
and the first serious competition came, we simply ran out of money. The company
eventually became a division of Norlin Music and, after being mishandled by a
string of managers with more testosterone than management smarts, dropped out
of the musical instrument manufacturing business about eight years ago.

At its peak, Moog Music had about 300 employees. How many overpriced, un- 14
derfeatured instruments would have to have been sold to well-meaning musicians
who wanted to "keep our neighbors employed and off welfare," even for one year?
Well, at an average salary of, say, $15,000 a year (back then), and manufacturing
labor being about 20% of an instrument's retail price, you musicians would have
had to cough up about $22 million just to keep Moog Music's employees off wel-
fare for one year! For sure, everybody was better off with the forces of competition
pushing my old company swiftly and mercifully into the ground.

An unusual story? Not at all. Moog's chief competitor, ARP Instruments, was 15
riding high during the early '70s. But by the late '70s, a combination of misman-
agement, bad product development decisions, and really nasty infighting in the
front office propelled the company into involuntary bankruptcy (the worst kind).
Lots of people were laid off. Should musicians have done their patriotic duty and
come to ARP's rescue by buying carloads of poorly conceived, overpriced products?
Are you kidding?

Another example is an Italian electronic keyboard manufacturer that I did 16
some work for about ten years ago. It was a well-established company, originally an
accordion manufacturer. But as electronic instruments increased in complexity, the
sophistication of their management still remained geared to the labor-intensive
practices of their earlier days. Shortly before its demise, the company was shipping
instruments that had a mean time between failures of three weeks! Still, the head

of the company would go on his daily rounds to turn out lights to save electricity, and to belittle the men and harass the women to remind everybody who was boss. So how many Italians stepped forward to buy the company's instruments "to keep their neighbors off welfare"? None that I know of.

17   Space limitations prevent me from regaling you with more stories of instrument manufacturers who are no longer in business. Like Moog Music, most of these companies did enjoy a few years of successful, profitable operation, but then failed because of a combination of inadequate marketing, manufacturing control, and financing. Most had been founded by engineers who were not trained managers. And more to the point of this editorial, no amount of "going out of one's way to buy American" would have saved any of these companies.

18   To be sure, there are many American instrument companies that have operated successfully for many years, who have grown, and who have consistently offered successful, desirable products. My hat is off in admiration to Peavey, E-mu, and Ensoniq, to name three companies who are doing the right kind of job for their employees, their customers, and their country.

19   Let me put down a few words about global competitiveness. Much of what we buy and use in our daily lives comes from outside our borders, because the production capacity to meet our needs does not exist here. Let's not get into why it doesn't exist, but merely note that if our supply of foreign petroleum, TV sets, sport shirts, computer printers, paper clips, rum, cheap shoes, expensive brandy, and thousands upon thousands of other items were to be cut off tomorrow, our domestic producers of these items could not keep up with our needs, and the conduct of our daily lives would be severely curtailed. To pay for all these foreign-made items, we have to export stuff that people in foreign countries want to buy. The more we export, the more foreign currency we have and the easier it is for us as a nation to afford the foreign goods that we need. This means that companies that make products that foreigners are willing to buy are helping us all to have foreign goods that we need.

20   Now, how do you help a company to be competitive in the world market? By saying that you'll buy its products just because they're made in America? No way! Any time a company perceives that it has a captive, unquestioning market, it becomes less competitive. I've seen it happen many times, especially in the early days of synthesizers. To take an extreme case, look what happened in the former Soviet Union and the Eastern bloc countries. They went one step beyond asking their citizens to give preference to their domestic goods. Through their import restrictions, they made it virtually impossible for their citizens to buy foreign goods. The result: Has anybody ever seen a Soviet consumer product that's competitive in the world market (except maybe for vodka or caviar)? What Soviet car would you buy? How about a nice Soviet jacket or portable stereo? None of these things exist as world-

marketable products, because the manufacturers of these products, having a captive domestic market, grew inefficient and unresponsive.

Here's my answer to how to help your fellow American instrument builders: 21
The next time you need an instrument, buy the best one for your needs that you can afford. If it happens to be an American product, great! Write to the marketing department of the instrument manufacturer, and tell them why you like their instrument. If they're on the ball (and they probably are if they got as far as making instruments that you like), they'll use your letter to fine-tune their product development program.

On the other hand, if you wind up buying a foreign-made instrument, it's your 22
patriotic duty to write to the American manufacturers whose products you didn't buy, tell them whose product you bought, and tell them why. If a company reads your letter and acts on it, then you have helped them to improve their product line, thereby helping them be more competitive worldwide. The day's pay or so that you denied some worker in that company because you bought a competitive product should be more than offset by the increased business that the company will enjoy because of the information you gave it. Or, if some company receives your letter and ignores it, then it won't last long anyhow, and the sooner its employees find employment elsewhere, the better it will be for them.

I'll close with a response to Marshall's crack about "the folks that gave us Pearl 23
Harbor." Yes, Japan gave us Pearl Harbor, no doubt about it. They were able to do it because their country was under the control of an imperialist, warmongering regime. As it turns out, the Japanese people paid dearly for their military adventures. Today, the political climate in Japan is decidedly pacifist. The Japanese people have directed their energies and their intelligence to economic, rather than military, achievements.

In our free market economy, playing our free market game, the Japanese have 24
made dramatic progress. In many cases, especially consumer electronics, they've gone far beyond us. They started out with the same technology that we had, but while we were keeping hundreds of thousands of people busy designing Star Wars Space Zappers and stockpiling nuclear weapons like so many bales of hay, Japanese engineers developed the technologies for portable DATs, professional-quality handheld video cameras, and, yes, digital keyboards. The Japanese nation has become wealthy by designing and making these things, and their products have given millions of people around the world great pleasure and enjoyment.

As a nation, we no longer need Space Zappers and thousands of nuclear 25
weapons. We no longer need a military-industrial complex of the size that has developed over the past 40 years. Now, for our own safety as well as our own economic well-being, we have to put a stop to being the world's arms purveyor and start designing and building products that people at peace want to buy.

Chapter Nine

Writing from Sources

At some time you may be asked to write a paper that does not spring entirely from your own mind. You may be expected to do research—to read fairly widely on a certain subject, to synthesize (to combine a number of different ideas into a new whole) and organize this information, and then to get your new knowledge down on paper in clear and coherent prose. The whole process may seem like busywork when assigned by your English instructor, but be assured: You will be learning a valuable skill, one that is essential in your advanced college classes and that will prove useful in compiling on-the-job reports.

Traditionally, research papers involve argument. You may be expected to choose a topic that is somewhat controversial, investigate the issues thoroughly on both sides, and take a stand. The writing process for a research paper is essentially the same as for any other, except that you begin with a thesis question that you later turn into a thesis statement. You still need to narrow the subject to a topic you can handle in the number of pages requested. And the bulk of the writing in the paper should be yours, stating your evaluation of what you have learned from your sources. You will quote from and give credit to the authors you have read, but a cut-and-paste job (in which you merely string together ideas and quotations from your sources) will not do.

Planning Your Research Paper

Writing a research paper is a time-consuming job. This is one paper that you simply cannot put off until the last minute. If you divide the project into units, you can keep the work under control.

Set Deadlines for Yourself

If your completed paper is due in, say, six weeks, you could put yourself on a schedule something like this:

1st week: Complete preliminary bibliography cards locating all your sources.
Try to narrow your topic down to a workable thesis question to investigate.

2nd week: Read and take notes.
Settle on a preliminary thesis question.
Try to come up with a preliminary outline.

3rd week: Continue reading and taking notes.

4th week: Complete reading and note-taking.
Turn your thesis question into a statement.
Wrestle the outline into shape.

5th week: Write the first draft.
Let it cool—rest yourself.
Begin revising and editing.
Get someone reliable to read your second draft and tell you whether every sentence is clear, every quotation properly introduced, and every paragraph nicely coherent.

6th week: Polish the paper.
Type the final draft.
Let it rest at least overnight.
Proofread it carefully.

That is a fairly leisurely schedule. You can, of course, do the work in a shorter time if required to. You will just have to be more industrious about the reading. Some instructors deliberately ask students to complete the project within a month in order to allow no chance for procrastination. Whatever your time limit, devise a schedule for yourself and stick to it.

Narrowing Your Topic

If you have an area of interest but no ideas about any way to limit that topic, your first step might be to consult a good encyclopedia. Perhaps your father recently underwent abdominal surgery; as a result of spending many hours with him, you have become interested in hospitals. An encyclopedia article on hospitals will briefly discuss their history, services provided, intern training, difficulties with sanitation, and cost of care, among other things. Remembering that your dad contracted a staph infection while recovering from his operation, you might decide to investigate the problem of infections in hospitals. Why have they become prevalent? What is being done about them? Or, as you read the article, you might encounter a new term and become interested in *hospices*—specialized hospitals that provide comfort and dignity for the dying. Are these proving successful? Should we have more of them in this country? Something in an encyclopedia article on your subject is likely to provide the spark needed to fire your curiosity and give you a focus for your research.

Expanding Your Associations

Once you have narrowed your topic, you may need briefly to expand it again in order to locate all the relevant information in the library. Since indexes and other reference tools do not necessarily classify information the way you do in your brain, you need to think of other headings under which your subject might be indexed. Before going to the library, you should make a list of topics related to your research subject. If you are planning to investigate hospices, your list might look like this:

Hospice	Geriatrics
Dying	Health care
Death	Old people
Aging	Euthanasia

EXERCISE

9.1

For each of the following subjects, list at least three related topics that you could look under in reference books.

1. No-fault divorce

2. High school students' legal rights

3. Fad diets

4. Detective fiction by women

5. Use of the word *ain't*

6. Tax shelters

7. Horror movies

Topics for Researched Writing

If your mind remains a blank and your instructor will allow you to borrow a topic from us, here are some ideas that we think might be interesting to research.

For Writing an Informative Paper

1. Research the history of a familiar product or object, such as Coca-Cola, Mickey Mouse, the dictionary, the typewriter, the nectarine, the title *Ms.,* black magic, vampire movies.

2. Research and analyze a fad, craze, or custom: fraternity hazing, pierced body parts, tattoos, fad diets, odd fashions, Power Rangers.

3. Research how a troubled group of people might be helped: autistic children, alcoholics, rape victims, anorexics, agoraphobics, battered women.

4. Research the history of some aspect of your home town: an industry, a landmark, street names, architecture.

5. Research some aspect of your hobby or job in order to inform someone unfamiliar with the activity.

For Writing About Literature

1. How effective is the ending of *Huckleberry Finn?*

2. Is the governess sane or insane in Henry James's "The Turn of the Screw"?

3. What are the characteristics of the "Hemingway hero"?

4. What are the mythological implications of Eudora Welty's short story "Moon Lake"?

5. What was Zola's contribution to literary naturalism?

6. Choose a popular author from any century and research his or her writing habits.

7. Have women's rights advocates been offended or pleased by Michael Crichton's novel *Disclosure* (1994)?

8. What is the real-life story behind David Henry Hwang's play *M. Butterfly?*

9. Why do some people say that someone else wrote Shakespeare's plays?

For Persuasion or Argumentation

A look at the tables of contents of news magazines like *The Nation, Time,* and *Newsweek* clues you in to matters of current public debate. Many of these will be beyond your scope due to the restrictions of your assignment and time; however, they can spur you to think of smaller, related issues. For example, the crisis of illiteracy in our nation has been headline news for some time now, but far too big a crisis to cover in a single paper. Some narrower aspects of this topic could be put into these questions:

1. Is illiteracy related to poverty?
2. What definition of *literacy* is appropriate to use in the context of national literacy?
3. If all grade schools taught children phonics thoroughly, would national literacy rise?
3. Are parents too busy these days to help their children learn basic reading skills?
5. How does U.S. literacy compare with other countries' literacy rates? What accounts for some of the differences?

Your best strategy for finding a persuasive topic is to develop a list of questions like these relating to a wider debate. Brainstorming with classmates and friends can help you devise the list. Then go to the library for a preliminary search to see which of your questions can be handled with materials available to you.

Some Clues on Using the Library

Once you have your deadlines set and your topic chosen, you need to get acquainted with your library. Most college libraries offer orientation courses to show students how to find material. If the course is not required, take it anyway. An orientation course is your surest bet for learning your way around a library. Some libraries have self-guided tours: you follow the guidebook's instructions to view all the parts of the library and see what is housed there. On your first visit to the library, go to the information desk and ask about orientations and self-guided tours; also, pick up a copy of the library handbook to study at home. After reading the handbook carefully, if you search and still fail to find what you need, ask for help. Librarians are seldom snarly about answering questions and will often take you in tow, lead you to the material you want, and give you valuable advice.

Locating the Major Resources

We can offer here some general instructions to help you find your way around the modern library.

The Public Access Catalog

In the old days, the first things you were likely to see upon entering a library were imposing rows of polished wood cabinets with small drawers: the card catalog. Even if your library still looks like that, it soon won't. Those cabinets are now being replaced with row upon row of computers. The computer version of the card catalog is called a *public access catalog (PAC)*.

The PAC terminal itself will direct you in how to use it: look for printed directions on a nearby card or on the opening screen. If you type in a general subject, such as FOOD ADDITIVES, you will get a screenful of subtopics from which to choose (for example, DYES, NUTRIENTS, PRESERVATIVES, and so on). Once you mark the subtopic you want, you will get a list that breaks that topic down further: under DYES, you would find topics like RED DYE #2, SAFETY HEARINGS, HYPERACTIVITY IN CHILDREN, and RELEVANT LAWS. Finally, the PAC will give you lists of specific titles of books, as well as the call number that you need to find it on the library's shelves. The computer will also tell you how many copies the library owns, whether or not any are checked out, and if so, when they are due back in. You can write down the call numbers you want by hand; however, many PACs let you use a printer to get a copy of what is on the screen.

The PAC's opening screen will also accept the name of a specific author or a specific title you seek and then present you with a list and publishing information.

Compact Disk Files

At the same computer terminal where you used PAC to find books, you can use *compact disk files* (CD-ROM) to find articles and further books. The ROM in CD-ROM means "Read Only Memory"; that is, you may read the files but can't type on them from your keyboard, which is a blessing. Many reference materials that used to be in long rows of fat dusty volumes, like the *Readers' Guide to Periodical Literature,* now exist as blips on a CD-ROM. One common system that combines several reference works—including the *Readers' Guide, Social Sciences Index, Humanities Index,* and nine others at last count—is called *Infotrac. Infotrac* provides you with titles, either popular or scholarly, in response to an author's name or a subject. Be sure to copy all the information down—or get a printout—because you will need it to find the periodical in which the article appears.

Systems like *Infotrac* are called "databases," and besides its listings on *Infotrac*, each academic field has its own specialized database (or more than one). If you are going into the field of physics, you will someday use *Scisearch* and *Spin*, for example. Your library's information desk will have a printed list of the databases it holds. These databases, like *Infotrac*, are updated frequently so that you can find the newest material on them. Often, the specialized databases aren't found through the main banks of computers; reasonably enough, they are kept in computers close to the areas where the books, periodicals, and references in the field are shelved. Many times, you must use specialized databases to find up-to-date research material in the field.

Indexes aren't the only dusty volumes that are now CD-ROM blips. You can read the full text of some materials, like the Bible, Shakespeare, *Grolier's Encyclopedia*, and the *New York Times* on CD-ROM. Again, your library will have a list of holdings on CD-ROM. Remember, when you use a source that you read on the screen, you still need to copy the information about where and when it appeared in print. This usually appears at the top of the first screen. You will also need to take note of the fact that you read it on CD-ROM, since you'll include that in your reference or works cited list.

Don't forget: most libraries still hold almost all this material in old-fashioned print. Even the *Readers' Guide* still comes out in paper form. If the computer terminals are crowded or out of commission—or if you simply want some peace and quiet while researching—your librarian can tell you where on the shelves the references you seek are kept.

National Vendors of Databases

If your library does not subscribe to a certain database, you may be able to connect through the telephone lines with a national vendor of databases. This service, which works through a computer modem, is commonly found at college libraries; however, it costs the library considerable money per minute of connection. The library may pass the charges on to you. Be sure to find out whether or not you will be charged when you ask the librarian to help you hook up. Remember that you will also be using a librarian's time when you use the national vendor, so employ this service only when it's obviously necessary. Most undergraduate papers will not require it.

Get It All Down

Every time you consult a new source, *copy or get printouts of all the information necessary for documentation* (that is, for indicating the source to your readers).

If you fail to record all the essential data, you may find yourself tracking down a book or an article weeks later in order to look up an essential publication date or volume number that you neglected to record initially. By this time, the book may be checked out, lost, or stolen, so get it all down the first time.

For whatever documentation system you are using, you will need to record the following.

For books

1. Author or editor
2. Title
3. Place of publication
4. Publisher
5. Date of publication (plus date of edition, if the book has more than one)
6. Library call number

For articles

1. Author (or "no author")
2. Title
3. Name of magazine, newspaper, or journal
4. Volume number (if a scholarly journal)
5. Date of issue
6. Complete pages the article covers

For the electronic form of either books or articles, you also need

7. Title of database (if relevant)
8. Medium (like CD-ROM)
9. Name of the vendor (if relevant)
10. Electronic publication date

On to the Reading

Using the list of sources you have developed so far, you next need to locate all the materials that look promising and try to decide which ones will be genuinely useful. As you are pondering what articles and books to study thoroughly and what ones to eliminate at this stage, you should give some thought to their reliability as well as their relevance to your thesis question. You have probably figured out by now that just because a statement appears in print, it is not necessarily honest or accurate. You need to be wary as you read.

Consider Your Sources

You might expect an unprejudiced analysis of an event from journalists who were present, but again you must stay alert because not all publications achieve—or even *try* to achieve—objective reporting. You may be certain that the conservative *National Review* will offer an appreciably different appraisal from that of the ultraliberal *Mother Jones.* And the *Congressional Record,* which sounds like an unimpeachable source, is actually one of the least reliable, since any member of Congress can have any nonsense whatsoever read into the *Record.* You must sample several authorities so that you are able to weigh the matter and discount the prejudices. This is one reason that many research papers require extensive bibliographies. You could probably scare up most of the facts from reading one unbiased source, but the problem is to discover a source that is unbiased—if one exists.

Do not make the mistake of embracing what you consider a reliable source and then placing your trust in it till death do you part. Too many of us do just this: we put our faith in the Bible, the *National Lampoon,* the *Wall Street Journal,* or *Time* magazine, and never bother to think again. You will discover writers and publications whose viewpoint is similar to yours. These will naturally strike you as the most intelligent, perceptive, reliable sources to consult. But be careful that you do not fall into the comfortable habit of reading these publications exclusively. And remember that book reviews can provide the most reliable information if you are trying to evaluate a book-length source.

The date of a publication often makes a difference in its value or reliability. If you are doing a paper analyzing the relative safety of legal and illegal abortions, you will find an article written in 1936 of little use. If, on the other hand, you are writing a paper on the *history* of the long struggle to legalize abortion, a 1936 article could be quite important. In general, we place the highest value on recent articles simply because the latest scholar or scientist has the advantage of building on all that has gone before.

EXERCISE

9.2

Find, photocopy, and read an article in *Newsweek* on some timely and controversial subject (some recent decision of the Supreme Court, for instance). Then find, photocopy, and read an article on the same subject in the *National Review.* Next, find, photocopy, and read an article on the same subject in *The Nation.* Look over the photocopies again, and make a list of any differences you discover. What can you say about the slant or the objectivity of each article from observing those differences? Which article do you consider the most objective? Why?

Making the Outline Easier

Keeping your thesis or thesis question in mind, you can get started on the reading. Have your note cards handy. At the same time you are doing research, you will be working out an outline. The note cards, each containing information related to a single idea, can be shuffled around later and slipped into appropriate sections of your outline. Taking notes consecutively on sheets of paper makes this handy sorting of ideas difficult.

Use Subject Headings

Chances are that your outline may not really take shape until you are well along with your reading—possibly not until you have finished it. As you take notes, put subject headings indicating in a word or two what each note is about in the upper-right-hand corner of your note cards. Eventually these subject headings probably will correspond to sections of your outline

As you collect more and more cards, leaf through them occasionally to see if they can be arranged into three or four main categories to form the major headings of an outline. The sooner you can get the organization worked out, the more efficient your research becomes. You know exactly what you are looking for and can avoid taking notes that would eventually prove off the point and have to be discarded.

If an idea sounds potentially useful, copy it down whether it fits exactly or not. If the idea recurs in your reading and gathers significance, you may decide to add a section to your outline or to expand one of the existing sections. Later, at the organizing stage, if you have cards with ideas that just do not seem to fit in anywhere, let them go. Let them go cheerfully. Do not ruin the focus and unity of your paper by trying to wedge in every single note you have taken. Unless you are an uncommonly cautious note-taker, you will have a number of cards that you cannot use.

Tips on Note-Taking

Of necessity you will do a considerable amount of reading for your research paper. If you remember that most published articles are put together according to the same advice we have given you in this book, you can summarize more efficiently. Read the introductory paragraphs of an essay quickly to discover the writer's thesis. If that main idea is relevant to your own thesis, continue reading carefully and jot down any useful ideas on note cards. Pay special attention to beginning and ending sentences of paragraphs; these will likely be topic sentences stating or summarizing major ideas.

If you are examining a book, the author's thesis will appear in the preface. You can thus get a quick clue concerning the usefulness of the volume. Usually a book will have a broader scope than your paper. You can tell from the table of contents which chapters may be useful to your investigation, and you need only consult those sections. If the book has an index, try to locate your topic there. You will then be directed to precisely the relevant pages and can treat yourself to a coffee break in the time saved.

Again, do not forget to record *on each card*

1. author's last name,
2. abbreviated title,
3. page number or numbers.

If you get in the habit of writing down these essentials before you take notes, there is less chance of forgetting an item.

Summarize the ideas in your own words, except when you think you might want to quote directly (verbatim), in which case copy the author's exact words and enclose them in quotation marks. If you carelessly forget the quotation marks and use those words in your paper, you will have committed a serious literary offense—*plagiarism* (see p. 177). Do not simply omit the specific examples when you summarize, because you are going to need some yourself. Remember that you must give credit for these examples, as well as for the ideas they illustrate, even if you put them in your own words when you incorporate them into your paper. Otherwise you will lapse into plagiarism. Your note cards should look something like the one shown in Figure 9.1.

FIGURE 9.1

Sample note card.

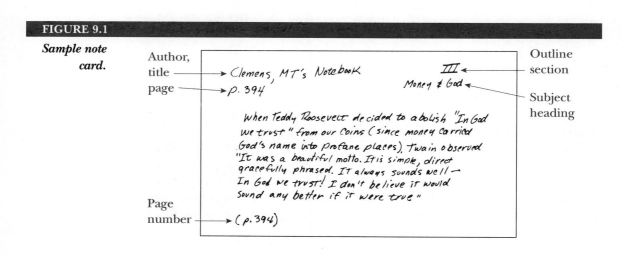

Author, title page

Outline section

Subject heading

Page number

The Photocopying Option

If the time you can spend in the library is limited and your finances are not, you might want to photocopy articles or pertinent portions of books in order to have these materials available to study at your convenience. You can then underline and make marginal notes without defacing the library's copy. And if later you want to check the accuracy of a quotation in your rough draft, you will be spared making yet another trip to the library to do so. But do not fail to note the source of the material directly on the photocopy.

How to Write a Quality Summary

Another kind of summary—much more exacting—is called a *précis* (pronounced *praý-see*). Précis writing is a valuable and challenging craft, highly useful in business and government work. Busy executives and top-level officials need precise summaries of the endless piles of papers that daily cross their desks. You would not take the trouble to write an actual précis when taking notes for a documented paper, but learning how to write a précis will sharpen your skills for summarizing in general. After mastering the art of the précis, you will be able to take ordinary notes more carefully and accurately. You cannot skim a passage and hope to produce a good précis, because you are expected to include all the important ideas from the original passage in your shortened version. Furthermore, you are expected to mention these ideas in the same order and in the same tone, using your own words. You may quote an impressive phrase or two, but *do not forget the quotation marks*.

Retain Only the Main Ideas

While you must write clear, coherent sentences in your précis, nobody expects the summary to be as stylistically pleasing as the original: the point is to make it considerably shorter. You need to eliminate all nonessential information by reading each paragraph carefully and setting down in your own words the main ideas that you remember. If you have not had much practice in summarizing, you should begin by working on a sentence at a time. Consider this one from Pete Axthelm's "A Really Super Bowl" (*Newsweek,* 22 Jan. 1979).

> In an effort to keep everyone buying tickets and watching television as far as possible into this elongated sixteen-game season, the NFL juggled its schedule so that strong teams faced the toughest tests and weaker members were able to kindle local hopes while playing fellow stragglers. [46 words]

Now ask yourself: What did he say? You might jot down something like this:

> To keep fans interested through the long season, the NFL scheduled teams against others of equal strength. [17 words]

Now, reread the sentence to see if you left out any important ideas. There is the bit at the beginning about buying tickets that is not included in the summary. Since finances no doubt provided the motivation for the unusually long season, the idea *is* important. You would do well to substitute *buying tickets* for the single word *interested*. Accuracy is more important than brevity.

After you have finished summarizing all the sentences in the passage, go back over your first draft and prune it down even more by combining sentences and dropping any unnecessary words. (See Chapter 11 for further help.) How much you can shorten a passage depends on the style and substance of the original. Naturally, you can condense the information in a paragraph by Ralph Waldo Emerson in fewer words than you can a passage of the same length by Ernest Hemingway. Most expository prose can be greatly reduced—usually by half, at least. You must, of course, resist the temptation to add comments of your own. Remember, you are *summarizing,* not *analyzing,* in a précis.

Here is a paragraph by journalist Christopher Hitchens on the peculiarities of the Nobel Prize awards, followed by a précis of the passage.

> There are further ironies in the way the Peace Prize is awarded. On several occasions it has gone to institutions rather than to individuals, but more often than not these recipients only serve to emphasize the element of futility in the donor. The International Red Cross, which won the prize in 1917, 1944, and 1963, is, after all, an organization which accepts war as inevitable and tries to palliate its effects. The same can be said of the Office of the United Nations High Commissioner for Refugees (1954). And it comes as a surprise to see some laureates, such as Theodore Roosevelt or Austen Chamberlain, on a list of peace crusaders. [111 words]

> Ironically, the Peace Prize has been given to institutions whose function underlines the futility of the award. The International Red Cross (winner in 1917, 1944, and 1963), and the United Nations High Commissioner for Refugees (1954), rather than working to prevent war, merely try to relieve the suffering. And some winners, like Theodore Roosevelt and Austen Chamberlain, appear strange choices as peacemakers. [62 words]

Tips on Avoiding Plagiarism

Plagiarism means using somebody else's writing without giving proper credit. Most teachers consider plagiarism close to a criminal offense. In some schools students may be expelled for plagiarism. The most lenient penalty is an F in the course. Deliberate plagiarism is, after all, a form of cheating.

You can avoid accidental plagiarism by using a moderate amount of care in taking notes. Put quotation marks around any material—however brief—that you copy verbatim. As you leaf through the note cards trying to sort them into categories, circle the quotation marks with a red pencil so you cannot miss them.

There remains the necessity of avoiding the author's phrasing if you decide not to quote directly but to paraphrase. This obligation is not so easily met. You naturally tend to write the idea down using the same phrasing, changing or omitting a few words. This close paraphrasing is still plagiarism. To escape it you must not even look at your source as you take notes that are not direct quotations.

We suggest that you use both methods—verbatim notes and summarizing notes—and let the summaries condense several pages of reading onto a single card. You will scarcely be able to fall into the author's phrasing that way. Or if your writer uses an eye-catching phrase—something like Thorstein Veblen's *code of pecuniary honor*—get that down in quotation marks in the middle of your summary. A summarizing note card will look something like the card in Figure 9.2.

FIGURE 9.2

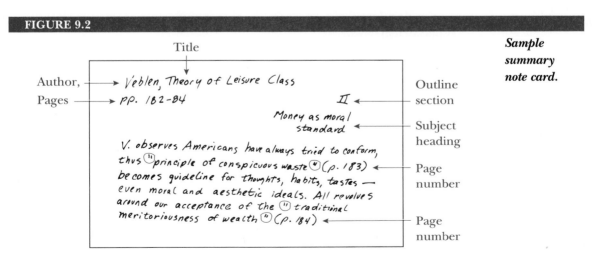

Sample summary note card.

Paraphrase Carefully

Sometimes, of course, you must do fairly close paraphrasing of important ideas. Since plagiarism is often accidental, we will give you a couple of examples to show you exactly what plagiarism is. Here is a passage from Deborah Tannen's *You Just Don't Understand*. Assume that you want to use her idea to make a point in your paper.

> Girls and women feel it is crucial that they be liked by their peers, a form of involvement that focuses on symmetrical connections. Boys and men feel it is crucial that they be respected by their peers, a form of involvement that focuses on asymmetrical status.

If you incorporate that material into your paper in the following way, you have plagiarized.

> Females feel that it is important to be liked, focusing on involvement in symmetrical connections, while males feel that it is important to be respected, focusing on asymmetrical status (Tannen 396).

The fact that the source is cited suggests that this plagiarism might have resulted from ignorance rather than deception, but it is plagiarism nonetheless. Changing a few words or rearranging the phrases is not enough. Here is another version, somewhat less blatant but still plagiarism.

> To girls and women, being liked by equal peers is crucial; to boys and men, being respected by peers, implying asymmetrical status, is crucial (Tannen 396).

Two phrases, "is crucial" and "asymmetrical status," are distinctly lifted from Tannen. The only way to save this version from plagiarism is to put quotation marks around the lifted phrases, thus:

> To girls and women, being liked by equal peers "is crucial"; to boys and men, being respected by peers, implying "asymmetrical status," "is crucial" (Tannen 396).

This solution is legal but stylistically clunky, as you can see. Notice, by the way, that the phrases "girls and women" and "boys and men" do not have quotation marks around them, even though they appear in the original passage. These phrases are so simple, so commonly used—and so nearly impossible to replace—

that quotation marks are unnecessary. Here is another acceptable version that doesn't violate rules of plagiarism or style.

> Girls and women place importance on equal friendships, while boys and men place importance on their position of respect among peers (Tannen 396).

Even though this version only repeats Tannen's ideas, not her words, the source note is absolutely necessary.

> REMEMBER: *If you are paraphrasing, put the passage into your own words; if you are quoting directly, put the passage within quotation marks.*

How to Write the First Draft

After you have read all the material you feel is necessary to cover your topic thoroughly, gather up your note cards and shuffle them to fit the sections of your outline. If your outline is still a flabby hulk, now is the time to whip it into shape and turn your thesis question into a thesis statement. The actual writing of the paper is the same as writing any other paper, except that you incorporate the material from the note cards into your text (either in your own words or through direct quotations) and give credit at the end to the original authors both for ideas borrowed and for actual passages quoted. Quickly review Chapters 3 through 8 if you are having difficulty at this stage.

To Quote or Not to Quote

Never quote directly unless (1) the material is authoritative and convincing evidence in support of your thesis, or (2) the statement is extremely well phrased, or (3) the idea is controversial and you need to assure your readers that you are not slanting or misinterpreting the source. You would want, for instance, to quote directly an observation as well put as this one:

> Bernard Rosenberg defines pragmatism as "a distinctly American philosophy whose only failing is that it does not work."

There is no need, however, for the direct quotation in the following sentence.

> The ICC, in an effort to aid the rail industry, has asked for a "federal study of the need and means for preserving a national passenger service."

You could phrase that just as well yourself. But remember, even after you put the statement into your own words, you still need to indicate where you got the information.

Quoting Quotations

Sometimes in your reading you will come across a quotation that says exactly what you have been hoping to find. If the quotation is complete enough to serve your purpose, and if you honestly don't think you would benefit from tracking down the original, then don't bother. Instead, include that quotation in the usual way. But notice that your citation will include "qtd. in" before the source and page number.

> George Cukor once told Scott Fitzgerald, "I've only known two people who eat faster than you and I, and they are both dead now" (qtd. in Latham 39).

> Mark Twain relates that he once knew a Miss Sexton, who pronounced her name "Saxton to make it finer, the nice, kindhearted, smirky, smily dear Christian creature" (qtd. in Wecter 103).

Indenting Long Quotations

If you're writing on a topic in the humanities using the MLA style, you are expected to set off quotations longer than four typewritten lines by indenting them one inch or ten spaces. *Omit the quotation marks* (since the spacing indicates that the material is quoted), and give the citation in parentheses two spaces after the period:

> In <u>Life on Earth</u>, David Attenborough describes the three-toed sloth this way:
>
> > It spends eighteen out of twenty-four hours soundly asleep. It pays such little attention to its personal hygiene that green algae grow on its coarse hair and communities of a parasitic moth live in the depths of its coat, producing caterpillars which graze on its moldy hair. (248)

If your quotation includes more than one paragraph, indent the paragraph a quarter inch or three spaces (instead of the usual five).

Notice that if you want to quote conversation, indenting the whole passage is a handy way of avoiding an untidy clutter of quotation marks within quotation marks.

Working Quotations in Smoothly

If you want your research paper to read smoothly, you must take care in incorporating quotations into your own writing. You must have ready a supply of introductory phrases with which to slide them in gracefully—phrases like "As Quagmire discovered," "Professor Clyde Crashcup notes," and "According to Dr. Dimwit." If you run through the examples in this section on quoting, you will find a generous assortment of these phrases. Borrow them with our blessing.

Notice, please, that the more famous the person, the less likely we are to use Mr., Miss, Mrs., or Ms. in front of the name. "Mr. Milton" sounds quite droll. If the person has a title, you can use it or not, as you think appropriate: Dr. Pasteur or Pasteur, Sir Winston Churchill or Churchill, President Lincoln or Lincoln.

Introduce Your Quotations

Most of the time you will introduce a quotation before beginning it.

As Mark Twain observed, "Heaven for climate, hell for society."*

But you may want to break one up in the middle every so often for variety.

"But if thought corrupts language," cautions George Orwell, "language can also corrupt thought."

Or you can make most of the sentence yours and quote only the telling phrases or key ideas of your authority.

Lily B. Campbell considers King Henry's inability to fight "a saintly weakness."

The play's effectiveness lies, as E. M. W. Tillyard points out, in "the utter artlessness of the language."

But do introduce your quotations, please. The standard MLA (Modern Language Association) documentation style suggests identifying the source within the citation immediately following the quotation. But we find that identifying the source before presenting the borrowed material allows the readers a clearer understanding of which ideas are yours and which come from sources.

---

*We have omitted many citations in this book, as is common practice outside of scholarly publications. But remember, you do not have this option in a documented paper. Whenever you quote directly, you *must* cite the source.

If you have difficulty introducing your authorities gracefully in the text of your paper, perhaps you are using too many direct quotations.

Make the Grammar Match

When you integrate a quotation into your own sentence, you are responsible for making sure that the entire sentence makes sense. You must adjust the way your sentence is worded so that the grammar comes out right. Read your quotations over carefully to be sure they do not end up like this one:

> When children are born, their first reactions are "those stimuli which constitute their environment."

"Reactions" are not "stimuli." The sentence should read this way:

> When children are born, their first reactions are to "those stimuli which constitute their environment."

What a difference a word makes—the difference here between sense and nonsense. Take particular care when you are adding someone else's words to your own; you get the blame if the words in the quotation do not make sense, because they *did* make sense before you lifted them out of context.

Use Special Punctuation

When you write a documented paper, you probably will need to use some rather specialized marks of punctuation: *ellipsis dots* (to show that you have omitted something from a quotation) and *brackets* (to make an editorial comment within a quotation). You will find both of these useful devices discussed fully in Chapter 14, "An A to Z Guide to Revision and Editing."

To Cite or Not to Cite

The main purpose of documentation—of citing sources used in a research paper—is to give credit for ideas, information, and actual phrasing that you borrow from other writers. You cite sources in order to be honest and to lend authority to your own writing. You also include citations to enable your readers to find more extensive information than your paper furnishes, in case they become engrossed in your subject and want to read some of your sources in full.

We are all troubled occasionally about when a citation is necessary. We can say with authority that you must include a citation for:

1. all direct quotations;
2. all indirect quotations;
3. all major ideas that are not your own; and
4. all essential facts, information, and statistics that are not general knowledge—especially anything controversial.

The last category is the one that causes confusion. In general, the sort of information available in an encyclopedia does not need a citation. But statements interpreting, analyzing, or speculating on such information should be documented. If you say that President Warren G. Harding died in office, you do not need a citation, because that is a widely known and undisputed fact. If you say that Harding's administration was one of the most corrupt in our history, most people would not feel the need for a citation, because authorities agree that the Harding scandals were flagrant and enormous. But if you say that Harding was sexually intimate with a young woman in the White House cloakroom while President of the United States, we strongly suggest that you cite your source. Because such information is not widely known and is also debatable, you need to identify your source so that your readers can judge the reliability of your evidence. Then, too, they might want further enlightenment on the matter, and your citation will lead them to a more complete discussion. Probably it is better to bother your readers with too many citations than to have them question your integrity by having too few.

Accuracy Is the Aim

After years of being told to be original, to be creative, to think for yourself, you are now going to be told—on this one matter, at least—to fall into line and slavishly follow the authorities. What you might consider a blessed bit of variety will not be appreciated in the slightest. If you put a period after the first citation, put a period after every one. Get the form correct every time, right down to the last comma, colon, and parenthesis.

The information (date, publisher, place of publication) necessary for completing a citation is located on the title page and on the back of the title page of each book. For magazines you usually can find it all on the cover.

When in Doubt, Use Common Sense

Keep in mind that the purpose of documentation is dual:

1. To give credit to your sources
2. To allow your readers to find your sources in case they want further information on the subject

If you are ever in doubt about documentation form (if you are citing something so unusual that you cannot find a similar entry in the samples here), use your common sense and give credit the way you think it logically should be done. Be as consistent as possible with other citations.

You will find instruction on the documentation styles for the MLA used in the humanities beginning on page 190 and the APA (American Psychological Association) used by the social sciences beginning on page 217.

How to Revise the Paper

Since a research paper requires the incorporation of other people's ideas and the acknowledgment of these sources, you need to take special care in revising.

Check the Usual Things

1. Be sure the introduction states your thesis.
2. Be sure each paragraph is unified, coherent, and directly related to your thesis.
3. Be sure the transitions between paragraphs are smooth.
4. Be sure your conclusion evaluates the results of your research; if the paper is argumentative, be sure the last sentence is emphatic.

Check the Special Things

1. Be sure that you have introduced direct quotations gracefully, using the name and, if possible, the occupation of the person quoted.
2. Be sure each citation is accurate.
3. Be sure that paraphrases are in your own words and that the sources are clearly acknowledged.
4. Be sure to underline the titles of books and magazines; put quotation marks around the titles of articles and chapters in books.
5. Be sure that you have written most of the paper yourself; you need to examine, analyze, or explain the material, not just splice together a bunch of quotations and paraphrases.
6. Be sure always to separate quotations with some comment of your own.
7. Be sure to use ellipsis dots if you omit any words from a quotation that your readers would not otherwise know were missing; never leave out anything that alters the meaning of a sentence.
8. Be sure to use square brackets, not parentheses, if you add words or change verb tenses in a quotation.
9. Be sure that you have not relied too heavily on a single source.
10. Be sure to indent long quotations ten spaces—without quotation marks.

Before you work on your final draft, give your entire attention to the following instructions on form.

Preparing the Final Draft

1. Provide margins of at least one inch at the top, bottom, and sides.
2. Double-space throughout.
3. Do not put the title of your paper in quotation marks.
4. Insert corrections neatly in ink *above the line* (if allowed by your instructor).
5. Put page numbers in the upper-right-hand corner. But do not number the title page. After the title page and the outline, count all pages in the total as you number. If you do not have a separate title page, begin pagination on the first page of the paper. Note correct page numbering on the sample published paper, pages 203–216.
6. Proofread. You may well be close to exhaustion by the time you finish copying your paper, and the last thing you will feel like doing is rereading the blasted thing. But force yourself. Or force somebody else. But do not skip the proofreading. It would be a shame to allow careless errors to mar an otherwise excellent paper.

Documentation Styles

We provide complete instruction for documenting papers according to the two most widely used academic styles:

1. MLA (Modern Language Association) for the humanities
2. APA (American Psychological Association) for the social sciences

If you are writing a paper using library sources for any of the remaining academic disciplines, you should identify a leading journal in that field and follow the style used there.

SAMPLES OF STUDENT WRITING FROM SOURCES

To give you a glimpse of what a research paper looks like, we include two brief samples in which students used sources. Notice that these students' papers are not just quotations from sources strung together with transitions between them: the students include their own observations and ideas. These samples are shorter than many college term papers. We provide them here to give you a sense of how material taken from sources works in each essay.

These essays use the MLA's system of citation, as published in the *MLA Handbook for Writers of Research Papers,* 4th ed. (New York: MLA, 1995). Remember that your Works Cited list should appear on a seperate page. We will also provide some examples from the American Psychological Association (APA) system later.

Drive-In Movies

Lisa Dill

1   At one time, almost every town had a drive-in movie theater. There was no better place to spend a Saturday night: a place where parents could take their children and share a family night out. Teenaged kids would sneak in through the bean fields to catch the double feature for free. Young lovers would snuggle together in the back of Dad's Chevy. What ever happened to movies at the drive-in?

2   According to journalist Neal Karlen, the first drive-in theater was erected in New Jersey in 1933. It had the capacity to hold 400 cars. But the fad didn't turn into an institution until the fifties, when baby-boom teenagers driving their parents' cars became an economic force. By 1961, the number of drive-in theaters in the United States reached an all-time high, with a total of 6,000 (Karlen 45).

3   Why were these movie theaters so successful in that decade? As Karlen wrote, "We had gone from Andy Hardy's front porch to the back seat of Dad's Chevy. In the fifties, nearly everybody had a car. No generation had ever had such opportunities to be alone together" (Karlen 45–46). It also provided cheap entertainment for large families. Dad and Mom had the front seat with a big tub of popcorn, and the kids curled up with sleeping bags in the back. It was gratifying to be able to enjoy a triple feature and stay out really late.

4   However, this pleasure is becoming less and less available. According to a recent article in the New York Times, over the last two decades the number of drive-in theaters in the United States has decreased from 3,700 to 900. The increase in land prices has led to real estate speculation and development and the disappearance of the theaters' habitat. The arrival of the VCR and cable has led to cheaper forms of similar entertainment (Wilkerson N1). And there has always been the problem of what you got to see at the drive-in. Theater owners have continuously struggled to afford first-run, top-quality movies. The increased popularity of R-rated and X-rated films, which were barred from screening at drive-ins, helped cause the disappearance of audiences.

As if in a time warp, the drive-in theater is still very popular in Texas and the   5
Southwest. Those still in business are dependent on a loyal audience, such as parents looking to save on baby-sitting expenses or young people in small towns with
no place else to go. An article in <u>American Film</u> noted that a number of technological improvements in screen and sound have been developed to make drive-ins
more attractive. For example, you can now tune into a radio station for the sound
instead of using the speaker that attached to the car window. There are bilingual
broadcasts and super screens that practically glow in the dark (Liftin 42).

I still go to drive-in theaters when I get the chance, and I hate to see them be-   6
come a thing of the past, I love the atmosphere of the drive-in. For some reason, a
kind of intimacy is possible there that isn't replaceable in any other setting: an intimacy that can only be achieved while sitting in a dark car in front of a big screen.

Works Cited

Karlen, Neal. "Rituals of Summer." <u>Minneapolis-St. Paul Magazine</u> Aug. 1992:
    44–46.
Liftin, Joan. "Films Alfresco." <u>American Film</u> July-Aug. 1986: 40–42.
Wilkerson, Isabel. "A Time Warp in Nebraska: Movies at the Last Drive-in." <u>New
    York Times</u> 8 Aug. 1992: N1+.

Children and Death
Jody Orrick

Although "Nothing is certain but death and taxes," people view these cer-   1
tainties quite differently. People talk openly about taxes. Taxes are publicly debated, and newspaper articles are written daily on the subject of taxation. Death,
however, is a subject that is rarely discussed. Perhaps people avoid discussion of
death because of its unhappy and depressing associations.

Death is confusing to a child. Children see adults as very powerful, and to   2
think of them as powerless against death and grief is threatening. Parents are reluctant to talk openly about death, and when someone close to the child dies, the
child is often sheltered and protected. Parents may assume that death is beyond
children's level of understanding and attempt to hide from them the anguish that
they themselves feel. Children are sensitive to such parental deceptions and wish
for explanations instead.

3   According to an article in Bloomington's <u>Pantagraph</u>, "Children Need to Know the Truth About Death," Earl Grollman states, "There are unhealthy explanations parents should avoid when discussing the death of a parent or grandparent" (C3). Some typical statements about death and the potential for damage:

<u>So-and-so has gone on a long journey for a long time</u>. The child could feel hurt, angry, and abandoned because someone they loved left without saying goodbye.

<u>So-and-so has been taken away by God because he's so good</u>. A child may feel the reward for goodness is death.

<u>So-and-so has died because she was sick</u>. A child may fear the normal illnesses they experience will kill them.

<u>So-and-so is in eternal sleep</u>. Equating sleep with death can cause bedtime problems. (C3)

All of these unhealthy explanations can leave a child feeling lonely, mixed up, and frightened.

4   Julius Segal, psychologist in child development, and Zelda Segal, school psychologist, in "Helping Children Deal with Death," suggest guidelines to follow:

Make sure that you answer their questions—not your own.

Be sincere. Answer as honestly and directly as you can.

Don't try to hide your own sadness over death when it is an event that the family shares.

Keep in mind that young children tend to personalize their concern about death, and may need an extra dose of warmth and intimacy more than a philosophical discussion.

Remember that fear and sadness over death can be expressed indirectly—so be patient. (147)

5   Answering children's questions about death can be a very difficult and traumatic experience. Parents shouldn't tell the child to be brave or not to cry. A death in the family is a sad situation, and the child should be allowed to express his or her sadness in the same way the adult does. Adults should talk to the children, and encourage them to talk as well. If the child is too young to talk about death, parents can still share their emotions. Hugging, kissing, and touching can still comfort young children who sense something is wrong.

6   A child's understanding of death grows with age. Dr. Gerald Schneiderman, the author of <u>Coping with Death in the Family</u>, says that children under the age of three tend to view death as a temporary separation and may become

angry when they think a parent who is gone rejected them (qtd. in Gray 29). Children three to five generally view death as reversible, according to psychologist Dr. Julius Segal. As Dr. Segal explains, "Children believe if a flattened cartoon character can get up and skip away, Dad could return, too" (112). Dr. Segal contends that six-to-eight-year-olds see death as permanent, although they don't believe it will happen until a person is quite old (112). "By ten or twelve," observes Dr. Gerald Schneiderman, "a child can accept death as a termination of life and struggles with the idea that death can happen to anyone at any age" (qtd. in Gray 29).

Children, regardless of age, should be reassured that although one parent or family member has died, other family members will be there; the child will sleep in the same bed, eat at the same table, and go to the same school. Children also have to be reassured that they are not the cause of a parent's death. If a loved one has died in an accident or of a disease, the cause of death should be explained, and the child should be reassured that they are healthy and won't die of the same disease, and that not many people die in accidents.   7

A child will express grief in many ways. In his study of grief, Dr. Julius Segal states that some children receive the news of a loved one's loss with only a shrug—or act as though nothing has happened (115). Following this surface indifference, behavior problems are not uncommon. Dr. Janice Cohn, psychotherapist in New York City, reports that some children may react with nightmares, stomachaches, and headaches. "Some children are so overwhelmed by anxiety or sadness that their emotions may freeze or reverse into giddiness," says Dr. Cohn (78). There is no right way to react to death, but according to Dr. Segal, "Whatever the reactions, parents are urged to accept the child's own grief" (115).   8

According to a leading group of psychologists, participation in the ritual of the final goodbye can help a child accept the loss. Some recommend that a child four and older be allowed to go to the funeral (Gray 29). A thorough explanation of what happens and what to expect should be made clear to the child ahead of time. Above all, if the child does attend the funeral, it would be a good idea to stay close and hold hands.   9

The process of grieving takes a long time. It is not a series of neat, organized stages, but more like an emotional roller coaster. There are no magic words that will ease the pain. Listening, touching, caring, and including the child in the process will not only help the child but will also help the parent come to terms with death.   10

Works Cited

"Children Need to Know the Truth about Death." <u>The Pantagraph</u> [Bloomington]
    30 Apr. 1989: C3.

Cohn, Janice. "The Grieving Student." <u>Instructor</u> Jan. 1987: 76–78.

Gray, Charlotte. "When a Young Child's Parent Dies." <u>Chatelaine</u> Apr. 1985: 29.

Segal, Julius. "When a Parent Dies." <u>Parents</u> June 1989: 112–18.

Segal, Julius, and Zelda Segal. "Helping Children Deal with Death." <u>Parents</u> June
    1988: 147.

The MLA Documentation Style for the Humanities

The simplified MLA documentation style resembles those used in other academic disciplines. It works like this:

A. Mention your source (author's last name and page number) within the text of your paper in parentheses, like this:

One of the great all-time best-sellers, <u>Uncle Tom's Cabin</u>, sold

over 300,000 copies in America and more than 2 million copies

worldwide (Wilson 3).

B. Your readers can identify this source by consulting your Works Cited list at the end of your paper (see items I through N). The entry for the information above would appear like this:

Wilson, Edmund. <u>Patriotic Gore: Studies in the Literature of the</u>

<u>American Civil War</u>. New York: Oxford UP, 1966.

C. If you are quoting directly or if you want to stress the authority of the source you are paraphrasing, you may mention the name of the source in your sentence. Then include just the page number (or numbers) at the end in parentheses, like this:

In <u>Patriotic Gore</u>, Edmund Wilson tells us that Mrs. Stowe felt

"the book had been written by God" (5).

D. If you must quote indirectly—something quoted from another source not available to you—indicate this in your parenthetical reference by using "qtd. in" (for "quoted in"). The following example comes from a book written by Donald Johanson and Maitland Edey.

> Richard Leakey's wife, Maeve, told the paleoanthropologist David Johanson, "We heard all about your bones on the radio last night" (qtd. in Johanson and Edey 162).

E. If you are using a source written or edited by more than three people, use only the name of the first person listed, followed by "et al." (meaning "and others"):

> Blair et al. observe that the fine arts were almost ignored by colonial writers (21).

F. If you refer to more than one work by the same author, include a shortened title in the citation in your text:

> (Huxley, <u>Brave</u> 138).

G. If the author's name is not given, then use a shortened title instead. In your abbreviation, be sure to use at least the first word of the full title to send the reader to the proper alphabetized entry on your Works Cited page. The following is a reference to a newspaper article titled "Ramifications of Baboon Use Expected to Become an Issue":

> The doctor observed that some people objected to the transplant on grounds that were emotional rather than rational ("Ramifications" A23).

H. If you are quoting more than *four* typed lines, you should indent the quotation ten spaces or one inch and omit the quotation marks. Cite the page number in parentheses after the period:

About Nora in Ibsen's <u>A Doll's House</u>, Liv Ullman writes,

> She says goodbye to everything that is familiar and secure. She does not walk through the door to find somebody else to live with and for; she is leaving the house more insecure than she ever realized she could be. But she hopes to find out who she is and why she is. (263)

I. On your last page, a separate page, alphabetize your Works Cited list of all sources mentioned in your paper. Use *hanging indention;* that is, after the first line of each entry, indent the other lines five spaces.

J. In your Works Cited list, in citing two or more works by the same author, give the name in the first entry only. Thereafter, in place of the name, type three hyphens and a period, then follow with the usual information. Alphabetize the entries by title.

Lewis, C. S. <u>The Dark Tower and Other Stories</u>. Ed. Walter

Hooper. New York: Harcourt, 1977.

---. <u>The Screwtape Letters</u>. New York: Macmillan, 1976.

K. Omit any mention of *page* or *pages* or *line* or *lines:* do not even include abbreviations for these terms. Use numbers alone.

L. Abbreviate publishers' names. See the list of abbreviations suggested by the MLA on pages 200–201.

M. Use regular arabic (not roman) numerals throughout. Exception: James I, Elizabeth II. Use *lowercase* roman numerals for citing page numbers from a preface, introduction, or table of contents. You may use roman numerals to indicate act and scene in plays: "In *Hamlet* III.ii, the action shifts. . . ."

N. Use raised note numbers for *informational notes* only (i.e., notes containing material pertinent to your discussion but not precisely to the point). Include these content notes at the end of your paper on a separate page just before your Works Cited list, and title them "Notes."

O. If you are writing about literature, you should cite the edition of the novel, play, short story, or poetry collection you are using in an informational note. Thereafter, include the page numbers in parentheses in the text of the paper. The note should read like this:

[1]Joyce Carol Oates, "Accomplished Desires," <u>Wheel of</u> <u>Love and Other Stories</u> (Greenwich: Fawcett, 1970) 127. All further references to this work appear in parentheses in the text.

Your subsequent acknowledgments in the text should be done in this way:

Dorie was not consoled, although Mark "slid his big beefy arms around her and breathed his liquory love into her face, calling her his darling, his beauty" (129).

Note the placement of the quotation marks—before the parentheses, which are followed by the period. *But* if the quotation is a long one that you need to indent without quotation marks, the period comes *before* the parentheses as shown in item H above.

Sample Entries for a Works Cited List

The following models will help you write Works Cited entries for most of but not all the sources you will use. If you use a source not treated in these samples, consult the more extensive list of sample entries found in the *MLA Handbook,* 4th ed., or ask your instructor.

BOOKS

1. Book by one author

    Abernathy, Charles F. <u>Civil Rights: Cases and Materials</u>. St. Paul: West, 1980.

2. Two or more books by the same author

    Gould, Stephen Jay. <u>The Mismeasure of Man</u>. New York: Norton, 1981.

    ---. <u>The Panda's Thumb: More Reflections in Natural History</u>. New York: Norton, 1980.

3. Book by two or three authors

    Brusaw, Charles, Gerald J. Alfred, and Walter E. Oliu. <u>The Business Writer's Handbook</u>. New York: St. Martin's, 1976.

    Ciardi, John, and M. Williams. <u>How Does a Poem Mean?</u> Rev. ed. Boston: Houghton, 1975.

4. Book by more than three authors

Sheridan, Marion C., et al. <u>The Motion Picture and the Teaching of English</u>. New York: Appleton, 1965.

[The phrase *et al.* is an abbreviation for *et alii,* meaning "and others."]

5. Book by an anonymous author

<u>Beowulf</u>. Trans. Kevin Crossley-Holland. New York: Farrar, 1968.

6. Book with an editor

Zaranka, William, ed. <u>The Brand-X Anthology of Poetry</u>. Cambridge: Apple-Wood, 1981.

[For a book with two or more editors, use "eds."]

7. Book with an editor and an author

Shakespeare, William. <u>Shakespeare: Major Plays and the Sonnets</u>. Ed. G. B. Harrison. New York: Harcourt, 1948.

8. Work in a collection or anthology

Firebaugh, Joseph J. "The Pragmatism of Henry James." <u>Henry James's Major Novels: Essays in Criticism</u>. Ed. Lyall Powers. East Lansing: Michigan State P, 1973. 187–201.

Pirandello, Luigi. <u>Six Characters in Search of an Author</u>. <u>The Norton Anthology of World Masterpieces</u>. Eds. Maynard Mack et al. 5th ed. Vol. 2. New York: Norton, 1985. 1387–432.

9. Work reprinted in a collection or anthology

Sage, George H. "Sport in American Society: Its Pervasiveness and Its Study." <u>Sport and American Society</u>. 3rd ed. Reading: Addison-Wesley, 1980. 4–15. Rpt. in <u>Physical Activity and the Social Sciences</u>. Ed. W. Neil Widmeyer. 5th ed. Ithaca: Movement. 1983. 42–52.

[First give complete data for the earlier publication; then add "Rpt. in" and give the reprinted source.]

10. Multivolume work

Blom, Eric, ed. <u>Grove's Dictionary of Music and Musicians</u>. 5th

ed. 10 vols. New York: St. Martin's, 1961.

11. Reprinted (republished) book

Malamud, Bernard. <u>The Natural</u>. 1952. New York: Avon, 1980.

12. Later (second or subsequent) edition

Gibaldi, Joseph. <u>MLA Handbook for Writers of Research Papers</u>.

4th ed. New York: MLA, 1995.

13. Book in translation

de Beauvoir, Simone. <u>The Second Sex</u>. Trans. H. M. Parshley.

New York: Knopf, 1971.

[Alphabetize this entry under *B*.]

NEWSPAPERS

14. Signed newspaper article

Krebs, Emilie. "Sewer Backups Called No Problem." <u>Pantagraph</u>

[Bloomington] 20 Nov. 1985: A3.

[If the city of publication is not apparent from the name of the newspaper, give the city in brackets after the newspaper's name.]

Weiner, Jon. "Vendetta: The Government's Secret War against

John Lennon." <u>Chicago Tribune</u> 5 Aug. 1984, sec. 3: 1.

[Note the difference between "A3" in the first example and "sec. 3: 1" in the second. Both refer to section and page, but in the first the pagination appears as "A3" in the newspaper, whereas in the second the section designation is not part of the pagination.]

15. Unsigned newspaper article

"Minister Found Guilty of Soliciting Murder." <u>New York Times</u> 2

Aug. 1984: A12.

16. Letter to the editor

> Kessler, Ralph. "Orwell Defended." Letter. <u>New York Times Book Review</u> 15 Dec. 1985: 26.

17. Editorial

> "From Good News to Bad." Editorial. <u>Washington Post</u> 16 July 1984: 10.

MAGAZINES AND JOURNALS

18. Article from a monthly or bimonthly magazine

> Foulkes, David. "Dreams of Innocence." <u>Psychology Today</u> Dec. 1978: 78–88.
>
> Lawren, Bill. "1990's Designer Beasts." <u>Omni</u> Nov.-Dec. 1985: 56–61.

19. Article from a weekly or biweekly magazine (signed and unsigned)

> Adler, Jerry. "A Voyager's Close-Up of Saturn." <u>Newsweek</u> 7 Sept. 1981: 57–58.
>
> "Warning: 'Love' for Sale." <u>Newsweek</u> 11 Nov. 1985: 39.

20. Article from a journal with continuous pagination

> Potvin, Raymond, and Che-Fu Lee. "Multistage Path Models of Adolescent Alcohol and Drug Use." <u>Journal of Studies on Alcohol</u> 41 (1980): 531–42.

21. Article from a journal that paginates each issue separately or that uses only issue numbers

> Sher, Steven. "Poetry and Its Visionary Necessity." <u>Oregon English Journal</u> 8.2 (Fall 1991): 3–6.
>
> [That is, volume 8, issue 2.]

OTHER SOURCES

22. Book review

Langer, Elinor. "Life under Apartheid: The Possible and the
Real." Rev. of <u>A Revolutionary Woman</u>, by Sheila Fugard.
<u>Ms</u>. Nov. 1985: 26–27.

23. Personal or telephone interview

Deau, Jeanne. Personal interview. 12 Mar. 1983.
Vidal, Gore. Telephone interview. 2 June 1984.

[Treat published interviews like articles, with the person being interviewed as the author.]

24. Published letter

Tolkien, J. R. R. "To Sam Gamgee." 18 Mar. 1956. Letter 184 in
<u>The Letters of J. R. R. Tolkien</u>. Ed. Humphrey Carpenter.
Boston: Houghton, 1981. 244–45.

25. Unpublished letter

Wharton, Edith. Letter to William Brownell. 6 Nov, 1907.
Wharton Archives. Amherst Coll., Amherst.
Updike, John. E-mail to the author. 5 Aug. 1995.

26. Anonymous pamphlet

<u>How to Help a Friend with a Drinking Problem</u>. American
College Health Association, 1984.
<u>Aaron Copland: A Catalogue of His Works</u>. New York: Boosey,
n.d.

["n.d." means "no date given."]

27. Article from a specialized dictionary

Van Doren, Carl. "Samuel Langhorne Clemens." <u>The Dictionary of American Biography</u>. 1958 ed.

[When citing commonly used resources, such as the *Dictionary of American Biography,* list only the year of publication and the edition, if stated. For less familiar references, give full publication information.]

28. Encyclopedia article (signed and unsigned)

Martin, William R. "Drug Abuse." <u>World Book Encyclopedia</u>. 40th ed. 1983.

"Scapegoat." <u>The Encyclopaedia Britannica: Micropaedia</u>. 1979 ed.

[The micropaedia is volumes 1–10 of the *Britannica*.]

29. Government publication

United States Dept. of Labor, Bureau of Statistics. <u>Dictionary of Occupational Titles</u>. 4th ed. Washington: GPO, 1977.

30. Film

<u>Wuthering Heights</u>. Dir. William Wyler. Perf. Merle Oberon and Laurence Olivier. Samuel Goldwyn, 1939.

[If you are citing the work of a director, composer, actor, or screenwriter, put that person's name first.]

31. Lecture

Albee, Edward. "A Dream or a Nightmare?" Illinois State University Fine Arts Lecture. Normal, Illinois. 18 Mar. 1979.

NOTE: *For any other sources (such as television shows, advertisements, recordings, works of art), you should remember to include enough information to permit an interested reader to locate your original source. Be sure to arrange this information in a logical fashion, duplicating so far as possible the order and punctuation of the entries above. To be on safe ground, consult your instructor for suggestions about documenting unusual material.*

ELECTRONIC SOURCES

If you use material from a computer database or online source, you need to indicate that you read it in electronic form. In your research, most or all of the items you read on screen have also appeared in print. Give the print information, followed by the computer source.

32. Article from a journal
[Cite the following information: Author. "Article Title." *Journal Title*. Volume. Issue (Year): paging or indicator of length. Medium. Available Protocol (e.g., HTTP): Site/Path/File. Access date.]

Inada, Kenneth. "A Buddhist Response to the Nature of Human
    Rights." Journal of Buddhist Ethics 2 (1995): 9 pars.
    Online. Available HTTP:
    http://www.cac.psu.edu/jbe/twocont.html. 21 June 1995.

33. Article from a magazine
[Cite the following information: Author. "Article Title." *Magazine Title*. Date: paging or indicator of length. Medium. Available Protocol (e.g., HTTP): Site/Path/File. Access date.]

Viviano, Frank. "The New Mafia Order." Mother Jones.
    May-June 1995: 72 pars. Online. Available HTTP:
    http://www.mojones.com/Mother_Jones/MJ95/viviano.html.
    17 July 1995.

34. Article from a newspaper
[Cite the following information: Author. "Article Title." *Newspaper Title*. Date, Edition (if given): paging or indicator of length. Medium. Information Supplier. *Database Name*. File identifier or number. Accession number. Access date.]

Howell, Vicki, and Bob Carlton. "Growing up Tough: New
    Generation Fights for Its Life: Inner-city Youths Live by
    Rule of Vengeance." Birmingham News. 29 Aug. 1993: 1A+.
    CD-ROM. 1994 SIRS. SIRS 1993 Youth. Volume 4. Article 56A.

[Access date is not needed when the medium is a CD-ROM.]

35. Article from an encyclopedia
[Cite the following information: Author/editor. "Part Title." *Title of Print Version of Work*. Edition statement (if given). Publication information (Place of publication: publisher, date), if given. *Title of Electronic Work*. Medium. Information supplier. Available Protocol (e.g., HTTP): Site/Path/File. Access date.]

Daniel, Ralph Thomas. "The History of Western Music."

Britannica Online: Macropaedia. 1995. Online Encyclopedia

Britannica. Available HTTP: http://www.eb.com:180/cgi-

bin/g:DocF=macro/5004/45/0.html. 14 June 1995.

[It is not necessary to give place of publication and publisher when citing well-known reference sources.]

36. Miscellaneous

Shakespeare. Editions and Adaptations of Shakespeare.

Interactive multimedia. Cambridge, UK: Chadwick-Healey,

1995. CD-ROM. Alexandria: Electronic Book Technologies,

1995.

"Silly." The Oxford English Dictionary. 2nd ed. CD-ROM.

Redmond: Microsoft, 1993.

NOTE: *For any other sources (such as diskettes, magnetic tape, or more than one source combined), follow the rules for citing a book, but add a description of the electronic source after the title.*

Models for Standard Abbreviations of Publishers' Names

University Presses

Columbia UP	Columbia University Press
Feminist	Feminist Press at the City University of New York
Harvard UP	Harvard University Press
MIT P	The Massachusetts Institute of Technology Press
Oxford UP	Oxford University Press

State U of New York P	State University of New York Press
U of Illinois P	University of Illinois Press
UP of Florida	The University Presses of Florida

Commercial Presses

Allyn	Allyn and Bacon, Inc.
Bantam	Bantam Books, Inc.
Harcourt	Harcourt Brace Jovanovich, Inc.
McGraw	McGraw-Hill, Inc.
NAL	New American Library, Inc.
New Directions	New Directions Publishing Corp.
Prentice	Prentice Hall, Inc.
St. Martin's	St. Martin's Press, Inc.
Simon	Simon and Schuster, Inc.

Specialized Presses

GPO	Government Printing Office
MLA	Modern Language Association of America
National Geographic Soc.	National Geographic Society
NCTE	National Council of Teachers of English
NEA	National Education Association
Sierra	Sierra Club Books
UMI	University Microfilms International

In order to practice composing entries for a Works Cited list, complete an entry for each of the works described below. You need to supply underlining or quotation marks around titles. The first example will show you how.

EXERCISE

9.3

1. The author of the book is Charles K. Smith.
   The title of the book is Styles and Structures: Alternative Approaches to Student Writing.
   It was published in 1974 by W. W. Norton and Co., Inc.

   Smith, Charles K. <u>Styles and Structures: Alternative Approaches to Student Writing</u>. New York: Norton, 1974.

2. Author: Robin Lakoff
   Title of the book: Language and Woman's Place
   Published by Harper and Row in New York in 1975

3. Author: Max Spalter
Title of the article: Five Examples of How to Write a Brechtian Play That Is Not Really Brechtian
Periodical: Educational Theatre
Published in the 2nd issue of 1975 on pages 220 to 235
Note: this periodical has continuous page numbering.

4. Author: Daniel S. Greenberg
Title of the article: Ridding American Politics of Polls
Newspaper: The Washington Post
Published on September 16, 1980, in section A, on page 17

5. Authors: Clyde E. Blocker, Robert H. Plummer, and Richard C. Richardson
Title of the book: The Two-Year College: A Social Synthesis
Published in Englewood Cliffs, New Jersey, by Prentice-Hall in 1965

6. How would your textbook, *The Practical Writer's Guide,* appear in a Works Cited list? Include the exact data.

7. In which order would the publications from 1 to 6 above appear in your list? Write the correct answer.

a) 5 6 4 2 1 3   b) 1 2 3 4 5 6   c) 4 3 6 1 5 2   d) 6 4 3 5 1 2

A Published Research Paper Illustrating MLA Style (Annotated)

The following research essay was published in *Journal of Physical Education, Recreation, & Dance* (1992). Merrill Melnick is a professor in the Department of Physical Education and Sport at the State University of New York—College at Brockport.

Male Athletes and Sexual Assault

Merrill Melnick

For your research papers, get a cover page format from your professor.

Are certain male athletes more prone than others to commit sexual assault crimes and, if so, what factors and/or elements within today's athletic environment encourage, support, and/or ignore such behavior? Such a question seems ridiculous at first glance given the popular notion that sports teach honesty, integrity, responsibility, self-discipline, and respect for authority. And yet the question needs to be seriously addressed given the recent spate of sexual abuse crimes involving high school football players, college basketball players, college football players, college lacrosse players, and professional ice hockey players.

Given the mass media's tendency to magnify crimes involving public figures (e.g., politicians, entertainers, religious leaders), it is easy to jump to irrational conclusions based on isolated cases and anecdotal evidence. This is certainly no less true for athletes. Their dalliances, moral improprieties, and deviances are especially fair game for those who control the flow of information to the public. Sensationalism sells newspapers and magazines and improves television ratings.

Abbreviations like, e.g. and i.e. are fine in parenthetical material—but write out in English elsewhere: "for example."

But having recognized the obvious, these disparate, seemingly unrelated examples of male athlete sexual abuse may, in fact, be part of a larger pattern of behavior with roots firmly planted in the very structure and culture of

Melnick 2

sport. Additional evidence is available from the following
sources:

• A recently completed three-year survey by the National
Institute of Mental Health found that athletes participated in
approximately one-third of 862 sexual attacks on college
campuses (Eskenazi 1).

Give credential when →
possible.

• Chris O'Sullivan, a Bucknell University psychologist,
studied 26 alleged gang rapes that were documented between
1980 and 1990 and found that most involved fraternity
brothers and varsity athletes, specifically football and

Author's last name and →
page number designating
where the information
can be found in the
source.

basketball players (Neimark 196).

• A survey of 1,050 athletes and more than 10,000
students by the Towson State University's Center for the
Study and Prevention of Campus Violence found that athletes
were 5.5 times more likely to admit committing date rape

Author's name (if not →
in sentence), page,
and section from a
newspaper.

(Weiberg 2C).

It is always dangerous to offer explanations for crimes such
as sexual assault because they can be misinterpreted as
alibis for the offender. The observations in this article are
not meant to excuse the perpetrators or to direct attention
away from the victims—females who have been violated.
However, if we are to fully understand the dynamics of
female sexual assault within the athletic environment, we
must look at the male sport experience.

Ask your professor
whether you may use →
headings and
subheadings.

Male Bonding

       Most experts agree that episodes of gang rape are
usually, but not always, associated with males bonding

Melnick 3

together in tightly knit groups (e.g., military platoons, ghetto gangs, college fraternities, rock groups). Such groups foster strong feelings of exclusivity, camaraderie, and solidarity. In the case of athletic teams, not only do the members play together, they frequently live and eat together. Group loyalty in all-male, small groups is often so strong that sometimes it can override personal integrity. With respect to gang rape, psychologist Bernice Sandler observed, "Group members will do anything to please each other; . . . they are raping for each other. The women are incidental" (qtd. in Toufexis 77). Why might they be raping for each other? Homophobia may be one of the root causes of the crime; that is, they may be willing participants in such a crime because they wish to remove any suspicions their peers may have about their sexual preferences. At the very least, not to participate in acts of deviance is to invite considerable peer pressure, suspicions concerning one's loyalty to the group, and often social ostracism. As Clair Walsh, director of the University of Florida's Sexual Assault Recovery Service, recently noted, "The pressure to be one of the boys can turn rape into a team activity" (qtd. in Weir 3C).

An authority quoted within a source.

Sports as a Masculine Proving Ground

Male bonding can become especially dangerous when coupled with pressure to prove one's masculinity. Male athletes are frequently beseeched by coaches, teammates, and peers to prove their manhood by being tough, aggressive,

Melnick 4

and dominating. In many ways, reports Michael Messner of the University of Southern California, an athletic team functions as a "masculine proving ground" for adolescent as well as adult males ("Boyhood" 429). It is possible that aggression on the playing field, sexist language and attitudes used in the locker room, and an inordinate need to prove one's maleness can combine in complex ways to predispose some male athletes toward off-the-field hostility. The net result, what some psychologists call "macho groupthink," can serve as a precursor to an act of sexual abuse.

Since there are two articles by Messner, use a short title to show which one was used.

Combative Sports and Violence

When we read of sexual assault cases involving athletes, they are, more often than not, participants in contact or combative sports. In these sports, players are encouraged and reinforced to beat, dominate, and control the opponent. Interestingly, one of the highest compliments that sport pays to a male participant who demonstrates a particular fondness and ability for bestial, brutish behavior is to call him an "animal."

Little is known about whether there is a correlation between on-the-field and off-the-field violence; yet, one has to wonder about the interpersonal consequences of sports which teach participants to use their bodies as instruments of force and domination (Messner, "When Bodies" 203). Whether physically aggressive, intimidating behavior taught and learned in some sport contexts transfers to nonsport

The other article by Messner is referred to here.

Melnick 5

situations must be researched further. In addition, while the social learning consequences resulting from participation in a particularly aggressive sport are well worth examining, researchers must also determine whether certain sports attract or recruit a particular type of male.

Not surprisingly, the social education of these same athletes is often neglected. Interestingly, sport psychologists at the University of California at Berkeley have found that the more physically aggressive the athlete, the less mature his moral reasoning tended to be (Bredemeier et al, 311). As Leavy observed in her book <u>Squeeze Play</u>, "You can't grow up if you spend your whole life perfecting the rhythms of childhood" (xxx).

Citation for a source with more than three authors.

The Athletic Justice System

The "athletic justice system" may also be part of the etiology of sexual assault crimes. Athletes' rules are often very different from the rules which govern the campus community or society. Too many athletes believe they can get away with anything, that "coach will take care of things." For example, in 1983, University of Maryland basketball coach Lefty Driesell attempted to persuade a coed to drop an accusation of sexual misconduct against one of his players. Driesell's action drew only a mild reprimand from the school. Given such an atmosphere of moral leniency, is it any wonder that some athletes fail to consider the consequences of their actions?

Information that is general knowledge—it was widely covered in the news.

Melnick 6

It is not only the "athletic justice system" that dismisses deviant acts committed by athletes. Society at large needs to shoulder some of the responsibility for the callous regard and even contempt some athletes have for normative structures. American society holds "star" athletes in such high regard that it is no wonder that these athletes expect, if not demand, differential treatment for their transgressions. The privileged status of star athletes begins in youth sports and extends all the way to the professional ranks. Some community leaders, law enforcement agents, and school officials are only too willing to "look the other way" or treat lightly crimes committed by star athletes.

Big-Man-on-Campus Syndrome

Because star athletes are held in such high esteem, they frequently find themselves worshipped by their adoring publics. This is no less true on college campuses today where the "big-man-on-campus" syndrome is still intact. It is very easy for star athletes to believe that all women who flirt with them are interested in sex. Many have become so accustomed to "easy sex" that they may find it difficult to accept the word "no" when their date decides the evening is over. In 1987, the NCAA assessed the "death penalty" against Southern Methodist University after it was revealed that boosters paid sorority women up to $400 a weekend to have sex with high school football recruits ("Sex-for-Athletes" 4D). A one-time Syracuse University basketball recruit who was

Article with no known author.

Melnick 7

indicted for a sexual assault he allegedly committed during his recruiting visit to the Southern Methodist campus said, "I thought the young woman was one of the team groupies who hang out with team members and do whatever [the team members] want" ("Ex-SU Recruit Indicted" 1A).

Clarifying words added to quotation by writer of article—put them within square brackets.

Athletes, as a category, are overrepresented among those college students who commit date and gang rape; however, sexual assault crimes committed by athletes are manifest at every level and should not be dismissed as insignificant or inconsequential. The following five suggestions and/or recommendations may help reduce the likelihood of such incidences:

1. <u>Abolish special residences for athletes</u>. Athletic dormitories contribute to the privileged status of athletes and frequently serve as the venue for sexual assault. Judged strictly from an educational perspective, it seems very difficult to defend a practice which physically, socially, and recreationally isolates a group from their classmates. Student athletes are either bona fide members of the student body or they aren't. Although some will argue, as Mississippi head football coach Billy Brewer does, that "in our part of the country, it's imperative that we have athletic dorms and training tables" (Reed 138), it is difficult to see how the practice can be justified. If a varsity football player has trouble deciding how best to select from among the four basic food groups, let him enroll in Nutrition 101. If he can't

Melnick 8

decide which fork to use with his salad, let him read a book
on table etiquette. It is time for big-time athletic programs to
stop infantilizing grown men. Encouragingly, the NCAA
addressed the privileged caste system for athletes and voted
at its 1991 convention to phase out all athletics dorms or
dorm wings by 1996. Training table meals will also be
reduced to one day by 1996.

2. <u>Eliminate all sexist talk from the sport</u>
<u>environment</u>. Bruce Kidd, professor of physical education at
the University of Toronto, observed that what is said among
and between males within the sports context contributes to
the degradation and exploitation of women (261). In a 1990
presentation to a Sociology of Sport meeting, Curry reported
discovering empirical support for Kidd's concerns when he
analyzed conversations held in two locker rooms at a large
midwestern university with a big-time sports program. He
found that, in general, locker room talk encouraged sexist
attitudes and the expression of hostility toward women. At
the extreme, such talk promoted a type of "rape culture."
Coaches should carefully monitor the language heard in and
around the game, practice field, and locker room. They must
make it perfectly clear to their players that sexist language
is totally unacceptable; they must be prepared to take
punitive action against those athletes who refuse to comply.
The explicit, omnipresent misogyny of the male locker room
must not go unchallenged. At the very least, the exclusion of

*Cite only page number if
the author's name
appears in the same
sentence.*

*A speech is listed on
the Works Cited page.*

Melnick 9

sexist language from the sport environment would represent a positive, initial step toward eliminating sexist views.

Consider sportswriter Lisa Olsen's heavily reported ◄—— *General knowledge,* locker room incident involving members of the New England *found in any news* Patriots football team. Recall how her charges of sexual *medium of the time.* harassment were muffled in favor of an extended and hot debate over whether female sportswriters should be allowed in male locker rooms. The humiliation and embarrassment Olsen was subjected to were essentially trivialized. Instead, she found herself vilified for "invading" the sanctuary of a male locker room. The misogyny of the male locker room was reinforced as Lisa Olsen, the victim, was stigmatized as the guilty party.

Coaches also must recognize that, whether they like it or not, they are role models for many of their athletes. That is why Indiana University head basketball coach Bobby Knight's flip and insensitive response to broadcaster Connie Chung's question about sexual assault on the college campus caused such an uproar a few years ago. Knight's advice to college coeds, as reported in the daily newspapers, was, "If rape is inevitable, relax and enjoy it."

3. <u>Impose tough, swift punishment for athletes who</u> <u>are found guilty</u>. Not only is rape the most unreported crime in the United States, but when a victim does press charges against an athletic assailant, all too often the response is one of delay and often stonewalling by athletic department

Melnick 10

officials and college administrators. In the worst cases, the crime is treated as having not happened. Often, the assailant's defenders will deny a gang rape took place; instead, they will argue that the victim was a willing participant in an episode of "group sex." Faced with the considerable muscle and prestige of the athlete's defense, victims will usually back off from prosecuting the case rather than face the psychological trauma and personal embarrassment of reliving the assault at one or more trials (a separate trial for each defendant). Male athletes must understand, in no uncertain terms, that the prosecution of sexual assault crimes will be swift, vigorous, and uncompromising and that the full weight of the law will fall on all guilty parties. To his credit, a federal judge in Missouri recently ruled that campus crime records must be open to the public and that withholding a crime investigation and incident report is unconstitutional ("End the Cover-up" 12A). The judge specifically responded to a rape allegedly committed by a star athlete at Southwest Missouri State University which was not disclosed and in which no charges were filed. In his action, the judge sent a clear signal that there is only one justice system for both athletes and nonathletes on college campuses in Missouri.

Unsigned newspaper article.

4. <u>Educate athletes for greater sensitivity to the problem</u>. In the same way that drug workshops and seminars are designed to heighten an athlete's sensitivity to the use

Melnick 11

and abuse of drugs, athletes should be required to attend mandatory, sensitivity-raising sessions dealing with date rape, group rape and related topics. For example, at the University of Colorado, football players are now required to attend date rape seminars after two team members were charged in 1990 with rape and sexual assault in separate incidents. Raising the athletic community's awareness of sexual assault crimes through seminars, workshops, film, and literature would be an important step in dealing with the problem. Such educational efforts could also be extended to include broader discussions of male bonding, men and masculinity, and heterosexual relationships.

5. Reformulate the male sport experience. As long as sport continues to be a proving ground for manhood and masculinity, it will continue to devalue and demean women. As long as the male sport experience is defined as a military operation whereby one team's success can only be achieved by the opposing team's destruction, humane values are not likely to flourish. On this point, Kidd speculated that "a sport culture that de-emphasized winning in favor of exploring artistry and skill and the creative interaction of 'rival' athletes would be much less repressive" (263). In such an environment, sport would become more inviting to everybody, expressive and instrumental player violence would be totally unacceptable, and sexist thought and practice would give way to a greater respect for, and

appreciation of, women. Such a humane sport environment could be a powerful counterpoint to the hostile and sexist feelings, attitudes, and actions which the current male sports model, either wittingly or unwittingly, exhibits.

For the sake of the athletes who commit sex crimes and, more importantly, for their victims, we must take a closer look at the male sport experience and its consequences. Possibly embedded within the very structure and culture of sport are several factors which may predispose or condition some male athletes to physically aggress against women: "macho groupthink," the inherently violent nature of contact sports, neglect of the athlete's "social education," a perverse system of athletic justice, and a system which gives star athletes carte blanche. These factors are offered as starting points for such an analysis.

Melnick 13

Works Cited

Bredemeier, Brenda Jo, David Shields, Maureen Weiss, and
Bruce Cooper. "The Relationship of Sport Involvement
with Children's Moral Reasoning and Aggressive
Tendencies." Journal of Sport Psychology 8 (1986):
304–18.

Curry, T. J. "Fraternal Bonding in the Locker Room: A
Dramaturgical Analysis of Talk about Competition and
Women." Paper presented at the 10th Annual
Conference of the North American Society for the
Sociology of Sport. Denver, CO. 7 Nov. 1990.

"End the Cover-up of Campus Crime." USA Today 14 March
1991: 12A.

Eskanazi, G. "The Male Athlete and Sexual Assault." New
York Times 3 June 1990, sec. 8: 1.

"Ex-SU Recruit Indicted on Sex Charges." Democrat and
Chronicle [Rochester] 16 Feb. 1991: 1A.

Kidd, Bruce. "Sports and Masculinity." Beyond Patriarchy:
Essays by Men on Pleasure, Power, and Change. Ed.
M. Lautman. Toronto: Oxford UP, 1987. 250–65.

Leavy, J. Squeeze Play. NY: Doubleday, 1990.

Messner, Michael. "Boyhood, Organized Sports, and the
Construction of Masculinities." Journal of
Contemporary Ethnography 18 (1990): 416–44.

---. "When Bodies Are Weapons: Masculinity and Violence in
Sport." International Review for the Sociology of Sport
25 (1990): 203–20.

*Your Works Cited should
begin on a new page.*

*Center the title 1″ from
the top of the page (your
page will be 8½″ × 11″);
use title capitalization
(upper and lower case);
do not underline or
boldface.*

*Reverse the order of the
first author's name only.*

*Give as much informa-
tion as possible when
noting a speech.*

*Alphabetize anonymous
articles by the first word
(other than a, the, an).*

*Article in a collection of
articles.*

*Scholarly journals need
volume numbers in
Works Cited.*

*A second source by the
same author as above.
Do not repeat the name.*

Melnick 14

Popular magazines use dates, not volume numbers. ——→ Neimark, Jill. "Out of Bounds: The Truth About Athletes and Rape." <u>Mademoiselle</u> May 1991: 196–99.

Reed, W. F. "Don't Hang It on Coaches." <u>Sports Illustrated</u> 3 Sept. 1990: 138.

Identify the city name if the title of the newspaper does not. ——→ "Sex-for-Athletes, Grade-fixing Schemes Reported at SMU." <u>Democrat and Chronicle</u> [Rochester] 24 March 1987: 4D.

Toufexis, A. "Sex and the Sporting Life." <u>Time</u> 6 Aug. 1990: 77.

Weiberg, S. "Campus Crime Study Not Kind to Athletes." <u>USA Today</u> 21 Feb. 1991: 2C.

Weir, T. "Athletes Must Play by Society's Rules." <u>USA Today</u> 17 May 1990: 3C.

The APA Documentation Style for the Social Sciences

The APA style puts more focus on the date of the source than the MLA style does. The year appears right in the parenthetical documentation, instead of only in the Works Cited list. Take a look at an excerpt of Melnick's published essay, shown here in APA format, and compare it to the same section in MLA format (pp. 204–206). Following this example, you will find a guide to using APA documentation.

<u>Male Bonding</u>

Most experts agree that episodes of gang rape are usually, but not always, associated with males bonding together in tightly knit groups (e.g., military platoons, ghetto gangs, college fraternities, rock groups). Such groups foster strong feelings of exclusivity, camaraderie, and solidarity. In the case of athletic teams, not only do the members play together, they frequently live and eat together. Group loyalty in all-male, small groups is often so strong that sometimes it can override personal integrity. With respect to gang rape, psychologist Bernice Sandler observed, "Group members will do anything to please each other; . . . they are raping for each other. The women are incidental" (Toufexis, 1990, p. 77). Why might they be raping for each other? Homophobia may be one of the root causes of the crime; that is, they may be willing participants in such a crime because they wish to remove any suspicions their peers may have about their sexual preferences. At the very least, not to participate in acts of deviance is to invite considerable peer pressure, suspicions concerning one's loyalty to the group, and often social ostracism. As Clair Walsh, director of the University of Florida's Sexual Assault Recovery Service, recently noted,

"The pressure to be one of the boys can turn rape into a team activity" (Weir, 1990, p. 3C).

<u>Sports as a Masculine Proving Ground</u>

Male bonding can become especially dangerous when coupled with pressure to prove one's masculinity. Male athletes are frequently beseeched by coaches, teammates, and peers to prove their manhood by being tough, aggressive, and dominating. In many ways, reports Michael Messner (1990a) of the University of Southern California, an athletic team functions as a "masculine proving ground" for adolescent as well as adult males (p. 429). It is possible that aggression on the playing field, sexist language and attitudes used in the locker room, and an inordinate need to prove one's maleness can combine in complex ways to predispose some male athletes toward off-the-field hostility. The net result, what some psychologists call "macho groupthink," can serve as a precursor to an act of sexual abuse.

Using APA Style

A. Always mention your source within the text of your paper in parentheses.

The study reveals that children pass through identifiable cognitive stages (Piaget, 1954).

B. Your readers can identify this source by consulting your References list at the end of your paper. The entry for the information in item A would appear like this:

Piaget, J. (1954). <u>The construction of reality in the child.</u> New York: Basic Books.

[Note the use of sentence capitalization for titles in the references section. Note also that APA style calls for you to underline the punctuation following underlined titles.]

C. On your last page, a separate page, alphabetize your References list of all sources mentioned in your paper. Use *paragraph indention:* that is, indent the first line of each entry and not the other lines.

D. In your References section, in citing two or more works by the same author, put the earliest work first. When more than one work has been published by the same author during the same year, list them alphabetically, according to name of the book or article, and identify them with an "a," "b," "c," etc., following the date. See p. 218 for an example of the in-text citation.

> Graves, D. (1975). An examination of the writing processes of seven-year-old children. Research in the Teaching of English, 9, 227–241.
>
> Graves, D. (1981a). Writing research for the eighties: What is needed. Language Arts, 58, 197–206.
>
> Graves, D. (1981b). Writers: Teachers and children at work. Exeter, NH: Heinemann Educational Books.

E. Use the following abbreviations: Vol., No., chap., Trans., ed., Ed., rev. ed., 2nd ed., p., pp. (meaning Volume, Number, chapter, translated by, edition, Editor, revised edition, second edition, page, and pages). Use official U.S. Postal Service abbreviations for states: IL, NY, TX, etc.

F. If you are quoting directly or if you want to stress the authority of the source you are paraphrasing, you may mention the name of the source in your sentence. Then include just the date in parentheses.

> In Words and Women, Miller and Swift (1976) remind us that using the plural is a good way to avoid "the built-in male-as-norm quality English has acquired . . ." (p. 163).

G. If you are using a source written or edited by more than two people and fewer than six, cite all authors the first time you refer to the source. For all following references cite only the surname of the first person listed, followed by "et al." (meaning "and others").

> Blair et al. (1980) observe that the fine arts were almost ignored by colonial writers.

When there are only two authors, join their names with the word *and* in the text. In parenthetical materials, tables, and reference lists, join the names by an ampersand (&).

```
Hale and Sponjer (1972) originated the Do-Look-Learn

theory.
```

```
The Do-Look-Learn theory (Hale & Sponjer, 1972) was taken

seriously by educators.
```

H. If the author's name is not given, then use a shortened title instead. In your abbreviation, be sure to use at least the first word of the full title to send the reader to the proper alphabetized entry in your References section. The following is a reference to a newspaper article titled "Ramifications of Baboon Use Expected to Become an Issue":

```
The doctor observed that some people objected to the transplant

on grounds that were emotional rather than rational

("Ramifications," 1979).
```

I. If you are quoting more than *forty* words, begin the quotation on a new line and indent the entire quotation five spaces, but run each line to the usual right margin. Omit the quotation marks. Do not single-space the quotation.

```
In Language and Woman's Place (1975) Lakoff observes

that

        men tend to relegate to women things that are not of

        concern to them, or do not involve their egos. . . . We

        might rephrase this point by saying that since women

        are not expected to make decisions on important matters,

        such as what kind of job to hold, they are relegated the

        noncrucial decisions as a sop. (p. 9)
```

J. For citing electronic sources, see Xia Li and Nancy Crane's *Electronic Style: A Guide to Citing Electronic Information* (Westport: Meckler, 1993), which is based on the APA style. (See also pp. 223–224.)

Sample Entries for a References List

The following models will help you write entries for your References list for most of the sources you will use. If you use a source not treated in these samples, consult the more extensive list of sample entries found in the *Publication Manual of the American Psychological Association,* 4th ed. (Washington, DC: APA, 1994), or ask your instructor.

Alphabetize your list by the author's last name. If there is no author given, alphabetize the entry by the title. Use regular paragraph indention. Use author's initials for given names. Note the major differences between APA and MLA: paragraph indention instead of hanging; dates following authors' names instead of at the end of the entry; and sentence capitalization of article and book titles instead of capitalizing all important words.

A. Book by one author

Abernathy, C. F. (1980). <u>Civil rights: Cases and materials.</u> St. Paul: West Publishing.

B. Two or more books by the same author (listed in chronological order)

Gould, S. J. (1980). <u>The mismeasure of man.</u> New York: Norton.

Gould, S. J. (1989). <u>The panda's thumb: More reflections on natural history.</u> New York: Norton.

C. Book by two or more authors

Cook, M., & McHenry, R. (1978). <u>Sexual attraction.</u> New York: Pergamon Press.

Brusaw, C., Alfred, G., & Oliu, W. (1976). <u>The business writer's handbook.</u> New York: St. Martin's.

[Note that in your list of references you use the ampersand sign instead of writing the word *and.*]

D. Book by a corporate author

White House Conference on Children and Youth. (1970). <u>The becoming of education.</u> Washington, D.C.: U.S. Government Printing Office.

E. Book with an editor

>Zaranka, W. (Ed.). (1981). <u>The brand-X anthology of poetry.</u> Cambridge: Apple-Wood Press.

[For a book with two or more editors, use "Eds."]

F. Article in a collection or anthology

>Emig, J. (1978). Hand, eye, brain: Some basics in the writing process. In C. Cooper & L. Odell (Eds.), <u>Research in composing: Points of departure</u> (pp. 59–72). Urbana, IL: National Council of Teachers of English.

G. Multivolume work

>Asimov, I. (1960). <u>The intelligent man's guide to science.</u> (Vols. 1–2). New York: Basic Books.

H. Later (second or subsequent) edition

>Gibaldi, J. (1995). <u>MLA handbook for writers of research papers</u> (4th ed.). New York: MLA.

I. Article from a journal

>Emig, J. (1977). Writing as a mode of learning. <u>College Composition and Communication, 28,</u> 122–128.

[Do not put quotes around article titles. Capitalize all important words in journal or magazine titles.]

OTHER SOURCES

J. Personal or telephone interview:
Not cited in Reference list, only within your paper.

K. Article from a specialized dictionary or encyclopedia:
Treat as an article in a collection (item F above).

ELECTRONIC SOURCES

L. Article from a journal

[Cite the following information: Author. (Year). Title. *Journal Title* [Type of medium], *volume* (issue), paging or indicator of length. Available Protocol (e.g., HTTP): Site/Path/File [Access date].]

Inada, K. (1995). A Buddhist response to the nature of human rights. Journal of Buddhist Ethics [Online], 2, 9 paragraphs. Available HTTP: http://www.cac.psu.edu/jbe/twocont.html [1995, June 21].

M. Article from a magazine

[Cite the following information: Author. (Year, month, day). Title. *Magazine Title* [Type of medium], *volume* (if given), paging or indicator of length. Available Protocol (e.g., HTTP): Site/Path/File [Access date].]

Viviano, F. (1995, May/June). The new Mafia order. Mother Jones Magazine [Online], 72 paragraphs. Available HTTP: http://www.mojones.com/MOTHER_JONES/MJ95/viviano.html [1995, July 17].

N. Article from a newspaper

[Cite the following information: Author. (Year, month day). Title. *Newspaper Title* [Type of medium], paging or indicator of length. Available: Supplier/Database name (Database identifier or number, if available)/Item or accession number [Access date].]

Howell, V., Carlton, B. (1993, August 29). Growing up tough: New Generation fights for its life: Inner-city youths live by rule of vengeance. Birmingham News [CD-ROM], p. 1A(10 pp.). Available: 1994 SIRS/SIRS 1993 Youth/Volume 4/ Article 56A [1995, July 16].

O. Article from an encyclopedia

[Cite this information: Author/editor. (Year). Title. In *Source* (edition), [Type of medium]. Producer (optional). Available Protocol (e.g., HTTP): Site/Path/File [Access Date].]

Daniel, R. T. (1995). The history of Western music. In <u>Britannica online: Macropaedia</u> [Online]. Available HTTP: http://www.eb.com:180/cgi-bin/g:DocF=macro/5004/ 45/0.html [1995, June 14].

An APA References List

Following is a References list for the Melnick article illustrating APA style.

NOTE: *Normally, as with the MLA example of a Works Cited list on pages 215–216, the References list in a research paper would begin on a new page.*

References

Bredemeier, B. J., Shields, D., Weiss, M., & Cooper, B. (1986). The relationship of sport involvement with children's moral reasoning and aggressive tendencies. <u>Journal of Sport Psychology, 8,</u> 304–318.

Curry, T. J. (1990, November 7). <u>Fraternal bonding in the locker room: A dramaturgical analysis of talk about competition and women.</u> Paper presented at the 10th Annual Conference of the North American Society for the Sociology of Sport, Denver, CO.

End the cover-up of campus crime. (1991, March 14). <u>USA Today,</u> 12A.

Eskenazi, G. (1990, June 3). The male athlete and sexual assault. <u>The New York Times,</u> Section 8, 1.

Ex-SU recruit indicted on sex charges. (1991, February 16). <u>Democrat and Chronicle</u> (Rochester), 1A.

Kidd, B. (1987). Sports and masculinity. In M. Lautman (Ed.), <u>Beyond patriarchy: Essays by men on pleasure, power, and change</u> (250–265). Toronto: Oxford University Press.

Leavy, J. (1990). <u>Squeeze Play.</u> New York: Doubleday.

Messner, M. (1990a). Boyhood, organized sports, and the construction of masculinities. <u>Journal of Contemporary Ethnography, 18,</u> 416–444.

Messner, M. (1990b). When bodies are weapons: Masculinity and violence in sport. <u>International Review for the Sociology of Sport, 25,</u> 203–220.

Neimark, J. (1991, May). Out of bounds: The truth about athletes and rape. <u>Mademoiselle,</u> 196–199.

Reed, W. F. (1990, September 3). Don't hang it on coaches. <u>Sports Illustrated,</u> 138.

Sex-for-athletes, grade-fixing schemes reported at SMU. (1987, March 24). <u>Democrat and Chronicle</u> (Rochester), 4D.

Toufaxis, A. (1990, August 6). Sex and the sporting life. <u>Time,</u> 77.

Weiberg, S. (1991, February 21). Campus crime study not kind to athletes. <u>USA Today,</u> 2C.

Weir, T. (1990, May 17). Athletes must play by society's rules. <u>USA Today,</u> 3C.

Part Three

A Handbook for Improving Your Writing

In this section of the book, we give advice about matters smaller than your essay as a whole. If you feel (or your instructor feels) that your paragraph development, sentence style, or word choice is less proficient than it could be, Part Three is the place to turn. Here you will find chapters devoted specifically to paragraphs, sentences, and words aimed to help you refine and improve your writing at these levels.

This section also includes information that we all wish we knew instinctively—but most of us need to look up. Chapter 13 provides a short background in grammar, since you may have had other things on your mind in junior high school. The "A to Z Guide to Revising and Editing" (Chapter 14) is just what it sounds like: an alphabetized handbook where you can easily look up your instructor's markings on your draft. You can also use it as a reference while you write. For example, if you are trying to decide whether you need a colon or a semicolon, look up both *colon* and *semicolon,* and check out the rules you find listed under each entry. Finally, the "Glossary of Usage" (Chapter 15) gives sample sentences showing the differences in meaning among similar words, such as *except* and *accept.* The Glossary, which is alphabetized for easy reference, will also answer questions such as, "Is it all right to use *you* in a paper?" and "How can I avoid sexist language?"

Chapter Ten

Writing Proficient Paragraphs

Defining the term *paragraph* is next to impossible unless you know the southern word *mess,* a unit of measure meaning "just the right amount of something"—as in "a *mess* of fried chicken" or "a *mess* of black-eyed peas." Once you know this word, we can explain that a paragraph is a mess of sentences about a single topic. Occasionally, though, for rhetorical reasons, a paragraph may be a single sentence, perhaps a single word. You see how tricky a simple definition can be.

Understanding the Basic Paragraph

Scarcely anyone is likely to ask you to *define* a paragraph; the important thing is to be able to *write* one that is unified, coherent, and complete. The average paragraph runs from about 100 words to 150 words—somewhat longer in formal writing, considerably shorter in newspaper stories where the small type in narrow columns requires frequent breaks to avoid eye strain and make for easier reading. In fact, writing specialist William Zinsser declares that "Short paragraphs put air around what you write and make it look inviting, whereas one long chunk of type can discourage the reader from even starting to read." Certainly, introductions and conclusions tend to be brief, but we'll get around to those after laying down some guidelines for writing solid, basic body paragraphs.

Making the Topic Clear

Every paragraph you write is going to be about something: It will describe something, question something, demand something, define something, reject something. That "something" can be identified in a topic sentence. Although professional writers do not always employ topic sentences, academic writers usually do. As a student, you will be wise to use them because instructors frequently expect them. They make your train of thought easier to follow.

Keeping the Ideas Unified

Topic sentences also serve to unify the ideas within the paragraph. Every idea, each detail in the paragraph, should relate to the idea mentioned in the topic sentence. And, as Mark Twain cautioned, "When in doubt, take it out."

If, for instance, you decide to write a paragraph about the undeserved good reputation of dogs, you might begin with this topic sentence: "Far from being our best friends, dogs are slow-witted, servile, slobbering beasts seldom deserving of their board and keep." Then you trot out examples of slavish spaniels and doltish Great Danes you have known in order to convince your readers that dogs are more trouble than they are worth. But if you then observe, "Cats are pretty contemptible also," you need a new paragraph. Or else you need to toss that bit of evidence out as being beside the point, the point being whatever idea you committed yourself to in the topic sentence.

You can, of course, broaden the topic sentence if you decide cats are essential to your argument. You can expand the topic sentence to read something like this: "Both dogs and cats are exceedingly disagreeable creatures to have around the house." Now the way is clear to discuss all the skittish cats of your acquaintance as well as those loutish dogs in a comparison/contrast paragraph.

> **REMEMBER:**   *The topic sentence should state the main idea of the paragraph, and all details, explanations, and descriptions in the paragraph should relate to the main idea.*

Adding the Details

A strategy that works for some writers is based on the theory that each sentence in a paragraph stems directly from the sentence before it and in some way responds to it. Thus, adding material in a paragraph becomes a matter of expectation and response: each sentence responds to the one before it as well as providing the expectation (or idea) that the next sentence will relate to. For example, say you begin with the following sentence.

> I encountered several problems when I took my pit bull to obedience school.

Now, ask yourself what your readers will expect from that sentence. They'll want to know about the problems, right? So, you provide the answer, which could be either the beginning of a list of difficulties or an explanation of the first problem. So, you might write:

> The first thing Bowser did was bite the instructor on the ankle.

Now, what do your readers expect? Probably a description of that biting incident, so off you go providing sentences about shredded trouser cuffs, mangled tennis shoes, flared tempers, and threatened lawsuits. After providing a suitable number of details, you will discover that you have written a nicely unified paragraph.

Choose one of the topic sentences below and write a paragraph of about 150 words using the "expectation and response" strategy for paragraph development explained in the preceding sections.

1. My "bargain" used car caused me no end of trouble in my first week of ownership.
2. When I offered to build a fire at our campsite, I thought I could have it roaring in about five minutes.
3. I know that claustrophobia is all in the mind, but, even so, I feel panic coming on when I'm in a closed space. [Substitute your own favorite phobia.]
4. If I'm having trouble getting started writing, I go through a few familiar rituals.
5. Since I am by nature a night person, having to get up at six in the morning brings out the worst in me.

PARAGRAPH
DEVELOPMENT
EXERCISE

10.1

Placing the Topic Sentence

You do not always have to make the topic sentence the first one in the paragraph—even though we think it may be the best place to put it when writing for college classes. You should become familiar, though, with the various ways of placing topic sentences so that your writing will exhibit a pleasing variety, when variety is appropriate.

At the Beginning

If you place your topic sentences at the start of each paragraph, your readers can grasp the outline of your essay just by glancing at the topic sentences—an arrangement that makes for clarity and rapid reading. We recommend this as the best way to position your topic sentences whenever you write *to inform* or *to explain,* as in writing on-the-job reports, directions, term papers, and essay exams.

Many paragraphs start out with the topic sentence, followed by examples, illustrations, explanations, evidence, or details, as in the following examples. (Topic sentences are set in boldface type.)

> **Among his colleagues at the Public Broadcasting Service, Moyers's obsession for the texture of language is a matter of legend.** Moyers revises. He edits. He revises again, tuning even the most functional introductory sentence until it resonates. You don't watch a Bill Moyers PBS special as much as you listen to it.
>
> —Ron Powers

At the End

Any time you develop a paragraph using *inductive reasoning* (gathering specific evidence and examples from which you draw a conclusion), the topic sentence will quite naturally come at the end, as in the following.

> In my mother's sun-belt apartment building, where the cost of utilities is included in the rent, air conditioners hum steadily, even when open windows would do the trick. "Why not?" they say. "The landlord's paying for it." City housing agencies around the country will tell you that the way to get tenants to conserve is to individually meter apartments. **It is amazing how much less of anything people will require when they have to pay the bill.**
>
> —Bernard Sloan

At the Beginning and the End

Occasionally, writers reinforce the ideas in a paragraph by restating the topic sentence—in different words, of course—at the end.

> **I've always been amazed at the nurturing emotional support that my wife can seek and return with her close female friends.** Often the most intimate

problems are shared and therefore diminished through empathy. Her three-hour talks with friends refresh and renew her far more than my 3-mile jogs restore me. **In our society it seems as if you've got to have a bosom to be a buddy.**

—Eliot Engel

Implying the Topic Sentence

Sometimes, especially in narrative and descriptive writing, you can get by just fine without a topic sentence because all the details in the paragraph relate to an idea that is easily understood by your readers. Occasionally an idea discussed in one paragraph is continued in the next, with the topic remaining quite clear. In the following narrative paragraph, the writer gives us the words of Cesar Chavez.

> There was this young waitress again. With either her boyfriend or someone close, because they were involved in conversation. And there was this familiar sign again, but we paid no attention to it. She looked up at us and sort of—it wasn't what she said, it was just a gesture. A sort of gesture of total rejection. Her hand, you know, and the way she turned her face away from us. She said: "Whattaya want?" So we told her we'd like to buy two hamburgers. She sort of laughed, a sarcastic sort of laugh. And she said, "Oh, we don't sell to Mexicans. Why don't you go across to Mexican town, you can buy 'em over there." And then she turned around and continued her conversation.

—Studs Terkel

Notice that the paragraph has unity, even though the topic sentence is unstated. All the details support the implied idea: "One day I experienced discrimination firsthand." Certainly the paragraph would not be improved by adding that sentence. It would be overkill.

REMEMBER: *All your paragraphs must achieve the simple, essential unity that comes from having every sentence relate to the idea in the topic sentence—even if your topic sentence is only implied.*

In each of the following paragraphs, identify the topic sentence and explain why you think it is placed where it is. If there are two topic sentences, one at the beginning and one at the end, explain why the writer uses both. If the topic sentence is implied, compose one to fit the material.

DISCUSSION
EXERCISE

10.2

1. The history of medicine is replete with accounts of drugs or modes of treatment that were in use for many years before it was recognized that they did more harm than good. For centuries, for example, doctors believed that drawing blood from patients was essential for rapid recovery from virtually every illness. Then, midway through the nineteenth century, it was discovered that bleeding served to weaken the patient. King Charles II's death is believed to have been caused in part by administered bleedings. George Washington's death was also hastened by the severe loss of blood resulting from this treatment.

    —Norman Cousins

2. "Man the Killer" and "Woman the Peacemaker" are symbols of two potentials in human nature. By focusing on the men in power who make war (and the men in armies who fight), we overlook the women who support and endorse war, making it possible. By focusing on male violence, we overlook the men who promote pacifism and negotiation. By regarding aggressiveness as an entrenched and exclusively male quality, and pacifism as an inherent feminine quality, we overlook the ways in which societies in turmoil create dangerous, violent men, and we conveniently forget that most of the great pacifists and reformers in history have been men. Archetypes are not blueprints; flesh-and-blood men and women conform to them in only the most general of ways.

    —Carol Tavris

3. Joint by joint, line by line, pill by pill, the use of illegal drugs on the job has become a crisis for American business. Football players do it, Hollywood stars do it, doctors do it—but you knew that. The more frightening development is that drugs have moved into airline hangars and chemical plants, textile mills and construction sites, boardrooms, courtrooms, newsrooms and nuclear plants: last week the Nuclear Regulatory Commission announced that 21 guards at the San Onofre nuclear facility in California had been suspended for suspected drug use. Companies of all sizes all around the country—General Motors in Detroit, Compugraphic in Wilmington, Mass., Humphrey & Associates in Dallas—all are being jolted by a dramatic amount of drug use among perfectly respectable, well-dressed people.

    —"Taking Drugs on the Job," *Newsweek*

4. It is taken for granted in country music that "men will be men" and "women will be women." In "I Can't Be Myself," Merle Haggard implies he'll be leaving a woman who wants him to change. George Jones demands, "Take Me As I Am," and Billy Ed Wheeler says straight out, "If you're expectin' me to change my old ways for the new / Baby, don't hold your breath until I do." Dottie West, however, is pictured on one of her album covers as a paper doll about to be cut out by a huge pair of scissors held by a big male hand ("Take your scissors and take your time / And cut along the dotted line"). She begs her man to keep his scissors in hand

and trim her edges now and then, and "Fit me in with all your plans / For I want to be what I'm cut out to be."

—Ann Nietzke

5. Beyond the road where the snakes sunned themselves was a dense young thicket, and through it a dim-lighted path led a quarter of a mile; then out of the dimness one emerged abruptly upon a level great prairie which was covered with wild strawberry plants, vividly starred with prairie pinks, and walled in on all sides by forests. The strawberries were fragrant and fine, and in the season we were generally there in the crisp freshness of the early morning, while the dew-beads still sparkled upon the grass and the woods were ringing with the first song of the birds.

—Mark Twain

Developing the Ideas Fully

The topic sentence states the main idea in each paragraph. To develop that main idea, you supply facts, figures, examples, and illustrations—in short, *concrete details*—that pertain to your topic sentence. You say that riding motorcycles is dangerous; then you show how you know this to be true. Cite statistics, if you have them, to prove how many cyclists are maimed and killed each year, but never forget that specific examples can be far more convincing than impersonal numbers. Mention the broken noses, the split lips, the fractured femurs, the spurting arteries, the dislocated elbows, the splintered teeth, the crushed pelvises, and your readers may well be convinced of the risk.

Descriptive Details

Descriptive details are usually intended to convey an impression—how something looked, smelled, tasted. They are especially common in eyewitness accounts of experiences, as in the following vivid picture of the plight of Chicago's poor during the Great Depression of the 1930s.

There is not a garbage dump in Chicago which is not diligently haunted by the hungry. Last summer in the hot weather when the smell was sickening and the flies were thick, there were a hundred people a day coming to the dumps, falling on the heap of refuse as soon as the truck had pulled out and digging in it with sticks and hands. They would devour all the pulp that was left on the old slices of watermelon and cantaloupe till the rinds were as thin as paper; and they would take away and wash and cook discarded onions, turnips, and potatoes. Meat is a more difficult matter, but they salvage a good deal of that, too. The best is the butcher's meat which has been frozen and hasn't spoiled. In the case of the other meat, there are usually bad parts that have to be cut out or they scald it and sprinkle it with soda to kill the taste and the smell.

—Edmund Wilson

Factual Details

You can use facts and figures if you have them, as do the writers of these next two paragraphs. The first one uses facts to support the topic sentence at the beginning.

No one change led to the virtual demise of the train robbery. A combination of stronger steel cars, modern law-enforcement techniques, and improved methods of transferring wealth made robbing trains too risky and unrewarding. Other forms of illegal activity in the 20th century occupied men (and a few women) who might have preyed on passenger trains 50 years ago. Bootlegging liquor, for example, seemed to be the 1930s equivalent of blowing up express cars.

—John P. Hankey

The second paragraph is developed by citing figures.

Although the Health Ministry projects that by the year 2002 Japan will have a cumulative total of eighteen thousand people who have AIDS or are HIV-positive, two Japanese epidemiologists who recently published a paper on the subject have reached a very different conclusion. They say that if the number of customers for prostitutes and the rate of condom use stay the same, "the estimated number of HIV-infected persons will reach a million three hundred thousand in 1996, which will result in two hundred and thirty thousand AIDS cases in 2000."

—Stan Sesser

Illustrations and Examples

Most of the time writers use illustrations and examples to flesh out paragraphs. Here is a paragraph developed by using a single illustration.

The case of Chicago accountant Howard F. MacNeil is especially chilling. He was assessed $36,000 personally for the taxes of a corporation that had been one of his clients. MacNeil refused to be bullied into a "compromise" and the IRS, as it had the power to do, without any court proceeding, attached his bank accounts and posted signs around his house proclaiming "KEEP OUT—Property of the US Government." He lost his business and went into debt as he waited years for his case to come to court. At the trial he was completely vindicated, but in the meanwhile the IRS had completely ruined him.

—Blake Fleetwood

This next paragraph includes a wealth of examples, all pertaining to the opening topic sentence.

On Wednesday morning at a quarter past five came the earthquake. A minute later the flames were leaping upward. In a dozen different quarters south of Market Street, in the working-class ghetto, and in the factories, fires started. There was no opposing the flames. There was no organization, no communication. The streets were humped into ridges and depressions and piled with debris of fallen walls. The steel rails were twisted into perpendicular and horizontal angles. The telephone and telegraph systems were disrupted. And the great water mains had burst. All the clever contrivances and safeguards of mankind had been thrown out of gear by thirty seconds' twitching of the earth's crust.

—Jack London

Achieving Unity and Coherence

If you want your writing to be clear and easy to follow, you must not let your readers get confused when you move from one point to the next or when you change the direction of your ideas. The techniques you can employ to make your writing *coherent*, to make it hang together, are fairly simple, yet they can often mean the difference between a first-rate essay and a merely passable one.

Stay in the Same Tense

No matter how skillfully you weave your sentences together, you will lose that smooth coherence if you carelessly change tenses without good reason. You may write in either present or past tense, depending on how you approach your material. This sentence, for instance, is written in present tense.

Scotty <u>is playing</u> a great game.

Past tense would be

> Scotty <u>was playing</u> a great game last night.

or

> Scotty <u>had been playing</u> well until he got hurt.

There is a good bit of variety within the two tenses, which we won't go into now, but the thing to remember is this: Pick either present or past tense and stay with it unless you have reason to change. Here is an example of a faulty tense switch.

> *(faulty)*   Scotty <u>was racing</u> toward the basket when suddenly he <u>is fouled</u>. He <u>whirled</u> and <u>shoots</u>, while the fans <u>roared</u>.

There is no call for the change from past to present tense. If Scotty *was racing,* then he also *was fouled* and he *shot.* You can, of course, switch tenses if you want to indicate a change occurring in time.

> Scotty <u>was angry</u> about the referee's call at first, <u>but now</u> he <u>says</u> it <u>was</u> fair.

Be sure to check when you edit your final draft to be sure you have not mixed tenses without meaning to.

Use Transitions

The main principle of good coherence lies in providing transitions—posting verbal signs to show your readers that you are moving to another point. The indention of a new paragraph does this visually, but indenting could also mean that you are going to expand on the same idea. And often your thought changes direction in midparagraph when organizing a comparison or when adding examples or mentioning exceptions.

So you need signals. These can be as pointed as *"Next, let us consider,"* or *"On the other hand, we must not overlook,"* or *"A related point is."* These are fairly obvious and formal transitions, but in an appropriate piece of writing, they will do just fine. You will find a number of transitional words neatly classified according to their function in Figure 10.1. Take note of the different types of transitions illustrated; then tuck in a bookmark in case you get stuck and need a transition to help you over a rough spot.

FIGURE 10.1

Useful Transitional Terms

To move to the next major point: *too, moreover, next, in the first place, second, third, again, besides, in addition, further, likewise, finally, also, furthermore, beyond this, admittedly, like*

> Examples: We *also* can see that the quality of most television programs is abysmal.
>
> *Furthermore*, the commercials constantly assault our taste and insult our intelligence.

To add an example: *for example, such as, that is, in the following manner, namely, in this case, as an illustration, for instance, in the same manner, at the same time, in addition*

> Examples: The daytime game shows, *for instance*, openly appeal to human greed.
>
> Soap operas, *in the same manner*, pander to many of our baser instincts.

To emphasize a point: *especially, without doubt, primarily, chiefly, actually, otherwise, after all, as a matter of fact, in fact, without question, even more, more important*

> Examples: The constant violence depicted on television, *in fact*, poses a danger to society.
>
> *Even more* offensive are deodorant commercials, *without question* the most tasteless on TV.

To contrast a point: *but, still, on the other hand, on the contrary, nevertheless, contrary to, however, nonetheless, conversely, yet, although, granted that, in contrast, neither*

> Examples: We abhor the violence, *yet* we cannot approve of censorship.
>
> *Although* commercials may enrage or sicken us, they do, *after all*, pay the bills.
>
> *Granted that* advertising picks up the tab, the deceptiveness of commercials remains indefensible.

To conclude a point: *consequently, so, accordingly, then, as a result, hence, in sum, in conclusion, in other words, thus, before, in short, in other words, finally, at last*

> Examples: Soap operas *thus* contribute to the subtle erosion of moral values.
>
> Commercials, *therefore*, are not worth the sacrifice of our integrity.
>
> Television, *in short*, costs more than society should be willing to pay.

Transitions Between Paragraphs

The transitions that you are most likely to notice are those that link ideas from paragraph to paragraph. Some of the more obvious conventions are not at all difficult to use (*First, Second, In conclusion*), but the more subtle ones require practice.

The "Bob-Type" Transition

An ultra-simple device is recommended by Jessica Mitford in her charming memoir, *A Fine Old Conflict* (1977). She explains that this "invaluable writer's aid consisting of a double space between paragraphs" was perfected by her husband Bob. Mitford testifies that this conspicuous blank space was the only transition her lawyer husband ever used, and that it worked just fine for him. We think, though, it may be a trifle *too* easy. Unless you are a lawyer or writing fiction, use it with caution.

The Rhetorical Question Transition

Another simple way to lead from one point to the next, from paragraph to paragraph, is to pose a rhetorical question and answer it, like this:

> How do we stop people from breeding? First, by not constantly brainwashing the average girl into thinking that motherhood must be her supreme experience. Very few women are capable of being good mothers; and very few men of being good fathers. Parenthood is a gift, as most parents find out too late and most children find out right away. So a change in attitude will help.
>
> —Gore Vidal

This device, useful though it is, will seldom work more than once in a paper. You must have others in stock.

The Short-Sentence Transition

Like the rhetorical question, the short-sentence transition should not be used often but comes in handy when you need it. You simply state briefly and graciously in advance what you intend to discuss next, like this:

> Europeans think more highly of Americans now than they ever did. Let me try to explain why.
>
> —Anthony Burgess

Here's a slightly more formal version (italics added):

> Economics, foreign policy, and some resulting questions of political style all require a special word. *To these matters I now turn.*
>
> —John Kenneth Galbraith

The Echo Transition

Sometimes you can get by without any clearly transitional term at all, if you adopt the echo method. This subtle technique also works within a single paragraph, but first let us show you how to touch on the idea from your previous paragraph as you introduce the idea for your next one. It sounds tricky, but it's worth working on if you want to write fluent, readable prose.

The following examples will show you precisely how it works. In the first example, the final sentence of a paragraph explaining America's fear of Communism in the 1920s is followed by the opening sentence of the next, explaining the reasons for the scare.

> It was an era of lawless and disorderly defense of law and order, of unconstitutional defense of the Constitution, of suspicion and civil conflict—in a very literal sense, *a reign of terror.*
>
> *For this national panic* there was a degree of justification.
>
> —Frederick Lewis Allen

Next, notice the easy transition from a paragraph concentrating on the deafening city noise to the next paragraph suggesting possible relief.

> Reveille is celebrated in New York these frantic days by *the commencement of pneumatic drills.*
>
> The only way to escape *the din of the asphalt bashers* is to move out or up.
>
> —Horace Sutton

Pneumatic drills are, of course, one kind of *asphalt basher.* As in the previous example, the echo is sounded by using a synonym. You can, if you wish, repeat the very same word, as the writer does in the next example.

Nowadays many cities contain block after block of empty stores, silent monuments to the epidemic of *business ripoffs.*

Arson, street crime, *business ripoffs.* They add up to a far more widespread and much more potentially lethal contagion than that of the previous decade.

—Michael Pousner

Transitions Within Paragraphs

This same echoing technique works to achieve coherence within paragraphs as well as between. You will rely on deliberately repeated words and the echo of pronouns as they refer to their antecedents. Most of this echoing happens automatically, but you need to understand the process in case you have to patch up a paragraph.

In the following example, we have set the transitional devices in boldface type and the repeated key term *addict* and the pronouns referring to it in italic type.

> **What to do about drug *addiction?*** I give you two statistics. England with a population of over fifty-five million has eighteen hundred *addicts.* The United States with over two hundred million has nearly five hundred thousand *addicts.* **What are the English doing right that we are doing wrong?** They have turned the problem over to the doctors. An *addict* is required to register with a physician who gives *him* at controlled intervals a prescription so that *he* can buy *his* drug. The *addict* is content. **Best of all,** society is safe. The Mafia is out of the game. The police are unbribed, and the *addict* will not mug an old lady in order to get the money for *his* next fix.
>
> —Gore Vidal

Notice that the third and fourth sentences (both citing statistics) are almost balanced in structure, which helps. And, besides the repetition of the word *addict,* we get echoes from *England . . . English . . . they;* from *United States . . . we . . . society;* and from *doctors . . . physicians . . . who.* Even more subtle are the echoes from *content* and *safe,* words with a similar reassuring meaning.

Another technique common in paragraphs presenting comparisons or contrasts involves putting a transitional term (shown here in boldface) in mid-paragraph.

> American teenagers seem to have inherited the worst of all possible worlds regarding their exposure to messages about sex: movies, music radio and TV

tell them that sex is romantic, exciting, titillating; premarital sex and cohabitation are visible ways of life among the adults they see and hear about; their own parents or their parents' friends are likely to be divorced or separated but involved in sexual relationships. **Yet, at the same time,** young people get the message good girls should say no. Almost nothing that they see or hear about sex informs them about the importance of avoiding pregnancy. For example, they are more likely to hear about abortions than about contraception on the daily TV soap opera. Such messages lead to an ambivalence about sex that stifles communication and exposes young people to increased risk of pregnancy, out-of-wedlock births and abortions.

—Alan Guttmacher Institute Report

Explain how the following paragraph gains coherence through the use of echoes and balanced structure.

DISCUSSION EXERCISE

10.3

> Where, after all, do human rights begin? In small places, close to home—so small that they cannot be seen on any map of the world. Yet they are the world of the individual person: the neighborhood . . . the school or college . . . the factory, farm, or office. Such are the places where every man, woman, and child seeks equal justice, equal opportunity, equal dignity without discrimination. Unless these rights have meaning there, they have little meaning anywhere.
>
> —Eleanor Roosevelt

Composing Special Paragraphs

Not all of your paragraphs are going to conform to the advice we have been giving you about the length and organization of typical paragraphs. Most notably, introductions and conclusions have special requirements, as do brief emphatic paragraphs and transitional paragraphs.

Advice About Introductions

A friend once told Robert Benchley, the humorist, that introductions were easy if you knew how to start. All you had to do was type "The" at the top of the page, and the rest would come by itself. Next morning Benchley tried it. Tap, tap, tap, t-h-e. Nothing came. He thought, he fidgeted, he fretted, he chewed his nails and popped his knuckles. Finally, in exasperation, he typed "hell with it" and abandoned the project.

Unlike Benchley, you cannot afford the luxury of abandonment. But postponing the introduction until you have gathered momentum and are writing at the height of your powers is probably a good idea. Usually you know the main idea of your paper by the time you begin your first rough draft, so put your thesis statement at the top of that blank page and get going. Think about the introduction in spare moments. Solicit divine inspiration, if possible. Something suitable will eventually come to you. Introductions need not be long. Two or three sentences leading up to the thesis will do nicely.

State Your Thesis

Although gaining your readers' attention is an important element of some introductions, the chief function is to let your readers know what the piece of writing is about. You will not always need a straightforward statement of your thesis, but the more formal the writing, the more likely you are to need a clear statement. In the following introduction the writer comes straight to the point.

> Today in the United States there is one profession in which conflict of interest is not merely ignored but loudly defended as a necessary concomitant of the free-enterprise system. That is in medicine, particularly in surgery.
>
> —George Crile Jr.

This whole introductory paragraph consists of only the thesis statement, as the second sentence just concludes the idea begun in the first. It is point-blank as introductions go.

Normally, you would take several sentences to introduce your controlling idea. You could give a little background information or begin with some fairly broad remarks about your subject, then narrow the focus down to the specific idea covered by your thesis. This method is used in the following introduction (thesis statements are italicized throughout this section).

> To her, tight jeans and no bra mean she's in style. To him, they mean she wants to have sex. So it goes among adolescents in Los Angeles, according to a survey by four researchers at U.C.L.A. Despite unisex hair salons, the women's movement, and other signs of equality between the sexes, *boys still read more sexual come-ons into girls' behavior than the girls intend.*
>
> —*Psychology Today*

The article then presents other examples of dress and behavior that are often misinterpreted, just as the introduction promises. Unless you are writing a narrative or developing your material inductively, it's a good strategy to give your readers the main idea of what your essay is going to be about somewhere near the beginning.

Get Your Readers' Attention

Unless you are writing in a business situation where others are required to read what you send them, you need an introduction that will spark your readers' interest in what you have to say. One good way involves putting a picture in their minds, as the writer does in this introduction.

> *Candid Camera* became so much a part of American culture in the 1960s that when a man hijacked a plane that producer Allen Funt was traveling on, the passengers stood and cheered, assuming—incorrectly—that the hijacking was a stunt staged for television. After *Candid Camera*'s seven-year run, CBS canceled it in 1967; *now Funt is not only developing new versions of the show but using old episodes to teach psychology and cure illness.*
>
> —*Newsweek*

The slapstick image of passengers applauding a hijacking is immediately engaging and establishes Funt's status as a celebrity. The last sentence, the thesis, tells the readers what the remainder of the article will be about.

Find Fascinating Facts

You can begin an essay with facts and figures—provided you can produce some real eye-openers.

> In our efforts to combat escalating crime, we have failed to acknowledge an elementary fact: one out of every five adult Americans is functionally illiterate.
>
> A substantial number of violent criminals are in prison for good reasons and should remain there. Yet many can be returned to society without jeopardizing the public's safety; they can even learn to lead useful and productive lives. *A renewed emphasis on literacy in prisons would enhance this prospect.*
>
> —Richard C. Wade

Setting off that first startling fact as a single-sentence paragraph gets our attention and keeps us reading until we arrive at the thesis statement at the end of the next paragraph. Here's another introduction that begins with—of all things—statistics, but they are shocking indeed.

> As the AIDS epidemic begins its second decade, it's time to face some unpleasant realities: AIDS is the number one health problem for men in the United States; it is the leading cause of death of men aged 33 to 45; it has killed more American men than were lost in the Vietnam War.
>
> —Michael S. Kimmel and Martin P. Levine

Begin with a Question

Many writers begin introductions by asking a question:

> *What is intelligence, anyway?* When I was in the army I received a kind of aptitude test that all soldiers took and, against a normal of 100, scored 160. No one at the base had ever seen a figure like that, and for two hours they made a big fuss over me. (It didn't mean anything. The next day I was still a buck private with KP as my highest duty.)
>
> —Isaac Asimov

Notice how handy those rhetorical questions are for sneaking in your main idea. You pose a question, then answer it yourself, and you're off. But be reasonable: Do not use something simpleminded (such as "What is sorority life?" or "Were you ever so mad you could scream?") just because it provides an easy way to get started.

Try a Definition

Another useful way to get started is by defining your subject, like this:

> The Indian and Hispanic people of Arizona and New Mexico eat blue tortillas, tissue-thin blue bread, and a blue milk-drink. *What gives these foods their color and much of their nutritional value is blue corn, a versatile corn that has been raised in the Southwest for centuries.* The farmers who have cultivated it so long have developed it into an extremely drought-tolerant, disease-resistant corn that can be steamed, boiled or roasted in the milk stage, and ground into a delicious meal when mature.
>
> —Richard Flint

Take care to introduce your definition gracefully. Many composition teachers threaten to slash their wrists if they encounter another paper beginning, "According to Webster's dictionary."

Avoid Mindless Generalizations

In your effort to begin with a general observation and narrow that down to a thesis statement, you want to avoid obvious generalizations like these:

Life can be very interesting.

People are funny sometimes.

If you begin with such clichéd observations, your readers may never get beyond the opening sentence.

Advice About Conclusions

Like introductions, conclusions ought to be forceful and to the point. Work especially hard on your last paragraph. Its effectiveness will influence the way your readers react to the whole paper. If you trail off at the end, they will sigh and feel let down. Avoid any sort of apology or hedging at this point. You want an impressive ending, but do not overdo it.

In fact, if you are writing a short paper and have saved your strongest point for the end, you may not need a whole new paragraph to conclude. In the following conclusion, the writer is still providing information and citing statistics. But notice that the last two sentences provide a sense of closure.

> A drug culture is once again emerging on college campuses, despite the existence of draconian mandatory minimums. Twelve years after the current war on drugs was declared, some rough numbers hint at its cost: $30 billion spent so far at the state, federal, and local levels to fight marijuana; two billion dollars' worth of assets seized in marijuana cases; four million Americans arrested for marijuana offenses; a quarter of a million people convicted of marijuana felonies and sent to prison for at least a year. Statistics can only suggest a portion of the truth. As I learned from the families of inmates, the human costs are not so easily measured.
>
> —Eric Schlosser

Echo Your Thesis Statement

What you want in a conclusion is a tidy ending that reinforces the point you set out to make in the beginning. An echo of your thesis statement can be perfect. Consider the conclusion of the article on misinterpreting sexual signals (the introduction appeared on page 244):

> The young people's ethnic backgrounds, ages, and previous dating and sexual experiences had almost no effect on their reactions. The girls' "relatively less-sexualized view of social relationships," the psychologists suggest, "may reflect some discomfort with the demands of the dating scene"; women do, after all, have more to lose from sexual activity, facing risks of pregnancy and/or a bad reputation. The girls in the study were much more likely than the boys to agree with the statement, "Sometimes I wish that guys and girls could just be friends without worrying about sexual relationships."
>
> —*Psychology Today*

The quotation at the end echoes the thesis idea ("boys still read more sexual come-ons into girls' behavior than the girls intend"), restating the thesis in different terms and giving the article a pleasing unity.

Suggest Solutions

If you are writing an analysis or a persuasive piece, a useful closing device involves offering suggestions—possible solutions for problems discussed in the essay. Naturally, this technique is valid only if you can come up with some sound ideas for solving problems. Here is the conclusion to the article suggesting reducing jail terms in exchange for learning to read and write (the introduction is on page 245):

> For such a small investment [in staff and libraries], it is hard to see where the public could get a larger return. It takes $2,000 to teach an adult to read and write: it costs $8,000 to put him on welfare, and $50,000 to put him in jail. What should a prudent society do?
>
> —Richard C. Wade

Although the final sentence is a question, it is clearly intended to lead the reader to agree.

Offer Encouragement

Especially in process writing, in which you are explaining how to do something, it's good to close with a few words of encouragement. Tell your readers how delicious they will find the cheesecake if they follow your instructions carefully. Or tell them how rewarding they will find growing their own tomatoes, as the writer does in this conclusion.

When you shop for tomato seeds or plants this season, consider trying at least one new variety. There are hundreds to choose from and if you keep looking, one of them may find a home in your garden. Even if you find nothing to match your favorite, you'll have fun, and the pleasure of gardening is not just in the eating.

—Mark Kane

Provide Advice

If you have written a paper that allows you to offer advice or a word of warning, you can produce a strong conclusion. An editor for *The Nation,* criticizing an announcement of new party policies, ends with this emphatic sentence:

Following the strategy outlined in this report may leave the Democratic Party flatter than a dead armadillo.

Speculate on the Future

Think about the long-term implications of what you have said in your essay. You might want to conclude by warning of hazards or by suggesting advantages. In the next example, the writer does both, as he argues that Americans need to become bilingual.

The benefits, not only in economic terms but also in terms of enhancing our understanding of other cultures and of ourselves, would be beyond measure. The costs, should we fail to act decisively, could eventually prove to be catastrophic.

—Daniel Shanahan

Advice About Short Paragraphs

Introductions and conclusions tend to be shorter than body paragraphs, but once in a while you may write a truly short paragraph—only one sentence long.

For Emphasis

At once you can see that a single sentence used as a paragraph calls attention to itself by departing from the normal length of a paragraph. Even a fairly long sentence set off as a paragraph will command attention. Consider using this strategy to emphasize a key point, but remember, you cannot use this device often. Its whole impact depends on its being used sparingly.

For Transition

If you are writing a long piece, you may need a short paragraph of pure transition—a sort of verbal bridge to get you from one main idea to the next. Vincent P. Norris, writing in *Media and Consumer,* establishes that in this country more money is spent on advertising than on higher education. Then he sets off a couple of rhetorical questions as a transitional paragraph.

What did we get for our money? Who knows?

In the next paragraph he begins to speculate on the answer.

Keep in mind that setting off a sentence gives your transition more emphasis than just attaching it to the next paragraph. Most of the time you will want to tuck your transitions within regular paragraphs.

Chapter Eleven

Writing Effective Sentences

Historian Barbara Tuchman says that "Nothing is more satisfying than to write a good sentence." But as writer Katherine Anne Porter points out, "Most people don't realize that writing is a craft. You have to take your apprenticeship in it like anything else." Crafting clear, interesting sentences takes time and effort. This chapter offers techniques to help you construct good sentences and revise those that aren't so good.

Developing a Mature Style

Just as choosing lively details will improve your writing, so will creating more interesting sentence structures. If too many of your sentences follow the same simple pattern, you should try sentence combining. If you notice that you are repeating words needlessly (often at the end of one sentence and the beginning of the next), sentence combining can eliminate the problem and add variety to your writing at the same time.

Sentence combining involves turning two or more sentences into one by tucking the less important ideas and details into subordinate or modifying positions. We will now explain how this process works.

Using Coordination and Subordination

In speaking and writing we link ideas together in various ways. *Coordination* involves giving essentially equal importance to two or more words, phrases, or clauses, often connecting them with *and* or *but*. But excessive coordination can be tedious.

> I was born in Iowa but grew up in the Chicago area, and I took my first trip to the Loop with my friends Casey and Linda, and we spent the whole day walking around the city and visiting the Art Museum and watching the boats on the lake and . . .

This is the way small children talk, with little variety, few modifiers, and no distinction between important ideas and passing details.

By the time we reach the third grade or so, we learn to use more complicated patterns, which employ *subordination* as well as coordination. Subordination lets us create different levels of importance. We can express major ideas in *independent* clauses and downplay other points by embedding them in *dependent* clauses, phrases, or single words. If you are in doubt about what makes a clause dependent or independent, Figure 11.1 will help you to review the differences.

Most of us subordinate details and ideas automatically. For example, what if we wanted to incorporate the following ideas into a single sentence?

> I baked a cake. I did it this afternoon. It fell. It was flat.

Scarcely giving the matter a thought, we would write:

> I baked a cake this afternoon and it fell flat.

But we might then tighten up the sentence this way:

> The cake that I baked this afternoon fell flat.

In the revision, we stressed the main idea in the independent clause—"The cake . . . fell flat"—and tucked the less important information about when the cake was baked into a dependent (adjective) clause—"that I baked this afternoon."

Combining Choppy Sentences

Too many short sentences, one after another, make your prose sound choppy. When you discover that you have written two or three short sentences beginning with the same word—or with a pronoun referring to that word—you may do well to combine the sentences. You have a number of techniques at your disposal. We will begin with some very simple ones.

FIGURE 11.1

*Kinds of
Clauses*

Clause: **a group of related words containing a subject and verb.**

1. *An independent (main) clause* has a subject and a verb and is not introduced by a subordinating word. It stands alone as an independent
sentence.

> *subject + verb:* The writer's style changes.

> *subject + verb + completer:* The writer's style changes the reader's
> point of view.

2. *A dependent (subordinate) clause* is an incomplete sentence that depends
on an independent clause to complete its meaning.

> A. A *noun clause* is used as a noun:

>> The author writes *what she believes.* (direct object)

>> *Whatever she writes* sounds sincere. (subject)

> B. An *adjective clause* modifies a noun or pronoun:

>> The essay *that I liked best* made its point humorously.

>> I did not like Randall's essay, *which was too long.*

> An adjective clause is introduced by a relative pronoun:
> *who, which, that, whose, whom.*

> C. An *adverb clause* modifies a verb, adjective, or adverb:

>> *After we read the essays,* we argue about them.

>> We can't discuss them rationally *because we're nervous.*

> An adverb clause is introduced by a subordinating conjunction:
> *after, although, as, as if, because, before, if, since, so as, as far as, so that,
> than, though, till, unless, until, when, whenever, while, whereas.*

(For more details on clauses, see pages 309–313.)

1. You can compress a simple sentence into a single word.

> A. *As an adjective:*

>> Doris bought a motorcycle.

>> It was maroon.

> Doris bought a maroon motorcycle.

B. *As a compound adjective:*

Fred is cleaning our yard.

The yard is cluttered with trash.

Fred is cleaning our trash-cluttered yard.

C. *As an adverb:*

Carmen conferred with her supervisor.

It was a brief conference.

Carmen conferred briefly with her supervisor.

D. *As a participle* (**a descriptive word ending in** *-ing, -ed,* **or** *-en*)**:**

(*-ing*)   Sam stirred the soup.

It was boiling.

Sam stirred the boiling soup.

(*-ed/-en*)   Monica has a sore wrist and a bad ankle.

She sprained one and broke the other.

Monica has a sprained wrist and a broken ankle.

E. *As a gerund* (**an** *-ing* **word that names an action**)**:**

Many people are on diets these days.

It has become a fad.

Dieting has become a fad with many people these days.

2. You can turn a whole sentence into a phrase.

A. *A prepositional phrase:*

Larry sets tile.

He takes great care and patience.

Larry sets tile with great care and patience.

B. *An appositive phrase:*

Dr. Cooley is a pioneer in transplant surgery.

He is a famous heart specialist.

Dr. Cooley, a famous heart specialist, is a pioneer in transplant surgery.

C. *A participle phrase:*

(*-ing*)   The TV movie was a sentimental tearjerker.

Lassie was the star.

The TV movie starring Lassie was a sentimental tearjerker.

(*-ed/-en*)   Candidates are swayed by flattery.

They promise victory at receptions.

Self-serving backers give the receptions.

Candidates swayed by flattery promise victory at receptions given by self-serving backers.

D. *A gerund phrase:*

Carlos works second shift.

He finds it difficult.

Working second shift is difficult for Carlos.

E. *An infinitive phrase* (**a phrase with** *to* **+ a verb**):

The test will be given on Tuesday.

It measures proficiency in writing.

The test to measure proficiency in writing will be given on Tuesday.

3. You can form clauses using *who, whom, whose, which, that, when,* **or** *where.*

A. *Who:*

Psychologists are studying the effects of malnutrition on intelligence.

They work with children.

Psychologists who work with children are studying the effects of malnutrition on intelligence.

B. *Whom:*

Nadene will be my new office mate.

I barely know her.

Nadene, whom I barely know, will be my new office mate.

C. *Whose:*

I want to invite Mickey.

I enjoy her company.

I want to invite Mickey, whose company I enjoy.

D. *Which:*

Marita fixed our radio.

It now works perfectly.

Our radio, which Marita fixed, now works perfectly.

E. *That:*

Nintendo is a madness.

It strikes adolescent boys.

Nintendo is a madness that strikes adolescent boys.

F. *When:*

You must wait till Tuesday.

The results of the audition will be posted then.

You must wait till Tuesday, when the results of the audition will be posted.

G. *Where:*

The town is known for its iris gardens.

I was born there.

The town where I was born is known for its iris gardens.

Skillful writers often use several of these techniques to craft a fluent, sophisticated sentence. With practice you can soon be doing the same. But remember: clarity remains the most important goal of expository writing. Do not get so enthusiastic in your use of subordination that you try to compress too much into a single sentence and obscure the meaning.

SENTENCE
COMBINING
EXERCISE

11.1

Combine each group of short sentences into one complex sentence. Put the most important idea into the main clause, eliminate needless repetition, and subordinate less important ideas as single-word modifiers, phrases, and dependent clauses. We will do the first one to be sure you have the idea.

1. The university dismissed the coach.
   The coach had questionable recruiting practices.
   The NCAA had questioned them.

   The university dismissed the coach whose recruiting practices the NCAA had questioned.

2. The drug epidemic is a cancer.
   It threatens the nation's survival.

3. The new Thunderbird features a button.
   The button is mounted on the console.
   It controls the suspension setting.

4. Senior citizens come to the clinic.
   They have suffered strokes.
   They come for speech therapy.

5. A firm has developed a computer keyboard.
   The keyboard relieves wrist pressure.
   The firm is in Miami.

6. The sociologist searched for materials.
   The materials describe the experiences of young women.
   The young women go through these experiences during adolescence.

The following sentences were written by students. Combine each pair into a single, concise sentence. Compare your combined sentences with those of your classmates.

SENTENCE
COMBINING
EXERCISE

11.2

1. The second type of day is a blah day. Most days, especially in the middle of the semester, fall into this category.

2. While the goals of music therapy are nonmusical, the activities prescribed to reach these goals are musical. Musical activities include singing, listening, playing instruments, writing songs, and dancing.

3. People should learn to profit from their mistakes. My sister-in-law makes the same mistakes over and over and never seems to learn anything from them.

4. One can approach this problem in two ways. Each approach has significant drawbacks.

5. The woman who lived next to us was Mrs. Wilding. She was a sensible woman who did her best with too little money.

6. My grandfather told me about a Christmas during the depression. For Christmas, each of the children in the family received only a banana or an orange from Santa Claus.

7. Kate Chopin wrote a short story called "The Storm." As the title suggests, the story is about a savage storm and shows how the characters respond to the storm.

8. I decided to stop living in the past. It was time to start looking toward my future once again.

9. On August 27, 1966, Sir Francis Chichester set out in a fifty-three-foot boat. He intended to sail the boat singlehandedly around the world.

10. Some movie stars become Hollywood playboys. Nick Nolte has resisted this.

The following sentences have been decombined from a paragraph by author Maya Angelou. Read through the entire passage; then, combining sentences, create a paragraph that is fluent and concise. You will probably not combine these repetitive sentences in exactly the same way that Angelou originally wrote them (she used only four sentences), but try to produce a version that you consider smooth and free from needless repetition.

> Lafayette County Training School was unlike the White high school.
> Lafayette County distinguished itself in several ways from the White high school.
> It had no lawn or hedges.
> It didn't have tennis courts or climbing ivy.
> There were two buildings.
> One held the main classrooms.
> The other contained the grade school and home economics.
> The buildings were set on a dirt hill.
> There was no fence to limit the school's boundaries.
> There was no limit to the boundaries of the bordering farms either.
> There was a large expanse to the left of the school.
> It was used as a baseball diamond.
> The diamond had to be unoccupied.
> Alternately, it was used as a basketball court.
> There were rusty hoops on swaying poles.
> They represented the permanent recreational equipment.
> But bats and balls could be borrowed from the P.E. teacher.
> The borrower had to be qualified.

Here is a list of traits supposedly possessed by people who are born under the astrological sign of Aquarius. Write a description of Aquarians that includes all these traits. Try to get all the information into three sentences.

> extremely open-minded about all things
> try not to judge other people
> believe that everyone has the right to lead his or her own life
> honesty and friendliness make them very popular
> thought by some people to be eccentric
> patient and pay attention to detail
> make good lawyers and scientists

Practicing with Models

Professional writers often consciously work at perfecting sentence structure by imitating effective passages from their reading. Writers as diverse as Ben Jonson, Benjamin Franklin, Robert Louis Stevenson, Abraham Lincoln, Winston Churchill, and Somerset Maugham all practiced during their apprentice years by copying and imitating selections from accomplished stylists.

To begin model imitation, you should select a sentence or short paragraph you admire (or one that we have chosen for you) and copy it precisely—right down to the commas, semicolons, dashes, and periods. Next, examine the model to discover how it is put together. What are the linguistic devices that shape it? For instance, does it use phrases or clauses in series? (If your memory about phrases and clauses needs refreshing, see p. 307.) Does it depend on deliberate repetition of some word or element? Does it provide a number of details or examples? Does it arrange points in order of increasing importance, building to a forceful point at the end?

After you discover the form, imitate it in a sentence using your own words and subject matter. Then, write more sentences just like it, changing the ideas each time. To achieve a lasting effect on your own prose, you must reproduce each model repeatedly—just as you would practice a melody while learning to play a musical instrument.

In the following simple example, music critic Michael Kernan describes the celebrated conductor, Leopold Stokowski.

> Again he clapped, the dry-handed clap that by now commanded instant attention.

The basic structure of this sentence can be illustrated this way:

> Again [main clause], the [noun phrase] that [dependent clause].

Notice that part of the effectiveness of Kernan's sentence depends on the deliberate repetition of the word *clap*. Try to duplicate that repetition when you imitate the pattern. You might come up with a sentence like this:

> Again the alarm went off, the meaningless alarm that sounded every day at this time.

Perhaps you noticed that imitation reverses the usual composing process in which writers begin with an idea and then try to find the best way to say it. But as language specialist Richard Graves points out, "Even though the activity seems alien, it is nevertheless valuable—like the batter swinging a weighted bat or the long-distance runner practicing with weights." When you work with models, you are exercising your language skills.

Developing Variety and Emphasis

In order to become an effective writer, you need a wide assortment of sentence structures at your command. First, you must be able to write straightforward everyday sentences, but you also must be able to come up with impressive sentences to give variety to your writing and emphasis to your important points.

Cumulative Sentences

Most of the time people do not pay much attention to sentence structure as they write. They begin with their main idea and add details until they reach the end of the thought, where they put a period and start in on the next thought. These sentences—like the one we just wrote—are called *cumulative* sentences and make up the bulk of most writing. The following cumulative sentence by George Orwell is typical.

> He was a Hindu, a puny wisp of a man, with a shaven head and vague liquid eyes.

This next longer cumulative sentence, written by essayist Judith Viorst, expands the main idea (having a precious friend) by adding an appositive and a series of *who* clauses.

> I have in my own life a precious friend, a woman of sixty-five who has lived very hard, who is wise, who listens well, who has been where I am and can help me understand it.

SENTENCE MODELING EXERCISE **11.5**	Carefully copy Orwell's sentence. Now write five of your own imitating this model. Then copy Viorst's sentence, and write three imitations of it. Try to choose details as effectively as Orwell and Viorst do. Compare your sentences with those of several classmates.

Periodic Sentences

Unlike cumulative sentences, which begin with the main idea, *periodic* sentences open with modifiers and withhold the main idea until the end. You can see the difference in this pair of sentences:

Cumulative: The bird sailed for hours, searching the blanched grasses below him with his telescopic eyes, gaining height against the wind, descending in mile-long, gently declining swoops.

— Walter Van Tilberg Clark

Periodic: Searching the blanched grasses below him with his telescopic eyes, gaining height against the wind, descending in mile-long, gently declining swoops, for hours the bird sailed.

Sometimes the meaning of a periodic sentence is not revealed until its very last word, as in these examples.

The memory of how apprehensive we were at the beginning is still strong.

— E. B. White

The only completely consistent people are dead.

— Aldous Huxley

Notice how the force of these sentences is diminished when we alter their structure.

The memory is still strong of how apprehensive we were at the beginning.

Only dead people are completely consistent.

Another common type of periodic sentence involves setting up the reader's expectations with background details at the beginning and then delivering the main idea in the final clause, as sports writer Murray Ross does here:

The pitcher's windup, the anticipatory crouch of the infielders, the quick waggle of the bat as it poises for the pitch—these subtle miniature movements are as meaningful as the home runs and the strikeouts.

You can see that you could not effectively use that unusual structure very often. Save periodic sentences to achieve variety, to emphasize a point, to round out a paragraph, or to conclude an essay.

SENTENCE
COMBINING
EXERCISE

11.6

Working individually or with another student, combine the information from each group of sentences below into a single emphatic sentence similar to the periodic sentences written by Walter Clark and Murray Ross. Remember to build to the most important idea at the end.

1. Eleanor showed great patience and courage.
   She had to take care of her little brother.
   Her mother was in the hospital.
   Her father was on the edge of a nervous breakdown.

2. Manuel went to Chicago last Tuesday.
   I went with him.
   We took the train.
   We were going to the Art Institute.
   There was a Monet exhibit there.

3. Two cars collided.
   The accident occurred on Saturday afternoon.
   It was at the intersection of Lincoln and University.
   The light was just changing.
   The dark blue car failed to stop.

4. Lucinda ran to him.
   She threw her aims around him.
   She kissed him passionately.
   Her skirt was fanning out behind her.
   Her cheeks were glowing.
   She ran ecstatically.

5. Michele and I made chicken spaghetti.
   We made it for Jamal's birthday.
   It took us two hours.
   We chopped the vegetables.
   We diced the cheese.
   We steamed the spaghetti.
   We served it in an elegant casserole.
   We forgot to put in the chicken.

Balanced Sentences

Another way to make your meaning emphatic and clear is to use *balanced* (or *parallel*) sentences. Balanced sentences depend on deliberate repetition—

sometimes of the same words, always of the same grammatical structures: phrases, clauses, sometimes whole sentences. We all remember Abraham Lincoln's "of the people, by the people, and for the people," even if we have forgotten the rest of the Gettysburg Address.

Balanced sentences create a forceful impression. They are particularly effective for showing contrasts and emphasizing choices, as these examples illustrate:

> To be French is to be like no one else; to be American is to be like everyone else.
>
> —Peter Ustinov

> Mankind must put an end to war, or war will put an end to mankind.
>
> —John F. Kennedy

In this next example, writer Nora Ephron's repetition of the same sentence three times accentuates her astonishment at being favorably impressed by a famous woman she expected to dislike.

> I did not expect to find her charming, and I did not expect to find her canny, and I certainly did not expect to find her moving. All of which she was.

Practical Patterns

Nora Ephron's pattern of pointed repetition and reversal, although forceful, is perhaps too dramatic to be useful in the kind of everyday writing that is appropriate for reports, case studies, proposals, business letters, and the like. Here is a more practical sentence composed by writing specialist Richard Lloyd-Jones that achieves the same emphatic purpose.

> The point, however, is not so much discovering the new but noticing the old.

The ability to write such sentences in which you emphasize an idea through contrast with another is essential to good writing of any kind.

Another practical use of balanced structure involves putting items in series. This sentence by George Orwell illustrates the basic technique:

> At each step his muscles slid neatly into place, the lock of hair on his scalp danced up and down, his feet printed themselves on the wet gravel.

Although the series elements in Orwell's sentence vary in length and precise structure, the repetition of the same basic pattern (determiner/noun/verb)

guides the reader through the description. A series of parallel structures is always an efficient way to present several important points in a single sentence, as
this example demonstrates:

> Medical researchers are trying to learn what causes the infection, how it
> enters the bloodstream, and whether it can be controlled.

SENTENCE
MODELING
EXERCISE

11.7

1. Carefully copy the sentence by Richard Lloyd-Jones. The structure is essentially
this:

The _____, however, is not _____
_____ but _____.

Write five sentences following this model, beginning with "The issue" or "The
problem" or "The reason," or follow the model by specifically stating your point,
your issue, or your problem, like this:

> The major problem with health care in this country is not the high cost but
> the lack of reasonable access.

2. Copy the sentences by Peter Ustinov, John F. Kennedy, and George Orwell. Write
two or three imitations of each one. Compare your sentences with those of your
fellow students.

Deliberate Repetition

We have, of course, been discussing deliberate repetition since the beginning of this chapter in our advice about balanced structure. But occasionally
you may want to repeat the same word for emphasis, as Edward Lawry does in
this rhetorical question.

> How are athletes true members of the student body when they have special
> computers, special tutors, special dorms, special food, special enrollment pro-
> cedures, and special counselors?

One caution, though, about repeating words: Be sure that the word deserves
emphasis, and be doubly sure that you have repeated it on purpose. Do not
allow careless repetition to creep into your sentences. For example:

> Some *child* psychologists claim that exposing a *child* to too much noise in
> the earliest stages of *childhood* can cause the *child* to become hyperactive.

You need to rewrite a sentence like this one to eliminate the annoying repetition of the word *child:*

> Some child psychologists claim that exposing infants to too much noise can cause hyperactivity.

Breaking the Pattern

Several times we have mentioned that you can produce emphasis by doing the unexpected. Part of the effectiveness of balanced structures depends on their being different from the ordinary sentences that people write. Following are several ways to gain emphasis by departing from the usual patterns.

Try a Short, Short Sentence

Really short sentences—from two to six words—are easy to write and catch your readers' attention because they are abrupt. Notice how well educator John Hurt Fisher makes his point in the short sentence that follows the longer one:

> Webster's dictionaries and the endless multiplication of handbooks and courses in English composition represent a desperate effort to prevent class distinction from revealing itself in language. And, of course, it has failed.

Jessie Birnbaum, writing in *Time* magazine, uses the same technique:

> Cavett's purpose was to ensure that I would suffer all the shocks, surprises, pitfalls, and confusions that afflict the host five shows a week. He succeeded.

Working alone or in a small group, combine each group of sentences below into one long sentence followed by an emphatic short sentence. Be sure to choose the most important or surprising idea for the short sentence.

1. My wife trained as a runner last semester.
  She practiced for hours.
  She ran every day.
  She ran in the rain.
  She lost the big race.
  My heart ached for her.

SENTENCE
COMBINING
EXERCISE

11.8

2. Mark has been out of college for years.
He decided he wanted to go to law school.
He wondered if he could get in.
He worried about passing the LSAT.
He scored in the ninety-ninth percentile.

3. Maynard came from Virginia to visit Sue.
They are old friends.
They seldom get to see each other.
They set off the smoke alarm.
Both are heavy smokers.
They talked for several hours.
They heard an ear-splitting sound.

Use Ands to Separate a Series

Most of the time writers use commas to separate items in a series, as Mark Twain does in this sentence:

Drays, carts, men, boys, all go hurrying from many quarters to a common center, the wharf.

Twain's brisk sentence suits the bustle that he is describing. Notice how columnist Ellen Goodman slows the pace in this sentence by replacing the usual commas with *ands:*

We made meals and changed diapers and took out the garbage and paid bills. While other people died.

The extra conjunctions help to convey the deliberate rhythm of everyday life. And the intentional fragment at the end gains shock value from both contrasts—in the rhetoric and in the meaning.

SENTENCE MODELING EXERCISE

11.9

Copy this sentence by biologist Rachel Carson:

A child's world is fresh and new and beautiful, full of wonder and excitement.

Then write a sentence of your own with the same structure. Try to choose a subject that merits emphasis. If you love music, you might write:

The first symphony is joyful and vibrant and sensuous, full of drama and surprise.

If you are an environmentalist, you might come up with something more like:

> The American coyote is threatened by drought and starvation and poisons and rifles, hunted for bounty and faced with extinction.

Repeat the process five times. Compare some of your sentences with the ones your classmates wrote.

Experiment with the Dash

Use dashes to set off material from the rest of a sentence. Because the end of a sentence is an emphatic position, you can use a dash there to good advantage, as philosopher Susan Sontag does:

> In the twentieth century it has become almost impossible to moralize about epidemics—except those which are transmitted sexually.

The dash is most useful for summarizing an idea or adding an explanation, as these examples show:

> That's what revision is—learning how to write.

> In walking, the average adult person employs a motor mechanism that weighs about eighty pounds—sixty pounds of muscle and twenty pounds of bone.

You can also produce considerable emphasis by interrupting the normal flow of your sentence with material set off by dashes, as essayist John McPhee does here:

> It rained all night at Seven Islands—heavily and steadily—but tapered in the early morning to drizzle and mist.

Using dashes to set off material in midsentence can simply be a handy way of slipping in a definition or some other important information, as economist Milton Friedman does:

> The real interest rate—the difference between the nominal rate and the rate of inflation—has averaged about three to four percent over long periods.

NOTE: *Like short sentences, dashes lose their emphatic effect if used too often.*

SENTENCE
COMBINING
EXERCISE

11.10

Combine the sentences in each of the following groups into a single sentence using dashes to set off any definitions, explanations, qualifiers, added thoughts, or other material that you think deserves emphasis.

1. Herman has quit smoking again.
   He has quit for the tenth time.

2. Sam took the sergeant's test.
   He took it three times.
   He finally passed it.
   He passed it with flying colors.

3. Cells in some organs suffer constant wear and tear.
   This can happen in the skin or in the intestinal lining.
   These cells grow and multiply all life long.

4. We complained to our printer.
   Some pages of our newsletter were over-inked.
   Some pages were too light.
   The color on some pages was out of register with the black print.
   Out of register means not lined up properly.

5. Putting a spin on an object gives it balance.
   Putting a spin on an object gives it stability.
   The object might be a top, a bullet, a satellite.

CUMULATIVE
SENTENCE
MODELING
EXERCISE

11.11

If you want to be a skilled writer, you will profit from imitating models as much as possible. Here are additional sentences for you to practice on. Copy down the model first; then write as many of your own sentences as you can, carefully imitating the structure of the model. Compare some of your sentences with those of your classmates.

1. Violence is immoral because it thrives on hatred rather than love. (Martin Luther King Jr.)

2. History became popular, and historians became alarmed. (Will Durant)

3. There is much in your book that is original and valuable—but what is original is not valuable, and what is valuable is not original. (Samuel Johnson)

4. No one can be perfectly free till all are free; no one can be perfectly moral until all are moral; no one can be perfectly happy until all are happy. (Herbert Spencer)

5. The care-takers—those who are helpers, nurturers, teachers, mothers—are still systematically devalued. (Ellen Goodman)

Developing Conciseness

All along we have stressed revision as one of the most important parts of the writing process. Now here is some concrete advice about revising and editing your sentences to make them clearer and more vigorous.

Revise for Wordiness

When you revise, try to make your writing clean, clear, and concise. Useless words can clog your sentences and make them hard to follow, like this:

> During the period of time in which Pia was learning the process of desktop publishing, she also discovered the benefits in regard to dealing with her fellow workers with something called thoughtfulness. (32 words)

You can say the same thing more forcefully with fewer words:

> While learning desktop publishing, Pia also learned to be more thoughtful toward her coworkers. (14 words)

Of course, if you edit your sentences too much, they may sound abrupt and awkward:

> Pia, learning desktop publishing, learned thoughtfulness for co-workers.

You want to take out unnecessary words but keep those that are required for your reader's understanding.

Cut Out Filler

Some words and phrases can be deleted without any loss of meaning. As your revise and edit, look for filler that stretches a single word or simple phrase into a wordy expression.

Wordy: The columns must be aligned *in an accurate manner.*

Concise: The columns must be *accurately* aligned.

Wordy: She demonstrated *the way in which to* gather a reliable sample.

Concise: She demonstrated *how to* gather a reliable sample.

Here are some other wordy expressions and their concise equivalents.

Wordy	Concise
regardless of the fact that	although
with regard to	about
in the event that	if
by means of	by
during the time in which	while
as a result of the fact that	because

Roundabout expressions like *it is* and *there is* can also produce wordiness:

Wordy: It is unfortunate that there are some parents who think their children are miniature adults.

Concise: Unfortunately, some parents think their children are miniature adults.

Compare these wordy expressions with some concise alternatives:

Wordy	Concise
It is obvious that	Obviously
There is no doubt that	Undoubtedly
It is probably true that	Probably
It may be that	Perhaps
It is believed by some that	Some people believe

Use Economical Verbs

Strung-out verb phrases, which include nouns and adjectives, are wordy and sound stuffy. Your writing will be clearer and more concise if you choose one-word, direct verbs. Study these examples:

Wordy verb phrase	Economical verb
put the emphasis on	emphasize
make a comparison to	compare
have an understanding of	understand
is reflective of	reflects
give permission to	allow
make an attempt to	try

Eliminate Redundancies

Be on the lookout for a special kind of wordiness called *redundancy,* which means saying the same thing twice—like *completely finished.* Because *finish* means *complete,* you don't need both words. Such phrases can sneak into your writing because they often sound impressive. But pay attention to meaning, and you will notice that the following familiar expressions all repeat the same idea.

absolutely essential	end result	necessary essentials
anticipate in advance	example to illustrate	past memories
audible to the ear	few in number	period of time
basic fundamentals	final outcome	reason is because
combine together	future plans	small in size
complete absence	general consensus	summarize briefly
completely unanimous	green in color	true fact
continue on	join together	various differences

Avoid Needless Repetition

Deliberate repetition, as we have pointed out, can be an effective device, but careless repetition may irritate your readers as much as wordiness. Ineffective repetition is often the result of inattention, as in this student's sentence.

> Walking up to the front door, I came upon the skull of a cow placed next to the front door.

The phrase *to the front door* isn't worth repeating. Revising the first phrase will solve the problem.

> Walking up to the house, I came upon the skull of a cow placed next to the front door.

Working with two or three other students, discuss revisions that will make the following sentences concise and readable. Then write a clear version of each sentence. We will show you how to revise the first one.

REVISING EXERCISE

11.12

1. It has been in the most recent past that many different groups of citizens have joined together in completely unanimous protest against the concept of nuclear war.

   Revised: Recently, many groups have joined in unanimous protest against nuclear war.

2. I would like you to call me Ishmael.

3. There is a general consensus that the paper that is judged to be the most original should be awarded the prize.

4. In actual fact, the main reason he lost the coaching position was primarily because of the poor job he did in winning an adequate number of games.

5. At future meetings, please do not request an exemption from the meeting.

6. We finally made a selection of a desk that was small in size and gray in color.

7. The participants who take part in the annual fund raiser every year seem to be few in number.

8. It is absolutely essential that we do something about the complete absence of members of minority groups among the members of our staff.

9. The reason that I personally think we should postpone our decision on this difficult problem is because this problem is a complex matter.

10. There was a feeling, at least on my part, based on a number of true facts that I had been reading, that the food we buy at the supermarket to eat may be poisoned with food additives.

Use Agent-Active Sentence Patterns

You can cut down on wordiness if you try consciously to write *agent-active* sentences. These are sentences in which your reader can tell immediately *who* is doing *what* to *whom*. You can see the difference in the following versions of the same sentence.

Not agent-active: The automatic response of public officials who are challenged is a denial of responsibility.

Agent-active: Public officials automatically deny responsibility when they are challenged.

Readers understand the second version more quickly because someone (public officials) is doing something (denying). Here is another example.

Not agent-active: Decisions in regard to the administration of medication rest only with the physician.

Agent-active: Only the physician can decide whether to administer medication.

In the first sentence it's hard to tell that the phrases *decisions in regard to the administration of medication* refer to somebody doing something. But when we make the agent ("physician") the subject of the sentence and link it with the action ("can decide"), the meaning becomes much clearer.

Rewrite these sentences in a more direct style. Use people as the agent of the action in each one. The first one is done for you as an example.

1. The burden of responsibility on the supervisor is primary.

   Revision: The supervisor bears the primary responsibility.

2. His expectation was for us to quit.

3. The discussion between the two sides concerned a salary cap.

4. Technological growth and the increase in mechanization have led to more consumption of energy by Americans.

5. A selection of a balanced diet of nutritious food is necessary for continued health and energy.

6. Determination of policy occurs at the executive level.

Change to Active Verbs

With an active verb, the subject performs the action:

The partners <u>broke</u> the agreement.

With a passive verb, the subject receives the action:

The agreement <u>was broken</u> by the partners.

As you can see, it takes more words to express an idea with a passive verb. In addition, the reader usually has to wait until the last part of the sentence to find out what is happening. Thus, "A decision on the matter has been made by the court" takes longer to read and process than "The court decided the matter."

When you write sentences with passive verbs you are also likely to increase your use of *nominalizations* (a word or word group functioning as a noun). In the following examples, notice how the nominalizations (underlined) disappear when we convert the passive verbs (in boldface) to active.

nom.

Passive: <u>An amendment to the by-laws</u> **was passed** by the members.

Active: The members amended the by-laws.

nom.

Passive: <u>The only examination of the problem</u> **has been undertaken** by women's groups.

Active: Only women's groups have examined the problem.

Even when passive verbs are not wordy, they sometimes allow a speaker or writer to omit important information. An official who announces that "it is recommended that a substantial pay cut be approved" is evading some crucial questions: Who recommended the pay cut? Who is being asked to approve it?

REVISING EXERCISE

11.14

Make the following sentences clearer and more concise by changing passive verbs to active and eliminating ineffective nominalizations. You may need to add active agents. We will get you started by doing the first one.

1. Discussion of the issues was carried out amicably by both sides.
   Revised: Both sides discussed the issues amicably.
2. The appearance of the candidates before the board will be made on January 10.
3. Explanations of difficult problems should be made by the teacher prior to the test.
4. Strict enforcement of the speed limit will be done by the police.
5. The demand for shirts bearing sports logos has been artificially stimulated by advertising.
6. It was stated by the author in the introduction that several approaches to grammar would be discussed.
7. Consideration of the firefighters' request will be given by the city council at its next meeting.
8. Your records have been seized and your assets have been frozen.
9. The prisoner was beaten severely.
10. It was decided that sick leave days would be canceled.

Use Passive Verbs Skillfully

Despite problems with length and vagueness, passive verbs can be useful and natural. Writers in the sciences and other academic disciplines often use passive verbs to focus on the object being studied rather than on the person doing the study. These sentences from an essay describing brain surgery illustrate this focus.

A curved incision *was made* behind the hairline so it *would be concealed* when the hair grew back. . . . Plastic clips *were applied* to the cut edges of the scalp to arrest bleeding.

—Roy C. Selby Jr.

Other writers use the passive voice when the action or the receiver of the action is more important than the agent.

President John Fitzgerald Kennedy was shot and killed by an assassin today.

The play was first performed in 1591.

Copy each sentence carefully. Then, choosing subject matter from your academic major, write several sentences imitating the passive structure of each of the originals. We will do the first one.

1. Certain things were not mentioned. (Jane O'Reilly)

   Imitiations: Pesticides were not used.
   Crop rotation was not advised.
   Early harvesting was not recommended.
   Organic methods were not tried.

2. All personal leaves have been canceled.

3. The SKIP option can be used in input and output statements.

4. The poor are slated to take the brunt of the federal budget cuts. (Barbara Ehrenreich)

5. Tygon catheters were implanted in the left atrium and aorta.

6. In the spring the upper trunk, branches, and leaves of the young Rough Lemon tree would be cut off altogether. (John McPhee)

7. All others, except apprentices, are excluded by law from the preparation room. (Jessica Mitford)

Repair Flawed Sentences

Many writers have difficulty in seeing their mistakes. Yet nothing is more important in the editing process than identifying and correcting flawed sentences. Ask a friend or classmate to read your draft and point out sentences that need attention.

Balance Coordinate Elements

You know about balancing elements to produce impressive sentences, but the technique is also fundamental to good everyday writing. If you put together a sentence involving two similar elements (or a series of them), your readers expect these parts to be balanced (or parallel). These structures occur whenever you join parts of sentences with any of the coordinating conjunctions (*and, but, or, for, nor, yet, so*).

> D. J. likes <u>to swim</u> and <u>climbing mountains</u>.

Your readers expect the elements joined by *and* to sound alike, to be phrased in the same way, like this:

> D. J. likes <u>to swim</u> and <u>to climb mountains</u>.

Or like this:

> D. J. likes <u>swimming</u> and <u>climbing mountains</u>.

Now look at a more typical example—the kind of sentence you are likely to write in a hurry and need to balance when you revise:

> The article explains the mayor's decision and how the city council responded to it.

In that sentence the two elements connected by *and* are a phrase (*the mayor's decision*) and a clause (*how the city council responded to it*). Both elements need to be the same:

> The article explains <u>the mayor's decision</u> and <u>the city council's response to it</u>. [2 phrases]

> The article explains <u>how the mayor made his decision</u> and <u>how the city council responded to it</u>. [2 clauses]

Usually, there are several ways to restore balance to sentences, all of which are equally good. In order to increase your revising and editing skills, try your hand at repairing the following faulty sentences.

The following sentences were written by students whose grasp of parallel structure was less than perfect. Read each sentence, decide which parts need to be parallel, and change the irregular part so it matches the grammatical structure of its coordinate part. The first is done for you as an example.

1. Politicians today face the difficult tasks of solving urban problems and how to find the money without raising taxes.

   Revised: Politicians today face the difficult tasks of solving urban problems and finding the money without raising taxes.

   Revised: Politicians today face the difficult tasks of how to solve urban problems and how to find the money without raising taxes.

2. This group is knowledgeable about lane conditions and choosing the proper bowling ball.

3. Roommates tell each other everything—even about work or who they're dating.

4. In the movies, all college men are portrayed as single and having other attractions, such as money, being good-looking, and a great personality.

5. Progressive education teaches children to be open-minded, self-disciplined, and how to do logical thinking.

Straighten Out Confused Sentences

Some sentence errors are impossible to categorize as anything other than messed up. These semantic puzzles are sometimes called *mixed constructions.* They apparently happen when a writer starts out in one sentence pattern and ends up writing another. Sentences like the following force readers to stop and go back, hoping for a better connection, although they may never get one.

> When students have no time for study or moral training also breeds a decadent society.

> The first planned crime will tell how well a boy has learned whether or not he is caught to become a juvenile delinquent.

You will lose more time trying to patch up troublesome sentences like these than you will rethinking the idea and starting again. Take that last example. It needs a completely different beginning—something like this:

> ***Revised:***   Whether or not a boy is caught in his first planned crime may determine if he becomes a juvenile delinquent.

Occasionally, a confused sentence can be easily revised, like this one:

> *Mixed:*   When opening and closing the oven door, it can cause a soufflé to fall.
>
> *Revised:*   Opening and closing the oven door can cause a soufflé to fall.

Although mixed constructions seem to reflect varying degrees of illiteracy, they usually result from lack of concentration. For this reason, we urge you to edit carefully.

<table>
<tr>
<td>

REVISING
EXERCISE

11.17

</td>
<td>

Working with two or three other students, try to figure out the following mixed constructions. Then write a clear version for each sentence. We will revise the first one.

1. Sherry, hoping to find a job that interests her, and so she doesn't have to type.

   Revised: Sherry is hoping to find a job that interests her—one that doesn't involve typing.

   Revised: Sherry is hoping to find an interesting job in which she doesn't have to type.

2. The Rites of Spring festival has been postponed because of too many students are sick with the flu.

3. Drunken drivers should stop being made into criminals.

4. Only through constant study will achievement of academic excellence be made.

5. By submitting to another person's influence is an acknowledgment of your own indecision.

6. Although six members quit during Wynton's first term as chair did not prevent him from being elected to a second term.

</td>
</tr>
</table>

<table>
<tr>
<td>

WRITING
EXERCISE

11.18

</td>
<td>

Write a paragraph titled "How I Relax." When you revise, check for clarity, sentence variety, effective subordination, active verbs, conciseness, concrete details, vivid word choice, and balanced structure.

</td>
</tr>
</table>

Chapter Twelve

Choosing Words Wisely

Language, as described by essayist Norman Cousins, is "the currency of communication." He is pleased that "our linguistic capital" is being constantly enriched by the addition of new words. But others who write about the state of the English language are far from happy. *Newsweek* reports that "Along with almost everything else, language is said to be slipping out of control in America. Inflation has eaten away our words; the bureaucrats in Washington churn them out by the millions, but they mean less and less."

Writing in a Human Voice

Lewis Lapham, editor of *Harper's* magazine, complains: "I have found that few writers learn to speak in the human voice, that most of them make use of alien codes (academic, political, literary, bureaucratic, technical)." Strive for a *human* voice when you write—your own. Of course, how much of your own personality you show in your technical reports or business memos is determined by where you work. Some institutions and some tasks (like group work) require that you suppress your individuality, but you still do not have to sound like an alien. Many people produce on paper a kind of artificial language known as *bafflegab* (from *baffle,* meaning "to confuse," and *gab,* meaning "to talk"). This language is much different from the kind people speak or the kind most professional writers use.

Bafflegab is vague, wordy, roundabout, stuffy, pompous, jargon-ridden—hence, difficult to understand. For instance:

> Desiring to assume a proactive posture yet realizing some reactive measures are inevitable, the Council plans to put the by-laws, as adopted by the faculty, to task in an attempt to become a functional liaison between the Dean (including college office staff) and the larger college faculty constituency.

Psychic powers far greater than ours are needed to divine meaning from that sentence.

> **REMEMBER:**   *Clarity is the keynote of good writing.*

Often bafflegab abuses the third-person approach to writing. (Writing in the third person means adopting an impersonal approach by using *one, he, she, it,* or *they,* instead of the more personal *I, we,* or *you.*) Here is an example of third-person bafflegab:

> One can observe that athletics can be beneficial to the health of one who participates as well as entertaining for one who watches.

Put that sentence into clear English and you get this:

> Athletics can be healthful for the players and entertaining for the fans.

Still in the third person, the second version avoids the word *one* to refer to people. There may, of course, be times when you will need to use the third-person approach. But be sure to check whether or not the occasion requires third person. If the assignment or request itself uses first or second person, your written response probably can, too. Here are examples of such assignments or requests:

- Bobby, will you let me know in writing which word processor you think is best for our staff and why?

- I'd like your committee's report on word processors by next Friday.

You can use *I* and *we* naturally in writing these responses. Now look at the way the requests would be written to demand less personal styles.

- To Bob Jimenez: A written report concerning the preferred word processor for the staff is needed. Reasons for the choice should be included in the report.

- The Office Management Committee is requested to report on word processors no later than Friday, September 15.

Those are fairly formal assignments, and your response would probably match them by avoiding *I* and *we* and using more impersonal forms.

If you glance at a few of the samples of good writing included in this book, you will discover that most professional writers use *I* and *we* when expressing their own opinions, and many of them address their readers directly as *you*. When you are free to do the same, you will find clarity and that human voice easier to achieve.

Avoiding Unclear Language

Be cautious about using words that sound impressive but have vague meanings. If you can say something plainly and clearly, do so. People who write "semantic and quantitative symbolizations" when they mean "words and numbers" are probably trying to impress their readers. But such pretentious language may destroy clear communication. Steven Pinker, author of *The Language Instinct* (Morrow, 1994), asserts that the major concern in language use today is "the clarity and style of written prose." Bafflegab is one of the aspects that needs changing.

Monstrous new phrases creep into the language via the federal bureaucracy, the educational establishment, the social sciences, the literary establishment, and computer science—phrases such as, "an increased propensity to actualize" (meaning "likely to occur"); a "combat emplacement evacuator" (meaning a shovel); a "combustion enunciator" (meaning a fire alarm); "to restructure one's external/internal reward system" (meaning "to take a cut in pay"); and "to facilitate the availability of funds" (meaning "to raise money"). A felonious friend of ours used to say he was in the business of "compulsory income and materials distribution adjustment." Guess what act sent him to prison.

Watch Out for Doublespeak

Some of the examples above are not just bafflegab, which obscures meaning accidentally by attempting to sound grand; they *purposely* conceal meaning to avoid saying something unpleasant, unpopular, or sexual. The robber's description of his activities quoted above does this.

These intentional smoke screens are called "euphemisms," and some of them are quite innocent. Rather than say bluntly, "He died of cancer," we say, "He passed away after a lingering illness." It takes the shudder out and cloaks the whole grim business of dying in a soothing phrase. Undertakers (or "funeral directors," as they prefer to be called) sometimes carry euphemism to grotesque extremes, such as calling the room where the body lies "the slumber chamber."

Such indirect language can be polite or amusing, but people also use an objectionable kind of euphemism called "doublespeak" to mask realities that ought not be concealed. A former president of the United States simply declared a false statement "inoperative" and thus avoided having to admit that he had lied to the American people. The CIA substitutes the bland phrase "terminate with extreme prejudice" for the ugly word *murder.* The Pentagon refers to weapons designed to kill people as "antipersonnel implements." Instead of "bombing," the Air Force speaks of "protective reaction strikes." Such transparent attempts to make sinister happenings sound inoffensive are dangerously misleading.

These deceptive euphemisms are becoming widespread in our society. The National Council of Teachers of English once conferred its annual Doublespeak Award on the nuclear power industry for coining these phrases:

an "energetic disassembly" (meaning an explosion)

a "rapid oxidation" (meaning a fire)

an "abnormal evolution" (meaning an accident)

If more and more individuals insist on the honest use of language, perhaps this slippery trend can be reversed. At least you in your own writing can be truthful both in what you say and in the way you say it.

**EDITING
EXERCISE**

12.1

A leaflet advertising a workshop for social workers (at $50-$75 a head) included the promotional material we reprint here. What characterizes the writing style? Why was this style used, do you think? See how briefly and clearly you can rewrite the passage, retaining the basic meaning. Make note of the problems you encounter in your efforts.

With increased demand for accountability in human services made by policymakers and the public, combined with the need to maximize the benefits of scarce resources, Quality Assurance becomes paramount in evaluating the effectiveness of programs in meeting objectives specified. The content of this workshop will focus on:

- the role of Quality Assurance as it applies to child care
- an examination of the questions to be addressed in planning a Quality Assurance study focused on child care
- defining and describing three alternative approaches to carrying out Quality Assurance work
- defining and describing key questions to be addressed in planning Quality Assurance studies
- identifying major characteristics of Quality Assurance work
- major difficulties/constraints of doing Quality Assurance work
- identifying and describing key tasks to be carried out in planning and conducting Quality Assurance studies
- a consideration of the role of the person doing Quality Assurance work, different practice styles
- questions to be addressed in planning a Quality Assurance study
- the desired characteristics of Quality Assurance work
- alternative ways to carry out Quality Assurance studies.

Be Careful about Using Jargon

Language used within a trade or profession that is understood perfectly well among that specialized group but not by outsiders is called *jargon.* Bridge players, for instance, mean something entirely different by *rubber, dummy,* and *slam* than the rest of us do. Among computer users, notes might be sent like, "I mistakenly saved this under wp6.0, but I've resaved it at 5.1 so you can read it," and no confusion would result. No tennis fan would be bewildered if a player called a let ball at 15–love. Before using jargon, consider your audience and your purpose. If your readers will find the terms familiar, and if these words help make your meaning clear, by all means, use them. If not, find more understandable terms, or else define the jargon (perhaps in parentheses following the word, as we often do in this textbook).

Find examples of euphemisms, bafflegab, doublespeak, or jargon in your own life, from your workplace, school, or reading material. How would you translate these examples into plain English? Why do you think plain English was not used in the first place?

DISCUSSION EXERCISE

12.2

Translate these sentences from bafflegab into clear, straightforward American English. You may have to guess at the meaning sometimes, but do your best. We will rewrite the first one to get you started.

1. The causal factors of her poverty become obvious when one considers the number of offspring she supports.

   Translation: She is poor because she has so many children.

2. This writer's report enjoyed a not unfavorable reception by the Resource Center Committee.

3. The administrators have designated a period of time within which one must respond to charges carrying threats of disciplinary action.

4. The level of radiation in the immediate vicinity of the nuclear power plant was evaluated and found to be within acceptable danger parameters.

5. One realizes as one progresses through life that a great many statements made by political figures are without substance or credibility.

6. The unacceptability of one's lifestyle can result in the termination of one's employment.

7. Police involvement in the conflict was considered to be an inhibiting factor to the peaceful progress of the protest.

8. It was with no little enthusiasm that one's peers inflicted various contusions and lacerations on members of the opposing affinity group.

9. One must recognize the enormous responsibilities that are to be assumed with an office of the public trust.

10. It is the feeling of the committee that the established priorities in management-employee relations are in need of realignment.

Selecting Usage Levels

The *level of usage* you select in writing and speaking depends on a number of stylistic choices, an important one being whether you use *I* and speak directly to your reader as *you,* or whether you use the more formal *one,* as in "One should not address the reader as *you* in formal writing." The nature of your audience and your purpose will determine your usage level. Certainly, when you write a letter to your best friend, your word choice will probably be different from the language you would use to write a business memo. The letter to your friend could be written on a *colloquial* (conversational) level, but the business memo would likely have to be *formal, general,* or *informal,* depending on the nature of the task. These levels of usage are considered appropriate on different occasions, just as for different events you would wear dress-up clothes, on-the-job clothes, blue jeans, and grubby old sweats that no one outside your family is allowed to see.

Formal Writing

There is not nearly so much call for formal writing as there once was, but it still has its uses. Many scholarly articles and books and a few magazines are written in formal English. Business communication that goes beyond the workplace, like to the stockholders or board of directors, may be formal, and legal documents are traditionally formal. The main characteristics of formal usage are

1. No contractions (uses *do not,* instead of *don't; he will,* instead of *he'll*)
2. No slang
3. Third-person approach (uses *one, he, she, it, they, a person, the committee*); no addressing the readers as *you*
4. No sentence fragments (look up *fragment* in the "A to Z Guide" if you do not know what one is)
5. A serious or neutral tone
6. Elevated word choice (*acceptable* rather than *all right; invent* rather than *make up,* for example)

In order to get the feeling of writing formally, try revising the sentences in the following exercise. The more you practice writing in third person, the more natural you will sound when you do have to use it.

The following sentences are written using the first person (*I* and *we*) and the informal second person (*you*). Rewrite each sentence more formally, eliminating first person and *you* as well as slang and contractions.

REWRITING EXERCISE

12.4

1. The point I want to make is quite simple.
   Revised: The point is quite simple.
2. "We hold these truths to be self-evident."
3. We must suppose, then, that the figures cited are O.K.
4. It seems as if I should encourage you to be more uptight in your style of dress.
5. You can't help expressing yourself, unless you live in a vacuum.

6. If you would hold the attention of your readers, you should come up with a pleasing style.

7. We shouldn't make editorial decisions based solely on our personal likes and dislikes.

8. If you attain high positions, your responsibility to other people goes up.

9. We could lack automobiles, banks, missiles, and computers, yet still be numbered among civilized peoples.

10. Poor old Bill looked like death warmed over.

General Writing

Most popular magazines on the newsstand are not written in formal English but are not quite informal either. For example, you might expect to see a sentence like "We hold these truths to be self-evident" or "If you attain high office, your responsibility to other people increases" in *Newsweek,* but you would be surprised to see a sentence like, "It seems as if I should encourage you to be more uptight in your style of dress." The general level of usage allows a *we* or indefinite *you* here and there to refer to people overall, and the word choice is not necessarily elevated; however, first person and contractions are still absent outside of editorial columns. General English may use some words that are not often spoken along with some very plain language. Think of the general level as covering the ground in between formal and informal, the next category to be described.

Informal Writing

Much of the writing you will be called on to do will probably be informal, which means ordinary, familiar, everyday writing. You can use *I* and *we* and address your readers as *you.* Contractions are fine. Slang is sometimes all right, but here you need to consider your audience. While poet Carl Sandburg admired slang as "a language that rolls up its sleeves, spits on its hands, and goes to work," satirist Ambrose Bierce called it "the grunt of the human hog." So be wary. Remember, you do not want to put off your readers; you want to communicate with them. We personally like slang but realize it sometimes comes close to being an in-group language known only to those of a certain age or background. As a matter of courtesy, you should never use slang that your readers are unlikely to understand or that they may find offensive.

By and large, your word choice in informal writing will consist of those serviceable, everyday words that everyone uses all the time. The main characteristics of informal usage are as follows.

1. Contractions are allowed.
2. Slang is sometimes acceptable if your audience will understand it and not be offended by it.
3. First-person approach (*I, we*) and use of *you* to refer to the readers are both all right—so long as *you* does indeed always refer to the readers.
4. Stylistically effective sentence fragments are usually acceptable, but consider your audience.
5. An informal, somewhat personal tone is appropriate. The tone may be obviously humorous or angry.
6. Word choice is everyday (not *residence,* but *house;* not *enervated,* but *tired* or even *worn out*). Notice that two-part verbs, like *gave up* or *found out,* are informal, while their one-word counterparts, like *surrendered* or *discovered,* are more formal.

Colloquial Writing

In colloquial writing, just about anything goes because it imitates everyday speech. The chief characteristics are slang, sentence fragments, and perhaps even nonstandard constructions. Your letter to a best friend and your private diary could easily be colloquial. In more public writing, colloquial writing comes in handy for reproducing actual speech in an otherwise informal essay. The following illustration is from humorist Larry L. King's description of an event in Texas.

> Sweetwater still holds the annual Rattlesnake Roundup, where contestants pay $10 each to catch live poisonous critters and tote their biggest, meanest captives to the judge's stand in gunnysacks. (The winners get to eat all the fried snake they want and a future almost guaranteed to be free of folks messin' with them.) But all that used to be commonplace and now it's considered downright eccentric. Long time ago they quit letting you fight duels without the courts meddlin' in it.

King was able to capture the flavor of the event by imitating regional speech rather than by writing in standard American English.

Figure 12.1 provides several examples of translations among levels of usage.

Establishing Tone

A mixture of purpose and audience will determine the appropriate *tone* for what you are about to write. Tone reveals your attitude toward your subject or your

*Usage Levels
for All
Occasions*

Formal: One should not admit defeat too easily.

General: I shall not admit defeat too easily.

Informal: We shouldn't give up too easily.
I won't give up too easily.

Colloquial: I'm not going to throw in the towel too easy.

Formal	General or Informal	Colloquial (slang)
automobile	car	wheels
homicide	murder	hit
comprehend	understand	get it
depart	leave	split
residence	house	crib
offensive	unpleasant	gross
exhausted	tired out	wasted
dejected	sad	down
hyperactive	jittery	wired
intoxicated	drunk	trashed
disparage	insult	diss

audience—or both. Primarily, tone involves choice of words and selection of details, but all aspects of style may come into play: usage level, sentence structure, organization, even punctuation. If, for example, you feel your point will best be communicated by making your readers laugh, you will use a *light, humorous* tone, as columnist Dave Barry does in this paragraph.

Today's Topic For Married People Is: Coping With Anger. Even so-called "perfect couples" experience conflict. Take Canada geese. They mate for life, so people just assume they get along well; when people see a goose couple flying overhead, honking, they say, "Oh, that's SO romantic." What these people don't realize is that honking is how geese argue. ("Are you SURE we're heading north?" "Yes, dammit." "Well, I think we should ask somebody.") The only reason they mate for life is that they can't afford lawyers.

Other humorous tones exist. A *sarcastic* tone uses humor to present caustic and bitter disapproval. In reviewing a novel whose characters attend a fancy private college, John Leonard wonders why the author even bothered

> . . . to set up shop in the big holes in the tiny heads of Sean, Paul, Lauren, and Victor, none of whom ever went to class, read a book, mustered a fierce feeling or surprised a coherent idea because they were all too busy doing drugs or committing suicide. Stoned, horny, ungrateful, uncomprehending, everybody in *The Rules of Attraction* seemed incapable of love, art, politics, unselfishness or even enthusiasm. It's taken most of us most of our lives, and several momentous occasions, ever to feel as bad for fifteen minutes as these kids have apparently felt since Pampers.

A *satiric* tone uses humor to point out human folly. Writer Frank Gannon is satiric when he rates famous authors as though he were a gossip columnist.

> Poor Thoreau. He spent so much time alone that he started to think he was the most interesting person in the room. Yes, Henry, do go on about your bean rows. Do you mind if I hang myself first? I once read Henry asking the pointed question, "Shall I go to heaven or a-fishing?" All I can say to someone who uses the word "a-fishing" is "Gaak!" I don't care which one it is, but *do* go, Henry. Goodbye.

In speaking, we often use an *ironic* tone. We say the opposite of what we mean and count on our listeners to understand (from our tone of voice as well as the reversed meaning) that we are being ironic. For instance, if the temperature is fifteen below zero, the streets are covered with ice, and snow is predicted, you can say, "Splendid weather we're having," and no one will misunderstand you. But in writing, irony is not so easily detected, because your readers cannot hear your tone of voice. You must be careful to provide clear verbal clues if you employ irony on paper. When author Edith Wharton writes, "The air in the corridor was rich in reminiscences of yesterday's dinners," we know that she means, "The hall smelled of stale cooking." Her ironic tone is carried in the phrase *rich in reminiscences,* words suggestive of something pleasant and desirable—not yesterday's dinners. Take care when using irony. If your readers miss your meaning, they will miss it completely and think you are saying the exact opposite of what you intend.

On the other end of the emotional range from humor is the *solemn* tone writers use for sad material. Essayist Alan Weisman wrote about exploring the area affected by the Chernobyl nuclear disaster in 1986, the deadliest nuclear accident in history.

We poked inside cottages, built centuries ago from stout, hewn timbers, whose painted doors and shutters now flapped uselessly. Their interiors attested to rapid evacuation: a plank floor strewn with crayoned pages from a child's geography lesson; a skeletal Christmas tree, tipped on its side; a barrel of apples, left to shrivel. The Geiger counter chattered in stove ashes, where radioactive kindling had been burned, and around drainspouts where rainwater laden with cesium 137 had poured off the eaves. In a former truck garden, feral, irradiated house cats lurked among rhubarb plants.

Weisman's grim details and word choice (*flapped uselessly, skeletal, shrivel*) set a solemn tone.

Quite often tone is not easy to detect. Most writing is done in a *neutral* tone that does not evoke any particular emotion. Following is a typical example written by psychologist Jane Adams. We might call it *straightforward* or *businesslike*, but basically the tone is neutral.

Parenthood doesn't end when children grow up and move out. Even when children are independent and mature, parents still worry about them and want what's best for them. Problems come when parents voice their concerns and children take their parents' concerns the wrong way. The result is a communication gap, which frequently leads to friction. Here's how to adjust your behavior so you can have a closer and healthier relationship with your grown children.

Most of your writing at school and at work will have this kind of neutral tone. Several assignments we suggest in this textbook, though, will allow you to experiment with other tones.

Temper Your Tone

Tone always depends to some extent on how the words are received by the readers. Always check over any writing you intend to share to make sure that the tone cannot be misunderstood. When we have to write a letter objecting to a policy or criticizing a decision, we always ask our coauthors to read it over to make sure that our irritation is not too obvious.

Sometimes it does you some good to express your negative feelings in writing, but remember, you want the good will of your readers. Try to adopt a tone that will not antagonize them. One friend of ours had spent a weary afternoon printing out and packaging his new novel to send to his agent. The printer malfunctioned; he found two typographical errors in the final copy; the right packing materials were hard to find; and it was a very hot day. When time finally came to write a cover letter to his agent, his first draft read this way:

Here's the next damn novel. Let me know when you've read it.

In exasperation, he asked his wife to revise the note, and she wrote this:

I'm happy to enclose my new novel. I'm eager to hear what you think of it.

Basically, the same message was worded in a much more friendly tone. Try to do the same sort of revising with your own writing. Work to achieve a tone that will allow you to be convincing, not offensive.

Compose your own brief memo of complaint or suggestion. Choose a situation at home, at work, or at school that could use some improvement. Write in a tone that will be effective in addressing the audience that will receive the memo. Use humor if you think your audience will respond well. Indicate at the top of the page both your audience and your purpose.

WRITING EXERCISE

12.5

Finding the Right Words

Mark Twain once observed that the difference between the right word and almost the right word is the difference between lightning and the lightning bug. Our language is full of synonyms—words that mean approximately the same thing, like *happy* and *glad*. But synonyms often have different shades of meaning. Although a *feeling* is a *sensation,* the two words are not always interchangeable. Neither are *witty* and *funny,* nor *visible* and *apparent,* nor *utensil* and *implement*—even though each pair of words shares an element of meaning.

Be especially careful not to confuse words that sound alike but mean different things—such as *uninterested* and *disinterested*—or you will mislead your readers. Sometimes, of course, the confusion can be amusing. We have a friend whose grandmother is continually crocheting "Africans." A co-worker with a herniated navel told us that his "biblical cord broke." A neighbor said that his wife went to Carle Clinic to have her breasts "monogrammed." These *malapropisms,* as such misused words are called, are often funny, but you want your readers laughing with you, not at you.

Say What You Mean

Sometimes the sense of a sentence becomes unclear because the writer fails to pay attention to what familiar words mean. The following sentences *sound* all right, until you realize they are nonsense. A local police officer recently announced in our local paper that

> We are trying to put some teeth into the law to help enforce narcotic abuse.

We hope he doesn't really intend to force everyone in town to abuse narcotics. More likely he meant "to help *curb* narcotics abuse," but he actually said just the opposite. One of our students made this observation in an essay:

> Many important factors are determined by the way one dresses—the person's personality, lifestyle, profession, age, and sex.

She couldn't seriously believe that changing one's manner of dress could also change one's profession, age, and sex, but that's what she *said*. Another student wrote this shocker:

> Researchers found that having sex education prolonged first sexual intercourse for six months.

Probably not even teenagers want the sex act to last *that* long. What researchers found was that teenagers with sex education *delay* first sexual intercourse for six months longer than teens without sex education. Again, the problem was a matter of not checking to make sure the words that were used meant what the writer intended to say.

Some people also confuse words that sound alike—which confuses readers who know what the words actually mean. If you write, "Tighten all the lose screws," people will understand you, but some of them will think *you* have a screw loose. Consult Chapter 15, the "Glossary of Usage," if you are in doubt about whether to write *effect* or *affect, lie* or *lay,* or any other words frequently confused.

When you write, pay attention to the words you choose. Be sure that each word in a sentence says exactly what you want it to say.

REWRITING
EXERCISE

12.6

In the following sentences, some words are used without regard for meaning. Point out what is wrong with each one, and then rephrase it accurately. You may need to revise some extensively in order to repair them. We'll rewrite the first one, which we saw on a sign in a parking lot at a grocery store.

1. Illegal Parking Will Be Towed Away At Their Expense.
   Revised: Illegally Parked Cars Will Be Towed At Owner's Expense.

2. Because she was disinterested in the novel's outcome, she called it boring.

3. Because of the newspaper report, Marvin's reputation exceeded him.

4. I cannot decide weather I like it or not.

5. Some teenagers have to hold jobs to help support the family's low income.

6. These figures deduce that the firm could expect a loss.

7. Wordwrap and Insert are among the first two problems a beginning word processor recounts.

8. I am going irregardless of what you say.

9. There is a variety of media under the classification of painting.

10. The rise in crime is a day that we all find regretful.

Choose the Right Idiom

An idiom is an expression of several words customarily used together in English, such as *regardless of* and *attitude toward*. Sometimes the short word, usually a preposition, gets confused with another preposition, since prepositions have such slippery meanings. So you may read a sentence like, "Regardless to what the weather report predicts, we're going to Charleston," or "Sandy has a poor attitude to her boss." Idioms are especially difficult when English is not your first language, since they follow tradition rather than logical rules. For example, why do we say "superior *to*" but "better *than*"? It's just language custom. Here are some idioms along with examples of ways they are sometimes misused.

> comply with (*not* comply to)
> regardless of (*not* regardless to)
> satisfied with (*not* satisfied of)
> similar to (*not* similar with)
> in contrast to *or* in contrast with (*not* in contrast against)
> insight into (*not* insight to)
> in my opinion (*not* to my opinion)

When you look up the main word in an expression, your dictionary will usually list the idioms that include that word. This way, you will find which words traditionally go together. The entry on Idioms in Chapter 14, "An A to Z Guide," gives additional examples.

Making Every Word Count

Even *Business Week* magazine advises writers to, "Be precise, be lively." A memo on your department's vanishing coffee fund and slovenly mug habits does not have to be dull, though the subject matter is unexciting.

When you revise, first make sure your sentences are clear; then look at the specific language you have used. Read through the rough draft, paying particular attention to the verbs. Look for forms of these overworked words:

> is (are, was, were, etc.)
> get
> do
> go
> come
> make
> have

Consider substituting a verb that presents an image, visual or otherwise, to your readers. For example, this version of a memo is correct but dull:

> The coffee fund is getting lower week by week, so please make sure you make a payment for each cup you drink.

Searching for a more precise and lively wording, you might write:

> The coffee fund dwindles week by week. Pay for your drinks, please!

Now the verbs are *dwindles* and *pay,* and the whole effect is more emphatic.

Writing soon becomes colorless and tiresome without vivid, specific details. When possible, substitute specific words for general ones. Here is a general statement:

> At a certain point, the coffee area has various items in it belonging to staff members.

Revised to be specific, the statement might look like this:

> By 4:30 P.M., your scummy mugs and sticky spoons litter the coffee area.

The revised statement gives the exact time, clarifies what the items are, and uses *litter* as the verb rather than *has.* Notice, too, that the revised statement is less likely to be misunderstood. The reader could not pretend that mugs and spoons are not the "various items" of complaint nor assume that some other "staff members" are the culprits.

Avoid Clichés

Be careful about writing down the first descriptive phrase that comes to mind, because it could be a *cliché,* an overused figure of speech that has lost its original force. *Cool as a cucumber, rugged individualist, frontiers of knowledge,* and *cutting edge* once produced images in readers' minds, but now we skim over such phrases without ever visualizing what they mean. Following is a list of some currently popular clichés you might be tempted to use. Try to resist the temptation.

acid test	have a nice day
at this point in time	history tells us
ballpark figure	high and mighty
bottom line	interface with
burning questions	in this day and age
crystal clear	last but not least
doomed to failure	paid my dues
few and far between	pretty as a picture
first and foremost	untimely death
for all intents and purposes	user-friendly

You may notice that in your workplace, one or more of the above weatherbeaten phrases appear all over the place. If certain clichés seem to be acceptable jargon in this setting, you might want to grit your teeth and use them.

Think About Connotations

Words are symbols that have *denotative* meanings—the actual concrete thing or abstract quality referred to—and *connotative* meanings—the emotional response attached to the word. The term *mother,* for instance, *denotes* a woman who gives birth to or adopts a child, but the term often *connotes* warmth, love, security, and comfort. Most of our words have connotations in varying degrees, some so strong that the words should be considered loaded. Whether you choose to refer to the President as a *statesman* or as a *politician* may well reveal your political leanings. Consider the connotations of these pairs of similar words:

smut	pornography
mob	gathering
smog	haze
egghead	intellectual
prudish	chaste
jock	athlete
foolhardy	courageous
nerd	specialist
gofer	assistant

Writer's attitudes are clearly revealed by whether they choose from the strongly negative words on the left or the more favorable words on the right.

We do not mean to suggest that you should avoid choosing words with strong connotations. Your writing would be lifeless if you did. But you must be aware of the hidden messages you convey with strongly connotative words. What does the following statement suggest about Mr. Patel?

> Fixating on office tidiness, Mr. Patel proposed a list of directives concerning the coffee area.

He sounds like a fussy, petty tyrant, does he not? The words *fixating* and *tidiness* make the issue sound unimportant, and the word *directives* suggests bossiness. Here is an alternative way of writing the same basic statement:

> Focusing on the professional appearance of the office, Mr. Patel suggested a list of guidelines concerning the coffee area.

Now Mr. Patel seems quite reasonable and helpful. Because ignoring connotations can produce regrettable effects, try to become sensitive to the emotional associations that some words carry.

Using Gender-Inclusive Language

In choosing words, you should be aware that many readers are offended by language that stereotypes females and males according to traditional roles. The major publishing companies and many large corporations such as State Farm Insurance Company now require writers to use language that clearly includes both sexes. Inclusive language entails avoiding the old generic use of *he* and *his* to refer to a mixed-gender group, as in this sentence:

> Each worker must wear his identification card clipped to his uniform collar at all times.

Since workers are both men and women, this usage reflects a male orientation that was once ingrained in our society. People used to think that everyone understood *he* to mean *he* or *she* in such sentences; however, psychological studies revealed that both children and adults really do think of *he* as a man, even when used generically.

Man also means *man,* the studies found, despite earlier claims that it included women. When the famous declaration "All men are created equal" was made, women were not allowed to vote and were held by law to be the property of their fathers or husbands. Clearly, "all men" did not include women—or non-white men, either.

Using the Plural and Other Inclusive Strategies

If you have gotten into the generic male habit, you may need to practice a few new ways to phrase things. The changes are minor enough to become natural to you quickly. Inclusive language is not clumsy, either; this entire textbook is written using gender-free language, and you probably have not even noticed. The most useful strategy is to write in the plural, since our plural *they* is gender-free.

> Workers must wear their identification cards clipped to their uniform collars at all times.

Another inclusive revision strategy just eliminates the pronouns entirely.

> Each worker must wear an identification card clipped to the uniform collar at all times.

If you must write in the singular and use pronouns (and sometimes you may need to), go ahead and use an occasional *he or she* or *his or her.* Used sparingly, the double pronoun is not all that cumbersome. Another solution is to use fictional examples, giving them female or male names, and alternate the sexes in your examples.

Sally D. is a model case of the at-risk employee. She is always late, never organized, and frequently too tired to listen to instructions. Joe S. exemplifies a different problem: he needs constant direction because he is too timid to make any decisions whatsoever.

Be careful that you do not sex-type your examples when you use this technique (for example, having Sally be the timid worker).

A number of compound words using the word *man* can be avoided with little difficulty.

Avoid	*Prefer*
chairman	chair, moderator, chairperson
congressman	representative, senator
councilman	council member
fireman	fire fighter
mailman	mail carrier
mankind	humanity, humankind
manpower	workforce
man the booth	staff the booth
manmade	artificial
policeman	police officer

Assuming a Mixed-Gender Audience

Some writers—even recent ones—sound as if they are speaking to both sexes but in reality address themselves only to males. They give themselves away in subtle ways, usually through references to *wives*. In our local newspaper a reporter, reviewing supposedly for the whole community a summer theater production, concluded: "Put the wife in the car and come out to spend an enjoyable evening in the park." We wonder if the wife could not get into the car by herself—or if she declined to go and had to be put in the car like the cat or the groceries. A published book review recently listed the footwear that resides in every suburbanite's closet: loafers, golf shoes, old sneakers, wingtips, and running shoes. What sex is "every suburbanite"?

Be aware of more subtle forms of assumed male dominance, as well. A discussion of pioneers' struggles may mention that "pioneers and their wives continued westward," implying that the men were the pioneers. If a married couple both work to operate a farm, he may be called the "farmer," she the "farmer's wife." Be sure not to refer always to a secretary or a grade school teacher as *she* and to an executive or an engineer as *he*. Learning to avoid old-fashioned gender stereotyping is absolutely necessary as women and men become free to break out of traditional roles.

Without changing the meaning or causing awkwardness, revise the following sentences to make them inclusive. We'll do the first one for you.

1. Man must work in order to eat.

    Revised: People must work in order to eat.

    A person must work in order to eat.

2. Anyone with a brain in his head can see the dangers of poorly marked highways.
3. The citizen may pay his water bill by mail or at the city hall.
4. The gregarious dog is man's best friend, but the more aloof cat keeps his own counsel.
5. He who laughs last laughs loudest.
6. "As long as man is on earth, he's likely to cause problems. But the man at General Electric will keep trying to find answers." [advertisement for GE]
7. Clyde was patched up by a lady doctor who stopped her car at the accident scene.
8. Juanita's mother is a computer repairman for IBM.
9. The hippopotamus is happiest when he is half submerged in mud.
10. The Native Americans were forced to leave their homes and move their wives and children to reservations.

Improving Your Command of Words: Using the Dictionary and Thesaurus

If you are going to become skilled in choosing words precisely, you need a dictionary large enough to provide reliable help. Abridged, pocket-sized editions are fine for carrying to class when you have to write a paper or take an essay test, but a small dictionary will not do for the thoughtful effort you must devote to revising any writing that needs to be polished and perfect.

Barbara Currier Bell, writing in the *New York Times,* agrees that you should buy a hardcover (rather than paperback) collegiate dictionary. *The Random House College Dictionary* (1984), for example, includes over one hundred seventy thousand entries. Be sure that your dictionary includes at least that number. So far, computer spell-checkers have fewer than half that many entries. This means they will frequently flag a word that you must then look up by hand.

The dictionary can be the best tool for increasing your vocabulary as well as improving your spelling. The more handy a dictionary is, the more likely you are to look up an unfamiliar word in your reading. How many times do you remember just skipping over a new word you encounter, or thinking that you will look it up later, when you are near a dictionary? The trick is to keep a dictionary nearby in all the places you read and write. We know two professional writers who have four dictionaries in their house (including one in the bathroom).

Using Your Dictionary

Myths abound concerning dictionaries. Many people believe that the first meaning listed for a word is the "best" one. Not true. The first meaning will often be the oldest meaning; hence, it could be the least common one. The same thing is true of alternative spellings. Unless a qualifier is inserted (such as *also* or *variation of*), multiple spellings are equally acceptable. And if the dictionary does not list parts of verbs, you know that those spellings are regular: only *irregular* plurals and verb forms appear in dictionary entries.

The only way to find out how your dictionary handles these matters is to read the explanatory notes—the "instruction manual" at the beginning. You might find out that you have been skipping some of the most interesting parts of the entry when you look up a word. Besides spelling, syllabification, parts of speech labels, pronunciation (check the bottom of each page for an explanation of the phonetic symbols), and definition, the entry may also give you the word's etymology (history); convenient examples of how the word is used; usage labels like *archaic, slang,* or *colloaquial;* and synonyms and antonyms. Most dictionaries also provide entertaining material in the back, like punctuation rules, pictures of the planets and stars, lists of abbreviations, lists of U.S. colleges, common given names with their meanings, and even rhyming words.

Using Your Thesaurus

If you often find yourself asking everyone you meet to give you that little short word that means something like *enthusiasm,* a thesaurus is just what you need. A thesaurus will probably come up with the word *zest* faster than your friends can. It does not define words; instead, it gives lists of synonyms—words that are similar in meaning. You might need a synonym if you can't think of the precise word you want or if you have used the same word three times already and are looking for a substitute. Some thesauruses are called "synonym finders" or "dictionaries of synonyms and antonyms."

Thesauruses, like dictionaries, are available in large, hardbound versions and in small, softcover volumes. Most word processing computer programs have on-screen thesauruses, too, although they are not as comprehensive as published ones. These electronic thesauruses are handy but may not provide all the help you need.

Remember that synonyms are not always interchangeable. Never, we repeat, never use an unfamiliar word without looking it up in a collegiate dictionary first to make sure it conveys the exact meaning you want. For instance, *fanaticism* is listed in the thesaurus under *enthusiasm,* but its connotations are quite different. A good dictionary will clear up distinctions between familiar words (*marvelous* and *excellent, dishonest* and *sly,* for example). The dictionary will also point out levels of usage so that you do not accidentally substitute a slangy synonym when writing on an otherwise general or formal level of usage.

A thesaurus entry for the threadbare word *nice* follows. Using the dictionary if necessary, choose the best synonym to substitute for *nice* in each of the sentences below. (The capitalized words indicate other entries to look up to find more synonyms.)

> **nice,** *adj.* pleasant, agreeable, amiable, lovely (PLEASANTNESS); precise, accurate (RIGHT); fine, subtle, hairsplitting (DIFFERENTIATION).
> —*The New Roget's Thesaurus in Dictionary Form* (1978)

1. Sandy's sentence provided a nice definition of "chauvinism."
2. We had a nice time at the party last night.
3. Joyce is usually a very nice person, but she always argues with Abdul.
4. She took a course to learn the nice points of constitutional law.
5. Autumn has nice weather.
6. I hate these endless bridge-table battles over nice rules of bidding etiquette.
7. You look quite nice in your new fake leopard-skin pillbox hat.

Chapter Thirteen

Background in Grammar

The ideal grammar of English would explain how human beings produce and understand the thousands of utterances they say and hear daily. That is a tall order, involving the study of language history, physiology, brain functions, gesture, tone, emphasis, and even silence—as well as the study of words and sentences. But you do not need a complete and thorough theory of grammar in order to write well.

What You Need to Know

What you do need is a basic vocabulary, shared by you and your teachers and other writers, in which you can talk about sentences. Learning the terminology of grammar and the concepts it describes can help you identify and correct sentence fragments, comma splices, and run-on sentences; it can help you decide where to put commas and semicolons and how to untangle sentences that are marred by dangling modifiers or piled-up prepositional phrases.

A Quick Look at the Parts of Speech

The sentence is the basic unit of communication in English. Sentences are, of course, made up of words, each of which can be classified as a *part of speech*. Learning these parts of speech and how they work will help you to understand how sentences operate. The following is a brief review of the traditional parts of speech.

NOUNS are names. A noun may name a person, place, thing, or idea: *Maria, brother, Chicago, beach, shoe, cat, daffodil, iron, courage.*

Most nouns can be made plural (*dog, dogs*) and possessive (my *dog's* name; the *dogs'* fleas). Subjects of sentences are usually nouns.

PRONOUNS replace or refer to nouns. The noun that a pronoun replaces or refers to is called the *antecedent* of that pronoun:

    ant. ◄——————————— *prn.*
    <u>Paula</u> took three suitcases with <u>her</u> to El Paso.

English has several different kinds of pronouns; the most frequently used are the *personal pronouns:* I, me, you, she, her, him, it, we, us, they, and them. Other types include *relative pronouns* (that, who, whose, whom, which), *indefinite pronouns* (each, some, many, one, few, everything, etc.), *demonstrative pronouns* (this, that, these, those), and *interrogative pronouns* (what, who, which, whose).

VERBS say something about the subject of a sentence. They express actions, describe occurrences, or establish states of being.

Action:	The umpire <u>called</u> the runner out.
Occurrence:	A hush <u>settled</u> over the stadium.
State of being:	The umpire <u>was</u> wrong.

A complete sentence always has a main verb. Many verbs combine with *auxiliary* (or *helping*) verbs to create verb phrases. The most common auxiliaries are forms of *be, have,* and *do:*

Silvio <u>is taking</u> a course in ballroom dancing. He <u>has taken</u> three lessons already. The instructor <u>did tell</u> him not to give up too soon.

Verbs can be transitive or intransitive. *Transitive* verbs transfer action to their objects to complete their meaning.

    vb.t.   d.obj.
    Tamara <u>fed</u> the <u>baby</u>.

Intransitive verbs make sense without objects.

    vb. int.
    The baby <u>swallowed</u> quietly.

ADJECTIVES describe or limit the meaning of nouns (and sometimes pronouns). Descriptive adjectives answer the question "what kind?":

<u>red</u> hair, <u>heavy</u> load, <u>foreign</u> car, <u>unbelievable</u> story

Limiting adjectives tell "which one" or "how many":

<u>this</u> problem, <u>any</u> car, <u>many</u> questions, <u>his</u> hair

Many adjectives change form to show a comparative and superlative degree: *happy, happier, happiest; expensive, more expensive, most expensive.*

ADVERBS usually modify verbs, describing *how, when, where,* and *how much* the action of the verb is performed:

Garfield ran <u>upstairs quickly</u>. Robert will arrive <u>soon</u>.

Some adverbs can modify an adjective or another adverb:

Mel is a <u>very</u> cautious driver. He drives <u>quite</u> carefully.

Although many adverbs in English are formed by adding *-ly* to an adjective (*happily, expensively*), many are not: *already, always, seldom, never, now, often, here, there, up, down, inside,* and so forth. Like adjectives, many adverbs change form to indicate the comparative and superlative degree: *carefully, more carefully, most carefully.*

PREPOSITIONS are connecting words. Each of the following prepositions shows a different relation between the noun *stump* and the actions expressed by the verbs:

The rabbit jumped <u>over</u> the stump, ran <u>around</u> the stump, sat <u>on</u> the stump, hid <u>behind</u> the stump, crouched <u>near</u> the stump.

The group of words beginning with a preposition and ending with a noun or pronoun (called its *object*) is called a *prepositional phrase.* For a list of common prepositions, see Figure 13.1.

CONJUNCTIONS join words or groups of words. A *coordinating conjunction* (*and, but, or, nor, for, yet, so*) joins words or word groups of the same kind and same importance:

FIGURE 13.1

*Common
Prepositions*

about	below	in	since
above	between	into	through
across	by	like	till
after	down	of	to
against	during	off	until
at	except	on	up
before	for	outside	upon
behind	from	over	with

Some prepositions are made up of more than one word and are called *compound prepositions*. Here is a list of familiar ones:

according to	in addition to	in spite of
because of	in back of	instead of
contrary to	in case of	on account of
except for	in front of	out of

Clovis forgot the extra nails <u>and</u> sealing tape. He also stepped on the drywall <u>and</u> ruined it. We wanted to fire him, <u>but</u> his dad owns the business.

A *subordinating conjunction* (*if, because, although, when,* etc.) joins a dependent (subordinate) group of words to an independent sentence:

<u>If you love me</u>, you will buy me a new car.

I love you <u>because you are so generous</u>.

Figure 13.2 gives a list of common subordinating conjunctions.

Conjunctive adverbs are adverbs used as conjunctions or transitional words. The most common are *however, thus, therefore, consequently, indeed, furthermore,* and *nevertheless.*

He used the wrong nails to put up the drywall; <u>thus</u>, they popped right out when spring came. His daughter told him to use special nails; <u>however</u>, he hated to follow her advice.

FIGURE 13.2

*Common
Subordinating
Conjunctions*

after	only	till
although	since	unless
as, as if	so as	until
because	so far as	when, whenever
before	so that	whereas
if	though	while

Putting the Words Together

Isolated words, as we have pointed out, often mean very little. The word *set* has different meanings for bridge players, tennis buffs, hairdressers, and math teachers. Only through considering the words around it and the social situation in which it's used can we decide with certainty what the word means. Knowing what part of speech a word belongs to tells us only part of the story. We must understand how the word operates in the pattern or structure of a particular sentence to get the full message.

The Six Basic Sentence Patterns

There are six basic patterns for sentences in English. Each pattern contains a subject and a verb. Depending on the nature of the verb, the pattern may also contain *objects* or *complements* that complete the meaning of the verb.

1. subject / intransitive verb

   S V
   Her tires squealed.

2. subject / transitive verb / direct object

   S V DO
   Flying gravel hit the sidewalk.

3. subject / transitive verb / indirect object / direct object

   S V IO DO
   Shana's driving gives her father the creeps.

4. subject / transitive verb / direct object / object complement

>   *S*   *V*   *DO*   *OC*
> Her driving makes him nervous.

>   *S*   *V*   *DO*   *OC*
> Shana calls her father a big worrywart.

5. subject / linking verb / subject complement

>   *S*   *V*   *SC*
> Her father was her driving teacher.

>   *S*   *V*   *SC*
> He usually seems calm.

6. subject / being verb / adverb of time or place

>   *S* *V*   *ADV*
> Shana is never here.

>   *S* *V*   *ADV PHRASE*
> She is usually in Chicago.

Phrases

A phrase is a string of related words that does *not* include a subject and verb combination. As a unit, a phrase acts as a part of speech (noun, adjective, or adverb) in a sentence. Let's look first at the seven kinds of phrases and then at how they function.

Types of Phrases

1. *Noun phrase:* a noun plus its modifiers
   a delicious six-foot submarine sandwich
2. *Prepositional phrase:* a preposition, its object, and the object's modifiers
   with dill pickles
3. *Infinitive phrase:* the base form of a verb preceded by *to,* plus any modifiers and complements
   to eat the delicious sandwich
4. *Gerund phrase:* an *-ing* verb form plus its modifiers and complements, used as a noun
   eating the six-foot sandwich
5. *Participle phrase:* an *-ing, -ed,* or *-en* verb form plus its modifiers and complements, used as an adjective
   having plenty of lettuce or mayonnaise
   topped with pickles and onions

6. *Verb phrase:* an action or being verb plus any related auxiliary verbs
   have eaten
   should be dieting
   will starve

7. *Absolute phrase:* a word group that modifies all or part of a sentence, but is not related to it with a conjunction or relative pronoun. An absolute phrase usually consists of a noun or pronoun and a participle.

<u>All told</u>, I ate two of those huge sandwiches.

<u>My diet ruined</u>, I vowed to skip lunch for three days.

The Roles of Phrases

Every phrase, short or long, acts like a single part of speech within a sentence.

1. *Phrases used as nouns.* Noun phrases, of course, perform the usual functions of nouns: subject, direct object, indirect object, subject complement, object complement, object of a preposition. But other phrases can act as nouns, too.

The best place to spend Sunday afternoon is <u>in bed</u>.

In bed is a prepositional phrase acting like a noun, in this case the subject complement (renaming "place").

<u>To read anything complicated</u> is unwise.

To read anything complicated is an infinitive phrase acting as a noun, the subject of the sentence.

I enjoy <u>drowsing off in midpage</u>.

Drowsing off in midpage is a gerund phrase used as the direct object of *enjoy.*

2. *Phrases used as adjectives.*

Most <u>of the newspaper</u> is too grim to read for fun.

Of the newspaper is a prepositional phrase used as an adjective modifying the indefinite pronoun *most.*

The best thing <u>to read in bed</u> is a Sherlock Holmes story.

To read in bed is an infinitive phrase used as an adjective modifying the noun *thing.*

<u>Tired of reading</u>, I can depend on Holmes to solve the murder without me.

Tired of reading is a participle phrase used as an adjective modifying the pronoun *I.*

3. *Phrases used as adverbs.*

I slumber peacefully <u>until suppertime</u>.

Until suppertime is a prepositional phrase used as an adverb modifying the verb *slumber.*

I am lucky <u>to have Sundays free</u>.

To have Sundays free is an infinitive phrase used as an adverb modifying the adjective *lucky.*

Clauses

Clauses contain both subjects and verbs plus all their related modifiers and complements. The two kinds of clauses are *independent* (sometimes called "main") and *dependent* (sometimes called "subordinate").

Independent Clauses

An independent clause is a complete sentence. It contains a subject and verb plus any objects, complements, and modifiers of that verb. We have already described the typical patterns for independent clauses: see The Six Basic Sentence Patterns, pages 306–307.

Dependent Clauses

A dependent clause does not sound like a complete sentence when it is spoken or written by itself. It *depends* on an independent clause to complete its meaning. The word that makes all the difference is the subordinating conjunction or relative pronoun that introduces the clause. For instance, suppose a stranger walked up to you and said,

I eat blue bananas.

You would understand those words as a complete, though odd, utterance. In contrast, suppose the stranger said

Since I eat blue bananas.

or

That I eat blue bananas.

or

> After I eat blue bananas.

You would think this even more unusual: you would want the stranger to finish the sentence. The words *since, that,* and *after* make the clauses dependent.

Like phrases, dependent clauses act as single parts of speech within a sentence. They can function as nouns, adjectives, or adverbs.

Noun Clauses

You can tell when a dependent clause is functioning as a noun by making up another sentence in which you substitute a single noun or pronoun for the clause. Noun clauses can be introduced by interrogative words (*how, when, where, why, what, where, whether, whatever*) as well as by the pronouns *who, which, whoever, whichever,* and *that.*

> *noun clause*
> *S   V*
> <u>What you told me</u> will remain locked in my heart.

> Your <u>secret</u> will remain locked in my heart.

The underlined parts act as the subject of each sentence.

> *noun clause*
> *S   V*
> Send letters to <u>whoever fills out the coupon</u>.

> Send letters to <u>everyone</u>.

The underlined parts are both objects of the preposition *to.*

Besides acting as subjects and as objects of prepositions, noun clauses can be direct objects and subject complements. Here are some examples:

> *noun clause (DO)*
> I know <u>who ate that banana</u>.

> *noun clause (SC)*
> His reason was <u>that he was hungry</u>.

> *noun clause (S)*
> <u>Why he ate it</u> does not concern me.

EXERCISE

13.1

Find the noun clauses in the following sentences. Underline each one and label it *subject, direct object, subject complement,* or *object of the preposition.*

1. I remember what you told me.
2. Their major disagreement was about which way he should turn.
3. Shana asked when she could go.
4. What you see is what you get.
5. The important question is why housewives leave home.

Adjective Clauses

An adjective clause is introduced by a relative pronoun (*who, which, that, whose, whom*) and directly follows the noun or pronoun it modifies.

> — *adj. clause* —
> The price, which was outrageous, included sales tax.

> — *adj. clause* —
> The lawyer whose donut you ate is famous.

Sometimes the relative pronoun *that* is dropped:

> The things we try most to forget are the things we always remember.

You can tell there's an adjective clause by noticing the subject-verb combination (*we try, we . . . remember*). Putting the *that* back in will confirm the presence of the clause.

> The things that we try most to forget are the things that we always remember.

EXERCISE

13.2

Identify the adjective clauses and the nouns or pronouns they modify in the following sentences.

1. She was the only student whose favorite subject was philosophy.
2. Her teachers liked having a student who was so enthusiastic.
3. These were memories that gave her pleasure.
4. She disliked Nietzsche, whom she considered depressing.
5. R. D. Laing's views were the ideas that seemed realistic to her.

Adverb Clauses

An adverb clause answers the same questions that any adverb does: When? Where? How? Why? How often? To what extent? To what degree? Under what conditions? Adverb clauses modify a verb, an adjective, another adverb, or a whole sentence. They are introduced by subordinating conjunctions, such as *if, because, when, although, unless, after, before, while,* and so forth. (For a more complete list of subordinating conjunctions, see page 306.)

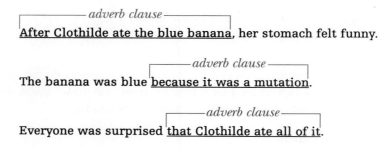

After Clothilde ate the blue banana, her stomach felt funny.

The banana was blue because it was a mutation.

Everyone was surprised that Clothilde ate all of it.

EXERCISE

13.3

Identify the adverb clauses in the following sentences.

1. If you learned grammar in seventh grade, this exercise should be easy.
2. When you study a foreign language, you will find your knowledge of English grammar helpful.
3. Transformational grammar is so unfamiliar that many students are frustrated by it.
4. Transformational grammar, however, is fascinating to some people because it challenges them.
5. Grammarians are welcome at parties because they are lively and eccentric.

COMPRE-HENSIVE EXERCISE

13.4

Label parts of speech, independent and dependent clauses, and phrases.

1. Many cures for insomnia exist.
2. Drinking warm milk is a common home remedy for sleeplessness.
3. Milk contains calcium, which is a natural tranquilizer.
4. When you heat the milk, you make the calcium in it easier for your body to absorb.
5. The warm milk cure does not work for everyone.

6. Some people believe in counting sheep.

7. This boring activity quickly makes them drowsy.

8. Others claim that long nineteenth-century novels will produce sleep efficiently.

9. Alarmed at such barbarism, nineteenth-century fiction scholars are frantically trying to find alternative sedatives.

10. Their most recent work, which is now in experimental stages, involves Wordsworth's *Prelude.*

Chapter Fourteen

An A to Z Guide to Revising and Editing

We do not expect you to sit down and read this chapter straight through. Use this alphabetized index to get quick advice during your revising process. For the convenience of both you and your instructor, the entries are keyed to common correction symbols. Figure 14.1 presents a punctuation guide as a quick reference for determining correct punctuation. We have also included exercises in this guide so you can get some practice on especially knotty problems.

Our advice covers current standard English, the language used by educated people in our society. While standard English is not necessarily any better than the language you may hear at the grocery store or in your local bar (it may, in fact, be less vigorous and colorful), standard English is the language usually required of college students and in the business world.

ab

Abbreviation

1. Abbreviate only the following terms in general or formal writing.

   A. *Personal titles:* Mr., Ms., Mrs., Dr.

   Abbreviate doctor only before the person's name: Dr. Dustbin—but never "The dr. removed my appendix."

   By the same token: St. Joan—*but:* "My mother has the patience of a saint."

   B. *Academic degrees:* Ph.D., M.D., D.V.M., R.N., M.S., or all can be written without periods.

FIGURE 14.1

Quick Punctuation Guide[*]

Between two whole sentences	Between a phrase or dependent clause and a whole sentence	In a whole sentence interrupted by a phrase or dependent clause	In a list or series
⊙ usually	⊙ if the phrase or dependent clause comes first and is long	◯~◯ no punctuation if the interrupter limits the meaning of the word before it	⊙ between each parallel item
⊙ if connected by *and, but, or, nor, yet, so, for*	◯ no punctuation if the whole sentence comes first followed by a phrase or clause	⊙~⊙ if the interrupter simply adds information or detail	⊙ between all items when one of the items already has a comma in it
⊙ if they are closely related in meaning		(~) to play down interrupter	
⊙ if the second one restates the first		⊖~⊖ to stress interrupter	
⊙ if followed by a conjuctive adverb (e.g., *however, thus, nevertheless*)			

[*]A glance at this table will solve most of (but not all) your punctuation quandaries. Decide which one of the four situations given in the column headings has you baffled and find the appropriate solution in the table.

C. ***Dates or time:*** 1000 B.C. or AD 150 (periods are optional here)
10:00 a.m., 3 p.m., or 10 A.M., 3:00 P.M.
(***but not:*** "Sylvester succumbed to exhaustion in the early a.m.")

D. ***Places:*** Washington, D.C. or DC, the U.S. economy (***but not:*** "Ringo flew to the U.S. on a jumbo jet.")

E. ***Organizations:*** IRS, FBI, ITT, UNICEF, YWCA.

Many organizations are commonly known by their abbreviations (usually written in capital letters without periods). If you are not certain whether your readers will recognize the abbreviation, write the name out the first time you use it, put the initials in parentheses following it, and use only the initials thereafter.

F. *Latin expressions:* e.g. (for example); i.e. (that is); etc. (and so forth)—but do not use etc. just to avoid thinking of other examples. In an essay, writing out the English phrase is preferred; it's OK to use abbreviations within parentheses.

2. **In Works Cited lists for papers that use sources, abbreviate the following (per MLA style).**

   A. The month (except for May, June, and July)

   B. The names of publishers (Yale UP for Yale University Press)

   C. The names of states, if cited (Boston, MA)

   D. The words *editor* (ed., eds.), *translator* (trans.), *compilers* (comps.), and *volume* (vol., vols.)

3. **Avoid using symbols (%, #, &).**

   In scientific papers, however, you are expected to use both numerals and symbols.

   See also *Numbers.*

Active Voice   See *Passive Voice.*

adv *adj* Adverb/Adjective Confusion

1. **Adverbs usually end in -ly.**

Adjective	Adverb
beautiful	beautifully
rapid	rapidly
mangy	mangily

   Naturally, there are exceptions—adjectives that end in *-ly* like *sickly, earthly, homely, ghostly, holy, lively, friendly, manly*—but these seldom cause difficulty. Also, there are adverbs that do not end in *-ly—now, then, later, there, near, far, very, perhaps*—but hardly anybody messes these up either.

2. **Adverbs modify verbs, adjectives, and other adverbs.**

	subj.	*vb.*	*adv.*
A. *Standard:*	The car	was vibrating	badly.

	subj.	*vb.*	*adj.*
Faulty:	The car	was vibrating	bad.

subj.   vb.   adv.   adv.

B. *Standard:*   The car was moving really rapidly.

subj.   vb.   adj.   adv.

Faulty: The car was moving real rapidly.

subj. vb.   adv.   adj.

C. *Standard:*   The car was badly damaged.

subj. vb.   adj.   adj.

Faulty: The car was damaged bad.

3. Adjectives modify *nouns* or *pronouns*.

n. vb.   adj.   n.

A. Fido is a frisky pup.

pron. vb.   adj.

B. She looks frisky.

4. Adjectives also follow linking verbs *(to be, to feel, to appear, to seem, to look, to become, to smell, to sound, to taste)* and refer back to the noun or pronoun subject.

subj. vlk.   adj.

A. Fido feels bad.

subj. vlk.   adj.

B. Fido smells bad.

Notice that a verb expressing action requires an adverb in what appears to be the same construction, but the adverb here modifies the verb:

subj. vb.   adv.

C. Fido eats messily.

subj.   vb.   adv.

D. Fido scratches frequently.

5. Some short adverbs do not need the *-ly* ending in informal writing.

Drive slowly!   Drive slow!
Yell loudly.   Yell loud.

6. The distinction between *good* and *well*.

Good is an adjective: it can be compared (*good, better, best*). *Well* can be an adverb (as in "Jamal writes well.") or an adjective (as in "Carla is well now.") What you want to avoid, then, is using *good* as an adverb.

A. *Wrong:*   Jamal writes *good.*
    Right: Jamal writes *well.*

B. *Wrong:*   Carla's job pays *good.*
    Right: Carla's job pays *well.*

Remember, though, that the linking verbs take predicate adjectives, so you are right to say:

linking *pred.*
subj. *vb.* *adj.*
C. Jamal looks good.

linking *pred.*
subj. *vb.* *adj.*
D. Carla's attitude is good.

E. I feel good.

F. I feel bad about my grade.

"I feel badly" means "I have a poor sense of touch," though people mistakenly use it to mean "I feel bad" emotionally.

If in doubt, find a more precise expression.

Jamal looks healthy (or happy or handsome).

Carla's attitude is positive (or cooperative or hopeful).

I feel frisky (or energetic or great).

EXERCISE

14.1

In the following sentences choose the correct form or forms to use in writing standard English.

1. Yoshi certainly dances (good, well).
2. The candidate talked too (loud, loudly).
3. Larry responds to requests (lazy, lazily).
4. Onion soup tastes (yummy, yummily).
5. Sodium nitrite reacts (dangerous, dangerously) in your stomach.
6. Reggie had been arguing (extreme, extremely) (loud, loudly).
7. Be (careful, carefully)!
8. Tamara appears to be (good, well).
9. Rhinoceroses seldom move very (quick, quickly).
10. (Rippling, ripplingly), the stream flowed through the park.

Agreement (Pronoun and Antecedent)

agr

1. **Pronouns should agree in number with their antecedents (the words they stand in for).**

   A. Charlene shucked *her* sweater.

   B. Charlene and Bianca shucked *their* sweaters.

   C. Neither Charlene nor Bianca shucked *her* sweater.

   Some indefinite pronouns can be singular or plural, depending on the construction.

   D. *All* my <u>money</u> <u>is</u> gone.

   E. *All* my <u>pennies</u> <u>are</u> spent.

   F. *Some* of <u>this toast</u> <u>is</u> burned.

   G. *Some* of <u>these peas</u> <u>are</u> tasteless.

2. **Some *indefinite* pronouns *sound* plural but have been decreed grammatically singular.**

anybody	none	someone	neither
anyone	no one	everyone	either

   Consider, for instance, the logic of these grammatically correct sentences:

   > Because everyone at the rally spoke Spanish, I addressed him in that language.

   > Everyone applauded, and I was glad he did.

   > After everybody folded his paper, the instructor passed among him and collected it.

   Robert C. Pooley points out in *The Teaching of English Usage* that grammarians since the eighteenth century have been trying to coerce writers into observing this arbitrary, often illogical, distinction. Professor Pooley, in summarizing his findings on current usage, reports:

   > It may be concluded, then, that the indefinite pronouns *everyone, everybody, either, neither,* and so forth, when singular in meaning are referred to by a singular pronoun and when plural in meaning are referred to by a plural pronoun. When the gender is mixed [includes both females and males] or indeterminate [possibly includes both sexes] the plural forms *they, them, their* are frequently used as common gender singulars.

Thus, we may now write in standard English,

A. *Everyone* should wear *their* crash helmets.

B. *Neither* of the puppies has *their* eyes open yet.

C. *None* of those arrested will admit *they* were involved.

That takes care of what used to be a really troublesome problem with pronoun agreement. But you should realize that there are still plenty of people around who will disapprove of this usage. Many people who learned standard English, say, twenty years ago will declare you wrong if you write *everyone* followed by *their.* If you prefer to avoid ruffling such readers, you can use both pronouns:

D. *Everyone* should wear *his or her* crash helmet.

E. *Neither* of the informers escaped with *his or her* life.

F. *None* of those arrested will admit *he or she* was involved.

There remains, too, the sticky problem of what pronoun to use if your indefinite pronoun is strictly singular in meaning. This dilemma occurs frequently because we are programmed to write in the singular. Some people would write

G. *Each* student must show *his* permit to register.

But the problem is easily solved by using the plural:

> *Students* must show *their* permits to register.

or, try this:

> *Each* student must show *a* permit to register.

The meaning remains the same, and you have included both sexes.

Occasionally, you may need to write a sentence in which you emphasize the singular.

H. *Each* individual must speak *his or her* own mind.

But the sentence will be just as emphatic if you write it in this way:

> *Each one of us* must speak *our* own minds.

Try to break the singular habit and cultivate the plural. You can thus solve countless agreement problems automatically.

For more tips on inclusive language, see *he or she* and *man/person* in Chapter 15.

In the following sentences, select one or more words suitable for filling in the blank in an inclusive way. If you cannot think of such a word, revise the sentence.

1. Everyone on the plane should fasten _____ seat belts.

2. Anyone living outside of town should leave _____ job early to avoid getting _____ car stuck in a snow drift.

3. A good student does _____ homework.

4. Someone has left _____ car lights on.

5. Our dog has lost _____ collar.

6. The writer must consider _____ audience.

7. Everyone must present _____ ID at the door.

8. Anyone wishing to improve _____ tennis game should work on _____ backhand.

9. After listening to the patient's heartbeat, the doctor removed _____ stethoscope.

10. Each person must cast _____ own vote.

Agreement (Subject and Verb)

agr

1. Subjects and verbs should agree in *number* (singular or plural).

plural   plural
subj.   vb.
A. Artichokes are a struggle to eat.

singular   singular
subj.   vb.
B. An artichoke is a struggle to eat.

NOTE: *The* to be *verb (am, was, were, being, been, etc.) agrees with the subject (a noun before the verb), not the predicate nominative (a noun following the* to be *verb).*

subj.   pred. nom.
C. My favorite fruit is peaches.

subj.   pred. nom.
D. Peaches are my favorite fruit.

2. Most nouns add *-s* to form the plural.

> snips and snails and puppy dogs' tails

But with most verbs, the singular form ends in *-s* and you drop it to form the plural.

> one squirrel gnaws, several squirrels gnaw

3. Do not let intervening modifiers confuse you.

Sometimes a modifier gets sandwiched in between subject and verb to trip the unwary, like this:

>   *subj.*   *vb.*
> **A. *Wrong:***   The full <u>extent</u> of his crimes <u>have</u> now <u>been</u> <u>discovered</u>.

"Crimes have been discovered" sounds fine, but *crimes* is *not* the subject of that sentence. The actual subject is the singular noun *extent,* with *crimes* serving as object of the preposition *of.* The sentence should read:

>   *subj.*   *vb.*
> **Right:**   The full <u>extent</u> of his crimes <u>has</u> now <u>been</u> <u>discovered</u>.

Here are more correct examples of sentences with intervening modifiers.

>   *subj.*
> **B.** The <u>bother</u> of packing clothes, finding motels, and searching for restaurants
>   *vb.*
>   <u>takes</u> the joy out of vacation.
>
>   *subj.*   *vb.*
> **C.** <u>Pictures</u> showing nude women and men having sexual contact <u>are</u> shocking.
>
>   *subj.*   *vb.*
> **D.** <u>Books</u> full of adventure <u>are</u> what Lucy likes.

4. Singular subjects connected by *and* require a plural verb.

>   *1*   +   *1 = plural*
> **A.** The <u>pitcher</u> and the <u>catcher</u> <u>are</u> both great players.

But sometimes we complicate matters by connecting singular subjects with *correlative conjunctions (not . . . but, not only . . . but also, neither . . . nor, either . . . or)* instead of *and.* Then the verb should be singular, although the idea may still come out plural.

B. Not only the pitcher but the catcher also is getting tired.

C. Neither the pitcher nor the catcher is still frisky.

D. Either the pitcher or the catcher is slowing down.

5. **Compound *plural* subjects connected by *or* require a plural verb.**

   <u>Fleas</u> or <u>ticks</u> <u>are</u> unwelcome.

6. **In the case of subjects joined by *or* or *nor*, if one subject is plural and the other singular, the verb agrees with the subject closest to it.**

   A. <u>Leather</u> or <u>hubcaps</u> <u>remind</u> me of you.

   B. <u>Hubcaps</u> or <u>leather</u> <u>reminds</u> me of you.

   WARNING: *Some constructions appear compound but really are not. Singular subjects followed by words such as* **with, like, along with, as well as, no less than, including, besides** *are still singular because these words are prepositions, not coordinating conjunctions. The idea in the sentence may be distinctly plural, but be advised that the subject and verb remain singular.*

   C. My <u>cat</u>, as well as my parakeet, <u>is</u> lost.

   D. <u>Seymour</u>, together with his St. Bernard, his pet alligator, and his piranha fish, <u>is</u> moving in with us.

   E. <u>Claudia</u>, no less than Carlyle, <u>is</u> responsible for this outrage.

7. **Always find the grammatical subject, and make the verb agree.**

   We do not always follow the usual subject-followed-by-verb sentence pattern.

   vb.   *subj.*   *vb.*
   A. Where <u>have</u> all the <u>flowers</u> <u>gone</u>?

   If the sentence is longer, you may have trouble.

   B. *Wrong:*   Where has all the hope, gaiety, yearning, and excitement gone?

   NOTE: *The adverb* **where** *can never be the subject of a sentence, so you must look further. The actual subject is compound: "hope, gaiety, yearning, and excitement," which means the verb should be* **plural**.

   Right: Where <u>have</u> all the <u>hope</u>, <u>gaiety</u>, <u>yearning</u>, and <u>excitement</u> <u>gone</u>?

   We often invert subject and verb for stylistic reasons.

                                                        vb.   *subj.*
   C. *Right:*   In poverty, injustice, and discrimination <u>lies</u> the <u>cause</u> of Juan's bitterness.

                vb.   *subj.*   *subj.*
   D. *Right:*   Here <u>are</u> my friend <u>Seymour</u> and his cousin <u>Selma</u>.

Like the adverbs *here* and *where,* the word *there* often poses alluringly at the beginning of a sentence, looking for all the world like the subject. Do not be deceived. *There* can never be the subject; it is either an adverb or an *expletive* (a "filler" word that allows variety in sentence patterns). So before you automatically slide in a singular verb after *there,* find out what the subject really is.

                   vb.   *subj.*

E. *Right:* There is great hope for peace today.

                   vb.   *subj.*

F. *Right:* There are two great hopes for peace today.

The pronoun *it* can also be an expletive, but unlike *there,* it can be the subject of a sentence and always takes a singular verb, even when functioning as an expletive.

G. *Right:* It is a mile to the nearest phone.

H. *Right:* It is miles to the nearest phone.

8. **Collective nouns can be singular or plural.**

   Some words in the language (*group, staff, family, committee, company, jury*) can be either singular or plural, depending on the context. To suggest that the members are functioning together as a single unit, you can write

   A. The office staff is working on the problem.

   B. The jury has agreed on a verdict.

   Or to suggest that individual members are functioning separately within the group, you can write

   C. The office staff are debating that proposal.

   D. The jury have not yet agreed on a verdict.

EXERCISE

14.3

In the following sentences, choose the correct word.

1. There (is, are) my cousin Ralph and his friend Rudy, jogging in the rain.
2. Where (has, have) the toothpaste and the hairbrush gone?
3. Not only adults but also children (has, have) problems.
4. Bananas and peanut butter (make, makes) a tasty sandwich.
5. Caffeine or cigarettes, in quantity, (cause, causes) damage to the body.

6. Cigarettes or caffeine, in quantity, (cause, causes) damage to the body.

7. The impact of these statistics (has, have) not yet been fully analyzed.

8. Movies packed with violence (is, are) still a favorite with the public.

9. In great poetry (lie, lies) many great truths.

10. Our family (is, are) in disagreement about where to spend our vacation.

Analogy

fig

An *analogy* is a form of comparison, either brief or extended.

A brief analogy will be a metaphor or simile. (See *Figures of Speech.*) An extended analogy provides a more thorough comparison and can be a means of organizing a paragraph, perhaps even a whole essay. You use something familiar to explain something unfamiliar. Geologists, for instance, often describe the structure of the earth's crust by comparing the layers to the layered flesh of an onion. Sometimes writers use analogy in an attempt to persuade, as advocates of legalizing marijuana are likely to argue that the present laws are as ineffective and unnecessary as prohibition laws in the twenties. Although analogy is not purely logical, you can certainly use analogy persuasively—so long as your analogy is indeed persuasive.

Antecedent   See *Agreement (Pronoun and Antecedent).*

Apostrophe

apos

1. **The apostrophe signals possession (except for the possessive pronouns, which do not need apostrophes: *ours, yours, its, theirs*).**

   Clarence's car
   the Joneses' junk
   Yeats's yearnings or Yeats' yearnings

2. **An apostrophe signals that some letters (or numbers) have been left out.**

   we've (for *we have*)
   something's (for *something has* or *something is*)
   mustn't (for *must not*)
   class of '75 (for *class of 1975*)
   o'clock (for *of the clock*)

3. **The *its/it's* confusion.**

Use the apostrophe only for the contraction. *It's = it is* or *it has.* If you use the apostrophe to form the possessive of *it* and write

That dumb dog chomped it's own tail.

you have really said

That dumb dog chomped it is own tail.

That dumb dog chomped it has own tail.

And your readers may wonder about you as well as the dog. Make a mental note to check every *its* and *it's* when you proofread if you tend to be careless about apostrophes. If you are writing on a computer, use the *search* command to find each *its* and *it's* and check them all.

REMEMBER: its = *"of it"—possessive (The dog chomped its tail.)*
it's = *"it is"—contraction (It's not an intelligent dog.)*

4. **Apostrophes are optional in forming the plural of numbers, titles, letters, and words used as words.**

The 1970's [or 1970s] proved quieter than the 60's [or 60s].
We hired two new Ph.D.'s. [or Ph.D.s]
Seymour makes straight A's.
Those two ***and***'s [or ***and***s] are ineffective.
You are learning the dos and don'ts of English usage.
Horace rolled three consecutive 7's [or 7s].

But no apostrophe in

Horace rolled three consecutive sevens.

EXERCISE

14.4

Choose the correct term in the following sentences.

1. The (Cox's, Coxes) will be gone for two weeks.
2. That donkey is not known for (it's, its) docility.
3. The (begonia's, begonias) have finished blooming.
4. Some lucky (dogs', dogs) houses are as warm as toast.
5. Mind your (ps and qs, p's and q's).
6. We want to be home before (its, it's) dark.
7. Steve smashed up Bill (Smiths', Smith's) car.

8. Kesha is learning the (ins and outs, in's and out's) of computer programming.
9. Hector's children are already in their (teens, teens').
10. Harold has gone to see the (Harrises', Harris's, Harris') new house.

Appositive

An appositive is a word or phrase that comes directly after a noun and identifies or supplements it. Appositives should have commas on both ends.

> Stella, ***the older sister,*** was quite intelligent, while Blanche, ***the younger sister,*** was courageous.

Also see *Case of Pronouns,* number 3.

Article

Articles are words used to limit or identify nouns: *a, an, the.*

Auxiliary Verb   See *Verbs,* page 303.

Bafflegab   See *Diction,* number 4.

Balanced Sentence

1. **A sentence that has balanced (or *parallel*) structure includes a series or pair of elements that are grammatically similar.**

   A. Series of prepositional phrases

   The juggler tosses ninepins <u>over</u> his head, <u>behind</u> his back, and <u>under</u> his knee.

   B. Series of three adjectives

   <u>Ignorant</u>, <u>sullen</u>, and <u>mean-spirited</u>, the young man did not seem to be a promising father.

   C. Pair of clauses

   She hoped <u>that she argued</u> the case well and <u>that she achieved</u> justice quickly.

2. Make items in series parallel.

Most of the time, similar grammatical constructions pair up naturally, but sometimes they get jumbled. You must then decide what grammatical construction you want and make the items in the series or pair fit that construction.

A. *Jumbled:*   She never got used to the drudgery, depression, and being so ill-paid for her work at the nursing home.

That example has two nouns and a gerund phrase.

Improved: She never got used to the drudgery, depression, and low pay of her work at the nursing home.

Now all are nouns.

B. *Jumbled:*   This new kind of therapy promises to make you happy, to improve your love life, and that it will make your hair shiny.

This one has two infinitive phrases and a clause.

Improved: This new kind of therapy promises to make you happy, to improve your love life, and even to make your hair shiny.

Now all three items are infinitive phrases.

C. *Jumbled:*   The bell was about to ring, the students closed their books, and watched the clock anxiously.

The third item is not a clause.

Improved: The bell was about to ring, the students closed their books, and everyone watched the clock anxiously.

Now all the items are independent clauses.

3. Balance sentences for effect and emphasis.

Practice writing parallel constructions for their beauty and impact. These qualities shine in the conclusion of a review of Dee Brown's *Bury My Heart at Wounded Knee,* a book detailing the deplorable treatment of Native Americans by White Americans who desired their land. The paragraph is effective for several reasons, but mainly because of the balanced structure:

The books I review, week upon week, report the destruction of the land or the air; they detail the perversion of justice; they reveal national stupidities. None of them—not one—has saddened me and shamed me as this book has. Because the experience of reading it has made me realize for once and all that we really don't know who we are, or where we came from, or what we have done, or why.

—Geoffrey Wolff

Put items in the following sentences into parallel constructions. Revise as much as you like.

1. The first part of the line dance consists of three steps backward, a touch step, and then stepping forward three times.

2. The dancer should remember to act unruffled, self-composed, and as though the steps came naturally.

3. After the dancer repeats the first part, a sideways two-step is executed, and the dancer two-steps back into the starting position.

4. Experienced dancers say that the hops and slides in the third part are the most exciting and also hard to teach to others.

5. The final step is executing a ninety-degree kick-turn and to start the pattern over from the beginning.

6. Yoshi knows all about how to pack a suitcase and finding clothes that wash easily.

7. Roommates are told everything from grades to who went out with whom the night before.

8. Armando's designs are simple in pattern and bold colors.

9. Mainly poor people, retired people, and those who have lost their jobs are protesting.

10. Horace leaps to his feet, runs upstairs, grabs his tennis racquet, and then a partner cannot be found.

Brackets

[ ]

Use brackets as a signal for readers in the following cases.

1. **To change verb tenses in a quotation.**

Usually you can adjust your phrasing to suit a quotation, but if the quotation is past tense and you are writing in present tense (or vice versa), it is considerably easier to change the verb in the quotation than to rewrite your paper. If you want to make a past tense quotation about H. L. Mencken fit your present tense essay, do it like this:

Original in past tense

"He defended prostitution, vivisection, Sunday sports, alcohol, and war."

Changed to present tense

"He defend[s] prostitution, vivisection, Sunday sports, alcohol, and war."

2. To clarify any word in a quotation.

Jessica Mitford remembered, "In those days [the early 1940s] until the post-war repression set in, the [Communist] Party was a strange mixture of openness and secrecy."

3. To enclose *sic.*

When you quote a passage that contains an error, you must copy the error. The word *sic* ("thus" in Latin) means, "Honest, it really was written that way." One edition of Stephen Crane's "The Open Boat" reads this way:

"The correspondent, as he rowed, looked down as [sic] the two men sleeping underfoot."

4. To enclose parenthetical material that is already within parentheses.

Use brackets this way only if you cannot avoid it, as in a scholarly aside, like this one:

(For an informed appraisal of her relationship with the Rev. Mr. Wadsworth, see Richard B. Sewall, *The Life of Emily Dickinson* [New York: Farrar, 1974], 444–62.)

cap

lc

Capitalization

1. Begin each sentence with a capital letter, including sentences you quote.

Ambrose Bierce says that "Diplomacy is the patriotic art of lying for one's country."

2. Begin each line of poetry with a capital letter only if the poet has used capitals.

3. Always capitalize the pronoun *I*.

4. **Use caution in capitalizing words to express emphasis or personification (Truth, Justice, Beauty), unless you are writing poetry.**

5. **Capitalize proper nouns—the names of specific persons, places, historical events and periods, organizations, races, languages, teams, and deities.**

Lowercase	Capitalized
the town square	Washington Square
go to the city	go to Boston
our club secretary	the Secretary of State
traveling east	visiting the Far East
a historical document	the Monroe Doctrine
reading medieval history	studying the Middle Ages
taking Latin, chemistry, and math	Latin 100, Chemistry 60, Math 240
an industrial town	the Industrial Revolution
a political organization	Common Cause
an ethnic group	a Native American
our favorite team	the Galveston Gophers
buttered toast	French toast
the gods	Buddha, Allah, Zeus

6. **Most people capitalize pronouns referring to the Christian God or Jesus.**

   Our Father, Who art in heaven, hallowed be Thy name . . .

   In His name, Amen.

7. **When in doubt, consult your dictionary.**

   If the word is capitalized in the dictionary entry, you should always capitalize it. If you find a usage label, like "often cap." or "usually cap.," use your own judgment. Occasionally, a word will acquire a different meaning if capitalized.

   Abraham Lincoln was a great democrat.

   Lyndon Johnson was a lifelong Democrat.

   The Pope is Catholic.

   Carla's taste is catholic (all-encompassing).

8. **Capitalize the *first* and *last* words of titles; omit capitals on articles, conjunctions, and prepositions of fewer than five letters.**

   If you are unable to tell an article from an artichoke or a preposition from a pronoun, see our Chapter 13, "Background in Grammar."

Pride and Prejudice
Gone with the Wind
Shakespeare Without Tears
Been Down So Long It Looks like Up to Me
One Flew Over the Cuckoo's Nest

9. Capitalize after colons.

Always capitalize the first word following the colon in a title.

Problems of Urban Renewal: A Reconsideration

A capital letter on the first word after a colon in a sentence is optional—unless a question or quotation follows; then capitalize.

case

Case of Pronouns

1. Pronouns change form with function.

Although nouns do not change form to show case when they move from being subjects to objects, pronouns do. We can write

A. Kesha resembles my sister.

B. My sister resembles Kesha.

But with pronouns, alas, we must use a different form for subjects and objects.

C. *She* resembles my sister.

D. My sister resembles *her*.

The case forms are easy:

Subjective	*Objective*	*Possessive*
I	me	mine
he	him	his
she	her	hers
you	you	yours
it	it	its
we	us	ours
they	them	theirs
who	whom	whose
whoever	whomever	whosever

Most of the time the possessives give no trouble at all, except for the confusion of the possessive *its* with the contraction *it's* (see *Apostrophe*, section 2). But problems like the following do come up.

2. **When the subject or object is compound, drop the noun momentarily to decide which case to use.**

   A. *Faulty:*   Sylvester and *me* went to a lecture.
      Preferred: Sylvester and *I* went to a lecture.

   B. *Faulty:*   Desiree sat with Sylvester and *I*.
      Preferred: Desiree sat with Sylvester and *me*.

   If in doubt about which pronoun to choose, drop the noun momentarily and see how the pronoun sounds alone:

   > *I* went?   or   *me* went?
   > Desiree sat with *me?*   or   Desiree sat with *I?*

   Your ear will tell you that "me went" and "sat with I" are not standard constructions.

   Remember that although prepositions are usually short words (*in, on, at, by, for*), a few are deceptively long (*through, beside, among, underneath, between*). Long or short, prepositions always take the objective pronoun.

   > between Homer and *me*
   > among Homer, Martha, and *me*
   > beside Martha and *me*

3. **When pronouns are used with appositives, drop the noun momentarily to decide.**

   A. *Faulty:*   *Us* cat lovers are slaves to our pets.
      Preferred: *We* cat lovers are slaves to our pets.

   B. *Faulty:*   Spring is a delight for *we* hedonists.
      Preferred: Spring is a delight for *us* hedonists.

   Once more, if in doubt about which pronoun to choose, drop the noun and your ear will guide you: "*We* are slaves to our pets," not "*Us* are slaves to our pets"; "Spring is a delight for *us*," not "Spring is a delight for *we*."

4. **When pronouns are used in comparisons, finish the comparison in your mind.**

      Faulty: Demon rum is stronger than me.
      Preferred: Demon rum is stronger than I.

   These comparisons are incomplete (or *elliptical*). If you finish the statement—at least in your mind—you will eliminate any problem. You would not be likely to write, "Demon rum is stronger than *me* am." Naturally, "stronger than *I* am" is standard English. How about "Henrietta's husband is ten years younger than her"? Younger than *her* is? No, younger than *she* is.

5. **When the choice is between *who* and *whom*, substitute *he* or *she* to decide the proper usage.**

Colloquial usage now allows *who* in all constructions because when we begin a sentence in conversation, we scarcely know how it's going to come out.

But in writing you can always see how your sentence comes out, so you need to know whether to use *who* or *whom*. When the choice occurs in midsentence, you can fall back on substitution. Replace the prospective *who* or *whom* with *she* or *her* in the following sentence, and your ear will tell you whether to choose the subjective or objective form.

> Kate Chopin was a superb writer (who, whom) literary critics have neglected until recently.

Ask yourself

> Critics have neglected *she*?

or

> Critics have neglected *her*?

We would all choose *her*, naturally. Since *her* is objective, the sentence needs the objective *whom:*

> Kate Chopin was a superb writer *whom* literary critics have neglected until recently.

There is also an easy way to avoid the choice. If you are writing an exam and have no time to think, try using *that:*

> Kate Chopin was a superb writer *that* literary critics have neglected until recently.

Although some people still find this usage distasteful, it is now standard English. But do not ever substitute *which* for *who* or *whom*. Standard usage still does not allow *which* to refer to people.

Preferred:	the woman **whom** I adore
Acceptable:	the woman **that** I adore
Faulty:	the woman **which** I adore
Preferred:	the woman **who** adores me
Faulty:	the woman **whom** adores me

Choose the correct pronoun in each sentence.

1. You can't win if you run against Coreen and (she, her).
2. At the next meeting Sherman and (I, me) are going to present a modern morality play.
3. For too long (we, us) taxpayers have been at the mercy of Congress.
4. Frasier is the one on (whom, who, which) I base all hope for humor on television.
5. (Who, Whom) is going to deliver the keynote address?
6. You will never persuade the people (who, whom, that) you need the most to go along with your proposal.
7. The very person (who, whom, that) you are trying to help is the least likely to accept your plan.
8. If you will agree to see us tomorrow, Sergi and (I, me) will go home now.
9. Stanley and (I, me) are planning to become transcendentalists.
10. The public should be spared commercials (who, whom, that, which) are an insult to our intelligence.

Clauses and Phrases

A *clause* is a group of words that has both a subject and a verb; a *phrase* does not have both.

Clauses:	after I lost my head
	I lost my head
	that I lost my head
Phrases:	having lost my head
	to lose my head
	after losing my head

Infinitive and gerund phrases can have a subject but will not have a finite verb:

the negatives to be developed

the film being shown

The subject within each phrase is underlined.

For a complete explanation of clauses and phrases, including their many functions, see pages 307–313 in Chapter 13.

Cliché   See *Triteness.*

coh

Coherence

Good writing must have *coherence*—a logical relationship among the parts. In short, it must *hang together.*

1. **Organize your ideas before, during, and after you write.**

   Each point should clearly follow the one before it. Make sure that all points pertain to the idea contained in your *thesis,* or main idea. (See also *Unity.*)

2. **Keep your audience in mind.**

   In order not to lose your readers when you move from one detail or example to the next (between sentences) or from one main idea to the next (between paragraphs), you must provide *transitions*—words like *for example, for instance, namely, next, besides, finally, otherwise, but, since, thus, therefore.* (See also our lists of subordinating conjunctions and conjunctive adverbs, pages 361 and 384).

3. **Use plenty of specific, concrete examples and discussion.**

   You cannot expect your readers to read your mind. Whenever you make a *generalization* (a general statement, a main point), be sure to follow it with specific examples or precise explanations to make sure that your readers can follow your thinking.

Collective Noun   See *Agreement* (*Subject and Verb*), number 8.

Colloquial   See page 287.

colon

Colon

⊙

For quick advice, see our handy punctuation chart on page 315.

1. **Use a colon to introduce lists of things: single words, phrases, or subordinate clauses.**

   A. A hawk sometimes catches small animals: chickens, rabbits, moles, and mice.

B. "It is by the goodness of God that in our country we have those three unspeakably good things: freedom of speech, freedom of conscience, and the prudence never to practice either of them."

—Mark Twain

2. **Use a colon to connect two independent clauses when the second enlarges on or explains the first.**

   A. The students had an inspired idea: they would publish a course guide.

   B. Only later did the truth come out: Bumper had gambled away his inheritance, embezzled the company funds, and skipped town with the manager's daughter.

   If the second clause poses a question, begin with a capital letter.

   The main question is this: What are we going to do about the nuclear arms race?

3. **In most cases, a colon should be used only after a complete sentence.**

   A. My favorite animals are the following: lions, tigers, aardvarks, and hippopotamuses.

   Many people, though, will stick in a colon without completing the first independent clause.

   B. *Faulty:* My favorite animals are: lions, tigers, aardvarks, and hippopotamuses.

   Careful writers would eliminate the colon in that sentence.

   Right: My favorite animals are lions, tigers, aardvarks, and hippopotamuses.

4. **Use a colon (or a comma) to introduce a direct quotation when your lead-in is a complete sentence.**

   Camus puts the matter strongly: "Without work all life goes rotten—but when work is soulless, life stifles and dies."

5. Use a colon to separate numerical elements.

Time: 9:35

Biblical chapter and verses: Revelations 3:7–16 *or*
                                 Revelations III:7–16

Act and scene: II:2

Act, scene, and line: IV:iii:23–27 *or*
                         IV, iii, 23–27

6. Use a colon after the salutation of business letters.

Dear Judge Ito:

Dear Credit Manager:

7. Use a colon between the title and subtitle of a book or article.

American Humor: A Study in the National Character

"The Money Motif: Economic Implications in *Huckleberry Finn*"

comb

Combine Sentences for Fluency

If your sentences tend to be fairly simple and monotonous in structure, combine one or two of them.

Say you are writing too many repetitious sentences like these:

Cucumber beetles begin their life cycle as white larvae. These larvae are hatched from yellowish eggs. The eggs are deposited in the soil around the cucumber plants.

What you need to do is combine the three ideas there into a single sentence, like this:

Cucumber beetles, which begin their life cycle as white larvae, are hatched from yellowish eggs deposited in the soil around the plants.

Or, if you want to emphasize instead the larval stage, you could combine the material this way:

Cucumber beetles, which are hatched from yellowish eggs deposited in the soil around the plants, begin their life cycle as white larvae.

For other material about combining ideas, see *Subordination and Coordination, Emphasis,* and *Overburdened Sentence.* And for a more thorough discussion of sentence combining, see Chapter 11.

Comma

comma

See also *Comma Splice.*

For quick advice, see the handy punctuation chart on page 315.

1. **Use commas to set off interrupters (nonrestrictive modifiers).**

   c1

   A word, phrase, or clause that interrupts the normal flow of the sentence *without changing the meaning* is nonessential or *nonrestrictive.* You need a comma both *before* and *after* the interrupter.

   A. Magnum Oil Company, our best client, canceled its account.

   B. Our instructor, who usually dresses conservatively, wore jeans and a headband today.

   C. "Being merciful, it seems to me, is the only good idea we have received so far."

   —Kurt Vonnegut

2. **Do not use commas around restrictive modifiers.**

   c2

   A. *Restrictive:*   Students who can't swim must wear life jackets on the canoe outing.

   B. *Nonrestrictive:* Melvin, who can't swim, must wear a life jacket on the canoe outing.

   Notice that "who can't swim" is essential to the meaning of the first example (it *restricts* the subject) but can easily be left out in the second without changing the basic meaning. Thus in sentence B the modifier "who can't swim" is nonrestrictive and is set off by commas. But commas around "who can't swim" in sentence A would mislead readers. The difference in meaning between restrictive and nonrestrictive modifiers should be clear in these two sentences:

   C. *Restrictive:*   Students who are lazy should be closely supervised.

   D. *Nonrestrictive:* Students, who are lazy, should be closely supervised.

c3

3. Use a comma for clarity.

After any longish introductory element (like a dependent clause or a long phrase), a comma makes the sentence easier to read.

A. Since we've run out of lemons, we'll have to make do with limes.

B. After all the trouble of sneaking into the movie, Arnold didn't like the film.

Once in a while you may write a sentence that needs a comma simply to make it easier to read, like these:

A. The main thing to remember is, do not light a match.

B. Smoking permitted, the passengers all lit up.

Do not write unclear sentences, though, and depend on a comma to make them intelligible. If in doubt, rewrite the sentence.

c4

4. A comma precedes a coordinating conjunction (*and, but, or, for, nor, yet, so*) that connects two complete sentences (*independent clauses*).

A. Myrtle splashed and swam in the pool, but Marvin only sunned himself and looked bored.

Notice, there are three coordinating conjunctions in that example, but a comma precedes only one of them. The *ands* connect compound verbs (splashed *and* swam, sunned *and* looked), not whole sentences the way the *but* does. Thus, a comma before a coordinating conjunction signals your readers that another complete sentence is coming up, not just a compound subject or object. Here are two more examples:

B. Curtis adores coconut cream pie, yet three times he has suffered ptomaine poisoning from eating it.

C. Harvey went to the library, so he may well be lost in the stacks.

c5

5. Use a comma to separate independent clauses if they are *short* and *parallel in structure*.

A. "We shall fight on the beaches, we shall fight on the landing grounds, we shall fight in the fields and in the streets, we shall fight in the hills; we shall never surrender."

—Sir Winston Churchill

B. "It was the best of times, it was the worst of times. . . ."

—Charles Dickens

6. Use a comma before a phrase or clause tacked on at the end of a sentence.

    A. "The universal brotherhood of man is our most precious possession, what there is of it."

—Mark Twain

    B. I just failed another math exam, thanks to Rob's help at the local bar.

    NOTE: *You can use a dash instead of a comma for greater emphasis.*

    C. I just failed another math exam—thanks to Rob's help at the local bar.

7. Use a comma to separate a direct quotation from your own words introducing it—if you quote a complete sentence.

    A. F. L. Lucas observes, "Most style is not honest enough."

Omit the comma if you introduce the quotation with *that* or if you quote only a part of a sentence.

    B. F. L. Lucas observes that "Most style is not honest enough."

    C. F. L. Lucas observes that in writing we are often "not honest enough."

If your introduction interrupts the quotation (as sometimes it should, for variety), you need to set off your own words with commas as you would any other interrupter.

    D. "Most style," observes F. L. Lucas, "is not honest enough."

8. Use commas to set off nouns of direct address and other purely introductory or transitional expressions.

    A. *Direct address*

        Mr. President, your proposal boggles the mind.

        Your proposal, Mr. President, boggles the mind.

        Your proposal boggles the mind, Mr. President.

    B. *Introductory and transitional words*

        Well, anywhere you go, there you are.

        Yes, we are now hopelessly lost.

        My, how the child has grown.

        In the first place, we must clean up the environment.

        We must, however, consider one thing first.

        We must first consider one thing, however.

c9

9. Use commas to separate elements in series.

A. Tabrina ordered tomato juice, bacon and eggs, pancakes, and coffee with cream.

B. Some of the old moral values need to be revived: love, pity, compassion, honesty.

NOTE: *For variety you can omit the* and, *as we did in sentence B. In sentence A the comma before* and *is now optional, but keep in mind it helps to avoid misreading.*

Another option: For emphasis, replace the commas with *ands.*

C. Some of the old moral values need to be revived: love and pity and compassion and honesty.

c10

10. Use a comma to separate adjectives in series before a noun if you can insert *and* between them.

Suppose you want to write

Tigers have thick short orange and black striped fur.

Can you say *thick and short?* You can. Can you say *short and orange?* Yes. What about *orange and and?* No way. *And and black?* Surely not. *Black and striped?* Sure. *Striped and fur?* No. So you need only three commas:

Tigers have thick, short, orange and black, striped fur.

Some series of adjectives read smoothly with no commas between them:

Sheila has short black hair styled in forty funny little spikes.

c11

11. Use commas to separate numerals and place names and to set off names of people from titles.

A. Eudora, who was born November 15, 1950, in Denver, Colorado, moved to Dallas, Texas, before she was old enough to ski.

B. You may write to Laverne at 375 Fairview Avenue, Arlington, TX 20036.

C. My friend Laverne lives in Arlington, Texas.

D. The committee chose Lola Lopez, attorney-at-law, to present their case.

See also *No Punctuation Necessary* for advice about where *not* to use a comma.

Try your hand at putting commas in the following sentences, if needed.

1. Your new hairstyle is stunning Reggie.

2. Oh I'll finish the job all right but it won't be because you inspired me.

3. My point however must not be misunderstood.

4. In the first place Heathcliff should never have taken the job.

5. Heathcliff should never have taken the job in the first place.

6. Although Irving takes his studies seriously he still flunks math regularly.

7. I said you made a slight miscalculation not a mistake.

8. The tall willowy red-haired girl with the short squinty-eyed long-haired dog is Jocasta.

9. Before getting all excited let's find out if the money is real.

10. He intends to help you not hinder you.

11. The principal without a shred of evidence accused Leonard of inciting the riot.

12. If you go out please get me some cheese crackers pickles and a quart of ice cream.

13. "Whatever you do" begged Florence "don't tell Fred."

14. Percy had a fearful time talking his way out of that scrape yet two days later he was back in trouble again.

15. Yolanda's new address is 1802 Country Club Place Los Angeles CA 90029.

Comma Splice

cs

cf

A comma splice (or *comma fault* or *comma blunder*) occurs when a comma is used to join ("splice") two independent clauses together, instead of the necessary semicolon or colon.

1. **Use a semicolon or possibly a colon—*not a comma*—to separate closely related independent clauses.**

   These sentences are correctly punctuated:

   A. Morris has been listless all day; he appears to have a cold.

   B. It's tough to tell when Morris is sick: he just lies around all day anyway.

   C. Tonight he skipped dinner; Morris must be sick if he misses a meal.

If you write comma splices, you are probably not paying attention to the structure of your sentences. You are writing complete sentences (independent clauses) without realizing it. Study the section on independent clauses in Chapter 13 to be sure you know what constitutes a simple sentence.

2. **Conjunctive adverbs cannot connect sentences.**

There's another devilish complication that can produce comma splices. Conjunctive adverbs—transitional words such as *indeed, therefore, nevertheless, however*—sound for all the world like coordinating conjunctions, *but they are not.* They cannot connect two independent clauses with only a comma the way coordinating conjunctions can. The solution to this seemingly baffling difficulty is to memorize the coordinating conjunctions: *and, but, or, for, nor, yet, so.* Then all you have to do is remember that all those other words that *sound* like pure conjunctions really are not; hence you need a semicolon.

A. It's tough to tell when Heathcliff is sick; indeed, he just lies around all day like a rug.

One final word of warning: try not to confuse the conjunctive adverbs (listed on page 384) with subordinating conjunctions (listed on page 361). A subordinating conjunction at the beginning of a clause produces a *dependent,* not an independent, clause. Thus, you do not need a semicolon in the following sentence because there is only one independent clause.

B. It's tough to tell when Heathcliff is sick because he just lies around all day anyway.

If you know you have difficulty with comma splices, slip a bookmark into your text to mark the list at page 361, and another at page 384. Get into the habit of checking your punctuation when you revise.

3. **Independent clauses (except short, balanced ones) must be separated by something stronger than a comma.**

You have all these options:

A. *Use a semicolon.*

Carlos feels better today; he's outside practicing chip shots.

B. *Use a period.*

Carlos feels better today. He's outside practicing chip shots.

C. *Use subordination to eliminate one independent clause.*

Carlos apparently feels better today since he's outside practicing chip shots.

D. *Use a comma plus a coordinating conjunction.*

Carlos feels better today, so he's outside practicing chip shots.

E. *Use a semicolon plus a conjunctive adverb.*

Carlos feels better today; indeed, he's outside practicing chip shots.

Correct any comma splices in the following sentences. Just to increase the challenge, we have included one that is already correct.

EXERCISE

14.8

1. We just passed Clark Kent, he was changing his clothes in a telephone booth.
2. Doris says she doesn't want to live on a cannibal isle, she'd be bored.
3. Once a week I go out into the country and fill my lungs with clean air, this outing gives me a chance to remember what breathing used to be like.
4. Henrietta spent a grim half hour shampooing Bowser to get rid of fleas, Bowser probably preferred to keep them.
5. Hunched over her typewriter, Flossie doggedly pecks out her term paper, it isn't even due until Monday.
6. Monroe complains that his history class offers little intellectual challenge, yet he never even reads the textbook.
7. This paper is due at nine o'clock in the morning, thus you'll have to go swimming without me.
8. You can't control your temper, Throckmorton, you shouldn't be teaching a Carnegie course.
9. Seymour's a polite young man, so far as I know, he never swears.
10. My opinion of Orville is not high, because he has a closed mind, I doubt that he'll be a good teacher.

Common Noun   See *Proper Noun.*

Comparison, Degrees of   See *Adjectives* and *Adverbs.*

comp

Comparisons, Incomplete or Illogical

1. **Comparisons must involve at least two things being compared.**

   A. *Incomplete:* Calculus is the hardest course.

   Improved: Calculus is the hardest course I've ever taken.

   B. *Incomplete:* Eloise has fewer inhibitions.

   Improved: Eloise has fewer inhibitions now that she's Maybelle's roommate.

   While the comparison in "improved" sentence B is still only implied, the meaning is easy to understand. But if you want to avoid all possibility of confusion, state the comparison flat out, like this:

   Better: Eloise has fewer inhibitions than she did before becoming Maybelle's roommate.

2. **The second element of any comparison must not be ambiguous, vague, or illogical.**

   Illogical: A passionate kiss is Scarlett O'Hara and Rhett Butler in <u>Gone with the Wind</u>.

   Improved: A passionate kiss is one like Rhett Butler gives Scarlett O'Hara in <u>Gone with the Wind</u>.

3. **Do not compare words that denote absolutes, like *unique, omnipotent, infinite.***

   Illogical: Clovis came up with a very unique design.

   Improved: Clovis came up with a unique design.

Complement   See pages 306–307.

Conciseness   See pages 269–271.

Concrete Examples   See *Coherence,* number 3.

mng?

Confused Sentence

conf

Take care that every sentence you write makes sense.

Be careful not to begin a sentence one way, lose track in the middle, and finish another way.

A. *Confused:*   The first planned crime will tell how well a boy has learned whether or not he is caught to become a juvenile delinquent.

Improved: Whether or not a boy is caught in his first planned crime may determine whether he will become a juvenile delinquent.

B. *Confused:*   When frequently opening and closing the oven door, it can cause a soufflé to fall.

Improved: Frequently opening and closing the oven door can cause a soufflé to fall.

Usually, such sentences result from sheer carelessness. You should catch them when you revise. *Do not forget to proofread.*

Try to straighten out the following confused sentences. Some of them are not easy to patch up. You will need to back off and begin again in a different way.

EXERCISE

14.9

1. The second qualification for my ideal roommate would have to be easy going.
2. Prison, bringing deprivation and degradation, is many hardships.
3. By driving too fast on the freeway, it can lower your gasoline mileage.
4. A political tone is dominant through reference to economic hardship.
5. People who are continually placed in a certain category, especially a dehumanizing one, in order to achieve an appropriate self-image.
6. We often treat strangers better than, how we relate to those in our own families.
7. The difficulty in achieving goals can be determined early in an individual's development of a problem personality.
8. The flooding gets really serious and will be difficult to keep emergency vehicles running.
9. Whether a person makes the choice to go to college or not has both its problems and rewards.
10. The judge ruled that the plaintiff, even though failing to appear since ill, she could not challenge the decision.

Conjunctions, Coordinating   See *Comma Splice,* number 2.

Conjunctions, Correlative   See *Agreement (Subject and Verb),* number 4.

Conjunctions, Subordinating

See *Comma Splice,* number 2.
See *Comma,* number 3.
For a list of subordinating conjunctions, see *Fragment,* number 2.

Conjunctive Adverb

See *Comma Splice,* number 2.
For a list of conjunctive adverbs, see *Semicolon,* number 2.

Connotation and Denotation

Words are symbols that often carry two meanings:

1. **Denotative meaning—the actual definition; the person, thing, or abstract quality referred to;** the term *mother,* for instance, denotes a woman who gives birth to or adopts and cares for a child.

2. **Connotative meaning—those feelings usually associated with the word;** the term *mother* suggests to most of us warmth, love, security, comfort, apple pie.

Whether you choose to refer to the president as a *statesman* or as a *politician* may well reveal your political sympathies. Consider, for example, Frederick Lewis Allen's description of Woodrow Wilson as a "Puritan Schoolmaster . . . cool in a time of great emotions, calmly setting the lesson for the day; the moral idealist . . . , the dogmatic prophet of democracy. . . ." The word *Puritan* suggests a moralist with no human warmth. Allen could have said *high-minded* and lessened the chill factor. And what does the word *schoolmaster* suggest that the neutral word *teacher* does not? Again, a strict, no-nonsense, unsmiling disciplinarian. The word *cool* reinforces this same feeling, as does *calmly.* The term *moral idealist* sounds at first totally complimentary—but is it? We associate idealists with good intentions, but a tinge of daydreaming impracticality clings to the word. *Dogmatic* denotes closed-mindedness. And *prophet* suggests an aura of fanaticism, since the biblical prophets were always exhorting the fun-loving Old Testament sinners to repent of their evil ways or face the wrath of Jehovah. Allen has told us perhaps more through connotation in the sentence than he did through denotation. He uses connotative words to convey a picture of Wilson that he feels is accurate—the image of a cold, determined, perhaps misguided man with the best intentions.

Without the use of emotion-laden words, writing becomes lifeless. But you must be *aware* of connotations as you choose lively words, or you run the risk of producing unfortunate effects. Ignoring connotations can produce regrettable sentences, like this one:

Sandor moped around for a week before he killed himself.

The connotations of the phrase "moped around" are too frivolous for that statement (unless the writer has no sympathy whatsoever for Sandor). This sentence might be better:

Sandor was deeply depressed for a week before he killed himself.

For more advice on connotations and tone, see pages 295–296 and 287–291.

Contraction   See *Apostrophe,* number 2.

Coordinating Conjunction   See *Comma Splice,* number 2.

Coordination   See *Subordination and Coordination.*

Correlative Conjunction   See *Agreement (Subject and Verb),* number 4.

Dangling Modifier

dm

A *modifier* is a word, a phrase, or a clause that describes, qualifies, or in some way limits another word in the sentence.

1. **Every modifier in a sentence needs a word to modify.**

    A. *Dangling:*   Staring in disbelief, the car jumped the curb and crashed into a telephone booth.

       Improved: While I stared in disbelief, the car jumped the curb and crashed into a telephone booth.

    B. *Dangling:*   When a girl of sixteen, we courted each other.

       Improved: When I was sixteen, we courted each other.

       Improved: When she was sixteen, we courted each other.

    C. *Dangling:* When only seven years old, her father ran off with another woman.

    Improved: When Marcella was only seven years old, her father ran off with another woman.

2. Be sure introductory elements have something to modify.

Unwise use of the passive voice often causes dangling modifiers. (In the last example here, *you* is understood as the subject of both *pin* and *cut*.)

Dangling: After carefully pinning on the pattern, the material may then be cut.

Improved: After carefully pinning on the pattern, you may then cut out the material.

Improved: First pin on the pattern; then cut the material.

In order to avoid dangling modifiers, think carefully about what you are writing. You can eliminate many of your modifier problems by writing consistently in the active voice: "I made a mistake," rather than "A mistake was made."

EXERCISE

14.10

Identify any dangling modifiers in the sentences below, and then revise to eliminate the problem.

1. After removing the reporters, the meeting resumed.
2. Driving through the lush, pine-scented forest, the air was suddenly fouled by the sulfurous belchings of a paper mill.
3. After bolting down lunch and racing madly to the station, the train left without us.
4. Looking back in history, Americans have often professed individualism while rewarding conformity.
5. The drive up there was quite scenic with its rolling hills and beautiful lakes.
6. I think love is when you get married and have children for the rest of your life.
7. Skiers like the wind blowing through their hair seeking adventure and excitement.
8. The poor child's face turns pure white and starts throwing up all over the place.
9. When writing on a formal level, dangling modifiers must be avoided.
10. After graduation, farming with a bank loan is my goal.

Dash

The dash—which requires your readers to pause—is more forceful than a comma. You can use dashes to gain emphasis, so long as you use them sparingly.

1. **Use a dash to add emphasis to an idea at the end of a sentence.**

   Emphatic: LaBelle had only one chance—and a slim one at that.
   Less emphatic: LaBelle had only one chance, and a slim one at that.

2. **Use dashes instead of commas around an interrupter to emphasize the interrupting material.**

   To take away emphasis from an interrupter, use parentheses.

   Emphatic: My cousin Caroline—the crazy one from Kankakee—is running for Congress.
   Less emphatic: My cousin Caroline, the crazy one from Kankakee, is running for Congress.
   Not emphatic: My cousin Caroline (the crazy one from Kankakee) is running for Congress.

3. **Use dashes around an interrupter if commas appear in the interrupting material.**

   All the dogs—Spot, Bowser, Fido, and even Old Blue—have gone camping with Cullen.

4. **Use a dash following a series at the beginning of a sentence.**

   Patience, sympathy, endurance, selflessness—these are what good mothers are made of.

   If you want to be more formal, use a colon instead of the dash.

   NOTE: Do not confuse the dash with the hyphen. *On your keyboard, strike two hyphens to make a dash. To use a hyphen when you need a dash is a serious mistake: hyphens connect, dashes separate.*

Denotation   See *Connotation and Denotation.*

mng?

d

Diction

Diction (meaning which words we choose and how we put them together) is vitally important since it affects the clarity, accuracy, and forcefulness of everything we write and say. (See also *Connotation and Denotation, Triteness, Wordiness.*)

1. Select exactly the right word.

Inaccurate: I was ***disgusted*** because rain spoiled our picnic.

Accurate: I was ***disappointed*** because rain spoiled our picnic.

Accurate: I was ***disgusted*** by the mindless violence in the movie.

Use your dictionary to be sure the word you choose really means what you want it to mean. If you cannot think of the perfect word, consult your thesaurus for suggestions; then check the dictionary meaning of the term you select to be certain you have the right one. Even synonyms have different shades of meaning: you must keep thinking and looking until you find the precise word.

2. Do not confuse words because they sound alike or are similar in meaning.

Wrong word: Today's society has been ***pilfered*** with a barrage of legalized drugs.

Improved: A barrage of legalized drugs has ***proliferated*** in today's society.

3. Use lively, concrete, specific terms.

Limp: We got into the car.

Improved: All four of us piled into Herman's Honda.

Limp: This dog came up, all excited.

Precise: "[A dog] came bounding among us with a loud volley of barks and leapt round us wagging its whole body, wild with glee at finding so many human beings together."

—George Orwell, "A Hanging"

4. Avoid bafflegab.

Bafflegab (or gobbledygook) is inflated, pretentious language that sounds impressive but obscures meaning.

Bafflegab: The production of toxic and noxious residue by hydrochloric acid obviates its efficacious application since it may prove incompatible with metallic permanence.

Translation: Don't use hydrochloric acid: it eats hell out of the pipes.

See also pages 279–281.

5. Avoid doublespeak.

Doublespeak is language that deliberately obscures the meaning with intent to deceive:

> "protection reaction strike" (meaning ***bombing***)
> "to terminate with extreme prejudice" (to ***assassinate***)
> "that statement is inoperative" (it is ***untrue***)

See also pages 281–282.

6. Be selective with euphemisms.

Euphemisms obscure meaning but in a benign way:

> powder room (meaning ***women's toilet***)
> unmentionables (***underwear***)
> passed away (***died***)
> sanitation engineer (***garbage collector***)

Consider your audience. If you think they would be shocked by blunt language, then use a harmless euphemism.

7. Be careful with jargon and slang.

Jargon can mean the same thing as gobbledygook. But *jargon* also means the technical language used in a trade, profession, or special interest group: *printer's jargon, medical jargon, sports jargon.* If you are certain your readers will understand such specialized language, go ahead and use it. Otherwise, stick to plain English, and define any technical terms that you cannot avoid.

Slang can contribute a lively tone to *informal* writing, but you need to be sure your readers will understand current slang. Remember also that today's slang is tomorrow's cliché. Do not write vague expressions, like these:

> Maybelle is simply far out.
> Clyde's a real cool cat.
> That movie just blew me away.

If you decide to use slang, do not apologize for it by putting it in quotation marks. Use it boldly. (See also pages 284–286.)

8. **Do not mix formal and colloquial language—unless you do so deliberately for effect.**

You will give your readers a considerable jolt if you write a basically formal sentence and drop in a slang term.

One anticipates that the Boston Symphony will deliver its customary *dynamite* performance.

See also pages 284–288.

EXERCISE

14.11

All the sentences below misuse words in various ways. Point out what is wrong with each sentence, and then revise it using more effective diction.

1. Euthanasia is a heavy decision.
2. Time was when the past wasn't nearly so nostalgic.
3. This disturbed sibling does not observe sociologically compatible behavioral parameters.
4. "We will continue to fight in Vietnam until the violence stops."
    —President Lyndon B. Johnson
5. The government apparently doesn't dig the potential disaster inherent in the problems of nuclear waste disposal.
6. The doctor asked to be appraised of any changes that might occur in the patient's condition, irregardless of the hour.
7. My dearly beloved Fido has departed this vale of tears.
8. We need to rethink this scenario in order to maximize resource utilization.
9. Several meanings can be implied from this poem.
10. Consumer elements are continuing to stress the fundamental necessity of a stabilization of the price structure at a lower level than exists at this point in time.

Digression   See *Unity.*

Doublespeak   See *Diction,* number 5.

Ellipsis Dots

. . .

1. Use three spaced dots if your readers will be unable to tell that you have omitted words from a direct quotation.

A. *Something left out at the beginning.*

About advice, Lord Chesterfield wrote ". . . those who want it the most always like it the least."

—Letter to his son, 1748

B. *Something left out in the middle.*

"The time has come . . . for us to examine ourselves," warns James Baldwin, "but we can only do this if we are willing to free ourselves from the myth of America and try to find out what is really happening here."

—*Nobody Knows My Name*

C. *Something left out at the end.*

Thoreau declared that he received only one or two letters in his life "that were worth the postage" and observed summarily that "to a philosopher all *news,* as it is called, is gossip. . . ."

—*Walden,* Chapter 2

NOTE: *The extra dot is the period.*

2. If you are quoting only a part of a sentence—and your readers can *tell*— do not use ellipsis dots.

Occasionally, like Eliot's Prufrock, we long to be "scuttling across the floors of silent seas."

Judge William Sessions describes himself as a "West Texas tough guy" and subscribes to a law-and-order philosophy.

3. Use either ellipsis dots or a dash to indicate an unfinished statement, especially in recording conversation.

"But, I don't know whether . . . ," Bernice began.

"How could you . . . ?" Ferdinand faltered.

Elliptical Construction   See *Case of Pronouns,* number 4.

Emphasis

Work especially hard on the beginnings and ends of things—of sentences, of paragraphs, of essays—because those are the positions that require the most emphasis.

Any time you vary the normal pattern of your writing, you gain emphasis. Try the following variations:

1. **Periodic sentences.**

   Save the word or words conveying the main idea until the end (just before the period):

   > One quality they definitely do not value in the military is individuality.

   See also page 261.

2. **Balanced sentences.**

   Make all grammatical elements balance precisely:

   > With this faith we will be able to work together, to pray together, to struggle together, to go to jail together, to stand up for freedom together, knowing that we will one day be free.
   >
   > —Martin Luther King Jr.

   See also pages 262–264.

3. *Ands* **to separate a series.**

   Instead of commas, use *ands* to emphasize items in series:

   > It is his privilege to help man endure by lifting his heart, by reminding him of the courage and honor and hope and pride and compassion and pity and sacrifice which have been the glory of his past.
   >
   > —William Faulkner

   See also pages 266–267.

4. **Dashes.**

   Set off with dashes elements you want to emphasize.

   A. *At the beginning:*

   Cardinals, blue jays, finches, doves—all come to frisk in the fountain.

B. *In the middle:*

> The trial allowed—indeed, required—a jury to pick between numerous flatly incompatible theories spun by credentialed experts.
>
> —George F. Will

C. *At the end:*

> Dandy ideas these—or so it seemed at the beginning.
>
> —John Hurt Fischer

See also pages 267–268.

5. **Deliberate repetition.**

Occasionally, repeat key words for emphasis:

> Her working-class, middle-aged life was buffeted by an abusive husband, an abusive son, and a series of abusive supervisors at a succession of low-level jobs.
>
> —Hugh Drummond, M.D.

6. **Short sentences.**

A short-short sentence following sentences of normal length will get attention:

> If there is to be a new etiquette, it ought to be based on honest mutual respect, and responsiveness to each other's needs. Regardless of sex.
>
> —Lois Gould

See also page 265.

7. **A one-sentence paragraph.**

Punctuate a single sentence as a paragraph to make it extremely emphatic. (See page 249.)

Euphemism   See *Diction,* number 6.

Exclamation Point   *!*

1. **Do not use exclamation points merely to give punch to ordinary sentences. Write a good, emphatic sentence instead.**

Ineffective: LeRoy's room was a terrible mess!
Improved: We declared LeRoy's room a disaster area.

2. Use exclamation points following genuine exclamations:

> O kind missionary, O compassionate missionary, leave China! Come home and convert these Christians!
>
> —Mark Twain, "The United States of Lyncherdom"

> I'm mad as hell, and I'm not going to take it anymore!
>
> —Paddy Chayefsky, *Network*

NOTE: *Avoid stacking up punctuation. Do not put a comma after an exclamation point or after a question mark.*

See also *Quotation Marks,* number 12.

Expletive

1. An *expletive* can be an oath or exclamation, often profane.

You will have no trouble thinking of the four-letter ones, so we will mention some socially acceptable ones: Thunderation! Tarnation! Drat! Oh, fudge! Use only when reproducing conversation.

2. The words *it* and *there*, also expletives, serve as "filler" words to allow for variety in sentence patterns.

> *It* is raining.
> *There* are two ways to solve the problem.

See also *Agreement (Subject and Verb),* number 7.

Figures of Speech

fig

Figures of speech involve the imaginative use of language and can give your writing greater vividness and clarity, if used effectively.

1. Metaphors and similes.

These imaginative comparisons are characteristic of poetry but are used frequently in prose.

A. *A metaphor is an* implied *comparison.*

Clarence was a lion in the fight.

B. *A simile is a* stated *comparison (with* like *or* as*).*

Clarence was like a lion in the fight.

The term *metaphor* now serves to describe both figures of speech. Here are some examples used in prose by professional writers:

New York is a sucked orange.

—R. W. Emerson

Like soft, watery lightning went the wandering snake at the crowd.

—D. H. Lawrence

His voice was as intimate as the rustle of sheets.

—Dorothy Parker

The medical case against smoking is as airtight as a steel casket.

—Barbara Ehrenreich

See also *Analogy.*

2. Extended metaphors.

Skillful writers sometimes write imaginative comparisons that go beyond a single comparison.

The intersection of IAA Drive and Vernon Avenue is like a heart attack waiting to happen. Clogged traffic arteries have prompted city officials to begin looking at ways to correct the motoring aneurysm.

—Kurt Erickson

3. Mixed metaphors.

Be careful of metaphors that do not compare accurately, that start off one way and end another way.

A. Our quarterback plowed through their defense and skyrocketed across the goal lines.

B. The FTC does nothing but sit on its hands and fiddle while Rome burns.

C. The fan really hit the ceiling.

REMEMBER: *Figures of speech should clarify the meaning through comparisons that increase understanding. Ambiguity fascinates the mind in poetry but tries the patience in expository prose. So, be creative; but when you revise, be sure that your metaphors clarify rather than confuse.*

4. Personification.

Personification means giving human characteristics to nonhuman things (objects or animals). Use with restraint.

> The missiles lurk in their silos, grimly waiting for the inevitable day when at last they will perform their duty.

5. Avoid *trite* figures of speech. See *Triteness*.

Formal Usage

See the discussion of levels of usage in the Glossary of Usage (pages 395–396).

Fragment

frag

1. A sentence fragment is only part of a sentence punctuated as a whole.

Many professional writers use fragments for emphasis, or simply for convenience, as in the portions we have italicized in the following examples.

> Man is the only animal that blushes. *Or needs to.*
>
> —Mark Twain

> I did not whisper excitedly about my Boyfriends. *For the best of reasons.* I did not have any.
>
> —Gwendolyn Brooks

> No member [of Congress] had ever been challenged or even questioned about taking the exemption. *Until my nomination.*
>
> —Geraldine Ferraro

> *Easy to say, but hard to practice.*
>
> —F. L. Lucas

> So Shelly asked her what was "real" and the student responded instantly. "Television." *Because you could see it.*
>
> —Harlan Ellison

2. Avoid fragments in formal writing (term papers, business reports, scholarly essays).

Fragment: Pollution poses a serious problem. *Which we had better solve.*
Complete: Pollution poses a serious problem—which we had better solve.
Complete: Pollution poses a serious problem which we had better solve.

NOTE: *If you write fragments accidentally, remember that a simple sentence beginning with one of the following subordinating words will come out a fragment:*

after	if	though	where
although	only	till	whereas
as, as if	since	unless	which
as far as	so as	until	while
because	so that	when	
before	still	whenever	

Fragment: Although I warned him time after time.

Complete: I warned him time after time.

Complete: Although I warned him time after time, Clyde continued to curse and swear.

NOTE: *Words ending in* -ing *and* -ed *can cause fragments also. Although such words sound like verbs, sometimes they're* verbals—*actually nouns or adjectives. Every complete sentence requires an honest-to-goodness verb.*

Fragment: Singing and skipping along the beach.

Complete: Juan went singing and skipping along the beach.

Fragment: Abandoned by friends and family alike.

Complete: Alice was abandoned by friends and family alike.

Complete: Abandoned by friends and family alike, Alice at last recognized the evils of alcohol.

3. Use fragments in asking and answering questions, even in formal writing:

When should the reform begin? At once.

How? By throwing self-serving politicians out of office.

4. Use fragments for recording conversation, since people do not always speak in complete sentences:

"I suppose that during all [my sickly childhood] you were uneasy about me?"
"Yes, the whole time."
"Afraid I wouldn't live?"
After a reflective pause, ostensibly to think out the facts, "No—afraid you would."

—Mark Twain, *Autobiography*

5. Be sure that two constructions connected with a semicolon are complete sentences.

Questionable: He looked a lot like Quasimodo; although I couldn't see him too well.

Improved: He looked a lot like Quasimodo, although I couldn't see him too well.

Improved: He looked a lot like Quasimodo; I couldn't see him too well, though.

EXERCISE

14.12

Some of the following constructions are not complete sentences. Correct the ones that you consider faulty. Defend the ones that you find effective.

1. Marion was late to his own wedding. To his eternal sorrow.
2. Broadcasting moment-by-moment, hour-by-hour, day-by-day reports.
3. What is the best policy? To do nothing—diplomatically.
4. Wealth, a taking advantage of another's resources by materialistic means.
5. A slow taking over, a slow control of the economy leading eventually into a loss of political principles.
6. The executive, who at the end of the day, can return to the comforts of home.
7. As an explorer with an intellectual curiosity, the scientific solver of a riddle by empirical means.
8. One in which she was dictator, and because she was dictator, she held the reins.
9. A society's ignorance of a condition of human wants and needs.
10. Our highways, bridges, and water systems must be repaired. Regardless of the cost.

Fused Sentence   See *Run-on Sentence.*

Generalizations   See *Coherence,* number 3.

div

Hyphen

Unlike exclamation points, hyphens are in fashion today as a stylistic device.

1. Hyphenate descriptive phrases used as a whole to modify a noun.

George needs to get rid of his holier-than-thou attitude.

2. Hyphenate compound adjectives when they come before the noun.

ivy-covered walls   up-to-date entries
high-speed railroads   lighter-than-air balloon

3. Omit the hyphen if the descriptive phrase comes after the noun.

walls covered with ivy   entries that were up to date
railroads running at high speed   a balloon lighter than air

4. Hyphenate most compound words beginning with *self-* and *ex-*.

self-employed   ex-wife
self-deluded   ex-slave
self-abuse   ex-President

5. Never use a hyphen in the following words.

yourself   himself   itself
themselves   herself   selfless
ourselves   myself   selfish
oneself (or one's self)

6. Consult your dictionary about other compound words.

Some words change function depending on whether written as one word or two:

Verb: Where did I **slip up?**

Noun: I made a **slipup** somewhere.

7. Use a hyphen to divide words at the end of a line.

Divide only between syllables. Consult your dictionary if in doubt. Never put a hyphen at the beginning of a line.

8. Use no hyphen between an adverb ending in *-ly* and an adjective.

Beauregard is a hopelessly dull person.

Idioms

Idioms are expressions peculiar to the language for which there are no grammatical explanations. For instance, we say, "I disagree **with** that statement," but "I disapprove **of** that statement." Most of the time native speakers have no trouble with idiomatic prepositions, the ones which cause considerable grief for adults trying to learn the English language from scratch. But sometimes even native speakers choose the wrong preposition and write bothersome sentences like this one:

> *Unidiomatic:*   The young couple soon became bored *of* each other.

That should read,

> *Correct:*   The young couple soon became bored *with* each other.

If you sometimes write unidiomatic expressions, you should, during the editing process, find someone to read your paper who can tell you if your prepositions are correct.

Idioms Often Misused*

Wrong	*Right*
comply to	comply with
to my opinion	in my opinion
regardless to	regardless of
insight to	insight into
to dispense of	to dispense with
first step of success	first step toward success
opportunity of work	opportunity to work
to identify to	to identify with
job on the field	job in the field
aptitude toward	aptitude for
education depends of	education depends on
satisfied of	satisfied with
on the future	in the future
insight on	insight into

Informal Usage   See the discussion of selecting usage levels on pages 286–287.

Interjection   See *Exclamation Point.*

Intransitive Verb   See page 303.

*Adapted from Mina Shaughnessy, *Errors and Expectations* (New York: Oxford UP) 192–93.

Irregular Verb   See *Tense,* number 6.

Italics   See *Underlining.*

Jargon   See *Diction,* number 7.

Levels of Usage   See pages 284–287.

Linking Verb

vlk

Linking verbs connect the subject of the sentence with the complement.

The most common linking (or copulative, as they used to be bluntly called) verbs are these: *to be, to feel, to appear, to seem, to look, to become, to smell, to sound, to taste.* See also *Adverb/Adjective Confusion,* number 4.

Logic

logic

In order to write convincingly, your thoughts must be logical. You should be aware of the most common pitfalls of slippery logic so that you can avoid them in your own thinking and writing, as well as detect them in the arguments of others.

1. **Avoid oversimplifying.**

   Most of us have a tendency to like things reduced to orderly, easily grasped *either-or* answers. The only problem is that things are seldom that simple. Be wary of arguments that offer no middle way—the "either we outlaw pornography or the nation is doomed" sort of reasoning.

2. **Avoid stereotyping.**

   Stereotypes involve set notions about the way different types of people behave. Homosexuals, according to the stereotype, are all neurotic, promiscuous, immoral people bent only on sex and seduction. Such stereotypes seldom give a truthful picture of anyone in the group and could never accurately describe all the members.

3. **Avoid faulty (sweeping or hasty) generalizations.**

   You will do well to question easy solutions to complex problems. A faulty generalization (broad statement) can result from stating opinion as fact.

Acid rock music causes grave social problems by creating an attitude of irresponsibility in the listener.

The statement needs evidence to prove its claim, and such proof would be nearly impossible to find. Since you cannot avoid making general statements, be careful to avoid making them without sufficient evidence. At least, *qualify* your statements.

Sweeping: *All* Siamese cats are nervous.
Better: *Many* Siamese cats are nervous.

Statements involving *all, none, everything, nobody,* and *always* are tough to prove. Instead, try *some, many, sometimes,* and *often.*

4. **Watch for hidden premises.**

Another sort of generalization that is likely to deceive involves a *hidden premise* (a basic idea underlying the main statement). This observation, upon first reading, may sound entirely plausible:

If those striking workers had left when the police told them to, there would have been no trouble, and no one would have been injured.

The hidden premise here assumes that all laws are just and fairly administered; that all actions of the government are honorable and in the best interest of all citizens. The statement presumes, in short, that the strikers had no right or reason to be there and hence were wrong not to leave when told to do so. Such a presumption overlooks the possibility that in a free country the strikers might legitimately protest the right of the police to make them move.

5. **Do not dodge the issue.**

People use a number of handy fallacies in order to sidestep a problem while appearing to pursue the point. One of the most effective—and most underhanded—involves playing on the emotional reactions, prejudices, fears, and ignorance of your readers instead of directly addressing the issue.

If we allow sex education in the public schools, the moral fiber of the nation will be endangered, and human beings will become like animals.

That sentence, which contains no evidence whatever to prove that sex education is either good or bad, merely attempts to make it sound scary.

In a variation of this technique (called "*ad hominem*"), people sometimes attack the person they are arguing with, rather than the issue being argued. They call their opponents "effete, effeminate snobs" and hope nobody notices that they have not actually said anything to the point.

Another favorite dodge is called "begging the question" or "circular argument." You offer as evidence arguments which assume as true the very thing you are trying to prove. You say that pornography is evil because pornography is evil, but you have to say it fancy, like this:

> If we want a society of people who devote their time to base and sensuous things, then pornography may be harmless. But if we want a society in which the noble side is encouraged and mankind itself is elevated, then I submit that pornography is surely harmful.
>
> —John Mitchell

6. **Keep an open mind.**

Thinking is your best defense against logical fallacies. Think while you are reading or listening and think some more before you write. Be prepared to change your mind. Instead of hunting for facts to shore up your present opinions, let the facts you gather lead you to a conclusion. And do not insist on a nice, tidy, clear-cut conclusion. Sometimes there isn't one. Your conclusion may well be that both sides for various reasons have a point. Simply work to discover what you honestly believe to be the truth of the matter, and set that down, as clearly and convincingly as you can.

See also *Analogy, Coherence, Connotation and Denotation,* and *Unity.*

Misplaced Modifier

mm

Keep modifiers close to what they modify (describe, limit, or qualify).

Faulty: I had been driving for forty years when I fell asleep at the wheel and had an accident.

Improved: Although I had driven safely for forty years, last night I fell asleep at the wheel and had an accident.

Faulty: DARE is sponsoring a series of presentations on drugs for local college students.

Improved: DARE is sponsoring for local college students a series of presentations on drugs.

In the following sentences move any misplaced modifiers so that the statements make better sense.

1. Also soft and cuddly, the main appeal of a kitten is its playfulness.

2. Registration assignments will not be accepted from students until the door attendant has punched them.

3. Although similar in detail, my purpose is to show how these two sea urchins differ.

4. Otis was robbed at gunpoint in the elevator where he lives.

5. At college I hope to start singing with a scholarship.

6. A crutch is a device to take the weight off an injured leg or foot by sticking it under the arm and leaning on it.

7. When I got there, I saw two men putting on ghost costumes just like the ones that robbed my house.

8. I found a marble that looked like candy walking home from church.

9. I do not see my Aunt Frieda much in Colorado.

10. Maribelle told her first falsehood in a panic by telephone.

Mixed Construction   See *Confused Sentence.*

Modifiers   See *Dangling Modifier.*
See *Misplaced Modifier.*

Nonrestrictive Clause   See *Comma,* number 2.

no punc

No Punctuation Necessary

Commas do not belong wherever you would pause in speaking. That rule doesn't always work; we pause far too often in speech, and different speakers pause in different places. Here are some situations where people are tempted to add unnecessary commas.

1. When main sentence parts are long.

Some writers mistakenly separate the subject from the verb or the verb from the complement, like this:

A. *Wrong:*   Tall people with large feet, are particularly good autoharp players.

B. *Wrong:*   By the end of the year we all understood, that using too many commas would make us grow hair on our palms.

Neither of those sentences should have a comma in it. In sentence B, the clause serves as the direct object of the verb *understood* and thus should not be set off with a comma.

2. **When a restrictive clause occurs in the sentence.**

   Putting a comma on one end of an adjective clause and no punctuation at all on the other end is never correct. Nonrestrictive clauses always need punctuation on both ends (see *Comma,* number 1), and restrictive ones need no punctuation. Avoid errors like this one:

   Wrong: Aretha's poem that compared a school to a prison, was the most moving one she read.

   No comma is necessary in that sentence.

3. **When the word *and* appears in the sentence.**

   Some people always put a comma before the word *and,* and they are probably right more than half the time. It's correct to put a comma before *and* when it joins a series or when it joins independent clauses. But when *and* does not do either of those things, a comma before it is usually inappropriate. This sentence should have no comma:

   Wrong: Mark called the telephone company to complain about his bill, and got put on "hold" for an hour.

Noun   See page 303.

Numbers

1. **Spell out numbers one hundred and under.**

2. **In general, write numbers over one hundred in figures.**

3. **Spell out round numbers requiring only a couple of words (two hundred tons, five thousand dollars).**

   If a series of numbers occurs in a passage, and some of them are over one hundred, use figures for all of them.

4. **Always use figures for addresses (27 White's Place), for times (1:05 P.M.), for dates (October 12, 1950), and for decimals, code and serial numbers, percentages, measurements, and source references.**

EXCEPTION: *Never begin a sentence with a numeral; spell it out or rewrite the sentence.*

Object   See *Prepositions,* page 304; *Complement,* page 306.

obs

Overburdened Sentence

Do not try to cram more into one sentence than it can conveniently hold.

> The plot concerns a small boy, somewhat neglected by his mother, a recently divorced working woman who is evidently having a difficult time keeping her family, her emotions, and her household together, who discovers by mysterious means and befriends a small, adorable extraterrestrial creature.

That's just too much. It should be divided into two more graceful sentences.

> Two of the story's characters are a small boy and his somewhat negligent mother, a recently divorced working woman who is evidently having a difficult time keeping her family, her emotions, and her household together. By mysterious means, the boy discovers and befriends a small, adorable extraterrestrial creature.

¶

Paragraph

The proofreader's mark ¶ means that your instructor thinks you should indent to begin a new paragraph at that point. When all your sentences are closely related, sometimes you forget to give your readers a break by dividing paragraphs.

Remember to indent when you shift topics or shift aspects of a topic. For instance, look at the break between the preceding paragraph and this one. Both of these paragraphs are on the same subject (paragraphing), but the topic shifts from *why* to begin a new paragraph to *when* to begin a new paragraph. Because of this shift, we indented.

When you notice that you have written a paragraph over eight sentences long, it may be time to look for places to break it into two separate paragraphs.

Parallel Structure   See *Balanced Sentences.*

paral

Parentheses

( )

1. **Use parentheses around parts of a sentence or paragraph that you would speak aloud as an aside.**

   A slight digression or some incidental information that you do not particularly want to emphasize belongs in parentheses.

   A. John Stuart Mill (1806–1873) promoted the idea of women's equality.

   B. Although Clyde has lapses of memory (often he forgets what he went to the store to buy), he is the best auditor in the company.

2. **Use parentheses around numerals when you number a list.**

   Her professor did three things that bothered her: (1) he called her "honey," even though he didn't know her; (2) he graded the class on a curve, even though there were only ten students; (3) he complained that male students no longer wore suit coats and ties to class.

3. **Punctuation goes inside the parentheses if it punctuates just the words inside.**

   Consumers can use their power by boycotting a product. (The word *boycott* is from Captain Charles C. Boycott, whose neighbors in Ireland ostracized him in 1880 for refusing to reduce the high rents he charged.)

4. **Punctuation goes outside the parentheses if it punctuates more than just the enclosed material.**

   The comma does this in example 1B above. A numbered list, like that in number 2, is the *only* case in which you may put a comma, semicolon, colon, or dash before an opening parenthesis.

Choose the best punctuation (parentheses, dashes, commas, or brackets) to put in place of the carats in the sentences below. Remember, dashes **stress,** parentheses *play down,* and commas *separate* for clarity.

EXERCISE

14.14

1. The 1960 *World Book* encyclopedia claims that smoking marijuana ∧ cannabis sativa ∧ causes fits of violence.

2. I tasted his omelette and found ∧ how disgusting! ∧ that it was runny inside.

3. Stewart Alsop ∧ who my mother claims is a distant relation of ours ∧ was a well-known conservative journalist.

4. People often mistakenly think that Lenin ∧ our black and white cat ∧ was named after John Lennon of the Beatles.

5. Bateson includes in his reading list the "elongated biographical pieties ∧ about Carlyle ∧ of D. A. Wilson." (Bateson is reviewing D. A. Wilson's book, and you added the phrase "about Carlyle" to Bateson's words.)

6. Maria ran the entire obstacle course in record time ∧ three minutes!

7. Hubert ∧ the coordinator of our newsletter ∧ says he will crack up unless we get more typists.

8. If you are going to get married ∧ and most people eventually do ∧ you must not develop rigid daily habits.

9. Edgar Allan Poe ∧ 1809–1849 ∧ believed that beauty was the goal of poetry.

10. He thought ∧ in fact, he knew ∧ that if he continued his life of crime, he would one day find himself at the bottom of the river.

Participle Endings

Do not omit the *-ed* from the ends of participles.
An adjective formed from a verb is called a participle. Examples are

> a tired writer (from ***tire***)
> an embarrassing moment (from ***embarrass***)
> a delayed reaction (from ***delay***)

Many of the participles ending in *-ed* are said aloud without the *-ed* sound; thus, sometimes you forget to put the ending on in writing. Some typical examples of this error are

> old fashion ice cream
> air condition theater
> vine ripen tomatoes
> prejudice attitudes

Those phrases should read:

> old-fashioned ice cream
> air-conditioned theater
> vine-ripened tomatoes
> prejudiced attitudes

Passive Voice

Passive voice contrasts with active voice as you can see in the following examples:

A. *Active:* My daughter solved the problem.

B. *Passive:* The problem was solved by my daughter.

C. *Passive:* The problem was solved.

In active voice, the agent of the action (the person who does the solving, in this case) is also the subject of the sentence. In passive voice, the agent of the action is not the subject of the sentence. In both example B and example C, even though the daughter did the solving, *problem* is the subject of the sentence, and in example C, the daughter is left out altogether and gets no credit for her ingenuity.

For further discussion—and an exercise—see pages 272–275.

Period

Use a period at the end of a complete declarative sentence and after most abbreviations (see *Abbreviation*).

If a sentence ends with an abbreviation, let its period serve as the final period of the sentence: Do not double up.

Personification   See *Figures of Speech.*

Phrase

A phrase is a string of words that does not include a subject and verb combination. See *Phrases,* pages 307–309.

Point of View   See *Shifts in Tense and Person.*

Possessives   See *Apostrophe.*
See *Case of Pronouns,* item D.

Possessives with Gerunds

1. A gerund is a verbal ending in *-ing* that serves as a noun in a sentence.

A. Squishing mud between your toes is a sensual pleasure.

Squishing is the subject of the sentence, and thus acts as a noun.

B. He got back at the telephone company by folding his computer billing card each month.

Folding is the object of a preposition, and thus acts as a noun.

2. **Use possessive nouns and pronouns before gerunds because gerunds act as nouns.**

You probably would not forget to use a possessive before a regular noun in a sentence like this:

A. I was embarrassed by John's coarse manners.

But you may forget to use the possessive before a gerund. The preferred usage is as follows:

B. I was embarrassed by John's snapping his fingers to attract the waitress's attention.

Not "*John* snapping his fingers."

C. I disapproved of his acting so rudely.

Not "*him* acting so rudely."
    If you have other problems with possessives, see *Apostrophe*.

Predicate

The predicate of a sentence is the verb plus the complement (if there is one).

*faulty
pred*

Predication, Faulty

1. **This error comes from not rereading your sentences closely enough.**

A sentence with faulty predication is one whose predicate adjective or predicate noun does not match the subject in meaning.

A. *Faulty:* Your first big city is an event that changes your whole outlook if you grew up in a small town.

B. *Faulty:* The importance of graceful movement is essential when doing ballet.

C. *Faulty:* Smoothness and precision are among the basic problems encountered by beginning dancers.

In sentence A, a city is not really an event; in B, the writer probably did not want to say something as banal as "importance is essential"; and in C, smoothness and precision are not problems.

To correct such errors, you can revise the subject, the predicate, or both to make them match up better. Here are possible revisions of our problem sentences:

A. *Improved:*   Your first visit to a big city is an experience that changes your whole outlook if you grew up in a small town.

B. *Improved:*   Graceful movement is essential when doing ballet.

C. *Improved:*   Roughness and imprecision are among the weaknesses of beginning dancers.

2. **Your predication can be merely weak instead of utterly illogical.** Important words should appear as the subject and predicate.

Weak: One important point of his speech was the part in which he stressed self-reliance.

The key subject and predicate words are *point . . . was . . . part,* which do not carry much meaning in the sentence. Here's an improvement:

Improved: At one important point, his speech emphasized self-reliance.

Now the key subject and predicate words are *speech . . . emphasized . . . self-reliance,* which are more meaningful.

Preposition   See page 304.

Pronoun   See page 303.
See *Agreement (Pronoun and Antecedent).*
See *Case of Pronouns.*
See *Reference of Pronouns.*

Proper Noun

A common noun names a class (*dog, city*); a proper noun names a specific person, place, or thing (*Rover, Chicago*).

Qualification

Avoid making absolute statements in writing:

Avoid: My gym instructor is never wrong.
Avoid: Cats are finicky.

Instead, qualify your remarks:

Better: My gym instructor is seldom wrong.
Better: Cats are often finicky.
Better: My cats are finicky.

Quotation Marks

quot

〰

1. **Put quotation marks around words that you copy just as they were written or spoken, whether they are complete or partial sentences.**

   A. "Gloria, please don't practice your quacky duck imitation while I'm trying to do my income tax," she said.

   B. She said that Gloria's barnyard imitations made her "feel like moving to New York for some peace and quiet."

2. **A quotation within a quotation should have single quotation marks around it.**

   I remarked, "I've disliked him ever since he said I was 'a typical product of the midwest,' whatever that means."

   NOTE: *Do not panic if you read a book or article that reverses double and single quotation marks (that is, uses single around quotations and double around quotations within quotations). The British do it the opposite of the American way, so that book or article is probably British.*

3. **If you paraphrase (i.e., change words from the way they were written or spoken), you are using indirect quotation and you need not use quotation marks.**

   A. She said that Gloria's pig grunt was particularly disgusting.

   Her actual words were, "Gloria's pig grunt is the worst of all."

   B. He told me that he loathed levity.

   He actually said, "I despise levity."

4. **When you write dialogue (conversation between two or more people), give each new speaker a new paragraph. But still put related nondialogue sentences in the same paragraph.**

> After our visitor finally left, I was able to ask my question. "What did he mean by 'a typical product of the midwest'?" I said.
> "Maybe he meant you were sweet and innocent," Mark suggested.
> "Fat chance," I replied. "He probably meant I was corny." I doubt that he was that clever, though.

5. **Put quotation marks around titles of works that you think of as *part* of a book or magazine rather than a whole by itself: articles, stories, chapters, essays, poems, T.V. episodes.**

   Do not put quotation marks around titles of your own essays.

   Examples:

   > "Petrified Man," a short story by Eudora Welty
   > "We Real Cool," a poem by Gwendolyn Brooks
   > "My View of History," an essay by Arnold Toynbee

6. **Underline the titles of works you think of as a *whole*: books, magazines, journals, newspapers, plays, T.V. series, and movies (*Walden*, The *New York Times, Star Trek, Casablanca*). Also underline the names of works of visual art (Dali's painting, *Civil War*).**

   NOTE: *Italics in print mean the same thing as underlining by hand or on a keyboard.*

7. **Do not use underlining or quotation marks around Preface, Appendix, Index.**

8. **Underline or put quotation marks around words used as words.**

   A. You used <u>but</u> and <u>and</u> too often in that sentence.

   B. He thought "sophisticated" referred only to stylishness.

9. **In general, do not put quotation marks around words that you suspect are too slangy.**

   A. *Weak:*   Phys ed was really a "drag."

   B. *Weak:*   On the first day of class, my philosophy instructor showed that he was really "hot" on the subject.

Do not use quotation marks as a written sneer, either. Learn to express your feelings in a more exact way.

10. Periods and commas always go inside quotation marks.

A. "Never eat at a restaurant named *Mom's*," my brother always said.

B. In James Joyce's story "Eveline," the main character is at once frightened and attracted by freedom.

C. "I must admit," Cosmo said, "that Gloria sounds more like a rooster than anyone else I know."

11. Colons and semicolons always go outside the quotation marks.

"If at first you don't succeed, try, try again"; "It takes all kinds"; "You can't get something for nothing": these shallow mottos were his entire philosophy of life.

12. Exclamation points and question marks go inside the quotation marks if they are part of the quotation and outside if they are not.

A. "That man called me 'Babycakes'!" Sandra screeched.

B. He said, "Hey there, Babycakes, whatcha doin' tonight?"

C. Isn't that what my father calls "an ungentlemanly advance"?

EXERCISE

14.15

Add single or double quotation marks or underlining to these items if needed.

1. Did you see the article Dietmania in Newsweek? she asked.
2. He called Gloria's performance an embarrassment to man and beast.
3. Until I heard Gloria, I thought that oink was the basic pig sound.
4. At first, Gloria said, I just did easy ones like ducks and lambs.
5. In March she mourned, I will never get the emu call right; however, by May she had learned it perfectly.
6. Deedee calls everything cute or nice.
7. Did you say a good life or a good wife? she asked.
8. After I read the story Death in the Woods, I reexamined my life.

9. The grass is always greener on the other side of the fence: I surely found this saying true.

10. Look! There's Elvis! the casino customer cried.

Redundance

Do not accidentally pile up two or more words that say the same thing.

emotional feelings
round in shape
earthtone shades of color
fatally murdered

To avoid this redundance, just *emotions, round, earthtones,* and *murdered* would be fine.

Redundant Prepositions

Avoid using a preposition at the end of any sentence involving *where.*

Colloquial: Can you tell me where the action's at?
Standard: Can you tell me where the action is?

Colloquial: Where is our money going to?
Standard: Where is our money going?

Reference of Pronouns

1. Make sure pronouns have clear antecedents.

Pronouns are useful words that stand in for nouns so that we do not have to be forever repeating the same word. Occasionally pronouns cause trouble, though, when readers cannot tell for sure *what* noun the pronoun stands for (or refers to). Say you write

A. Seymour gave Selina her pet parrot.

There's no problem: *her* clearly means Selina. But suppose you write instead

B. Seymour gave Clyde his pet parrot.

Instant ambiguity: *his* could mean either Seymour's or Clyde's. In order to avoid baffling your readers in this fashion, you must rephrase such constructions in a way that makes the pronoun reference clear.

C. Seymour gave his pet parrot to Clyde.

or

D. Clyde got his pet parrot from Seymour.

If you have difficulty with vague pronoun reference, start checking pronouns when you proofread. Be sure each pronoun refers clearly to only *one* noun. And be sure that noun is fairly close, preferably in the same sentence.

2. **Use *this* and *which* with care.**

Whenever you use the word *this,* try to follow it with a noun telling what *this* refers to. Too often *this* refers to an abstract idea or to a whole cluster of ideas in a paragraph, and your readers would require divine guidance to figure out exactly what you had in mind. So, if you write

A. The importance of this becomes clear when we understand the alternatives.

at least give your reader a clue: "this *principle,*" "this *qualification,*" "this *stalemate*" or "this *problem.*"

Which causes similar problems. Often this handy pronoun refers to the entire clause preceding it. Sometimes the meaning is clear, sometimes not. Suppose you write

B. Jocasta has received only one job offer, which depresses her.

That sentence can be interpreted in two different ways:

C. Jocasta is depressed about receiving only one job offer, even though it *is* a fairly good job.

or

D. Jocasta has received only one job offer—a depressing one, at that.

Look up *Agreement (Pronoun and Antecedent)* for a discussion of more pronoun problems.

EXERCISE

14.16

Revise the following sentences to eliminate unclear pronoun reference.

1. He prepared a delicious meal for Al and then criticized his cooking throughout dinner, which irritated him immensely.

2. Juan told Al that his soufflés never rose as high as his.

3. Al asked if Juan allowed a speck of egg yolk or a particle of grease to pollute the egg whites. This might keep the whites from fluffing up as much as they should.

4. Al also suggested making a foil collar for the soufflé pan, which encourages the soufflé to puff higher.

5. Juan told Al that he might as well just give up and try quiche instead.

6. The problems with elaborate cooking projects are so serious that Shontel dreads them.

7. Eating a simple meal in an outdoor setting, which I prefer, relaxes both host and guests.

8. This makes the evening enjoyable and free from anxiety.

9. She told her that her husband simply refused to eat casserole dishes.

10. The chefs were eager to discuss their problems with white sauce, but they were not very serious.

Regular Verb   See *Verbs,* page 303.
See *Tense.*

Repetition

rep

Carefully designed repetition of terms can add emphasis and coherence to a passage, as it does in this one by Dr. Hugh Drummond:

> I watched a woman slip into madness recently. Her working-class, middle-aged life was buffeted by an abusive husband, an abusive son, and a series of abusive supervisors at a succession of low-level jobs. She would come home day after day, year after year from her file-clerk tedium, exhausted by the subway commute and the stained city's air, only to begin caring for her indulged, soured men; with their impatient appetites and their bottom-rung entitlements, they waited for her like beasts in a lair.

The repetition reflects the tedious repetitiousness of the woman's life.

Careless repetition, though, lends emphasis to a word or phrase awkwardly and unnecessarily:

A. After the performance, we went to Karl's house to discuss whether or not it was an effective performance.

B. The length of his hair adds to the wild appearance of his hair.

Those sentences need revision because the repeated words have no reason to be emphasized.

A. After the performance, we went to Karl's house to discuss whether or not our production was effective.

B. The length of his hair adds to its wild appearance.

Restrictive Clause   See *Comma,* number 2.

Run-on, Fused, or Run-together Sentence

run-on

Do not run two sentences together without a period between them.

Fused: Horace has a mangy dog without a brain in his head his name is Bowser.

When you proofread, make sure that each sentence really *is* an acceptable sentence.

Revised: Horace has a mangy dog without a brain in his head. His name is Bowser.

Those sentences are standard English, but a good writer would revise further to avoid wordiness.

Revised: Horace has a mangy, brainless dog named Bowser.

EXERCISE

14.17

Put end punctuation where it belongs in the following items, and revise to avoid wordiness where necessary.

1. Playing blackjack is an absorbing hobby it might even absorb your bank account if you're not careful.
2. Blackjack is the only Las Vegas game in which the house does not have an overwhelming advantage in fact the players have an advantage if they use a system.
3. The best blackjack system involves remembering every card that has turned up the player keeps a running count of what cards are left in the deck and makes high or low bets accordingly.
4. The system is based on statistical tables compiled by computer expert Julian Braun of the IBM Corporation Braun does not play blackjack himself.
5. System players must be dedicated learning the system well takes two hundred hours of memorization and practice.

6. Slot machines, on the other hand, are quite simple they do not require any practice.

7. However, the house has a stupendous advantage over the slot machine player the slot machine addicts cannot quite believe this.

8. Slot machine addicts are always hoping for the big jackpot these hopes are encouraged by the design of the machines.

9. Each machine boasts of its jackpot prize in large letters and pictures each one also makes loud noises whenever any payoff, however small, is won.

10. In spite of my wisdom I did start to play slots more often after January 1989 that is when I saw a man win a Cadillac on a machine at the El Cortez.

Semicolon

semi

For quick advice, see the punctuation chart in Figure 14.1.

1. The semicolon, which is similar to a period, means stop briefly; then go ahead.

Complete sentences connected by semicolons should be closely related.

> When angry, count four; when very angry, swear.
>
> —Mark Twain

2. Use a semicolon (instead of only a comma) when sentences are joined with a conjunctive adverb rather than with a coordinating conjunction (*and, but, or, for, nor, yet, so*).*

---

*This rule may seem senseless, but there *is* a reason for the distinction. A conjunctive adverb is not a pure connective in the way a coordinating conjunction is. *However,* it can be picked up and moved to several other spots in the sentence. You could write:

> The prisoners have a valid point; I can't, however, condone their violence.

or

> I can't condone their violence, however.

or even

> I, however, can't condone their violence.

You cannot take such liberties with the coordinating conjunctions without producing nonsentences like these:

> I can't, but, condone their violence.
> I can't condone their violence, but.
> I, but, can't condone their violence.

Here is a list of the most commonly used conjunctive adverbs.

accordingly	indeed	nonetheless
besides	instead	otherwise
consequently	likewise	then
furthermore	meanwhile	therefore
hence	moreover	thus
however	nevertheless	too

3. **The following sentences appear to require identical punctuation, but in standard usage the first requires a semicolon, the second only a comma, because *however* is a conjunctive adverb and *but* is a coordinating conjunction.**

   The prisoners have a valid point; however, I can't condone their violence.

   The prisoners have a valid point, but I can't condone their violence.

   It's easy to tell the difference between the pure conjunctions and the conjunctive adverbs if you'll just memorize the seven coordinating conjunctions: *and, but, or, for, nor, yet, so.* Then all the other words that seem like coordinating conjunctions are actually conjunctive adverbs.

4. **Do not use a semicolon to connect an independent clause with a dependent clause (a fragment).**

   Faulty: He looked a lot like Robert Redford; although I couldn't see him too well.

   Improved: He looked a lot like Robert Redford, although I couldn't see him too well.

5. **The semicolon substitutes for the comma in separating items in series when any of the items listed *already contain commas*.**

   Ann went to college and dropped out; lived with her parents for a year; worked as a veterinarian's assistant, a teacher's aide, and a clerk; and finally found her niche as an organic farmer.

   Sometimes the series may follow a colon.

   Cosmo made several New Year's resolutions: to study harder, sleep longer, and swear less; to eat sensible, well-balanced meals; and to drink no more rum, tequila, or gin.

Add semicolons to the following items where appropriate.

1. He believed that spicy foods were good for the heart, therefore, he ate jalapeña peppers for breakfast each morning.

2. He was tall, handsome, and rich, everyone loved him.

3. She divided her life into four distinct eras: blissful childhood, 1940–1954, care-free student life, 1954–1964, motherhood, 1964–1974, and, finally, liberation, 1974 to the present.

4. He forgot to add oil, thus finding himself the victim of thrown rods and other serious malfunctions.

5. Seymour asked me to bring wine, preferably a rosé, baby Swiss cheese, and rolls, ideally fresh-baked whole wheat ones, little did he know I'd already packed peanut butter sandwiches, strawberry Koolaid, and cheese curls.

6. The picnic, however, was a smashing success.

7. We had to coax George out of the fountain in front of City Hall, he was about to get arrested.

8. Our high spirits were due to good food, weather, and company, a citywide air of celebration, fun, and song, and a holiday from work.

9. Although George made a fool of himself, no one cared.

10. We ended the day with a swim at the gravel pit, then everyone went home.

Sentences   See *Balanced Sentence.*
See *Fragment.*

Shifts in Tense and Person

shift

Sometimes your prose gets rolling along, and you shift into the wrong gear while you are moving, which results in an unpleasant grinding noise in your readers' heads. These shifts occur in tense and point of view.

1. Choose either present or past tense and stay with it unless you have a reason to change.

Here's an example of faulty tense switch.

Faulty: Maris was quietly cleaning the dining room when in comes Sue with a bunch of her loud friends and puts on her Nine Inch Nails CD at full volume. Maris had to go upstairs and sulk.

There's no call for the change from past to present tense. If Maris *was cleaning*, then Sue *came* in and *put* on the CD. You can, of course, switch tenses to indicate a change occurring in time:

Revised: Maris was cleaning the dining room, but now she is sulking.

Just be sure that you do not mix tenses without meaning to.

2. **When you are writing about literature, be especially careful about mixing past and present tense in your discussion of what happens in the book.**

It's traditional to describe literary happenings in the present tense (called the "historical present"):

> Kingsley Amis's hero, Lucky Jim, *has* an imaginative humor that constantly *gets* him in trouble.

3. **Shifting *point of view* in a passage is a similar error.**

Faulty: As students we learn the ghastly effects of procrastination. You find out that you just cannot assimilate ten chapters of geography the night before a test. Most students know the grim thud in the gut that they feel when they stare at an exam and do not even understand the questions.

In that example the writer refers to the students in three different ways: *we* (first-person plural), *you* (second person), and *they* (third-person plural). To revise the passage, stick to one pronoun.

Revised: As students, we learn the ghastly effects of procrastination. We find out that we just cannot assimilate ten chapters of geography the night before a test. We become familiar with the grim thud in the gut that we feel when we stare at an exam and do not even understand the questions.

EXERCISE

14.19

Correct the tense and person shifts in the following passages.

1. At the end of *Jane Eyre,* Jane is rewarded for her courage and virtue. She found happiness in an egalitarian marriage.

2. People often forget to file a change-of-address card at the post office when you move.

3. I saw that he was growing angry, so I jump up and leave the room.

4. My sister could not stand it when I wear her favorite jeans, but what can you do when all of yours are dirty?

5. Everyone who reads knows that government is corrupt. You can never be sure, though, that we know just how corrupt it is.

6. Lynette's new haircut is badly mangled, but I don't know what you can do about it.

7. Steve arrives, obnoxious as usual, and insulted the people at Arlo's party.

8. Jamal wants to go see the play but claims that he didn't have time.

9. The philosophy students had a potluck last Friday, but then they ruin it by arguing whether the food exists or not.

10. Alfredo's truck needed alignment, but he complains constantly about the cost.

Simile   See *Figures of Speech.*

Slang   See *Diction,* number 7.

Spelling   *sp*

Use your spell-checker or your dictionary.

If you get certain pairs of words confused, like *accept* and *except,* or *affect* and *effect,* the Glossary of Usage, beginning on page 395, will help you.

Subject   See *Agreement (Subject and Verb).*

Subordination and Coordination   *sub*

1. **You can enrich a sentence or series of sentences by subordinating some of the clauses—that is, by changing independent clauses to dependent ones or phrases.**

   Plain simple and compound sentences may be the easiest ones to write, but they do not always get across the relationships between your ideas in the clearest way possible. And if you use simple sentences too often, you will have a third-grade writing style. Here are a couple of plain simple sentences.

   Lucy forgot how to spell *exaggerated.* She used the word *magnified* instead.

The idea in one of those sentences could be subordinated in these ways:

A. *By using subordinating conjunctions and adverbs (after, when, because, if, while, until, unless, etc.)*

<u>Since Lucy forgot how to spell *exaggerated*</u>, she used the word *magnified* instead.

B. *By using an adjective clause*

Lucy, <u>who forgot how to spell *exaggerated*</u>, used the word *magnified* instead.

C. *By using a participial phrase or an adjective*

<u>Having forgotten how to spell *exaggerated*</u>, Lucy used the word *magnified* instead.

2. **Avoid stringing together simple sentences with coordinating conjunctions.** Subordinate some of the ideas, using parallel structure (see also *Balanced Sentence*).

Ineffective: Phoebe got a hot tip on the phone, and she grabbed her tape recorder and hurried to the corner and an angry mob was gathered there, and she ran to a phone booth and called the paper's photographer and said, "Dave, get down here quick!"

Improved: After getting a hot tip on the phone, Phoebe grabbed her tape recorder and hurried to the corner where an angry mob was gathered. She ran to a phone booth, dialed the paper's photographer, and said, "Dave, get down here quick!"

EXERCISE

14.20

The following sentences are examples of excessive coordination. Revise each sentence, using subordination.

1. Moose is my cat, and he has stripy fur and is inordinately lazy, but he is busy now and is washing himself.

2. Clarence has a new motorcycle, and it's a huge Harley-Davidson, and he went to a wild party on it and drank six beers, and then crashed into a tree at sixty miles per hour.

3. Rae was lonely, so she joined the YWCA, signed up for line dancing and has been practicing her bored expression and has got her hip movement perfect and is now the life of the party.

4. Our firefighters went on strike and are now in jail because they want a written contract and better working conditions and also they want their lieutenants in the union, but the town council opposes the firefighters' demands, so the situation is at a stalemate.

5. Joyce Carol Oates writes superb short stories and is interested in women and in their fear of loneliness and she shows that women perpetually fear rape and violence and abandonment and she seems to suggest that women feel this way because they have few options and thus seek connections with men to give meaning to their lives.

6. Our trip to Bloomington was perfect and we had iced tea and spinach salads and stayed up late but we felt great the next day anyway.

7. Carlos is out running errands and he plans to go to the bank and then he will stop and talk to his boss and then he needs to pick up some papers from my office.

8. I always remember my mother's birthday but I have a hard time figuring out what to get her and sometimes I'm afraid I got her the same thing I got her last year.

9. Laurie plays lead guitar in a rock 'n' roll band and all the band members are female and they choose old songs that are from the male point of view and rewrite the lyrics to reflect the female point of view.

10. Maria has a job at a gift shop and it is much more demanding than it sounds and she has to take inventory and arrange displays and do the bookwork and work as a cashier also.

Thesis Statement

A successful essay needs a *thesis,* or controlling idea, either expressed in a single sentence in the introduction or implied, as in narrative or descriptive writing.

1. **Narrow the topic.**

   If you're assigned a 500-word paper on "Solving the Energy Shortage," you need to find a suitable thesis idea that you can handle within the word limit. You might, for instance, focus on the need to develop alternative energy sources. But that still is too broad a topic to cover in 500 words. You could then narrow your idea to one neglected source, like solar energy. But you will need an approach—a *focus*—for your paper.

2. **Give the direction of your thinking.**

   Your thesis should state more than just your general topic. Do not settle for just "solar energy" or even "the need for solar energy." Write a complete sentence—with a *verb* as well as a subject—to indicate what you plan to say about the subject. You might propose the need for solar energy like this: "Our economy needs to convert to solar power because it remains our only nonpolluting source of energy."

3. Make all ideas relate to your thesis.

Once you've decided on a clear, concise thesis statement, make sure that every major and minor point in the paper relates directly to that controlling idea so that your essay will be unified.

4. Be flexible.

As you write your paper, be prepared to broaden, narrow, or change your thesis if you discover a better direction or focus.

This and Which   See *Reference of Pronouns,* number 2.

Title Tactics

Your title should tell the readers, so far as possible, what the paper is about.

1. Do not use a complete sentence but give more than a hint about your topic.

Vague: The Teacher and Research
Better: The Teacher and Research in Education
Good: Practical Research Ideas for High School Teachers

2. Experiment with a colon.

Grass Roots Organization: A Key to Political Success

Legal Liability: What Everyone Needs to Know about Mercy Killing

3. Do not put quotation marks around your own essay title.

See also *Quotation Marks,* numbers 5, 6, and 7, for advice on punctuating other people's titles.

Topic Sentence

The topic sentence expresses the central idea of a paragraph. Most of your paragraphs should have one. See pages 230–235.

Transitions

trans

1. Transitional words are verbal signals that help your readers follow your thought.

Some of the most useful ones function this way:

A. *To move to the next point:* also, besides, too, furthermore, moreover, next, in the first place, second, third, again, in addition, further, likewise, finally, accordingly, at the same time, first, to begin with.

B. *To add an example:* for instance, for example, in the same manner, such as, that is, in the following manner, namely, in this case, as an illustration.

C. *To emphasize a point:* in fact, without question, especially, without doubt, primarily, chiefly, actually, otherwise, after all, as a matter of fact.

D. *To contrast a point:* yet, although, after all, but, still, on the other hand, on the contrary, nevertheless, contrary to, however, nonetheless, conversely, granted that, in contrast, in another way.

E. *To conclude a point:* thus, therefore, in short, consequently, so, accordingly, then, as a result, hence, in sum, in conclusion, in other words.

2. Use special transitional techniques when moving from one point to the next.

A. Occasionally, you can pose a question for yourself and answer it, like this:

> How does vitamin E work to repair body tissues? Nobody knows for sure, but . . .

B. A more useful method is the *echo transition* in which you touch on the idea from the previous paragraph as you introduce the idea for your next one, like this:

> He also *gave up coffee, cigarettes, and alcohol.*
>
> Despite *this new health program,* Sylvester continued to be depressed until . . .

Transitive Verb   See *Verbs,* page 303.

Triteness

trite

A *cliché* is a worn-out series of words which usually expresses a simple-minded or trite idea: "It takes all kinds to make a world." But you can express superficial ideas without using clichés too. Here is an example of a sentence your reader might think trite.

Motherhood is a joyful experience that no woman should miss.

The writer has not thought very deeply about the idea. Is motherhood joyful for a poor woman with nine children? Are women's personalities so alike that such a generalization could be true?

We all find ourselves mindlessly writing down unexamined ideas once in a while. A thoughtful rereading of whatever you write can help you avoid making this weakness public.

¶ dev   Underdeveloped Paragraphs

A friend of ours says that throughout college she got her papers back marked with "Underdeveloped ¶" in the margins. To correct this problem, she would carefully restate the topic four or five different ways in each paragraph, and she would still get "Underdeveloped ¶" marked in her margins.

Our friend finally realized, too late, what *underdevelopment* meant. She resents the fact that her teachers never wrote in her margins, "Add an example or illustration here," or, "Give some specific details," or, "Describe your reasoning step by step." She would have understood *that.*

When you find one of your skimpy paragraphs marked *undernourished* or *lacks development,* you will know what it means: add examples, provide specific details, describe your reasoning, or do all three.

und
ital   Underlining

Underlining by hand or on a keyboard is the same as italics in print. It is used three ways:

1. **To indicate titles of long works.**

   See *Quotation Marks* for a list of what titles to underline and what titles to enclose in quotation marks.

2. **To point out words used as words.**

   A. <u>Manipulative behavior</u> is my therapist's favorite phrase.

   B. You have used twelve <u>in other words</u>'s in this paragraph.

3. To indicate foreign words.

In informal writing, you do not have to underline foreign words that are widely used, like et cetera or tortilla or tango.

But underline foreign words when they are less familiar or when you are writing formally.

> After graduation, Jocasta seemed to lose her joie de vivre.

Unity

un

Unity is something we never require of casual conversation: it's fine if you wander a little off the track and tell about the Bluebird Saloon in Denver in the middle of a discussion about Humphrey Bogart films.

But in an expository essay, unity is important: you must not go on about the Bluebird in the middle of an essay about Bogart films, even though you had a beer there after seeing *The Maltese Falcon* at a nearby theater. Such a departure from the main subject is called a "digression." A paragraph or essay has unity if it sticks to the main point. It lacks unity if it wanders across the street for a drink.

See also *Coherence.*

Usage   See *Levels of Usage,* pages 395–396.
    See *Diction,* number 8.

Variety   See *Developing Variety and Emphasis,* pages 260–268.

Verb   See *Verbs,* page 303.
    See *Agreement (Subject and Verb).*
    See *Linking Verb.*

Word Division   See *Hyphen.*

Wordiness

w

A *wordy* sentence has words and phrases that add nothing to its meaning; in fact, extra verbiage can actually blur the meaning and spoil the style of a sentence. Here, for instance, is a wordy rewriting of the last sentence:

> A sentence that is wordy usually consists in part of words and phrases
> that do not add anything in the area of meaning; in fact, the meaning of

a sentence, in addition to its style, can be blurred or otherwise spoiled due to the fact that it is wordy.

To cure your writing of wordiness, practice sentence-by-sentence revision, hacking and slashing zealously. Passive voice makes a sentence wordy (see *Passive Voice*). So does using canned phrases such as *due to the fact that* instead of *because* and *in addition to* instead of *and*.

For further discussion and some exercises to practice on, see pages 269–275 in Chapter 11.

Chapter Fifteen

Glossary of Usage

In this section we distinguish between a number of words that people often confuse, like *sit* and *set, effect* and *affect.* We also describe the current usage of some terms that are questionable standard American English, like the word *irregardless* and the use of *quotes* as a noun. In making decisions on usage, we have been guided by Robert C. Pooley, *The Teaching of English Usage;* Roy H. Copperud, *American Usage: The Consensus; Webster's Dictionary of English Usage; The American Heritage Dictionary of the English Language,* 4th ed.; several widely used composition handbooks; and sometimes our own generous hearts.

Levels of Usage

Usage simply means the way the language is used. But different people use the language in different ways. And even the same person uses the language differently on different occasions. You probably speak more carefully on the job or in the classroom than you do when relaxing among friends. Good usage, then, is a matter of choosing language *appropriate* to the purpose and the occasion. In this chapter, we give you clues about which expressions are appropriate for various occasions. Although we have already discussed the levels of usage in some detail in Chapter 12, we will review them again briefly.

• *Standard:* Safe for any level of usage—formal, informal, or colloquial. Be sure *all* terms are standard if you are writing on the formal level.

- *Formal:* Some of your college writing and business writing must be done on a formal level. This means only standard American English is appropriate. Do not use slang or contractions (no *can'ts* or *don'ts*). Completely formal writing requires one to write in the third person (as we just did in this sentence).

- *General:* Most college and business writing is not strictly formal but not quite informal either. This level of usage, which is used in popular magazines, allows the use of *we* or even *you* to refer to people in general.

Formal: One can observe . . . ; This writer believes . . .

General: We can observe . . . ; You can see . . .

General usage does not usually include slang, contractions, or the use of the first-person singular (*I*), but it does employ plain, ordinary language (rather than elevated vocabulary).

- *Informal:* You get considerable leeway in informal writing. Some slang is acceptable, depending on the tolerance of your audience, and you may be able to use a few contractions. This textbook is written on an informal level.

- *Colloquial:* Since *colloquial* means the language of everyday speech of educated people, both contractions and slang are all right. But there is not much call for colloquial writing in your college courses, and it would be highly inappropriate in most business writing. Use with caution.

- *Nonstandard:* Most nonstandard phrasing (*it don't*) will get you into big trouble when writing. Most dialectical expressions (*"You hadn't ought," "She might could do it," "I been gone"*) are also considered nonstandard. Some dictionaries even label nonstandard constructions as *illiterate,* which seems harsh to us, but you should be aware that many people have strong prejudices against nonstandard English. Avoid it in writing.

If you are in doubt about any terms that do not appear in this glossary, consult your trusty collegiate dictionary—but be sure it is of recent vintage. Even the best of dictionaries become out-of-date on usage within ten years.

a/an

Use *a* before words beginning with consonant sounds; use *an* before words beginning with vowel sounds (*a, e, i, o, u*). For words beginning with *h:* use *a* if the *h* is pronounced; use *an* if it is silent.

a martini	an Irish coffee
a tree toad	an armadillo
a hostile motorist	an hour exam (the *h* is silent)

a one-car accident   an only child
   (*o* sounds like *w*)
a history test   an historical date
                        (exception to the rule)

accept/except

Accept, a verb, means "to receive or to agree with."

> We *accept* your excuse with reluctance.

Except as a preposition means "but" or "excluding."

> Everyone has signed a contract *except* Dinsmore.

Except as a verb means "to leave out"; it is used rarely, mainly in passive constructions.

> Senior citizens *are excepted* from paying an admission fee.

advice/advise

When you *advise* someone, you are giving *advice.*

>   *vb.*
> We *advise* you to stop smoking.

>   *n.*
> Mavis refuses to follow our good *advice.*

affect/effect

The verb *affect* means "to influence." The noun *effect* means "the result of some influence."

>   *n.*   *vb.*
> The *effect* on my lungs from smoking should *affect* my decision to quit.

>   *vb.*
> Smoking adversely *affects* our health.

>   *n.*
> Carleton cultivates a grungy appearance for *effect.*

Just to confuse things further, *effect* can also be a verb meaning "to bring about." And *affect* can be a verb meaning "to put on or simulate" or a noun meaning "emotional response."

>   *vb.*
> We need to *effect* [bring about] some changes in the system.

vb.

He *affects* [puts on] the disdainful petulance of a rock star.

n.

Psychologists say that inappropriate *affect* [emotional response] is a feature of schizophrenia.

These last three meanings are seldom confused with the more widely used words above. Concentrate on getting those first common meanings straight.

ain't

Still regarded as a mark of illiteracy. Do not use it in writing unless you are creating dialogue or trying to get a laugh.

all right/alright

For some reason *all right,* which is usually pronounced as if it were a single word, did not follow the same development in spelling as *already* and *altogether. Alright* is still not accepted as standard usage.

Alright is definitely not *all right* with everybody.

allude/refer

To *allude* means "to *refer* indirectly or briefly."

Mark *alluded* to some previous shady dealings by the mayor but focused on the present scandal.

Refer is more direct.

Mark then *referred* to the mayor's indictment for tax evasion.

allusion/illusion

An *allusion* is an indirect reference.

The movie's title contains an *allusion* to a nursery rhyme.

An *illusion* is a deception or fantasy.

My brother-in-law clings to the *illusion* that he looks like Tom Cruise.

almost/most

Do not write *most all;* standard usage still requires *almost all.*

Cesar drank *almost* all the Gatorade. Mel sloshed down *most* of the iced tea.

a lot/alot/allot

Even though *alike* is one word, *a lot* remains two.

> Sound-alike words can cause you *a lot* of trouble.

Allot, a verb, means to assign or parcel out.

> They *allotted* each speaker twenty minutes.

already/all ready

Already means "before, previously, or so soon."

> The children were *already* asleep when we got home.

All ready means "fully prepared."

> They were *all ready* for bed before we left.

altogether/all together

Altogether means "entirely, thoroughly."

> Issac's analysis is *altogether* sound.

> We lost the TV signal *altogether.*

All together means "as a group." Don't use this phrase unless you can rewrite the sentence with *all* and *together* separated by other words.

> Let's sing it *all together* from the top.

> Let's *all* sing it *together* from the top.

A.M./P.M.   See *Abbreviation,* number 1C, in "An A to Z Guide to Revising and Editing," Chapter 14.

ambiguous/ambivalent

Both of these words refer to a double meaning or a confusing message. But *ambiguous* emphasizes uncertainty and is usually applied to external things.

> I was so frustrated by the *ambiguous* directions that I never did learn to program the VCR.

> Her reputation as a Broadway star remains *ambiguous.*

Ambivalent stresses conflict and is usually applied to internal things (like feelings or attitudes).

> Many Americans are *ambivalent* about raising taxes to cut the deficit.

among/between

Use *among* when referring in general terms to more than two.

> Maureen found it difficult to choose from *among* so many delectable goodies.

Use *between* when referring to only two.

> She finally narrowed it down to a choice *between* the raspberry torte and the lemon pie.

You can use *between* when naming several persons or things individually.

> Elspeth vacillates *between* the key lime pie, the Bavarian cream, and the amaretto cheesecake.

amount/number

In formal writing, be sure to use *amount* to refer to things in a mass or in bulk; use *number* to refer to things that can be counted.

> Armando bought a huge *amount* of sugar, which David used to make a considerable *number* of cookies for the bake sale.

and

Be careful not to write *an* when you mean *and*.

> ***Careless:***   We want a pizza with mushrooms *an* pineapple.
>
> ***Accurate:***   We want a pizza with mushrooms *and* pineapple.

And do not get lazy and use the symbol *&*. Write the word out, except when taking notes and listing references in APA style.

any more/anymore

Some authorities consider only the two-word expression acceptable. But recent dictionaries cite *anymore* (one word) as standard. Use it only in negative sentences.

> Alice doesn't live here *anymore*.

The use of *anymore* in a positive sentence to mean "nowadays" is considered colloquial or even nonstandard.

> ***Nonstandard:***   We used to wash all the dishes by hand, but *anymore* we put them in the automatic dishwasher.

anyways/anywheres

Nonstandard. Use *anyway* and *anywhere*.

apprise/appraise

To *apprise* means "to inform or serve notice."

> Before arresting us, the officer *apprised* us of our rights.

To *appraise* means to "evaluate or judge."

> Zena *appraised* the situation carefully and caught the next plane to Brazil.

as

To avoid misinterpretation, do not use *as* to mean *because.*

> *Unclear:* As the charges were dropped, Zena returned from Brazil.

Did Zena return "at the same time" the charges were dropped or "because" they were dropped?

> *Clear:* Because the charges were dropped, Zena returned from Brazil.

as/like   See *like/as.*

as to

Many people feel this phrase is a clumsy borrowing from legal jargon. You can probably substitute the single word *about.*

> *Clumsy:*   They questioned the speaker *as to* his first marriage.
>
> *Improved:* They questioned the speaker *about* his first marriage.

author

You will have no trouble finding people who dislike *author* used as a verb.

> *Colloquial:*   Felicia *authors* our monthly newsletter.
>
> *More acceptable:* Felicia *writes* our monthly newsletter.

Interestingly, few people object to using *coauthor* as a verb.

> She and a colleague *coauthored* a genetics textbook.

awhile/a while

Written as one word, *awhile* is an adverb.

> Socks frolicked *awhile* with Bowser.

A while is an article plus a noun.

> After *a while,* Socks got bored and chased Bowser off.

bad/badly   See *Adverb/Adjective Confusion,* Chapter 14.

being as/being that

Do not use either of these phrases. Write *because* or *since.*

beside/besides

Beside (without an *-s*) means "at the side of."

He leads me *beside* the still waters.

Besides (with an *-s*) means "in addition to."

Bumper has a math exam tomorrow *besides* his physics test.

better/best

Use *better* when comparing two people or things.

Mickey is a *better* dancer than Langston.

Use *best* when comparing more than two.

Mickey is the *best* dancer in the place.

This rule holds true for all comparative adjectives: *prettier/prettiest, little/littlest, sadder/saddest,* and so on.

between/among   See *among/between.*

busted

Do not write *busted* in formal writing if you mean *broke* or *burst.*

Colloquial: Chris *busted* his leg skiing.
Standard: Chris *broke* his leg skiing.
Colloquial: Lulu's balloon got *busted.*
Standard: Lulu's balloon *burst.*

There are a number of slang meanings for *busted* that you should not use in formal writing.

Slang: Norman got *busted* for jay-walking.
Sergeant Snafu got *busted* to private.
Sedgewick is flat *busted.* (no money)
Maribelle is flat-*busted.* (no bosom)

can/may

Few people recognize the distinction between these two words anymore (if they ever did), but in formal usage *can* means "to have the ability."

> Percy *can* sleep through a thunderstorm.

May is used to suggest a possibility or to request (or grant) permission.

> Percy *may* be awake by now.
>
> *May* I wake him, if he's not?
>
> Yes, you *may.*

can't help but/cannot help but

Technically, this expression is a double negative; hence some people object to it in formal writing.

> ***Informal:***   I *can't help but* question Jose's intentions.
>
> ***Formal:***   I *cannot help* questioning Jose's intentions.

center on/center around

The traditional rule holds that the verb *center* may be freely used with the prepositions *on, upon, in,* or *at.* Its use with *around* is denounced as "illogical" and "physically impossible."

> ***Questionable:***   The discussion *centered around* the need for more money.
>
> ***Acceptable:***   Our hope *centers on* a tax increase.
>
> Their trade is *centered in* Amsterdam.

choose/chose

Choose (rhymes with *ooze*) means a decision is being made right now or all the time.

> Ruby always *chooses* to take the train rather than fly.

Chose (rhymes with *toes*) means a choice has already been made.

> The last time she *chose* to stay home rather than ride with those boors in her department.

compare/contrast

These words overlap in meaning. When you *contrast* two things, you are making a comparison. But as most instructors use the terms on examinations or in writing assignments, *compare* generally means to focus on similarities; *contrast* means to focus on differences.

> *Compare* the human brain to a computer.

> *Contrast* the realistic early plays with the later fantasies.

complected

This term for "having a particular facial complexion" used to be considered nonstandard, but it is now acceptable in informal writing, especially in compounds like "dark-complected" or "light-complected."

> ***Informal:*** "A white-haired and ruddy-*complected* priest stood on the deck of one of the trawlers." (*New York Times*)

> ***Formal:*** A priest with white hair and a ruddy *complexion* stood on the deck of one of the trawlers.

complement/compliment

A *complement* is something that completes or brings to perfection.

> The colorful centerpiece was a stunning *complement* to the beautifully set table.

A *compliment* is an expression of praise or courtesy.

> We received many *compliments* on our beautiful table setting.

continual/continuous

These adjectives both mean "occurring over and over again during a period of time." *Continual* stresses what is intermittent or repeated at intervals.

> The *continual* banging of the pipes nearly drove me crazy.

Continuous implies a lack of interruption.

> He suffered a *continuous* bout with the flu all winter long.

could of/should of/would of

Nonstandard. Use *could have, should have, would have* in writing.

> I *should have* [not *should of*] stopped at the grocery store.

deduce/infer/imply

Deduce and *infer* mean essentially the same thing—to reach a conclusion through reasoning.

Theodore *deduced* (or *inferred*) that Juanita was angry with him when she poured a pitcher of water over his head.

Do not confuse these words with *imply,* which means "to state indirectly or hint."

Juanita had *implied* several times earlier in the evening that she was displeased.

differ from/differ with

To *differ from* means "to be different."

Victoria's preferences in music *differ from* Steve's.

To *differ with* means "to disagree."

Victoria *differs with* Steve on the immigration question.

different from/different than

To be safe, stick with *different from* in formal writing.

Turtles are *different from* terrapins in several ways.

You can save words, though, by introducing a clause with *different than;* this usage is now widely accepted.

Wordy: Your hair looks *different from* the way I remembered.

Improved: Your hair looks *different than* I remembered.

disinterested/uninterested

Although educated people often confuse these two words, the distinction between them is clear-cut. *Disinterested* means "impartial or unbiased."

We need a totally *disinterested* person to judge the debate.

Uninterested means "not interested."

Albert is totally *uninterested* in the moral ambiguities of Jacobean drama.

effect/affect   See *affect/effect.*

enthused

Many people still object to the use of *enthused* as a modifier. Stick with *enthusiastic.*

Colloquial: Hector is *enthused* about jogging.

Standard: Hector is *enthusiastic* about jogging.

etc.

Do not use this abbreviation (for the Latin meaning "and so on") unless you have a list in which the other examples are obvious (such as large cities: Paris, London, Rome, New York, etc.). Do not ever write *and etc.,* because *etc.* means "*and* so forth," so you are saying it twice. In an essay, write in English: "and so on," "for example," "that is," rather than *etc., e.g., i.e.*

everyday/every day

Use *everyday* as an adjective to modify a noun.

> Jamal is wearing his *everyday* clothes.

Use *every day* to mean "daily."

> It rains here almost *every day.*

except/accept   See *accept/except.*

farther/further

Although the distinction is not always easy to make, *farther* should be used to indicate physical or literal distances and *further* should be used for nonphysical dimensions.

> Mars is *farther* from Venus than Saturn is.

> Nothing could be *further* from the truth.

To indicate something additional, use *further.*

> The judge would hear no *further* arguments.

fewer/less

The traditional rule says to use *fewer* with things that can be counted and *less* with qualities or things that cannot be counted.

> ***Countable:***   Marvin catches *fewer* colds than Marlene.

> ***Not countable:***   Stanley has *less* patience than Travis.

However, *less than* is standard in phrases involving countable measures of time, amount, and distance.

> ***Acceptable:***   We were there *less than* three weeks, we spent *less than* $400, and we traveled *less than* fifty miles.

former/latter

Unless you are a skillful writer, do not use these terms. Too often readers must look back in order to recall which was the former (the first mentioned) and which the latter (the second mentioned). For greater clarity, repeat the nouns.

get

This verb has many colloquial meanings. In writing, you should try to find more precise verbs.

Colloquial: Romantic music really *gets to* me.

Better: Romantic music really *affects* [or *moves*] me.

Colloquial: What *gets* me is his lack of self-discipline.

Better: What *annoys* me is his lack of self-discipline.

Colloquial: She finally *got back* at him.

Better: She finally *took her revenge* on him.

Colloquial: Cherise *got sick* with the flu but eventually *got* better.

Better: Cherise *became ill* with the flu but eventually *recovered*.

hanged/hung   See *hung/hanged*.

has got/have got

The *got* is unnecessary; drop it.

Nonstandard: You *have got* only one more chance to prove yourself.

Standard: You have only one more chance to prove yourself.

he or she/his or her

In order to include women in the language, many socially conscious people deliberately use *he or she* (instead of simply *he*) or *his and her* (instead of simply *his*) when referring to nouns that are not specific to either gender (like *teacher* or *lawyer* or *doctor*). Other people find the double pronoun cumbersome, as indeed it can be if used ineptly.

Awkward: The student must have his or her schedule signed by an adviser before he or she picks up his or her class cards.

But that sentence can be easily revised to eliminate the excess pronouns.

Improved: The student must have his or her schedule signed by an adviser before picking up class cards.

Better yet, that sentence can be recast in the plural to eliminate the problem altogether.

> ***Improved:***   Students must have their schedules signed by an adviser before picking up class cards.

Notice that the *idea* in the previous example was plural all along, even though the first two versions were written in the singular. We are taught early on to write in the singular even when we mean the plural. We write sentences like this:

> A child should memorize *his* multiplication tables.

Really we mean *all* children should memorize *their* multiplication tables. We need to kick that singular habit and cultivate the plural, since our language has perfectly good nonsexist pronouns in the plural—*they, them, their, theirs.*

If you cannot avoid using the singular—and sometimes you can't—try to eliminate unnecessary pronouns.

> ***Avoid:***   The winner should pick up *his* prize in person.
>
> ***Better:***   The winner should pick up the prize in person.

If you cannot eliminate the pronoun, an occasional *his or her*—or *her or his*—is quite acceptable in current usage. Or you can alternate throughout your essay, using *him* in one example and *her* in another.

See also *man/person.*

hisself

Nonstandard. Do not use it unless writing dialect. Use *himself.*

hopefully

Many writers use this adverb as a sentence modifier.

> *Hopefully* the contracts will be signed by next week.

Although *hopefully* causes no more problems with clarity and precision than other accepted sentence modifiers (*mercifully, interestingly, happily, frankly,* etc.), many critics still do not approve of it. If you think your audience may include such people, you will do well to rephrase your sentence.

> We *hope* the contracts will be signed by next week.

hung/hanged

If you are talking about hanging inanimate objects, then *hung* is the correct past and past participle.

The people at the art museum *hung* the pictures upside down.

But if you are referring to executing people by suspending them by the neck, then *hanged* is the correct past and past participle.

They *hanged* the prisoner at dawn.

illusion   See *allusion/illusion.*

imply/infer   See *deduce/infer/imply.*

in/into/in to/in two

To be precise, use *in* to show location; use *into* to indicate movement.

I was *in* the back seat when our car crashed *into* the train.

Often we use *in* not as a preposition (see previous example) but as an adverb functioning almost as part of a verb: *to go in, to sleep in, to give in.* With these fused verb-adverb constructions, keep *to* as a separate word.

Do not give *in* to pressure. (adverb)

Do not play *into* their hands. (preposition)

In two is an expression that means "in two separate parts" or "in half."

We cut the sandwich *in two.*

irregardless

Most people still steadfastly refuse to accept *irregardless* as standard English. Do not use it; say *regardless* or *nonetheless.*

is when/is where

Do not use *is when.*

Avoid: In tragedy, catharsis *is when* the audience feels purged of pity and fear.

Improved: In tragedy, catharsis involves purging pity and fear from the audience.

Use *is where* only when you mean a place.

That *is where* I lost my keys.

Avoid: An accident *is where* someone gets careless.

Improved: Accidents *occur* when people get careless.

its/it's

Do not confuse these two terms. Memorize the two definitions if you have trouble with them, and when you proofread, check to be sure you have not confused them accidentally. *Its* is a possessive pronoun.

> That dog wags *its* tail whenever *its* owner walks into the room.

It's is a contraction of *it is* or *it has.*

> *It's* a great day for taking the dog for a walk.

> *It's* been a long time since you walked the dog.

If you never can keep the two straight, quit using the contraction. If you always write *it is,* then all you have to remember is this: no apostrophe in *its.*

kind of/sort of

Colloquial when used instead of *rather* or *somewhat* to qualify adjectives.

> ***Colloquial:***   Ricardo is *sort of* touchy today.
>
> ***Standard:***   Ricardo is *somewhat* touchy today.

The phrases can be used in standard English to modify nouns.

> ***Standard:***   What *kind of* snacks does Myrtle like?

Be careful, though, to avoid wordiness.

> ***Wordy:***   Myrtle prefers a less salty *sort of* snack.
>
> ***Improved:***   Myrtle prefers a less salty snack.

Never use *kind of a* or *sort of a* in writing.

> ***Avoid:***   Grandpa is *kind of a* grouch today.
>
> ***Improved:***   Grandpa is rather grouchy today.

latter/former   See *former/latter.*

lay/lie

To lay means to put or place; *to lie* means to recline. Be sure you know the principal parts; then decide which verb you need.

> *to place*   lay, laid, laid, laying
> *to recline* lie, lay, lain, lying

Remember that *lay* requires a direct object: you always *lay* something. But you never *lie* anything: you just *lie down,* or *lie quietly,* or *lie under a tree,* or *lie on a couch.*

No direct object: Selma *lies* in the hammock.

Direct object: Selma *lays* her weary body in the hammock.

The problem usually comes with the past tense and past participle of *lie;* many people use the colloquial *laid* instead of *lay* and *lain.*

Colloquial: Selma *laid* in the sun all day yesterday.

Standard: Selma *lay* in the sun all day yesterday.

Colloquial: She *has laid* in the sun every day this week.

Standard: She *has lain* in the sun every day this week.

lead/led

Pronunciation causes the confusion here. *Lead* (rhymes with *bed*), a noun, means a heavy, grayish metal.

Our airy hopes sank like *lead.*

Lead (rhymes with *seed*) is present tense of the verb meaning *to guide.*

He *leads* me beside the still waters.

Led (rhymes with *bed*) is the past tense of the verb *lead.*

Leroy *led* the march last year, but he vows he will not *lead* it again.

leave/let

Standard usage allows either "*Leave* me alone" (meaning "go away") or "*Let* me alone" (meaning "stop bothering me"). But since *let* really means *to allow,* "*Leave* me give you some advice" is definitely nonstandard. Use "*Let* me give you some advice before you *leave.*"

lend/loan

You may now correctly ask a loved one either to *lend* you some socks or to *loan* you some socks. Only a traditionalist would be likely to object to *loan* as a verb.

less/fewer   See *fewer/less.*

lie/lay   See *lay/lie.*

like/as

Although writers since the thirteenth century have used *like* as a conjunction (to introduce clauses), many modern critics scorn this usage. You would be wise to use *as* instead, especially in formal writing.

> *Informal:*   The critics complained *like* we expected them to.
>
> *Formal:*   The critics complained *as* we expected them to.

Like is more acceptably used as a conjunction with the verbs *look, seem, feel, sound,* and *taste.*

> It looks *like* we are in for a rough time.

No one complains about using *like* as a preposition (to introduce a phrase).

> He saves things *like* old newspapers and pieces of string.

likely/liable

Although these words are virtually interchangeable today, many writers are careful to use *likely* when they mean "quite possibly" and *liable* when they want to suggest responsibility.

> Your roommate is *likely* to be upset since she is *liable* for damages.

lose/loose

This is another problem in pronunciation and spelling. *Lose* (rhymes with *ooze*) is a verb meaning "to fail to keep something."

> If we *lose* our right to protest, we will ultimately *lose* our freedom.

Loose (rhymes with *goose*) is an adjective meaning "not tight."

> The noose is too *loose* on your lasso.

man/person

The generic *man* (as the term is called) is supposed to include both sexes—all human beings. But unfortunately the same word, *man,* also means simply "a male human being." Thus the term is ambiguous. Sometimes it includes both sexes; sometimes it does not—and sometimes no one can tell. To avoid this subtle sexism, use *person* or *people* when you mean a person or people, not just males.

> *Exclusive:*   We want to hire the best *man* for the job.
>
> *Inclusive:*   We want to hire the best *person* for the job.

A number of compound words using *man* can be avoided with little difficulty.

Avoid	*Prefer*
chairman	chairperson, chair, moderator
congressman	representative, senator
councilman	council member
fireman	firefighter

foreman	supervisor
mailman	mail carrier
manpower	work force
manmade	artificial, manufactured
policeman	police officer
salesman	salesperson

See also *he or she/his or her.*

may/can   See *can/may.*

most/almost   See *almost/most.*

myself

Properly used, *myself* is either an intensive (I am going to fix the faucet *myself*) or a reflexive pronoun (I cut *myself* shaving). Do not use *myself* in place of *I* or *me.*

Colloquial: Jasmine and *myself* are going to be partners.

Preferred: Jasmine and *I* are going to be partners.

Colloquial: Will you play tennis with Jasmine and *myself?*

Preferred: Will you play tennis with Jasmine and *me?*

number/amount   See *amount/number.*

prejudice/prejudiced

Prejudice (without the *-d*) is a noun.

   Prejudice remains engrained in our society.

Prejudiced (with the *-d*) is the past participle of the verb *to prejudice;* it means "affected by prejudice." Do not leave off the *-d* when using this word as an adjective.

   adj.   *n.*
A *prejudiced* person is someone who harbors *prejudice.*

         pred. adj.
Our society remains *prejudiced* against minorities.

principal/principle

Although we have numerous meanings for *principal,* the word *principle* means a rule: a person of high moral *principle,* a primary *principle* of physics. You can remember the *-le* spelling by association with the *-le* ending of *rule.* All other uses end with *-al:* a high school *principal,* the *principal* of a loan, a *principal* cause or effect, the *principal* (main character) in a film or play.

probable/probably

The adjective *probable* (sounds at the end like *capable*) and the adverb *probably* (ends with a long *e* sound, like *capably*) both mean "likely."

    adj.   *adv.*

    The *probable* involvement of the CIA in the uprising *probably* caused the rebels to lose.

quite/quiet

Be careful not to confuse these words. *Quite,* a qualifier, means *entirely, truly; quiet* means the opposite of *loud.*

    Charla was *quite* ready to yell, "Be *quiet,* please!"

quotes

As a verb, *quotes* is standard English.

    Louella *quotes* Shakespeare even in bed.

But as a shortened form of *quotations* or *quotation marks,* the term *quotes* is still considered colloquial.

    Avoid: You no longer need to put *quotes* around slang.

raise/rise

You never *rise* anything, but you always *raise* something. *Rise* is an intransitive verb (prices *rise,* spirits *rise,* curtains *rise*); *raise* is a transitive verb (you *raise* cain or *raise* corn or *raise* prices).

    vbi.   *vbt.*

    Taxes are *rising* because Congress has *raised* the defense budget again.

If you cannot keep these verbs straight, avoid them.

    Taxes are going up because Congress has increased the defense budget again.

See Verbs, page 303.

real/really

Do not use *real* as an adverb or qualifier in writing.

    Colloquial: Li-Yung saw a *real* interesting movie.

    Standard: Li-Yung saw a *really* interesting movie.

reason is because

You should write "The reason is that. . . ."

Avoid: The reason he lost the sale was because he forgot his sample case.

Standard: The reason he lost the sale was that he forgot his sample case.

Or you can rewrite your sentence to eliminate the word *reason.*

Improved: He lost the sale because he forgot his sample case.

refer   See *allude/refer.*

rise/raise   See *raise/rise.*

she or he   See *he or she/his or her.*

should of   See *could of/should of/would of.*

sit/set

You seldom *sit* anything. *Sit* is an intransitive verb; its principal parts are *sit, sat, sat, sitting.* We *sit* down or *sit* a spell or *sit* in a chair. One notable exception: *sit* can mean "to cause to be seated." Thus, it's quite correct to write: "The teacher *sat* Buffy down and gave her a lecture."

Set is a transitive verb; its principal parts are *set, set, set, setting.* We *set* a glass down or *set* a time or *set* the table. Exceptions: in some common phrases, *set* does not have an object—the sun *sets,* jello and concrete *set,* hens *set*—but people seldom have a problem with these uses.

sometime/some time/sometimes

Sometime is an adverb meaning "at an indefinite or unstated time."

We will meet *sometime* tomorrow afternoon.

Some time is a two-word phrase made up of the determiner *some* and the noun *time.* It means "a period of time."

We haven't had a meeting for *some time.*

Sometimes is also an adverb; it means "at times, now and then."

We *sometimes* meet in the executive conference room.

sort of   See *kind of/sort of.*

split infinitive

Split infinitives have always been acceptable in English, although some people still object to them. Sometimes avoiding a split infinitive will make a sentence easier to read.

> *Awkward:*   Some managers are unable *to* with troublesome employees *take* decisive action.
>
> *Improved:*   Some managers are unable *to take* decisive action with trouble-some employees.

supposed to/used to

Since we never hear the *-d* sound in these phrases when we talk, the *-d* is easy to forget in writing. Whenever you write either term, be sure to add the *-d.*

than/then   See *then/than.*

that   See *who/which/that.*

their/there/they're

These words are easy to confuse because they sound exactly alike. But their meanings and uses are very different. *Their* is a possessive modifier or pronoun.

> *Their* dog is friendly. That dog is *theirs.*

There is an adverb or an expletive.

> *Adverb:*   Sylvia is over *there.*
>
> *Expletive:*   *There* is no one with her.

They're is a contraction of *they are.*

> *They're* gone now.

If you have trouble spelling *their,* remember that all three (*they're, there,* and *their*) start with *the-.*

theirselves

Do not use it unless writing dialect. The accepted form is *themselves.*

then/than

These words have quite different meanings. *Then* is an adverb or adverbial conjunction denoting time.

First we need to pick up the ice; *then* we can get the ice cream salt.

Than is a conjunction used in comparisons.

No one talks more *than* Michael does.

Claudia would rather talk *than* eat.

thusly

Do not use it: Always simply write *thus*.

to/too/two

To is usually a preposition and sometimes an adverb; it also introduces an infinitive.

to the depths, push the door *to, to* swing

Too is a qualifier or an adverb meaning "also."

Don't make *too* much noise. (qualifier for "much")

Selma is going *too*. (means "also")

Two is the number.

two paychecks, *two* miles

try and/try to

Although we frequently say, "We must *try and* get this work finished," the usage is colloquial. In writing, stick with *try to*.

We must *try to* get this work finished.

uninterested/disinterested   See *disinterested/uninterested*.

used to   See *supposed to/used to*.

very

Avoid this colorless, exhausted word. Use a more exact and expressive qualifier (extremely, considerably, fully, entirely, completely, utterly) or leave it out. See also *real/really*.

weather/whether

Weather is what goes on outside; *whether* introduces an alternative.

> We cannot decide *whether* the *weather* will be suitable for a picnic.

while   See *awhile/a while.*

who/which/that

Use *who* to refer to people (or to animals you are personifying).

> The person *who* lost the car keys . . .
>
> Lenin, *who* is Susie's cat, . . .

Use *which* to refer to animals and nonliving things.

> The earth, *which* blossoms in the spring, . . .
>
> The cat, *which* is sitting in the window, . . .

Use *that* to refer to either people or things.

> The person *that* lost the car keys . . . (*who* is preferable in formal usage)
>
> The earth *that* blossoms in spring . . .
>
> The cat *that* is sitting in the window . . .

> See *Comma,* numbers 1 and 2, in Chapter 14.
>
> If you are in doubt about whether to use *who* or *whom,* see *Case of Pronouns,* number 5, in Chapter 14.

would of   See *could of/should of/would of.*

you (indefinite)

In informal writing, you may address your readers as *you* (as we have done in this sentence). Somewhat questionable, though, is the use of *you* to mean just anyone (the indefinite *you*).

> In France if *you* buy a loaf of bread, *you* get it without a wrapper.

If writing on a formal level, you should use the third-person singular *one.*

> In France if *one* buys a loaf of bread, *one* gets it without a wrapper.

your/you're

Your is a possessive determiner or pronoun.

> Here is *your* book; this book is *yours.*

You're is a contraction of *you are*.

>   Let me know when *you're* leaving.

A. Words frequently confused

The following sentences contain words that sound alike but have different meanings. In each sentence, select the appropriate word from the choices in parentheses.

1. I have been (lead, led) astray again.
2. Tristan is plumper (then, than) a teddy bear.
3. (Its, It's) not the money; (its, it's) the (principal, principle) of the thing that bothers me.
4. Those most in need of (advice, advise) seldom welcome it.
5. Darryl cannot study if his room is (to, too) (quiet, quite).
6. The automobile is a (principal, principle) contributor to air pollution.
7. Our spirits (rose, raised) with the sun.
8. They had a frisky time when (there, their) mongoose got (lose, loose).
9. Let's (lie, lay) down and talk this over.
10. That (continual, continuous) drip from the faucet is driving me to drink.
11. You ought to (appraise, apprise) the situation carefully before you decide (weather, whether) to file a complaint.
12. (You're, Your) decision could (affect, effect) your career.
13. If you (choose, chose) to file, you should not harbor the (illusion, allusion) that all (your, you're) problems will be solved.
14. Why don't we (sit, set) this one out?
15. (Your, You're) going to be sent to the boondocks if you (accept, except) this job.
16. The IRS is really (uninterested, disinterested) in Virgil's (continual, continuous) complaints.
17. I could (infer, imply) from his complaints that he owes back taxes.
18. If the (weather, whether) improves, (then, than) we will plant the garden.
19. Any news program will usually (appraise, apprise) you of a late frost.
20. Snow peas will not be (affected, effected) by a light frost.
21. I (advice, advise) you to pick them young.
22. The dean has (lain, laid) down firm rules concerning class attendance.
23. I (chose, choose) strawberry last time, and it was (alright, all right), (accept, except) there weren't any strawberries in it.
24. Sherman was (quiet, quite) outraged by LaDonne's (illusion, allusion) to his bald spot.
25. How did that dog (lose, loose) (its, it's) tail?

26. Call me (sometime, sometimes) next week, and we'll spend (sometime, some time) together.
27. Please (set, sit) that plant over (their, there) near the window.
28. Whenever I (lie, lay) down for a nap, the children outside (rise, raise) a ruckus.
29. Miguel is a person of firm moral (principle, principal) who should (rise, raise) to national prominence.
30. He (implied, inferred) that using artificial chocolate (sometimes, sometime) (affects, effects) the taste of the cookies.
31. Which would you rather (loose, lose)—your mind or your heart?
32. In her paper, Candice (inferred, implied) that John Milton is a crashing bore, but *Paradise Lost* (affects, effects) me deeply.
33. A large (amount, number) of students love English courses.
34. There are (few, less) differences (among, between) trashy romantic novels.
35. The (principle, principal) cause of indigestion is overeating.

B. Assorted matters of usage

Most of the sentences below contain examples of questionable usage. Revise those sentences that need changing in order to be acceptable as standard American English. Some contain more than one dubious usage.

1. My roommate and myself moved in a new apartment.
2. We need to quickly, thoroughly, and painstakingly perform the analysis again.
3. Did Everett author that report all by hisself?
4. Having been raised on a farm, Henrietta is disinterested in urban entertainment.
5. George baked a considerable amount of cookies.
6. You could of busted the lawn mower on that huge rock.
7. For once, try and do what you're suppose to.
8. Hopefully, we are already to go now.
9. I am going to put quotes around this slang expression, irregardless of what the book says.
10. Most everyone which is liable to come has all ready got here.
11. A banquet is where you eat alot of food and can't help but be bored by the speeches.
12. If we go altogether, we should be alright.
13. A person may buy his or her ticket from his or her union representative.
14. You would of had less problems if you would of centered around the main issue better.
15. The real reason I am not coming is because I am not interested anyways.
16. My ideas are all together different than those of the speaker.

17. If you live in Rome, you should do like the Romans do.

18. Clarence and Claudia got theirselves involved in a accident all ready on their new motorcycle.

19. Kim use to be enthused about the virtues of step aerobics.

20. Can I loan you my exercise tape?

21. If you turn the key, thusly, the engine will start.

22. Being as you are between a rock and a hard place, you do not have much choice anymore, do you?

23. In areas where muggers, rapists, etc., abound, a large dog really is man's best friend.

24. Sally and Serena both wrote poems about air pollution; Sally's was best.

25. If I had known you were coming, I would of left.

Appendixes on Special Skills

I n this section of the book, we provide supplementary material you may need. Depending on your situation, you may benefit from our advice on word processing and study skills, and on writing job application letters and résumés.

Appendix A

Writing with a Word Processor

You will probably be doing some or all of your writing on a computer or on a word processor (a computer that only performs writing tasks). With a computer, you will eventually find writing more fun, revising easier, and your printed pages more beautiful. We have found that even people with severe computer phobia convert to word processing with remarkable enthusiasm. The advantages of writing on a computer come from several nifty features that all the word processing programs we know of share.

The Novelty Factor

Writing on a computer can boost your skills simply because you may be more willing to sit down at the keyboard than to sit down at your desk. Writers at any level can benefit from practice—more than they can from instruction, in many cases. Once you have gone through the initial frustration of learning your program, you may find you enjoy snatching a session at the computer in your free time.

One of the new things you will be getting used to is working with a program. A program, which is a set of rules and directions that the computer memorizes, makes the computer operate according to built-in instructions. For example, in a word processing program there is always a way to set the margin where you want it, even after you have typed your document. The keyboard operations that you do to make the computer obey you are called "commands," and designing the appearance of your document on the screen is called "formatting" it.

You do not have to memorize the commands (though you'll probably know the most-used ones by heart very soon). You can make command lists appear on the screen in order to choose the one you want. These lists are called "menus." Learning to find the right menu and get it on the screen is half the battle of mastering your program. If you are a bit old-fashioned, you can always look up the commands in the manual that comes with your program.

What You Need to Know About Your Program

To get the most use out of word processing, you need to find out how to perform several valuable operations. Use your manual or the help of an experienced user to learn these functions.

Insert Mode

Admit it. There have been times when you knew you needed another example, detail, or explanation in a paragraph and have said to yourself, "I can't bear retyping that page. I'll just let it go the way it is." With a word processor, you will not have to retype—you can go back and add as much as you like by using your program's *insert* mode. You simply move your cursor (the marker on the screen that shows where you are working) to the spot where you want to make a change. When you set the machine on insert mode, whatever you type at that point will appear, and the rest of the writing will move over to make room.

The opposite of insert mode is *typeover* mode, in which your new writing erases and replaces the old writing. It is a good idea to choose insert mode and to use that one consistently, even though you will have to get used to it at first. That way, if you are touch typing and not looking at the text, you will not accidentally overwrite any material.

New technology creates new demands, and the insert mode means that your instructor will not feel kindly about underdeveloped ideas, since it is so easy to go back and add details and examples.

Cut and Paste

Your organization can improve instantly with word processing, too. If you wonder whether the paragraphs you have written would make more sense in a different order, you can experiment on the screen before you print. This type of operation is sometimes called "cutting and pasting," because people used to actually cut their papers in pieces and rearrange them by pasting them in a different order. The rearranging also goes by the name *block move* in some programs, since you are moving a block of type.

Usually, your program gives you a way to mark, or *select*, a section of type. Then you move your cursor to a new place and press a button that moves the section. Now you can read your work over and decide whether to make the change or not. You can always move the section back or try a new place. Your instructor will expect that you have thought through your organization and considered several possibilities on-screen.

Search and Replace

Word processing programs always have an ingenious way to find every instance of a certain word or phrase, and the function is usually called simply *find* or *search*. This function is great when you know that you have certain words you tend to confuse—such as *affect* and *effect,* or *its* and *it's.* You can ask your computer to show you each occurrence of each word on the screen, and you can check to see whether you have used the right word.

You can also use the search command to check whether or not you have overused your favorite words or phrases. For example, if you tend to use the word *therefore* to indicate all cause-and-effect relationships, you can ask the computer to point out all the instances of *therefore,* and you can change some of them if there are too many.

Your program can combine searching and replacing. Let's say you wrote a whole paper with a lot of conversation in it, and then noticed in the revision guide that commas are always supposed to go *inside* quotation marks, after you put them all *outside.* Instead of combing through your printout, you can ask your computer to find each instance of ", and automatically change them all to ,". This obviously is a real boon whenever you have made a certain error throughout your paper or when you want to change something throughout—for example, if you have referred to women as "Miss" or "Mrs." and decide to use the more progressive title "Ms."

Save and Name

One of the most crucial things to learn about word processing is that nothing you have written is remembered by the computer unless you save it. What you see on the screen is *only* on the screen until you hit the buttons that move it into the machine's memory. This means that if you have typed six pages and your cat dashes by and jars the electric plug loose, those six pages are gone forever if you have not saved. This is an experience that you (and your cat) want to avoid. The *save* command consists of one or two keystrokes, which you should learn immediately.

Make saving into an automatic gesture like buckling your seat belt. We save whenever we pause to reread or think about what to write next—about every two minutes or so. Most word processors have a way to set the program so that it automatically saves for you at regular intervals. Check your manual for directions if this feature appeals to you.

When you save a document or *file,* you will have to name it something so that you can recall it to the screen later. Some programs restrict you to eight letters or digits for your file name, and many won't let you include spaces. Be sure to give your documents names that will help you remember what they are. When we first began computing, we named our documents after our favorite foods, like *tostado* and *burrito*. We found that not many documents later, we could not figure out which file contained what, even though the names were appetizing. Now we settle for boring but informative titles like *ch.-1* and *app-a.pwg*.

When you make large scale revisions, saving old versions of the file can be a good idea. Just save the new revision under a new name, so that you have, say, *tostado* and *tostado2*. This way, you will still have access to pieces that you deleted in the revision, in case you decide that you want them after all. Saving several versions also guards against disaster when something terrible happens to the one on-screen: your old versions are still good.

We highly recommend printing a hard copy of what you have written, even if it's unfinished, when you quit a writing session. Hard disk crashes, floppy disk failures, and nasty hackers do exist, and if you have a hard copy (*paper* copy), you will only have to retype should your computer file be lost.

Spell-Check and Word Count

The computer's spell-checker is a blessing to students and teachers alike. A blessing, not a miracle. The checker reads through your essay and points out every word it does not recognize. Each program has a word list, significantly shorter than a print dictionary's. When a word in your paper is flagged, that simply means it's not in the program's word list.

At this point, you need to use your dictionary to decide whether or not it is spelled wrong or simply not in the list, but right anyway. For example, our word processor flags the words *typeover* and *repaginate,* which we use in this appendix. The terms are too specialized to be in the computer's word list. Like most spell-checkers, ours has a way that we can put *typeover* and *repaginate* into the word list so that they are not flagged continually. Consult your manual to find out how to add specialized terms you often use to your program's word list.

We wrote that the checker reads your essay, but it really does not. It looks at every word separately. The program recognizes *their, there,* and *they're* as correct—but you may have written the wrong one for your context. Correctness in matters of usage like this one are still your responsibility. If you make a typo that just happens to form a real word, the program will not find that typo. For example, in the previous sentence, we could have mistakenly typed "work" and "type" instead of "word" and "typo," and the program would not tell us that we had written a mighty weird sentence. It also will not catch mechanical problems, like capitalization, spacing errors, and words left out. Careful proofreading of the final copy by a human is still a necessity, and probably it always will be.

As we pointed out in Chapter 2, the existence of spell-checkers has raised standards of correctness among most instructors. A misspelling is now not just an error but a kind of moral failure, since you did not have the fortitude to use your program thoroughly.

When your program is done with its spelling check, it will probably tell you how many words you have typed. This way, you know whether you are within the limits of your assignment. Most programs also have a menu heading for *word count*, where you can get a report without running the spell-checker. Some even have a reading level estimate, so you can get a general idea of what grade level audience could read your writing.

On-Screen Formatting

Instructors' standards have also risen concerning the overall appearance of your written work, with the advent of on-screen formatting. Here are the basic formatting tools you need to have handy.

Double Spacing

Most computer screens cannot show a full page of type, so you may want to type single-spaced in order to see more, then double space later. Most of your college work, at least, requires double spacing. There is no need to retype in order to change the line spacing: your computer has a method for doing this. Usually, you select or mark the whole document and then give a command that changes it in a flash.

Centering

You may remember the days when you had to count the letters and spaces in a title, divide them in half, and use backspacing in order to get the thing centered. Now, your computer has a command to center either before you type the title or after you have already typed it. This command usually involves just a couple of keystrokes. Be sure to find out how to turn the centering command *off,* too, so that you can return to regular typing.

Underlining

In typewritten form, underlining is used instead of italics for titles, words used as words, emphasis, and so on. Like the centering command, your underlining command on the computer can be set before or after you type the material to be underlined. If you have already typed the material, you will need to mark or select it before you execute the command, so that the whole document is not underlined. Again, be sure you know how to turn underlining off as well as on.

Margins

You get to class on Thursday in a glow of accomplishment, having already completed the next day's essay assignment on your computer. Your instructor casually says, "And I hope you all remembered that your papers must have one-and-a-half-inch margins all around, so I have room for my comments." But your word processor sets only one-inch margins! No problem. You can still change the margins on your paper without retyping.

Remember that you are dealing with $8\frac{1}{2}$-by-11-inch paper: therefore, you need to reset the margins to $1\frac{1}{2}$ inches (left), 7 inches (right), $1\frac{1}{2}$ inches (top), and $9\frac{1}{2}$ inches (bottom). Your computer has a menu heading called something like *page setup* or even *margins* where you type in the numbers. With some word processors, you do not even need to do the math; they provide a visual way to shift margins.

Headers and Page Numbers

The *header* is the line within the top margin of your page that usually includes an identifying word or phrase (like your name) and a page number. Word processors do not make you type these onto each page. You create the header separately, and the program automatically pops one onto each page. No matter how much you add, subtract, and rearrange within your paper, the header will end up putting the correct page numbers on the final copy. Headers will not show on your screen, but they will appear on the printed version. The necessary commands are usually found under the term *header* or *page format*. (A *footer* is similar, only at the bottom of each page.)

Page Breaks

Your word processor automatically makes a new page every fifty-four or fifty-five lines: you do not have to worry about typing beyond the bottom of a page or starting too high or low on the next page. What an improvement over the old Selectric.

However, sometimes you do not want the page to divide (break) at the automatic spot. For example, when you are completing a paper using sources, you need to start a new page for the Works Cited or References list. You may also need to change the natural page break when a title or heading unfortunately falls at the very bottom of a page, which looks odd. So you need to learn your word processor's command for *page breaks*. Usually, you move your cursor to the point where you would like the pages to divide and then execute a command that puts in a break there. Then the rest of the document *repaginates* to compensate for the new page break. Behind the scenes, your header repaginates, too.

Be warned that in most word processors, making a page run short is much, much easier than making a page run long. Squeezing extra stuff onto the bottom of a page is frowned upon aesthetically.

Page Preview

Your word processor has a feature that will show you a picture of the pages you type. It will be so small that you probably cannot read the words, but you will see the block of type, the margins, and the header or footer. You will see how much room you have left on the page you are typing, which is handy if you do not want to flow over onto a new page. (We use this when we write business letters; frequently we want to restrict them to one page in length.)

This preview is especially helpful when you are creating a title page. You can tell whether or not you guessed right about where your typing appears vertically on the page, then go back to regular view and move it closer to the middle if necessary.

The command for such a preview is usually listed under *page preview* or *print preview* on your menu (or in your manual). In some word processors, you need to give the *print* command (even though you do not want to print yet), and the preview option will appear on the next screen.

Glorifying

It will not take long before you realize that your word processor has a huge variety of type styles, sizes, and options like boldface and italics. You can make your document look like a sleazy circus leaflet if you want. But don't. This tendency to fancy up your document is called "glorifying." It makes experienced computer users laugh at you, and it irritates most writing instructors. A tasteful and consistent use of some design features can surely improve the appearance of your writing, but do not get too lavish. Be sure to check with your instructor or supervisor to see what level of decoration is appropriate.

Explore Additional Features

Your word processor may come supplied with many, many more options to help you write effectively. It may include a thesaurus and a dictionary that you can call up on screen while you are writing. Some systems include grammar or style checkers that analyze your prose (however, these are often confusing and may be misleading; you need a lot of knowledge to decide whether or not they are giving you good advice). Brainstorming and outlining programs can help you plan your paper on screen. Split-screen options let you look at two documents at once. There are even programs that put bibliographical information into the proper MLA or APA format. We have described only the most basic word processing features in this appendix, but you may enjoy learning more elaborate ones.

Compose at the Keyboard

You may insist that you cannot write perfectly polished prose except with your favorite felt-tip pen on wide-lined, legal-sized paper. You may be certain that inspiration will fail you if you are facing a keyboard and a screen instead. But do try it anyway. Force yourself, if necessary, to try composing a few pieces of writing from start to finish on a word processor. Then consider the ease with which you can revise. Consider the time saved by not having to retype the last draft. Consider the handsome appearance of your final copy. You may find yourself converting to word processing for at least some stages of your writing process.

Appendix B

Studying in College

Your college classes require much reading, and some people continue reading regularly after college to satisfy curiosity or to form educated opinions. In this section, we will recommend methods for improving your reading and for managing the chores every college student needs to do: studying, taking notes, and taking tests.

Improving Your Reading

If you are not a good reader, you will be hampered throughout your college career. We have some suggestions to help you get more out of what you read. The most important piece of advice is to look over the reading material carefully before you actually read it. Let us explain how.

Reading a Textbook: Survey, Read, and Write

1. Get to know your book. Textbooks often provide chapter summaries at the end or study questions that help to focus your attention on the main points. Find these before you start so that you will be able to concentrate on learning what you need to know when you have finished the reading.
2. Use the table of contents and the section headings to get an overview of the material. Those section headings (and subheads) are designed to direct you to the key ideas in each chapter.
3. Write a preliminary outline of the chapter, using the headings and subheadings as a guide.

4. Read the chapter and fill in your outline *in your own words* as you go. If you simply copy sentences from the text, you may be fooling yourself into thinking you understand passages that would baffle you if you had to supply the information out of your own head.

5. Use these outlines to study for tests and examinations.

If you are assigned to do outside reading from books that lack the reading aids provided in textbooks, you should still look over the material first and study the preface or introduction to discover the main idea or purpose of the book. Then read the first line of each paragraph of the first chapter, looking for the general content and structure. Next, write a rough outline for this prereading, and then read the chapter, filling in the outline in your own words.

Expanding Your Study Skills

In *How to Study* (4th rev. ed., New York: McGraw, 1994), the authors analyze the most common difficulties students have when they try to study. These experts suggest that a study schedule can solve many such problems. Following is a summary of their advice.

Scheduling Your Study Time

As a typical student, you have probably run into the following troubles:

1. Even though you try, you do not study as much as you know you should.
2. When you finally sit down to study, you waste time or try to do too much in too short a period.
3. It's hard to start studying; things keep interfering with getting down to work.

All of these problems come from slipshod use of time. A schedule for studying can help you make the best possible use of your time.

To help you develop a plan of your own, we have designed a sample schedule for a person who takes five college courses and works nineteen hours a week (see Figure B.1). This sample schedule contains the following features, which will help make your studying time more efficient:

1. *Most of the study time is in one-hour blocks.* Psychological research shows that people work well when they work steadily for a period of time and then rest

	Monday	Tuesday	Wednesday	Thursday	Friday	Saturday	Sunday
8:00–9:00		Economics class		Economics class			
9:00–10:00	Literature class	Study economics	Literature class	Study economics	Literature class	Study economics	
10:00–11:00	Biology class	Study biology	Biology class	Study biology	Biology class		
11:00–12:00	Study biology		Study biology		↓		
12:00–1:00							
1:00–2:00	Study Spanish	Study Spanish	Study Spanish	Study Spanish	Study Spanish	Work	Work
2:00–3:00	Spanish class	Spanish class	Spanish class	Spanish class	Spanish class		
3:00–4:00							
4:00–5:00	Work	Health class		Health class			
5:00–6:00		Study health		Study health			
6:00–7:00						↓	↓
7:00–8:00		Study literature		Study literature			Study literature
8:00–9:00	↓						

This student works part time and has five classes. The gaps are for catch-up study, library time, or fooling around. When you devise your own schedule, consider your preferences and habits. For instance, if you study well late at night, your chart will not be so empty at the bottom. Realize that you need flexibility: you won't be able to follow your plan exactly week after week.

or change tasks. For studying, the best arrangement is forty or fifty minutes of work followed by ten minutes of rest.

2. *Study hours are set aside for specific subjects.* That way, you will not waste time figuring out what to do, and you can plan to have the appropriate study materials on hand. Scheduling regular hours for specific subjects also helps break the unproductive cycle of falling behind in one class while cramming for another.

3. *Studying is spread out.* Research shows that you learn and remember better if you distribute eight hours of study over a week's time rather than study eight hours in a row.

4. *Less time is given to easy subjects (health) and more to difficult ones (biology).*

5. *Study is placed at the best possible time for each course.* In general, studying a subject close to its class helps. For a lecture course (like health or economics), the best time to study is after class. For a recitation course (like Spanish) the best time to study is before class.

Once you face the grim facts that you have to study and that it takes time, it is possible to find satisfaction in developing your study techniques to peak efficiency.

Analyze Your Study Habits

Research supports the idea that each of us has our own cycles of energy and alertness. The factors involved in these peaks and valleys are too numerous to figure out scientifically, but if you pay attention to your own successes and failures, you may learn valuable lessons. Whenever you have a particularly good or bad study session, take note of the following four factors:

1. *Time of day.* One study of college students identified two peak learning periods: between 9 and 11 in the morning and 3 and 4 in the afternoon. The students were at their worst right after lunch. You may or may not fit this pattern, but you probably have one of your own. Record the times of your best and worst study sessions, and see if you can adjust your schedule accordingly.

2. *Your stomach.* Many people feel alert when they are a bit hungry; others cannot concentrate on anything but a snack. If hunger does not make you feel perky, a high-protein morsel (peanuts, cheese, yogurt) may help.

3. *Your worries.* Letting anxieties interfere with your efforts is probably one of the most common problems. If worries get in your way, try fifteen minutes of meditation, music, or exercise; a brief chat with a friend; or even a page or two of freewriting about your problem. Eventually you have to get down to work, but sometimes a half hour of self-therapy will allow hours of attentive studying.

4. *Your setting.* Do your good study sessions happen at a clean, bare desk or among a sea of stimulating clutter? Do you work better sitting in the library or lying on the couch? What kind of music or background noise, if any, do you like? The differences among people are immense, but being sensitive to your own quirks will help you to design a study system that works. And you can avoid situations in which learning is hopeless for you.

Note-Taking

Two kinds of note-taking are usually called for in college: note-taking from lectures and note-taking from texts. Taking clear, well-organized notes can save you time when you study for tests, because writing plants the details and ideas more firmly in your mind.

Our clever note-keeping system is designed for those read-the-book, listen-to-the-lecture, take-the-test courses that are so plentiful in your first years of college. We assume that you use a spiral or three-ring notebook and have a separate section for each of your subjects. This system integrates what you learn from books and what you learn from lectures by placing your notes on them conveniently next to each other: use the left-hand side for textbook notes and the right-hand side for lecture notes, as shown in Figure B.2.

If you read the textbook assignment before the related lecture, you will have the backs of several pages filled with notes when you go to class. Take your

FIGURE B.2

Note-taking System

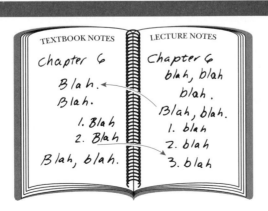

lecture notes on the blank pages facing each of those filled pages, right across from the information you got from the book. If you read the text after hearing the lecture, do it the other way around. You can even draw little arrows to point out relationships between the two sets (when, for instance, your teacher brings up a different and better example of some general principle that the book discusses).

If you work regularly on a word processor, you can still use this double-entry system. Enter your textbook notes in a narrow column on the left side of the page, print the notes out, punch holes in the pages, put them in your notebook, and take the pages to class, where you can record the teacher's comments in the space next to the column of typed notes. If you read the book after hearing the lecture, type up your lecture notes in a narrow column on the word processor and then add notes from the textbook, either on the screen or by hand on printed copy. Whatever way you do it, the two sets of notes reinforce your knowledge and understanding.

Lecture Notes

Good lecturers start the class by previewing the topic or main points to be covered that day, and you can write these important items (and the date) at the top of the page. Your class syllabus will often tell you what the topic of the day is.

Next, you have to figure out the lecture's outline—the main points and the details connected with them. Some lecturers list their main points on the blackboard, which makes it easy. Between main points, some teachers pause, look through their notes, change their tone of voice, or use transitions such as "The next solution has three drawbacks," in which case you can get ready to note the solution and list three items under it.

Do not, of course, try to take down every word. Record only key words, and use abbreviations and symbols to save time (so long as you can be sure to remember their meaning later), like this note from an accounting lecture:

> Diff. in cost & selling price = *gross margin* or *profit gross*. $$ used to pay operating exp. Prod. cost = exp. matched w/sales rev.

As you read this note back to yourself, you reconstruct it in your mind this way:

> The difference between the cost and the selling price is the *gross margin* or *profit gross*. This money is used to pay the operating expenses. The cost of the product is the expense that is matched with sales revenue.

You are in much better shape if you have read and taken notes on the relevant textbook assignment before the lecture. Then you will not furiously struggle to get down the details from the lecture that also appear in the book. Writing down the main points more than once, though, will help you remember them.

Textbook Notes

Taking notes from textbooks is much more comfortable. Writers usually provide headings and subheadings that tell you what the important concepts are. Many experts on study skills suggest that you look over a chapter's headings, sub-headings, and emphasized type. Then jot down questions that you suspect the chapter will answer. As you read the chapter, note the answers to the questions.

If the book or article you are studying does not provide helpful headings, remember that a paragraph usually has a stated or implied topic sentence. Trying to find and note down these topics can be a healthy exercise. You will end up with a skeleton of the chapter or article, and as a result be able to see clearly how it's put together, what the logic underlying it is.

Note-taking can help you focus on the major, minor, and supporting points of a lecture or reading selection. Highlighting or underlining in your book will not do you as much good because it does not require such a high level of involvement (psychologically or physically). If you develop your note-taking skills, you will find that you can cut your studying time for an exam in half. You will also double the length of time that you recall what you have learned.

Tips on Taking Tests

Hardly anyone likes tests, but for many courses in college, your grades are likely to be determined by testing. In this section, we summarize some of the best advice we have heard, which can transform you into a calm, cool, and competent taker of tests.

Scoring High on an Objective Test

Objective tests consist of true-false statements, items to be matched, multiple-choice questions, fill-in-the-blank sentences, and other devices teachers think up. In other words, tests in which you are not required to write sentences.

Before the Test

To prepare for an objective test, review the cleverly organized notes you took from your textbook and class lectures (see pages 437–439). There is no substitute for knowing the course material. You should have studied everything once already, before you begin to review for the test. If you have not, you need to work on your study habits. As you review, take notice of topics you do not remember clearly or in much detail; then reread the parts of your textbook that deal with those topics. Try making a list of special terms, key concepts, and their definitions. Making such a list, by the way, will help you on any kind of test.

Armed with a good night's sleep and a satisfied stomach, you are ready to take the test. Get to the testing place a little early, so you can sit and relax before the ordeal; you do not want your mind all muddled from rushing about. Be sure that you have a watch or that a clock is visible so you can schedule your time.

During the Test

When you get the test, do the following:

1. Check out what kinds of questions there are and how many of each, so you can get an idea of how long you should spend on each part.
2. Go back to the beginning and read the instructions very carefully. Filling out your answer sheet incorrectly can make your best efforts worthless.
3. Next, go through the test and answer all the easy questions. This will help build your self-confidence and will get your mind in the right mood to tangle with the tough ones. If you are doing multiple choice, begin by eliminating the choices you know are wrong, and you will then have a better chance of choosing the right one.
4. After you have finished the easy questions, estimate how much time you can spend on each of the hard ones. For instance, if you have twenty minutes left and sixteen unanswered questions, you should puzzle over each one for only about a minute.

As you go through the test answering the hard questions, you may have the urge to change some of your earlier answers. One school of thought says you should trust your first response. But you may have a perfectly good reason to change it, like having misread the question the first time or finding your memory sharper on that point. Do not change your answers on a shaky basis, like panic. And do not keep going back over and over them looking for details you might have missed: that will just rattle you. In most cases, though, you will do better to guess at an answer than to leave one blank.

Writing a Successful Essay Examination

The skills you need to write a good essay examination may seem irrelevant to life in the world outside college. But in other situations you will sometimes have to come up with impromptu, one-draft writing (like memos, on-the-spot job forms, teacher evaluations).

Before the Test

To prepare for an essay test, study your text and your notes, as you would for an objective test. But remember that this time you do not just have to *recognize* all those facts; you have to *recall* them. A little more memorization of details and definitions might be a good idea. In the process, ponder possible essay questions, and think about how you could organize your knowledge in writing.

During the Test

When you get your test, survey it first. Look for instructions about how long each answer should be. Sometimes your teacher will ask for one- or two-sentence answers, sometimes for one well-developed paragraph, and sometimes for an essay of several paragraphs. These length differences are likely to be related to point distribution—for instance, on a mixed (both objective and essay) test, an essay may net a maximum of 30 points, while a short answer, no matter how clever, will provide a paltry 5 points.

If you have several short essays to write, immediately mark those questions that look most attractive (or least repulsive) to you.

The most unnerving thing about essay exams is lack of time. You can ease this problem a little by scheduling. Of course, you should distribute your time in proportion to the number of points assigned to each answer. Some teachers furnish a time schedule along with the test, but in other cases you are left on your own. If the written instructions do not assign points to questions, ask your instructor for the point distribution.

Here's a sample proportional schedule for an hour test worth 90 points on your grade.

$$\frac{90 \text{ points}}{60 \text{ minutes}} = 3/2 = \text{about 2 minutes for every 3 points}$$

	Points	*Minutes*	
5 short identification items, 5 points each	25	15	(3 minutes each)
1 short essay (paragraph)	15	10	
1 long essay	$\underline{50}$	$\underline{33}$	
	90	58	

This sample reveals how important time planning is. If you did not survey the test and make a schedule, you might be tempted to write for five minutes each on the identification items—and that extra ten minutes would really cut down on your time for the long essay, which has the most possible points.

After planning your time, plan your answers. Every test expert we consult agrees that the time you spend making a scratch outline of your essay is well worth it. Even though your answer may turn out shorter than it would be if you attacked the page immediately, your essay will be more pointworthy because of its clear organization and lack of sloppy repetition (which is sometimes suspiciously called "padding").

As you plan, pay attention to the *verb* in the essay question: *list, explain, compare, evaluate, give examples.* Do what the verb tells you to do. If you are supposed to compare two kinds of cockroaches, a brilliant essay about cockroach habits simply won't do. And be careful not to miss a part of the instructions. If you are asked to *define* and *evaluate* five methods of cockroach extermination, and you just define them, you can expect only half credit for your answer.

In any course you may feel that you have a firm grasp of the general principles or trends or methods, but your teacher is not for a minute going to believe you do unless you follow up every general statement you make with a U-Haul full of specific details (names, dates, examples, quotations) that you have painstakingly memorized for this very purpose. Do not make the mistake of thinking that you need to know such "picky little stuff" only for objective exams. A mass of generalizations is boring and unimpressive to a teacher who is plowing through thirty essay exams over the weekend. A little life and color is certainly welcome (and likely to be rewarded) on those deadly Sunday afternoons.

In short, remember these three steps next time you must wrestle with an essay test:

1. Calmly survey the exam.
2. Schedule time according to point distribution.
3. Make a scratch outline of your essay.
   a. Do what the verb in the question tells you to do.
   b. Include lots of juicy details.

EXERCISE

B.1

1. Figure out a time schedule for taking the following tests:

   a. Test time: 50 minutes

	Points	Total points
10 short definition items	5 each	50
5 short essays	10 each	50

b. Test time: 2 hours (120 minutes)

	Total points
15 true-false questions	15
20 multiple-choice questions	40
2 short essays (30 points each)	60
1 long essay	50

2. Here's a sample half-hour essay examination based on Scheduling Your Study Time (pages 434–436). Read the section again. Then plan your time and take the test without looking back to the section.

Short-answer essays (10 points each)

a. List three advantages of setting up a study schedule.

b. Identify the best unit of time for most college study, and tell why it is good.

c. When should you review for a recitation class? When should you review for a lecture class? Why?

Longer essay (30 points)

Summarize the studying problems that writers identify. From your own experience, discuss whether that list of problems is true to life.

Analyze any difficulties you had with scheduling or planning your answers. Trade papers with other students, and see how they handled the answers.

Getting Extra Help: Useful Reference Books

Laird, Donald A., and Eleanor C. Laird. *Techniques for Efficient Remembering*. New York: McGraw, 1960.

Miller, Lyle L. *Increasing Reading Efficiency*, 5th ed. New York: Holt, 1984.

Morgan, Clifford T., James Deese, and Ellin K. Deese. *How to Study*, 4th rev. ed. New York: McGraw, 1994.

Robinson, Francis P. *Effective Study*, 4th ed. New York: Harper, 1970.

Smith, Genevieve L. *Spelling by Principles: A Programmed Text*. New York: Appleton, 1966.

Appendix C

Writing to Find a Job

Sooner or later, you're going to decide that you need a job—or, if you already have one, you'll try to find a better one. As part of this life-improvement project, you'll need to write a job application letter and put together a résumé. The following advice will help you complete the task with confidence when the time comes.

Producing a Persuasive Job Application Letter

Here are some general principles for writing an effective letter of application:

1. *Keep your reader firmly in mind.* You are trying to convince your prospective employer that you can be of service. Concentrate on what you can do for that organization.

2. *Adopt a polite and confident tone.* You want to present your best qualifications in the most favorable light. But if you appear too self-confident, too assertive, employers may worry that you won't be able to get along with the mere mortals they already employ. However, do not go to the other extreme and plead for a job because you have a family or an aging parent to support. Such appeals simply do not work.

3. *Follow a standard business letter format.* Most people in business judge job applicants to some extent on the way their letters look. At the end of this section, you'll find a couple of sample job application letters. Copy either format faithfully in your own letter.

4. *Make sure your letter is error free.* Any errors in typing, grammar, or usage will count against you in a competitive job market. Most of us have trouble spotting our own mistakes, so find a literate person to help you proofread—and read it several times.

5. *Keep your letter brief.* Limit yourself to one typewritten page consisting of three or four short paragraphs. Since you will include a résumé with the letter, most of the factual information about your qualifications can appear there.

6. *Do not send out photocopies—except for the résumé.* Using a word processor, you can easily send letters that appear to have been written specifically for the person addressed, even if you are fishing for a job opening. Although you will be working with a form letter, try to individualize it each time you reprint it. For instance, be sure to mention the name of the company you are applying to somewhere in the body of the letter, or perhaps say that you would like to live in the city where the company is located.

The following guidelines will suggest how to handle each section of your application letter. (Sample application letters, Figure C.1 and C.2, appear on pages 448–449.)

Write to a Specific Person

If possible, address your letter to a specific person, usually the head of the department you are interested in or the company's personnel manager. When you're fishing for a job, the task can be difficult. Try calling the company and asking for the name and title of the person who handles the hiring in your area. This personal touch shows you are serious, knowledgeable, and sufficiently energetic to locate the name. If you are writing out-of-town firms and can't afford the long-distance charges, addressing the "Director of Personnel" or "Personnel Manager" will do.

Write an Effective Opening

Often the best way to begin your letter is the most direct way, something like this:

My training and experience as a proofreader and copy editor should be useful to the *Daily Clarion*.

This opening makes clear what kind of job you want, why you are qualified for it, and how your skills can be valuable to the employer. Naturally, if you are applying for a job that was advertised, you will say so in your opening paragraph. If you know someone in the organization who will agree to recommend you, by all means mention that person's name.

Another way of opening your application letter is to ask a question: "Does the *Daily Clarion* need an excellent, experienced proofreader and copy editor?" That catches the reader's attention and gets right to the point. Then, explain how skillful you are in the next paragraph or two.

Present Your Qualifications

The heart of your application letter is the proof that you can do for a prospective employer what you say you can do. Since your résumé will supply the details, you should mention in the letter only those things that best qualify you for the job. That usually means experience.

> For two summers I worked as a proofreader on the *Daily Texan* in Austin, Texas, and for three years served as a part-time advertising copywriter on the same newspaper while attending the University of Texas.

If you do not have much work experience, you can emphasize your training (and your grades, if they are good). Or ransack your past for other useful experience. Many jobs require you to deal with the public. If you sold popcorn at a theater or shoes in a department store, mention those jobs to show you have experience dealing with people. Another skill that business needs is organizational ability. If you planned activities at a summer camp or managed the fund drive for the humane society, you can list those as examples of your ability to organize. Be resourceful in evaluating your skills, but don't exaggerate them.

If you have a long-range career goal, you might mention it as an indication of your commitment. Employers like employees who are dedicated to their work.

> My experience with various writing and proofreading assignments could prove useful to your paper, and this job would further my aim to become a professional editor.

You might want to refer to your present status.

> When I finish school in June, . . .

or

> A position in your accounting department would offer me more opportunity for advancement than I have with my present firm.

Notice that you should explain your desire to change jobs in a positive way. Employers take a dim view of employees who change jobs because of personal disagreements or disputes over how to run the place.

Never Mention Money

Salary is a subject that should not be dealt with in application letters. If an advertisement asks for your monetary requirement, suggest that the matter be discussed during your interview.

Set Up an Interview

The real object of your application letter is to obtain an interview, since few good jobs are handed out without one. Conclude your letter by offering to be interviewed at the company's convenience, explain how you can be reached by telephone, and add a polite word of thanks.

> I would welcome a personal interview. Being a student, my schedule varies from day to day, but any weekday after 3:00 p.m. would be the best time to contact me by phone at (303) 555-1212.
>
> Thanks for taking the time to consider my materials. I look forward to your response.

Write a Follow-Up Letter

After you have had your interview, you should write a brief follow-up letter to the interviewer. In this letter you could comment on some feature of the company that impressed you, but primarily you should thank your interviewers for their time and consideration. Since your purpose is mainly to keep your name in the interviewer's mind, a few brief, friendly lines will do. If, however, the interview ended on a "Don't call us, we'll call you" note, no follow-up letter is likely to help.

FIGURE C.1

*A Sample
Letter Using
Block Form*

22 Fuller Avenue
Bloomington, IL 61701
January 5, 1996

Mr. James Williams
Principal
McLean School District #19
4th & Mason Streets
McLean, IL 61754

Dear Mr. Williams:

As a proven, effective teacher, I hope to bring my abilities and ideas to an elementary classroom in District #19. If you have any vacancies, or anticipate any in the immediate future, please consider my qualifications.

As you can see from the enclosed résumé, my teaching experience encompasses K–8 and includes a strong computer curriculum for grades five through eight. Math, science, phonics, and reading are my primary focus areas. Most of the children I worked with at Lake Shore Academy in Oshkosh, Wisconsin, came from immigrant families in lower socioeconomic levels; at Blooming Grove, I taught students whose parents came from Iran, the Philippines, Japan, Brazil, Australia, China, Guatemala, and Africa; therefore, multicultural experience has enhanced my understanding of children and their learning abilities. I consider myself a creative, caring, and competent teacher who would make a positive contribution to the District 19 faculty.

If I can provide any additional information about my candidacy, please contact me at 309/555-1977. I appreciate your taking the time to consider my application and look forward to hearing from you.

Sincerely,

Deborah Livingston

Enclosure: Résumé

FIGURE C.2

A Sample Letter Using Modified Block Form

901 West Hemstead
Belleville, IL 67623
January 28, 1996

Director of Personnel
Personnel Department
Cook County Public Defender's Office
200 West Adams
Chicago, IL 60606

Dear Personnel Director:

Following my May 10, 1996, graduation from Southern Illinois University, I hope to serve a summer internship with the Cook County Public Defender's Office. The internship would fulfill the final six hours of coursework for my B.S. degree in political science with emphasis on pre-law.

This internship would be mutually beneficial. The research skills obtained in my pre-law courses and my strong work ethic would enable me to make a significant contribution to the Cook County Public Defender's Office while proving my abilities both to the office and to myself. In turn, I would be gaining valuable experience for my future career. The internship would be a positive move for both me and the Cook County Public Defender's Office.

A copy of my résumé is enclosed. Please feel free to contact me if additional information is desired.

I would welcome a personal interview. Being a student, my schedule varies from day to day, but any weekday after 3:00 p.m. would be the best time to contact me by phone at (309) 555-2620.

Thank you for taking the time to consider my materials. I am looking forward to your response.

Sincerely,

Damon A. Cross

Enclosure: Résumé

Creating an Effective Résumé

A résumé (or *vita,* in academic circles) is a listing in easy-to-read form of everything about you that might be useful to an employer: work experience, education and/or technical training, personal details, and special skills such as computer expertise or fluency in a foreign language.

Make It Attractive

Format is crucial here. Consult our samples at the end of this section to see some appealing arrangements. If you use a word processor, you should be able to create your own résumé. On the other hand, if you can afford it, you might do well to hire a professional to create the résumé from information you supply. Either way, it's quite acceptable to have the finished product duplicated on good quality paper.

What to Include

Examine the sample résumés included at the end of these guidelines to see examples showing several ways of formatting each category.

1. *Personal Data:* Your name, both present address and a permanent address if you are a student, and a telephone number for each address. These belong at the top.

2. *Career Objective (optional):* State the kind of position you hope to land, but do not just list the job. Instead, write a brief statement in which you indicate what position you hope to fill while subtly conveying to the employer what strengths you can bring to the organization.

3. *Education:* List your college degree (or degrees) and the school, plus the graduation date. If you have more than one degree, list the most recent one first. If you graduated with honors or belong to an honor society, be sure to mention it.

4. *Experience:* List jobs held before your graduation from college as "Work Experience," beginning with the most recent and summarizing if you worked at several different places. List positions held since graduation as "Professional Experience," beginning with the most recent and explaining briefly what your duties were.

5. *Special Skills:* List any skills that you think a prospective employer would find useful, from computer knowledge (very important these days) to skill in dealing with people.

6. *Memberships/Activities:* List membership in professional organizations, academic clubs, offices held, and functions you have organized. Omit church and political groups, but include sports participation if you think it could help (for instance, if you are going into sales, you might mention being an avid golfer).

7. *References:* In the past, applicants used to list the names of three or four people who had agreed to write letters of recommendation (i.e., references) for the applicant. Now, simply state "References available upon request." Most references are handled by telephone these days, but academic employers may still want letters. Before mailing out your job applications, you must contact the people you choose to vouch for you. You need to get their consent and alert them that someone may be calling to ask about your qualifications.

JOSE TORRES

PRESENT ADDRESS *(until May 10, 1995)*   **PERMANENT ADDRESS**
302 West Vernon   548 North Westwood
Normal, IL 61761   Hebron, IL 60133
(309) 555-3554   (708) 555-1212

OBJECTIVE   To obtain a challenging position in which my skills in marketing, business, and communication can be applied to benefit the organization.

EDUCATION   **Illinois State University,** Normal, IL
Bachelor of Science, May 1995
Major: Marketing; Minor: Business Administration

College of DuPage, Glen Ellyn, IL
1991–1993
General Studies

EMPLOYMENT   *College expenses financed:* 100% (work, loans)

April 1985–   <u>Pine Valley Country Club</u>, Pine Valley, IL
present   **Caddie**—consecutive summers for 10 years

June 1992–   <u>7-Eleven</u>, Hebron, IL
present   **Store manager**—part-time employee in family-owned business.
Purchase merchandise, interview applicants, and handle inventory control.

**COMPUTER   IBM and Macintosh; software usage includes Lotus 1-2-3, dBase, and
SKILLS**   WordPerfect.

**MEMBERSHIPS   Alpha Kappa Lambda Fraternity, active member since 1993.
&   • Interfraternal Council Representative
ACTIVITIES**   American Marketing Association, student member
Active in intramural sports including softball, football, basketball, volleyball, hockey, and golf.
Avid golfer with an eight handicap.

REFERENCES   Available upon request.

Jamal Nadeem

75 South Main, Apt. #1
Miami, FL 20613
Home: (202) 549-2583
Work: (202) 288-3033

CAREER EXPERIENCE

3/91-present   Mercedes Benz of North America, 870 South Park Avenue, Miami, FL 20631
     3/91-present   **Financial Analyst, Southern Region**
- Monitor regional performance and communicate results
- Review financial and operational detail to create useful reports
- Assist with business plan compilation and presentation
- Supervise budget preparation and implementation

1/89–3/91   LaMere Partners, 11 South Monroe, Chicago, IL 60603
                     Corporate Real Estate Services
                     Investment Management and Development Group
    10/89–3/91   **Portfolio Controller**—in charge of the accounting for four investment funds owning a total of $250 million of U.S. commercial real estate property.
    1/89–10/89   **Senior Accountant**
- Organize production schedule to meet established deadlines
- Coordinate reporting to external investors and internal managers
- Supervise staff

7/85–1/89   KPMG—Peat Marwick, 110 First National Bank Bldg., Woodstock, IL 61614
    6/87–1/89   **Senior Accountant**
    6/86–6/87   **Staff Accountant**
    7/85–6/86   **Assistant Accountant**
- Organized and conducted audits, created and monitored time budgets, and supervised assistants
- Analyzed data, interviewed clients, prepared audit reports

MANAGEMENT & COMPUTER SKILLS

- Manage in a caring, supportive manner, promoting individual growth while meeting the goals of the organization
- Flexible in adapting to a growing, changing environment
- Ability to listen and analyze
- Budget time wisely
- Microcomputer skills: IBM PS/2 and Apple Macintosh. Software usage includes Microsoft Excel, Lotus 1-2-3, WordPerfect

EDUCATION

Western Illinois University (Macomb, IL), Bachelor of Arts—Accounting, May 1985
GPA: 3.5/4.0
College work/study program—4 years

Passed Certified Public Accountants exam on first attempt

ACTIVITIES & INTERESTS

American Cancer Society volunteer   Chicago Anti-Hunger Federation
Boys and Girls Club of Chicago   Enjoy reading, running, and golf

References available upon request

DON ROBERTS

904 Pershing
Wheaton, IL 60187
708/653-6669

OBJECTIVE

To obtain a challenging position in which my strengths of organization, trustworthiness, and responsibility can be applied to benefit the organization.

EDUCATION

Illinois State University, Normal, IL
Bachelor of Science, August 1993
Major: **Mass Communication**

1987–88

Columbia College, Chicago, IL
Major: **Communication**
Technical courses in television production, directing, camera work.

WORK EXPERIENCE

3/92–12/93

Illinois State University Golf Course, Normal, IL
Head Cashier
Employed part-time during school; full-time during the summer and following graduation. Responsibilities included:
- Opened and closed the Pro Shop
- Assisted with monthly inventory, concessions, and special merchandise orders
- Comanaged a staff of twelve student workers
- Assumed duties of starter and concession employee as needed

7/87–1/91
Summers &
holidays

School District #200, Wheaton, IL
Crew Manager
Duties included cleaning, painting, hauling and other responsibilities in maintaining the upkeep of fourteen district schools.

10/88–6/89

Gary Wheaton Bank, Wheaton, IL
Document Messenger
Full-time position. Responsible for prompt and dependable pick-up and delivery of bank documents and mail for seven district banks.

SPECIAL SKILLS

Computer knowledge—Macintosh, WordPerfect
Trained in telecommunication sales
Filmed high school football and basketball games for cable television while at
    Columbia College
Adept at dealing with people
Hard working

INTERESTS

Travel, golf, ice hockey

REFERENCES

Available upon request

CARMEN J. BALLIE

PRESENT ADDRESS
101 West Standish, #2
DeKalb, IL 60142
309/555-1226

PERMANENT ADDRESS
469 Brainard Drive
West Point, IL 60090
708/555-0351

CAREER OBJECTIVE

To obtain a challenging position where my organizational abilities, time-management skills, and communication background can be utilized within a progressive environment.

EDUCATION

May 1993   Bachelor of Science in Public Relations, Northern Illinois University (NIU), DeKalb, IL
Minor: Business Administration   Major GPA: 3.0/4.0

PROFESSIONAL EXPERIENCE

Spring 1993   NIU Student Body Board of Directors, DeKalb, IL
Internship—One semester, 9 hours per week
Assisting the Director with various activities involving student/town liaison including planning and coordinating the Student United Way campaign.

Fall 1992   Occupational Development Center, Sycamore, IL
Internship—one semester, 9 hours per week
Composed and edited the quarterly newsletter; served on the fundraising committee; helped with initial planning for the spring fundraiser.

WORK EXPERIENCE

The following part-time positions have been held during summers and school holidays from 1987 to 1992. Besides providing money to continue my education, this employment has taught me how to be a team player, how to work effectively with the public, and how to perform efficiently and responsibly in varied work environments.

Waitress, Chi Chi's Mexican Restaurant, Deerfield, IL
Sales Associate, Compagnie International Express, Prospect Heights, IL
Lifeguard, Lincoln Club Property and McGill Management
Receptionist, Tom Todd Chevrolet, Wheeling, IL

ACTIVITIES

Aug. 1990–   Chi Omega Sorority
present   Editor and coordinator of alumni/parent newsletter, Spring 1993
Community service committee member
Career development committee member
Home Sweet Home volunteer (prepared and served food to the homeless)
Captain, field hockey intramural team

REFERENCES AVAILABLE UPON REQUEST

KATHERYN CHO

222 Fullerton Avenue
Rockford, IL 60321
(708) 828-6554

OBJECTIVE

To be an elementary teacher who:
- provides a warm environment that encourages participation and builds self-esteem
- communicates effectively and builds trusting relationships
- is sensitive to each child's learning style and special needs
- is creative and implements innovative techniques
- develops stimulating interactive lessons that lead to curiosity and inquiry

EDUCATION

Bachelor of Science in Education, Northern Illinois University, DeKalb, IL, 1986
Minor: Biological Sciences (31 hours); Social Studies (24 hours)

Illinois Standard Certification Type 03

TEACHING EXPERIENCE

1990–present   <u>Blooming Grove Academy</u>, Rockford, IL

Recess teacher (K–6); selective teacher volunteer (map class; Gifts for Giving)	1994–present
Kindergarten teacher (whole language, Math Their Way, Char L Phonics, parenting classes, Developing Capable People Workshop)	1993–1994
First grade teacher (all of above plus High Scopes Training)	1992–1993
First/second grade teacher (whole language; Math Their Way, Char L Phonics, selectives, parenting classes)	1991–1992
Kindergarten/first grade teacher (summer program: reading, math)	June–Aug 1991
First grade teacher (whole language, Math Their Way, Char L Phonics, selectives, parenting classes)	1990–1991

1989–1990   <u>Bloomington, El Paso, Gridley, Downs</u>, Normal, IL
Substitute Teacher

1987–1989   <u>Lake Shore Academy</u>, Oshkosh, WI

Computer teacher (proposed, designed and taught curriculum including computer care, use and parts; use of BASIC language, Apple graphics, the keyboard, word processor, database, spreadsheet, and telecommunications)	8/88–6/89 8/87–6/88
Third grade teacher	8/88–8/89
Sixth grade teacher	8/87–6/88

1987   <u>Rainbow Path</u>, Libertyville, IL
Head Teacher—preschool (3–4 year olds)

RELATED ACTIVITIES

Initiated school council for K–5 students
Organized and implemented two after-school computer clubs for junior high
Organized fund raisers involving students and parents for computer materials
Participated in peer facilitator training for students
Member of Heartland Whole Language Group
Teacher for CCD classes (junior high) and Logos Program (preschool)
Worked with physically and mentally challenged students
Cofacilitated parenting classes
Developed family education nights

CREDENTIALS

Available upon request from Career Planning & Placement Center, 210 Swen Parson Hall, North, Northern Illinois University, DeKalb, IL 60115

Part Four

Additional Readings

Description, Narration, and Process

Exemplification and Definition

Classification and Division

Martin Luther King Jr.   "Three Types of Resistance to Oppression"
Phillip Lopate   "What Friends Are For"
William Lutz   "Doublespeak"
Margaret Mead   "New Superstitions for Old"

Comparison and Contrast

Rachel Carson   "A Fable for Tomorrow"
Richard Cohen   "Glittering Alice and Sad Eleanor"
Suzanne Britt   "That Lean and Hungry Look"
Carol Tavris   "Are Women Wimps?"

Cause-and-Effect Analysis

Carl M. Cannon   "Honey, I Warped the Kids"
Ellen Goodman   "The Company Man"
Elizabeth Rapoport   "The Story of Z"
Roger Rosenblatt   "Sexual Bigotry"
Brent Staples   "Black Men and Public Space"

Persuasion

Nikki Giovanni   "Campus Racism 101"
Ricardo Chavira   "The Rise of Teenage Gambling"
Eric Marcus   "Ignorance Is Not Bliss"
Joy Overbeck   "Sex, Kids, and the Slut Look"

Description, Narration, and Process

WIND!

William Least Heat-Moon

*William Least Heat-Moon gave up his career as a professor of English at the
University of Missouri to become a writer. His first book,* Blue Highways
*(1982), describes in lyrical detail a journey across the United States. In the
following selection, taken from a longer essay in the September 1991 issue of
the* Atlantic Monthly, *the author uses vivid description to bring to life the
tale of a couple who were actually carried aloft by a rip-roarin' Kansas
tornado.*

Paul and Leola Evans are in their early seventies but appear a decade younger,   1
their faces shaped by the prairie wind into strong and pleasing lines. They have no children. Paul speaks softly and to the point, and Leola is animated, the kind of woman
who can take a small smoldering story and breathe it into bright flame. Paul listens to
her in barely noticeable amusement and from time to time tosses tinder to her.

Leola says: "It was 1949, May. Paul was home from the Pacific. We'd made it   2
through the war, then this. We were living just across the county line, near Americus,
on a little farm by the Neosho River. One Friday night I came upstairs to bed, and
Paul gawked at me. He said, '*What* are you doing?' I was wearing my good rabbit-fur
coat and wedding rings, and I had a handful of wooden matches. It wasn't cold at
all. I said I didn't know but that something wasn't right, and he said, 'What's not
right?' and I didn't know.

"We went to bed and just after dark it began to rain, and then the wind came   3
on and blew harder, and we went downstairs and tried to open the door, but the air
pressure was so strong Paul couldn't even turn the knob. The wind had us locked
in. We hunkered in the corner of the living room in just our pajamas—mine were
new seersucker—and me in my fur coat. The wind got louder, then the windows
blew out, and we realized we were in trouble when the heat stove went around the
corner and out a wall that had just come down.

"We clamped on to each other like ticks, and then we were six feet in the air,   4
and Paul was hanging on to my fur coat—for ballast, he says now—and we went up
and out where the wall had been, and then we came down, and then we went up
again, longer this time, and then came down in a heap of animals: a cow and one
of our dogs with a two-by-four through it. The cow lived, but we lost the dog.

5   "We were out in the wheat field, sixty yards from the house, and Paul had a knot above his eye that made him look like the Two-Headed Wonder Boy. Splintered wood and glass and metal all over, and the electric lines down and sparking, and here we were barefoot. Paul said to walk only when the lightning flashed to see what we were stepping on. We were more afraid of getting electrocuted than cut. We could see in the flashes that the second story was gone except for one room, and we saw the car was an accordion, and our big truck was upside down.

6   "The old hog was so terrified she got between us and wouldn't leave all the way up to the neighbors'. Their place wasn't touched. They came to the door and saw a scared hog and two things in rags covered with black mud sucked up out of the river and coated with plaster dust and blood, and one of them was growing a second head. The neighbors didn't know who we were until they heard our voices."

7   Paul says, "That tornado was on a path to miss our house until it hit the Cottonwood and veered back on us. The Indians believe a twister will change course when it crosses a river."

8   Leola: "The next morning we walked back home—the electric clock was stopped at nine-forty, and I went upstairs to the room that was left, and there on the chest my glasses were just like I left them, but our bedroom was gone, and our mattress, all torn up, was in a tree where we'd have been."

9   Paul: "We spit plaster for weeks. It was just plain imbedded in us."

10   I'm thinking, What truer children of Kansas than those taken aloft by the South Wind?

DARKNESS AT NOON

Harold Krents

Harold Krents, an attorney, has a second career in writing. His autobiography was the basis for the Broadway play, later a film, Butterflies Are Free. *This essay provides several narratives to make a point about how blind people are treated.*

Blind from birth, I have never had the opportunity to see myself and have been completely dependent on the image I create in the eye of the observer. To date it has not been narcissistic. 1

There are those who assume that since I can't see, I obviously also cannot hear. Very often people will converse with me at the top of their lungs, enunciating each word very carefully. Conversely, people will also often whisper, assuming that since my eyes don't work, my ears don't either. 2

For example, when I go to the airport and ask the ticket agent for assistance to the plane, he or she will invariably pick up the phone, call a ground hostess and whisper: "Hi, Jane, we've got a 76 here." I have concluded that the word "blind" is not used for one of two reasons: Either they fear that if the dread word is spoken, the ticket agent's retina will immediately detach, or they are reluctant to inform me of my condition of which I may not have been previously aware. 3

On the other hand, others know that of course I can hear, but believe that I can't talk. Often, therefore, when my wife and I go out to dinner, a waiter or waitress will ask Kit if "*he* would like a drink" to which I respond that "indeed *he* would." 4

This point was graphically driven home to me while we were in England. I had been given a year's leave of absence from my Washington law firm to study for a diploma in law degree at Oxford University. During the year I became ill and was hospitalized. Immediately after admission, I was wheeled down to the X-ray room. Just at the door sat an elderly woman—elderly I would judge from the sound of her voice. "What is his name?" the woman asked the orderly who had been wheeling me. 5

"What's your name?" the orderly repeated to me. 6

"Harold Krents," I replied. 7

"Harold Krents," he repeated. 8

"When was he born?" 9

"When were you born?" 10

"November 5, 1944," I responded. 11

"November 5, 1944," the orderly intoned. 12

This procedure continued for approximately five minutes at which point even my saint-like disposition deserted me. "Look," I finally blurted out, "this is 13 absolutely ridiculous. Okay, granted I can't see, but it's got to have become pretty clear to both of you that I don't need an interpreter."

14   "He says he doesn't need an interpreter," the orderly reported to the woman.

15   The toughest misconception of all is the view that because I can't see, I can't work. I was turned down by over forty law firms because of my blindness, even though my qualifications included a cum laude degree from Harvard College and a good ranking in my Harvard Law School class.

16   The attempt to find employment, the continuous frustration of being told that it was impossible for a blind person to practice law, the rejection letters, not based on my lack of ability but rather on my disability, will always remain one of the most disillusioning experiences of my life.

17   Fortunately, this view of limitation and exclusion is beginning to change. On April 16, the Department of Labor issued regulations that mandate equal-employment opportunities for the handicapped. By and large, the business community's response to offering employment to the disabled has been enthusiastic.

18   I therefore look forward to the day, with the expectation that it is certain to come, when employers will view their handicapped workers as a little child did me years ago when my family still lived in Scarsdale.

19   I was playing basketball with my father in our backyard according to procedures we had developed. My father would stand beneath the hoop, shout, and I would shoot over his head at the basket attached to our garage. Our nextdoor neighbor, aged five, wandered over into our yard with a playmate. "He's blind," our neighbor whispered to her friend in a voice that could be heard distinctly by Dad and me. Dad shot and missed: I did the same. Dad hit the rim: I missed entirely: Dad shot and missed the garage entirely. "Which one is blind?" whispered back the little friend.

20   I would hope that in the near future when a plant manager is touring the factory with the foreman and comes upon a handicapped and nonhandicapped person working together, his comment after watching them work will be, "Which one is disabled?"

ONLY DAUGHTER

Sandra Cisneros

Sandra Cisneros, the daughter of a Mexican father and a Mexican American mother, has published two collections of short stories: The House on Mango Street *(1984) and* Woman Hollering Creek *(1991). In this essay, she tells of her struggle to win her father's approval for her writing career.*

Once, several years ago, when I was just starting out my writing career, I was asked to write my own contributor's note for an anthology I was part of. I wrote: "I am the only daughter in a family of six sons. *That* explains everything." 1

Well, I've thought about that ever since, and yes, it explains a lot to me, but for the reader's sake I should have written: "I am the only daughter in a *Mexican* family of six sons." Or even: "I am the only daughter of a Mexican father and a Mexican-American mother." Or: "I am the only daughter of a working-class family of nine." All of these had everything to do with who I am today. 2

I was/am the only daughter and *only* a daughter. Being an only daughter in a family of six sons forced me by circumstance to spend a lot of time by myself because my brothers felt it beneath them to play with a *girl* in public. But that aloneness, that loneliness, was good for a would-be writer—it allowed me time to think and think, to imagine, to read and prepare myself. 3

Being only a daughter for my father meant my destiny would lead me to become someone's wife. That's what he believed. But when I was in the fifth grade and shared my plans for college with him, I was sure he understood. I remember my father saying, "*Que bueno, ni'ja,* that's good." That meant a lot to me, especially since my brothers thought the idea hilarious. What I didn't realize was that my father thought college was good for girls—good for finding a husband. After four years in college and two more in graduate school, and still no husband, my father shakes his head even now and says I wasted all that education. 4

In retrospect, I'm lucky my father believed daughters were meant for husbands. It meant it didn't matter if I majored in something silly like English. After all, I'd find a nice professional eventually, right? This allowed me the liberty to putter about embroidering my little poems and stories without my father interrupting with so much as a "What's that you're writing?" 5

But the truth is, I wanted him to interrupt. I wanted my father to understand what it was I was scribbling, to introduce me as "My only daughter, the writer." Not as "This is only my daughter. She teaches." *Es maestra*—teacher. Not even *profesora.* 6

In a sense, everything I have ever written has been for him, to win his approval even though I know my father can't read English words, even though my father's only 7 reading includes the brown-ink *Esto* sports magazines from Mexico City and the bloody *¡Alarma!* magazines that feature yet another sighting of *La Virgen de Guadalupe* on a tortilla or a wife's revenge on her philandering husband by bashing his skull in with a *molcajete* (a kitchen mortar made of volcanic rock). Or the *fotonovelas,* the little picture paperbacks with tragedy and trauma erupting from the characters' mouths in bubbles.

8   My father represents, then, the public majority. A public who is uninterested in reading, and yet one whom I am writing about and for, and privately trying to woo.

9   When we were growing up in Chicago, we moved a lot because of my father. He suffered bouts of nostalgia. Then we'd have to let go our flat, store the furniture with mother's relatives, load the station wagon with baggage and bologna sandwiches and head south. To Mexico City.

10   We came back, of course. To yet another Chicago flat, another Chicago neighborhood, another Catholic school. Each time, my father would seek out the parish priest in order to get a tuition break, and complain or boast: "I have seven sons."

11   He meant *siete hijos,* seven children, but he translated it as "sons." "I have seven sons." To anyone who would listen. The Sears Roebuck employee who sold us the washing machine. The short-order cook where my father ate his ham-and-eggs breakfasts. "I have seven sons." As if he deserved a medal from the state.

12   My papa. He didn't mean anything by that mistranslation, I'm sure. But somehow I could feel myself being erased. I'd tug my father's sleeve and whisper: "Not seven sons. Six! and *one daughter.*"

13   When my oldest brother graduated from medical school, he fulfilled my father's dream that we study hard and use this—our heads, instead of this—our hands. Even now my father's hands are thick and yellow, stubbed by a history of hammer and nails and twine and coils and springs. "Use this," my father said, tapping his head, "and not this," showing us those hands. He always looked tired when he said it.

14   Wasn't college an investment? And hadn't I spent all those years in college? And if I didn't marry, what was it all for? Why would anyone go to college and then choose to be poor? Especially someone who had always been poor.

15   Last year, after ten years of writing professionally, the financial rewards started to trickle in. My second National Endowment for the Arts Fellowship. A guest professorship at the University of California, Berkeley. My book, which sold to a major New York publishing house.

16   At Christmas, I flew home to Chicago. The house was throbbing, same as always; hot *tamales* and sweet *tamales* hissing in my mother's pressure cooker, and everybody—my mother, six brothers, wives, babies, aunts, cousins—talking too loud and at the same time, like in a Fellini film, because that's just how we are.

17   I went upstairs to my father's room. One of my stories had just been translated into Spanish and published in an anthology of Chicano writing, and I wanted to show it to him. Ever since he recovered from a stroke two years ago, my father likes

to spend his leisure hours horizontally. And that's how I found him, watching a Pedro Infante movie on Galavisión and eating rice pudding.

There was a glass filmed with milk on the bedside table. There were several 18 vials of pills and balled Kleenex. And on the floor, one black sock and a plastic urinal that I didn't want to look at but looked at anyway. Pedro Infante was about to burst into song, and my father was laughing.

I'm not sure if it was because my story was translated into Spanish, or because 19 it was published in Mexico, or perhaps because the story dealt with Tepeyac, the *colonia* my father was raised in and the house he grew up in, but at any rate, my father punched the mute button on his remote control and read my story.

I sat on the bed next to my father and waited. He read it very slowly. As if he 20 were reading each line over and over. He laughed at all the right places and read lines he liked out loud. He pointed and asked questions: "Is this So-and-so?" "Yes," I said. He kept reading.

When he was finally finished, after what seemed like hours, my father looked 21 up and asked: "Where can we get more copies of this for the relatives?"

Of all the wonderful things that happened to me last year, that was the most 22 wonderful.

A HANGING

George Orwell

George Orwell is best known for his novel 1984 *(1949). The social criticism in that book is also apparent in his narratives about experiences as a British colonialist in India, such as "A Hanging."*

1   It was in Burma, a sodden morning of the rains. A sickly light, like yellow tinfoil, was slanting over the high walls into the jail yard. We were waiting outside the condemned cells, a row of sheds fronted with double bars, like small animal cages. Each cell measured about ten feet by ten and was quite bare within except for a plank bed and a pot of drinking water. In some of them brown silent men were squatting at the inner bars, with their blankets draped round them. These were the condemned men, due to be hanged within the next week or two.

2   One prisoner had been brought out of his cell. He was a Hindu, a puny wisp of a man, with a shaven head and vague liquid eyes. He had a thick, sprouting moustache, absurdly too big for his body, rather like the moustache of a comic man on the films. Six tall Indian warders were guarding him and getting him ready for the gallows. Two of them stood by with rifles with fixed bayonets, while the others handcuffed him, passed a chain through his handcuffs and fixed it to their belts, and lashed his arms tight to his sides. They crowded very close about him, with their hands always on him in a careful, caressing grip, as though all the while feeling him to make sure he was there. It was like men handling a fish which is still alive and may jump back into the water. But he stood quite unresisting, yielding his arms limply to the ropes, as though he hardly noticed what was happening.

3   Eight o'clock struck and a bugle call, desolately thin in the wet air, floated from the distant barracks. The superintendent of the jail, who was standing apart from the rest of us, moodily prodding the gravel with his stick, raised his head at the sound. He was an army doctor, with a grey toothbrush moustache and a gruff voice. "For God's sake hurry up, Francis," he said irritably. "The man ought to have been dead by this time. Aren't you ready yet?"

4   Francis, the head jailer, a fat Dravidian in a white drill suit and gold spectacles, waved his black hand. "Yes sir, yes sir," he bubbled. "All iss satisfactorily prepared. The hangman iss waiting. We shall proceed."

5   "Well, quick march, then. The prisoners can't get their breakfast till this job's over."

6   We set out for the gallows. Two warders marched on either side of the prisoner, with their files at the slope; two others marched close against him, gripping him by arm and shoulder, as though at once pushing and supporting him. The rest of us, magistrates and the like, followed behind. Suddenly, when we had gone ten

yards, the procession stopped short without any order or warning. A dreadful thing had happened—a dog, come goodness knows whence, had appeared in the yard. It came bounding among us with a loud volley of barks, and leapt round us wagging its whole body, wild with glee at finding so many human beings together. It was a large woolly dog, half Airedale, half pariah. For a moment it pranced round us, and then, before anyone could stop it, it had made a dash for the prisoner, and jumping up tried to lick his face. Everyone stood aghast, too taken aback even to grab at the dog.

"Who let that bloody brute in here?" said the superintendent angrily. "Catch it, someone!" 7

A warder, detached from the escort, charged clumsily after the dog, but it danced and gambolled just out of his reach, taking everything as part of the game. A young Eurasian jailer picked up a handful of gravel and tried to stone the dog away, but it dodged the stones and came after us again. Its yaps echoed from the jail walls. The prisoner, in the grasp of the two warders, looked on incuriously, as though this was another formality of the hanging. It was several minutes before someone managed to catch the dog. Then we put my handkerchief through its collar and moved off once more, with the dog still straining and whimpering. 8

It was about forty yards to the gallows. I watched the bare brown back of the prisoner marching in front of me. He walked clumsily with his bound arms, but quite steadily, with that bobbing gait of the Indian who never straightens his knees. At each step his muscles slid neatly into place, the lock of hair on his scalp danced up and down, his feet printed themselves on the wet gravel. And once, in spite of the men who gripped him by each shoulder, he stepped slightly aside to avoid a puddle on the path. 9

It is curious, but till that moment I had never realised what it means to destroy a healthy, conscious man. When I saw the prisoner step aside to avoid the puddle, I saw the mystery, the unspeakable wrongness, of cutting a life short when it is in full tide. This man was not dying, he was alive just as we were alive. All the organs of his body were working—bowels digesting food, skin renewing itself, nails growing, tissues forming—all toiling away in solemn foolery. His nails would still be growing when he stood on the drop, when he was falling through the air with a tenth of a second to live. His eyes saw the yellow gravel and the grey walls, and his brain still remembered, foresaw, reasoned—reasoned even about puddles. He and we were a party of men walking together, seeing, hearing, feeling, understanding the same world; and in two minutes, with a sudden snap, one of us would be gone—one mind less, one world less. 10

The gallows stood in a small yard, separate from the main grounds of the prison, and overgrown with tall prickly weeds. It was a brick erection like three sides of a shed, with planking on top, and above that two beams and a crossbar with the rope dangling. The hangman, a greyhaired convict in the white uniform of the prison, 11 was waiting beside his machine. He greeted us with a servile crouch as we entered. At a word from Francis the two warders, gripping the prisoner more closely than ever, half led, half pushed him to the gallows and helped him clumsily up the ladder. Then the hangman climbed up and fixed the rope round the prisoner's neck.

12   We stood waiting, five yards away. The warders had formed in a rough circle round the gallows. And then, when the noose was fixed, the prisoner began crying out to his god. It was a high, reiterated cry of "Ram! Ram! Ram! Ram!", not urgent and fearful like a prayer or a cry for help, but steady, rhythmical, almost like the tolling of a bell. The dog answered the sound with a whine. The hangman, still standing on the gallows, produced a small cotton bag like a flour bag and drew it down over the prisoner's face. But the sound, muffled by the cloth, still persisted, over and over again: "Ram! Ram! Ram! Ram! Ram!"

13   The hangman climbed down and stood ready, holding the lever. Minutes seemed to pass. The steady, muffled crying from the prisoner went on and on. "Ram! Ram! Ram!" never faltering for an instant. The superintendent, his head on his chest, was slowly poking the ground with his stick; perhaps he was counting the cries, allowing the prisoner a fixed number—fifty, perhaps, or a hundred. Everyone had changed colour. The Indians had gone grey like bad coffee, and one or two of the bayonets were wavering. We looked at the lashed, hooded man on the drop, and listened to his cries—each cry another second of life; the same thought was in all our minds: oh, kill him quickly, get it over, stop that abominable noise!

14   Suddenly the superintendent made up his mind. Throwing up his head he made a swift motion with his stick. "Chalo!" he shouted almost fiercely.

15   There was a clanking noise, and then dead silence. The prisoner had vanished, and the rope was twisting on itself. I let go of the dog, and it galloped immediately to the back of the gallows; but when it got there it stopped short, barked, and then retreated into a corner of the yard, where it stood among the weeds, looking timorously out at us. We went round the gallows to inspect the prisoner's body. He was dangling with his toes straight downwards, very slowly revolving, as dead as a stone.

16   The superintendent reached out with his stick and poked the bare body; it oscillated, slightly. "*He's* all right," said the superintendent. He backed out from under the gallows, and blew out a deep breath. The moody look had gone out of his face quite suddenly. He glanced at his wristwatch. "Eight minutes past eight. Well, that's all for this morning, thank God."

17   The warders unfixed bayonets and marched away. The dog, sobered and conscious of having misbehaved itself, slipped after them. We walked out of the gallows yard, past the condemned cells with their waiting prisoners, into the big central yard of the prison. The convicts, under the command of warders armed with lathis, were already receiving their breakfast. They squatted in long rows, each man holding a tin pannikin, while two warders with buckets marched round ladling out rice; it

seemed quite a homely, jolly scene, after the hanging. An enormous relief had come upon us now that the job was done. One felt an impulse to sing, to break into a run, to snigger. All at once everyone began chattering gaily.

The Eurasian boy walking beside me nodded towards the way we had come, with a knowing smile: "Do you know, sir, our friend (he meant the dead man), when he heard his appeal had been dismissed, he pissed on the floor of his cell. From fright.—Kindly take one of my cigarettes, sir. Do you not admire my new silver case, sir? From the boxwallah, two rupees eight annas. Classy European style." 18

Several people laughed—at what, nobody seemed certain. 19

Francis was walking by the superintendent, talking garrulously: "Well, sir, all hass passed off with the utmost satisfactoriness. It wass all finished—flick! like that. It iss not always so—oah, no! I have known cases where the doctor wass obliged to go beneath the gallows and pull the prisoner's legs to ensure decease. Most disagreeable!" 20

"Wriggling about, eh? That's bad," said the superintendent. 21

"Ach, sir, it iss worse when they become refractory! One man, I recall, clung to the bars of hiss cage when we went to take him out. You will scarcely credit, sir, that it took six warders to dislodge him, three pulling at each leg. We reasoned with him. 'My dear fellow,' we said, 'think of all the pain and trouble you are causing to us!' But no, he would not listen! Ach, he wass very troublesome!" 22

I found that I was laughing quite loudly. Everyone was laughing. Even the superintendent grinned in a tolerant way. "You'd better all come out and have a drink," he said quite genially. "I've got a bottle of whiskey in the car. We could do with it." 23

We went through the big double gates of the prison, into the road. "Pulling at his legs!" exclaimed a Burmese magistrate suddenly, and burst into a loud chuckling. We all began laughing again. At that moment Francis's anecdote seemed extraordinarily funny. We all had a drink together, native and European alike, quite amicably. The dead man was a hundred yards away. 24

HOW TO WRITE A PERSONAL LETTER

Garrison Keillor

Best known for his creation on radio of the mythical Lake Wobegon, the town where "all the children are above average," Garrison Keillor is also author of numerous short stories and several books, including The Book of Guys *(1993). In typical Keillor style, this essay makes interesting a topic that is often bland and boring.*

1   We shy persons need to write a letter now and then, or else we'll dry up and blow away. It's true. And I speak as one who loves to reach for the phone and talk. The telephone is to shyness what Hawaii is to February, it's a way out of the woods. *And yet:* a letter is better.

2   Such a sweet gift—a piece of handmade writing, in an envelope that is not a bill, sitting in our friend's path when she trudges home from a long day spent among wahoos and savages, a day our words will help repair. They don't need to be immortal, just sincere. She can read them twice and again tomorrow: *You're someone I care about, Corinne, and think of often, and every time I do, you make me smile.*

3   We need to write, otherwise nobody will know who we are. They will have only a vague impression of us as A Nice Person, because, frankly, we don't shine at conversation, we lack the confidence to thrust our faces forward and say, "Hi, I'm Heather Hooten, let me tell you about my week." Mostly we say "Uh-huh" and "Oh really." People smile and look over our shoulder, looking for someone else to talk to.

4   So a shy person sits down and writes a letter. To be known by another person—to meet and talk freely on the page—to be close despite distance. To escape from anonymity and be our own sweet selves and express the music of our souls.

5   We want our dear Aunt Eleanor to know that we have fallen in love, that we quit our job, that we're moving to New York, and we want to say a few things that might not get said in casual conversation: *Thank you for what you've meant to me. I am very happy right now.*

6   The first step in writing letters is to get over the guilt of *not* writing. You don't "owe" anybody a letter. Letters are a gift. The burning shame you feel when you see unanswered mail makes it harder to pick up a pen and makes for a cheerless letter when you finally do. *I feel bad about not writing, but I've been so busy,* etc. Skip this. Few letters are obligatory, and they are *Thanks for the wonderful gift* and *I am terribly sorry to hear about George's death.* Write these promptly if you want to keep your friends. Don't worry about the others, except love letters, of course. When your true love writes *Dear Light of My Life, Joy of My Heart,* some response is called for.

7   Some of the best letters are tossed off in a burst of inspiration, so keep your writing stuff in one place where you can sit down for a few minutes and—*Dear Roy,*

I am in the middle of an essay but thought I'd drop you a line. Hi to your sweetie too—dash off a note to a pal. Envelopes, stamps, address book, everything in a drawer so you can write fast when the pen is hot.

A blank white 8″ × 11″ sheet can look as big as Montana if the pen's not so   8
hot—try a smaller page and write boldly. Get a pen that makes a sensuous line, get a comfortable typewriter, a friendly word processor—whichever feels easy to the hand.

Sit for a few minutes with the blank sheet of paper in front of you, and let your   9
friend come to mind. Remember the last time you saw each other and how your friend looked and what you said and what perhaps was unsaid between you; when your friend becomes real to you, start to write.

Write the salutation—*Dear You*—and take a deep breath and plunge in. A sim-   10
ple declarative sentence will do, followed by another and another. As if you were talking to us. Don't think about grammar, don't think about style, just give us your news. Where did you go, who did you see, what did they say, what do you think?

If you don't know where to begin, start with the present: *I'm sitting at the kitchen*   11
table on a rainy Saturday morning. Everyone is gone and the house is quiet. Let the letter drift along. The toughest letter to crank out is one that is meant to impress, as we all know from writing job applications; if it's hard work to slip off a letter to a friend, maybe you're trying too hard to be terrific. A letter is only a report to someone who already likes you for reasons other than your brilliance. Take it easy.

Don't worry about form. It's not a term paper. When you come to the end of   12
one episode, just start a new paragraph. You can go from a few lines about the sad state of rock 'n' roll to the fight with your mother to your fond memories of Mexico to the kitchen sink and what's in it. The more you write, the easier it gets, and when you have a True True Friend to write to, a soul sibling, then it's like driving a car; you just press on the gas.

Don't tear up the page and start over when you write a bad line—try to write   13
your way out of it. Make mistakes and plunge on. Let the letter cook along and let yourself be bold. Outrage, confusion, love—whatever is in your mind, let it find a way to the page. Writing is a means of discovery, always, and when you come to the end and write *Yours ever* or *Hugs and Kisses,* you'll know something you didn't when you wrote *Dear Pal.*

Probably your friend will put your letter away, and it'll be read again a few   14
years from now—and it will improve with age.

And forty years from now, your friend's grandkids will dig it out of the attic and   15
read it, a sweet and precious relic of the ancient Eighties that gives them a sudden clear glimpse of the world we old-timers knew. You will have then created an object of art. Your simple lines about where you went, who you saw, what they said, will speak to those children and they will feel in their hearts the humanity of our times.

You can't pick up a phone and call the future and tell them about our times.   16
You have to pick up a piece of paper.

Exemplification and Definition

PRIDE'S PARADOX

Regina Barreca

An English professor, Regina Barreca is the author of Perfect Husbands
(And Other Fairy Tales) *(1995). The article we reprint here is from a
series Barreca wrote on the seven deadly sins, which appeared in the*
Chicago Tribune *in 1995–96.*

1 Pride, I am proud to say, doesn't come easily to me. I'm terrible at pride.
Shame, guilt, a squirming sense of undeserving—now those I've got a real talent
for; I could teach workshops in "Low Self-Esteem," although nobody would want to
sign up for them. If pride is truly the considerable vice everybody says it is—many
claim pride is the big original sin, coming before the fall, sort of like winter fashions—
then I'm all set for heaven. Saying I'm all set for heaven, however, smacks of boasting, and there I am, shut out again.

2 Associated with positive images of self-esteem in everything from sexuality ("Gay
Pride") to race ("Black Pride") to employment ("Made With Pride in the USA"), pride
is valued by our culture in a way usually reserved for simple pleasures and not complex sins. The fact is, we don't have "humility" seminars to bone up on self-effacement,
and I haven't yet heard of a company bringing in a consultant at a zillion dollars a day
to teach the employees to blush shyly at a mention of the institution's success.

3 America loves pride: We scream "We're No. 1" at everything from football
games to the reclaiming of the Persian Gulf for Kuwait. We've heard that Joe
Kennedy told his sons, "Show me a good loser, and I'll show you a loser," which
probably didn't encourage them to get in touch with their soft, vulnerable sides.

4 We've grown up listening to commercials informing us that we deserve only
the best hot dogs (made from the best cow lips, presumably), best mayonnaise (with
the most fabulous cholesterol) and the best beer (superior to the rest insofar as you
can fall down faster with this one than the others). We want to be proud of our pets
(First in Show), cars (would you rather show up at your high school reunion in a
Jaguar or a Pinto?) and spouses ("Honey, how about wearing that great red tie/skirt/
hat/garter belt tonight?"). Thriving on competition and lapping up the cream of
others' envy, we've been taught to advertise ourselves by blowing our own horns
loud enough to be heard above the rest of the band. Pride waves the baton at the

head of the parade, twirling our images of ourselves deftly and catching them in one hand before they fall.

Is this a bad thing? Since it would appear un-American to stop waving this lit- 5 tle "Hooray for us" flag in my hand, I hardly dare pause to consider. But when I stop the frantic movement and avoid all the cheering, in the vacuum of sound one can hear the pin of self-destruction falling somewhere in the distance. Pride, say the sin scholars, is what led to our being expelled from Eden; Eve was flattered and ate. Adam (like many of his progeny) clearly didn't want to bother making his own meal, and so he ate, too. Pride made Lucifer into the bad guy in the first place; declaring in Milton's version of the fall that he'd rather rule in hell than serve in heaven, he went from being merely head chef in paradise to owning the first barbecue fran- chise. As much as history has sycophantically worshipped at the altar of success, it also delights in the downfall of the great, the boastful and the powerful.

Act a little too cocky, a little too arrogant and the dogs of ruin begin yapping 6 at your heels, led by someone just slightly less cocky and arrogant than you. Act a little too sanctimonious, and not only will the mob eventually rise up against you, but even your best friends will cheer them on. It's tougher to destroy the reputation of someone who says "I'm it for power and money" than it is to destroy the reputa- tion of someone who says "I'm in it because I have been called to show you all the best way to live your life" and then follows that phrase with "Please make all checks payable in my name."

When Jimmy Swaggart turned out to be, in some folks' opinions, living up to 7 his last name—a combination of "swag," meaning "loot," and "braggart," meaning "television evangelist"—not too many ordinary citizens grieved at his collapse. He had strutted his hour upon the stage full of the conviction of his own righteousness, and when the shrapnel of scandal blew through that façade, it made as grand a sound as, say, a pricked balloon. If a regular guy was caught with a babe in a hotel room, there would not have been as profound a reaction, because the regular guy had not been boasting about personally meeting the obligation for fidelity or purity as one of his selling points.

What are causes for pride in our lives? The easiest pride is the stuff we give 8 away—pride in a child's sweet singing voice or a husband's homemade cake or even a favorite co-worker's success—and such pride is downright accessible. But it's harder to be proud of yourself in the right way. And although there are no rights and wrongs in life, there really *are* rights and wrongs in life—it's like when I tell a student who thinks Danielle Steele is the world's best writer, "There's no such thing as a wrong answer—but if there were, that would be one." There are better ways to be proud of yourself than the guy I knew in college who wore a T-shirt saying "Yes, I Am Everything You've Ever Hoped For," to which I could only mutter beneath my breath, "That makes you a bag of Snickers and a hundred-dollar bill."

9   There's no telling what will constitute grounds for pride. My cat is proud when she catches a wadded-up piece of paper in one paw, but then, so is my lawyer. My niece is proud of herself because she can spell well; I've never been able to spell well, and I am proud of that. My aged aunt is proud of never having had sex with anyone besides her husband, and my rapidly aging friend is proud because she has a new liaison going outside her marriage. You might be proud to own a fur coat, whereas your neighbor might wrap an inherited mink in a Hefty bag before throwing it away because she's a card-carrying member of PETA (People for the Ethical Treatment of Animals).

10   One of the worst feelings in life is to once have been proud of something that later causes you shame: a love affair you bragged about that goes wrong; a career track you ostentatiously discussed that careens into a nose dive; an accomplishment you traded on that suddenly appears meaningless compared to someone else's more substantial or original achievement. And one of the most triumphant moments can occur when something you fear might embarrass you suddenly somersaults and turns into a matter of pride.

11   Unlike lust or envy, pride seems as much a virtue as a vice. If we are too proud to behave like cowards or hypocrites or cheapskates, then pride has saved us from worse sins; if we are too proud to be vicious, callous or vengeful, then pride has offered itself to us as the least of all evils, a little bit of possible wickedness injected into our lives the way a little bit of a virus is injected in an inoculation to ward off graver illness.

12   When Pride shows up like a character out of Edgar Allan Poe's "The Masque of the Red Death," however, all dressed up and ready to defy mortality itself, then it might indeed be a good time to edge your way out the door. There are usually a number of reliable indications signaling the moment at which Pride runs away with itself. It wasn't a good sign that the builders of the Titanic apparently claimed "God Himself could not sink this vessel," for example, and I for one would have wagged my finger reprovingly at Frankenstein when he was getting ready to create a whole new race of beings to call him master. Interesting to see that the world usually does more than wag its collective finger at those creators of the master race, whether they attempt this with their own community's approval or not. When one group becomes so swollen with pride that it considers itself immune from the slings and arrows of ordinary existence and so looks to others to carry its burden for it, it appears that the rest of us cannot stand it and thus bring the pedestal down. Such is the paradox of pride: a vice that is its own reward.

SHAME

Dick Gregory

*Dick Gregory is a well-known entertainer and political activist who ran for
U.S. president as the Peace and Freedom Party candidate in 1968. In
1965, he published* Nigger: An Autobiography, *from which this essay
came.*

I never learned hate at home, or shame. I had to go to school for that. I was   1
about seven years old when I got my first big lesson. I was in love with a little girl
named Helene Tucker, a light-complexioned little girl with pigtails and nice manners. She was always clean and she was smart in school. I think I went to school then
mostly to look at her. I brushed my hair and even got me a little old handkerchief.
It was a lady's handkerchief, but I didn't want Helene to see me wipe my nose on
my hand. The pipes were frozen again, there was no water in the house, but I washed
my socks and shirt every night. I'd get a pot, and go over to Mister Ben's grocery
store, and stick my pot down into his soda machine. Scoop out some chopped ice.
By evening the ice melted to water for washing. I got sick a lot that winter because
the fire would go out at night before the clothes were dry. In the morning I'd put
them on, wet or dry, because they were the only clothes I had.

Everybody's got a Helene Tucker, a symbol of everything you want. I loved her   2
for her goodness, her cleanness, her popularity. She'd walk down my street and my
brothers and sisters would yell, "Here comes Helene," and I'd rub my tennis sneakers on the back of my pants and wish my hair wasn't so nappy and the white folks'
shirt fit me better. I'd run out on the street. If I knew my place and didn't come too
close, she'd wink at me and say hello. That was a good feeling. Sometimes I'd follow her all the way home, and shovel the snow off her walk and try to make friends
with her Momma and her aunts. I'd drop money on her stoop late at night on my
way back from shining shoes in the taverns. And she had a Daddy, and he had a good
job. He was a paper hanger.

I guess I would have gotten over Helene by summertime, but something hap-   3
pened in that classroom that made her face hang in front of me for the next twenty-
two years. When I played the drums in high school it was for Helene and when I
broke track records in college it was for Helene and when I started standing behind
microphones and heard applause I wished Helene could hear it, too. It wasn't until
I was twenty-nine years old and married and making money that I finally got her out
of my system. Helene was sitting in that classroom when I learned to be ashamed of
myself.

It was on a Thursday. I was sitting in the back of the room, in a seat with a   4
chalk circle drawn around it. The idiot's seat, the troublemaker's seat.

5   The teacher thought I was stupid. Couldn't spell, couldn't read, couldn't do arithmetic. Just stupid. Teachers were never interested in finding out that you couldn't concentrate because you were so hungry, because you hadn't had any breakfast. All you could think about was noontime, would it ever come? Maybe you could sneak into the cloakroom and steal a bite of some kid's lunch out of a coat pocket. A bit of something. Paste. You can't really make a meal of paste, or put it on bread for a sandwich, but sometimes I'd scoop a few spoonfuls out of the paste jar in the back of the room. Pregnant people get strange tastes. I was pregnant with poverty. Pregnant with dirt and pregnant with smells that made people turn away, pregnant with cold and pregnant with shoes that were never bought for me, pregnant with five other people in my bed and no Daddy in the next room, and pregnant with hunger. Paste doesn't taste too bad when you're hungry.

6   The teacher thought I was a troublemaker. All she saw from the front of the room was a little black boy who squirmed in his idiot's seat and made noises and poked the kids around him. I guess she couldn't see a kid who made noises because he wanted someone to know he was there.

7   It was on a Thursday, the day before the Negro payday. The eagle always flew on Friday. The teacher was asking each student how much his father would give to the Community Chest. On Friday night, each kid would get the money from his father, and on Monday he would bring it to school. I decided I was going to buy me a Daddy right then. I had money in my pocket from shining shoes and selling papers, and whatever Helene Tucker pledged for her Daddy I was going to top it. And I'd hand the money right in. I wasn't going to wait until Monday to buy me a Daddy.

8   I was shaking, scared to death. The teacher opened her book and started calling out names alphabetically.

9   "Helene Tucker?"

10   "My Daddy said he'd give two dollars and fifty cents."

11   "That's very nice, Helene. Very, very nice indeed."

12   That made me feel pretty good. It wouldn't take too much to top that. I had almost three dollars in dimes and quarters in my pocket. I stuck my hand in my pocket and held onto the money, waiting for her to call my name. But the teacher closed her book after she called everybody else in class.

13   I stood up and raised my hand.

14   "What is it now?"

15   "You forgot me."

16   She turned toward the blackboard. "I don't have time to be playing with you, Richard."

17   "My Daddy said he'd . . ."

18   "Sit down, Richard, you're disturbing the class."

19   "My Daddy said he'd give . . . fifteen dollars."

She turned around and looked mad. "We are collecting this money for you   20
and your kind, Richard Gregory. If your Daddy can give fifteen dollars you have no
business being on relief."

"I got it right now, I got it right now, my Daddy gave it to me to turn in today,   21
my Daddy said . . ."

"And furthermore," she said, looking right at me, her nostrils getting big and   22
her lips getting thin and her eyes opening wide, "we know you don't have a Daddy."

Helene Tucker turned around, her eyes full of tears. She felt sorry for me.   23
Then I couldn't see her too well because I was crying, too.

"Sit down, Richard."   24

And I always thought the teacher kind of liked me. She always picked me to   25
wash the blackboard on Friday, after school. That was a big thrill, it made me feel
important. If I didn't wash it, come Monday the school might not function right.

"Where are you going, Richard?"   26

I walked out of school that day, and for a long time I didn't go back very often.   27
There was shame there.

Now there was shame everywhere. It seemed like the whole world had been   28
inside that classroom, everyone had heard what the teacher had said, everyone had
turned around and felt sorry for me. There was shame in going to the Worthy Boys
Annual Christmas Dinner for you and your kind, because everybody knew what a
worthy boy was. Why couldn't they just call it the Boys Annual Dinner, why'd they
have to give it a name? There was shame in wearing the brown and orange and white
plaid mackinaw the welfare gave to three thousand boys. Why'd it have to be the
same for everybody so when you walked down the street the people could see you
were on relief? It was a nice warm mackinaw and it had a hood, and my Momma
beat me and called me a little rat when she found out I stuffed it in the bottom of
a pail full of garbage way over on Cottage Street. There was shame in running over
to Mister Ben's at the end of the day and asking for his rotten peaches, there was
shame in asking Mrs. Simmons for a spoonful of sugar, there was shame in running
out to meet the relief truck. I hated that truck, full of food for you and your kind.
I ran into the house and hid when it came. And then I started to sneak through al-
leys, to take the long way home so the people going into White's Eat Shop wouldn't
see me. Yeah, the whole world heard the teacher that day, we all know you don't
have a Daddy.

SHITTY FIRST DRAFTS

Anne Lamott

Journalist and novelist Anne Lamott, having worked through many writing problems herself, shared her experiences in the best-selling book Bird by Bird: Some Instructions on Writing and Life *(1994). This selection is a chapter about getting started.*

1   Shitty first drafts. All good writers write them. This is how they end up with good second drafts and terrific third drafts. People tend to look at successful writers, writers who are getting their books published and maybe even doing well financially, and think that they sit down at their desks every morning feeling like a million dollars, feeling great about who they are and how much talent they have and what a great story they have to tell; that they take in a few deep breaths, push back their sleeves, roll their necks a few times to get all the cricks out, and dive in, typing fully formed passages as fast as a court reporter. But this is just the fantasy of the uninitiated. I know some very great writers, writers you love who write beautifully and have made a great deal of money, and not *one* of them sits down routinely feeling wildly enthusiastic and confident. Not one of them writes elegant first drafts. All right, one of them does, but we do not like her very much. We do not think that she has a rich inner life or that God likes her or can even stand her. (Although when I mentioned this to my priest friend Tom, he said you can safely assume you've created God in your own image when it turns out that God hates all the same people you do.)

2   Very few writers really know what they are doing until they've done it. Nor do they go about their business feeling dewy and thrilled. They do not type a few stiff warm-up sentences and then find themselves bounding along like huskies across the snow. One writer I know tells me that he sits down every morning and says to himself nicely, "It's not like you don't have a choice, because you do—you can either type or kill yourself." We all often feel like we are pulling teeth, even those writers whose prose ends up being the most natural and fluid. The right words and sentences just do not come pouring out like ticker tape most of the time. Now, Muriel Spark is said to have felt that she was taking dictation from God every morning—sitting there, one supposes, plugged into a Dictaphone, typing away, humming. But this is a very hostile and aggressive position. One might hope for bad things to rain down on a person like this.

3   For me and most of the other writers I know, writing is not rapturous. In fact, the only way I can get anything written at all is to write really, really shitty first drafts.

4   The first draft is the child's draft, where you let it all pour out and then let it romp all over the place, knowing that no one is going to see it and that you can

shape it later. You just let this childlike part of you channel whatever voices and visions come through and onto the page. If one of the characters wants to say, "Well, so what, Mr. Poopy Pants?" you let her. No one is going to see it. If the kid wants to get into really sentimental, weepy, emotional territory, you let him. Just get it all down on paper, because there may be something great in those six crazy pages that you would never have gotten to by more rational, grown-up means. There may be something in the very last line of the very last paragraph on page six that you just love, that is so beautiful or wild that you now know what you're supposed to be writing about, more or less, or in what direction you might go—but there was no way to get to this without first getting through the first five and a half pages.

I used to write food reviews for *California* magazine before it folded. (My writing food reviews had nothing to do with the magazine folding, although every single review did cause a couple of canceled subscriptions. Some readers took umbrage at my comparing mounds of vegetable puree with various ex-presidents' brains.) These reviews always took two days to write. First I'd go to a restaurant several times with a few opinionated, articulate friends in tow. I'd sit there writing down everything anyone said that was at all interesting or funny. Then on the following Monday I'd sit down at my desk with my notes, and try to write the review. Even after I'd been doing this for years, panic would set in. I'd try to write a lead, but instead I'd write a couple of dreadful sentences, xx them out, try again, xx everything out, and then feel despair and worry settle on my chest like an x-ray apron. It's over, I'd think, calmly. I'm not going to be able to get the magic to work this time. I'm ruined. I'm through. I'm toast. Maybe, I'd think, I can get my old job back as a clerk-typist. But probably not. I'd get up and study my teeth in the mirror for a while. Then I'd stop, remember to breathe, make a few phone calls, hit the kitchen and chow down. Eventually I'd go back and sit down at my desk, and sigh for the next ten minutes. Finally I would pick up my one-inch picture frame, stare into it as if for the answer, and every time the answer would come: all I had to do was to write a really shitty first draft of, say, the opening paragraph. And no one was going to see it.

So I'd start writing without reining myself in. It was almost just typing, just making my fingers move. And the writing would be *terrible*. I'd write a lead paragraph that was a whole page, even though the entire review could only be three pages long, and then I'd start writing up descriptions of the food, one dish at a time, bird by bird, and the critics would be sitting on my shoulders, commenting like cartoon characters. They'd be pretending to snore, or rolling their eyes at my overwrought descriptions, no matter how hard I tried to tone those descriptions down, no matter how conscious I was of what a friend said to me gently in my early days of restaurant reviewing. "Annie," she said, "it is just a piece of *chick*en. It is just a bit of *cake*."

7   But because by then I had been writing for so long, I would eventually let my-self trust the process—sort of, more or less. I'd write a first draft that was maybe twice as long as it should be, with a self-indulgent and boring beginning, stupefying descriptions of the meal, lots of quotes from my black-humored friends that made them sound more like the Manson girls than food lovers, and no ending to speak of. The whole thing would be so long and incoherent and hideous that for the rest of the day I'd obsess about getting creamed by a car before I could write a decent second draft. I'd worry that people would read what I'd written and believe that the accident had really been a suicide, that I had panicked because my talent was wan-ing and my mind was shot.

8   The next day, though, I'd sit down, go through it all with a colored pen, take out everything I possibly could, find a new lead somewhere on the second page, fig-ure out a kicky place to end it, and then write a second draft. It always turned out fine, sometimes even funny and weird and helpful. I'd go over it one more time and mail it in.

9   Then, a month later, when it was time for another review, the whole process would start again, complete with the fears that people would find my first draft be-fore I could rewrite it.

10   Almost all good writing begins with terrible first efforts. You need to start somewhere. Start by getting something—anything—down on paper. A friend of mine says that the first draft is the down draft—you just get it down. The second draft is the up draft—you fix it up. You try to say what you have to say more accu-rately. And the third draft is the dental draft, where you check every tooth, to see if it's loose or cramped or decayed, or even, God help us, healthy.

11   What I've learned to do when I sit down to work on a shitty first draft is to quiet the voices in my head. First there's the vinegar-lipped Reader Lady, who says primly, "Well, *that's* not very interesting, is it?" And there's the emaciated German male who writes these Orwellian memos detailing your thought crimes. And there are your parents, agonizing over your lack of loyalty and discretion; and there's William Burroughs, dozing off or shooting up because he finds you as bold and ar-ticulate as a houseplant; and so on. And there are also the dogs: let's not forget the dogs, the dogs in their pen who will surely hurtle and snarl their way out if you ever *stop* writing, because writing is, for some of us, the latch that keeps the door of the pen closed, keeps those crazy ravenous dogs contained.

12   Quieting these voices is at least half the battle I fight daily. But this is better than it used to be. It used to be 87 percent. Left to its own devices, my mind spends much of its time having conversations with people who aren't there. I walk along defending myself to people, or exchanging repartee with them, or rationalizing my behavior, or seducing them with gossip, or pretending I'm on their TV talk show or whatever. I speed or run an aging yellow light or don't come to a full stop, and one

nanosecond later am explaining to imaginary cops exactly why I had to do what I did, or insisting that I did not in fact do it.

I happened to mention this to a hypnotist I saw many years ago, and he looked   13
at me very nicely. At first I thought he was feeling around on the floor for the silent alarm button, but then he gave me the following exercise, which I still use to this day.

Close your eyes and get quiet for a minute, until the chatter starts up. Then   14
isolate one of the voices and imagine the person speaking as a mouse. Pick it up by the tail and drop it into a mason jar. Then isolate another voice, pick it up by the tail, drop it in the jar. And so on. Drop in any high-maintenance parental units, drop in any contractors, lawyers, colleagues, children, anyone who is whining in your head. Then put the lid on, and watch all these mouse people clawing at the glass, jabbering away, trying to make you feel like shit because you won't do what they want—won't give them more money, won't be more successful, won't see them more often. Then imagine that there is a volume-control button on the bottle. Turn it all the way up for a minute, and listen to the stream of angry, neglected, guilt-mongering voices. Then turn it all the way down and watch the frantic mice lunge at the glass, trying to get to you. Leave it down, and get back to your shitty first draft.

A writer friend of mine suggests opening the jar and shooting them all in the   15
head. But I think he's a little angry, and I'm sure nothing like this would ever occur to you.

MOTHER TONGUE

Amy Tan

Author of The Joy Luck Club *(1989) and* The Kitchen God's Wife
*(1991), Amy Tan grew up in California as the daughter of Chinese
immigrants. In "Mother Tongue," Tan brings out a truer definition of the
phrase than we usually apply.*

1   I am not a scholar of English or literature. I cannot give you much more than
personal opinions on the English language and its variations in this country or
others.

2   I am a writer. And by that definition, I am someone who has always loved language. I am fascinated by language in daily life. I spend a great deal of my time
thinking about the power of language—the way it can evoke an emotion, a visual
image, a complex idea, or a simple truth. Language is the tool of my trade. And I
use them all—all the Englishes I grew up with.

3   Recently, I was made keenly aware of the different Englishes I do use. I was giving a talk to a large group of people, the same talk I had already given to half a dozen
other groups. The nature of the talk was about my writing, my life, and my book, *The
Joy Luck Club.* The talk was going along well enough, until I remembered one major
difference that made the whole talk sound wrong. My mother was in the room. And
it was perhaps the first time she had heard me give a lengthy speech, using the kind
of English I have never used with her. I was saying things like, "The intersection of
memory upon imagination" and "There is an aspect of my fiction that relates to thus-
and-thus"—a speech filled with carefully wrought grammatical phrases, burdened, it
suddenly seemed to me, with nominalized forms, past perfect tenses, conditional
phrases, all the forms of standard English that I had learned in school and through
books, the forms of English I did not use at home with my mother.

4   Just last week, I was walking down the street with my mother, and I again found
myself conscious of the English I was using, the English I do use with her. We were
talking about the price of new and used furniture and I heard myself saying this:
"Not waste money that way." My husband was with us as well, and he didn't notice
any switch in my English. And then I realized why. It's because over the twenty years
we've been together I've often used that same kind of English with him, and sometimes he even uses it with me. It has become our language of intimacy, a different
sort of English that relates to family talk, the language I grew up with.

5   So you'll have some idea of what this family talk I heard sounds like, I'll quote
what my mother said during a recent conversation which I videotaped and then
transcribed. During this conversation, my mother was talking about a political gangster
in Shanghai who had the same last name as her family's, Du, and how the gangster

in his early years wanted to be adopted by her family, which was rich by comparison. Later, the gangster became more powerful, far richer than my mother's family, and one day showed up at my mother's wedding to pay his respects. Here's what she said in part:

"Du Yusong having business like fruit stand. Like off the street kind. He is Du like Du Zong—but not Tsung-ming Island people. The local people call putong, the river east side, he belong to that side local people. That man want to ask Du Zong father take him in like become own family. Du Zong father wasn't look down on him, but didn't take seriously, until that man big like become a mafia. Now important person, very hard to inviting him. Chinese way, came only to show respect, don't stay for dinner. Respect for making big celebration, he shows up. Mean gives lots of respect. Chinese custom. Chinese social life that way. If too important won't have to stay too long. He come to my wedding. I didn't see, I heard it. I gone to boy's side, they have YMCA dinner. Chinese age I was nineteen."

You should know that my mother's expressive command of English belies how much she actually understands. She reads the *Forbes* report, listens to *Wall Street Week,* converses daily with her stockbroker, reads all of Shirley MacLaine's books with ease—all kinds of things I can't begin to understand. Yet some of my friends tell me they understand 50 percent of what my mother says. Some say they understand 80 to 90 percent. Some say they understand none of it, as if she were speaking pure Chinese. But to me, my mother's English is perfectly clear, perfectly natural. It's my mother tongue. Her language, as I hear it, is vivid, direct, full of observation and imagery. That was the language that helped shape the way I saw things, expressed things, made sense of the world.

Lately, I've been giving more thought to the kind of English my mother speaks. Like others, I have described it to people as "broken" or "fractured" English. But I wince when I say that. It has always bothered me that I can think of no way to describe it other than "broken," as if it were damaged and needed to be fixed, as if it lacked a certain wholeness and soundness. I've heard other terms used, "limited English," for example. But they seem just as bad, as if everything is limited, including people's perceptions of the limited English speaker.

I know this for a fact, because when I was growing up, my mother's "limited" English limited *my* perception of her. I was ashamed of her English. I believed that her English reflected the quality of what she had to say. That is, because she expressed them imperfectly her thoughts were imperfect. And I had plenty of empirical evidence to support me: the fact that people in department stores, at banks, and at restaurants did not take her seriously, did not give her good service, pretended not to understand her, or even acted as if they did not hear her.

My mother has long realized the limitations of her English as well. When I was fifteen, she used to have me call people on the phone to pretend I was she. In this guise, I was forced to ask for information or even to complain and yell at people who had been rude to her. One time it was a call to her stockbroker in New York. She had cashed out her small portfolio and it just so happened we were going to go to New York the next week, our very first trip outside California. I had to get on the phone and say in an adolescent voice that was not very convincing, "This is Mrs. Tan."

11   And my mother was standing in the back whispering loudly, "Why he don't send me check, already two weeks late. So mad he lie to me, losing me money."

12   And then I said in perfect English, "Yes, I'm getting rather concerned. You had agreed to send the check two weeks ago, but it hasn't arrived."

13   Then she began to talk more loudly. "What he want, I come to New York tell him front of his boss, you cheating me?" And I was trying to calm her down, make her be quiet, while telling the stockbroker, "I can't tolerate any more excuses. If I don't receive the check immediately, I am going to have to speak to your manager when I'm in New York next week." And sure enough, the following week there we were in front of this astonished stockbroker, and I was sitting there red-faced and quiet, and my mother, the real Mrs. Tan, was shouting at his boss in her impeccable broken English.

14   We used a similar routine just five days ago, for a situation that was far less humorous. My mother had gone to the hospital for an appointment, to find out about a benign brain tumor a CAT scan had revealed a month ago. She said she had spoken very good English, her best English, no mistakes. Still, she said, the hospital did not apologize when they said they had lost the CAT scan and she had come for nothing. She said they did not seem to have any sympathy when she told them she was anxious to know the exact diagnosis, since her husband and son had both died of brain tumors. She said they would not give her any more information until the next time and she would have to make another appointment for that. So she said she would not leave until the doctor called her daughter. She wouldn't budge. And when the doctor finally called her daughter, me, who spoke in perfect English—lo and behold—we had assurances the CAT scan would be found, promises that a conference call on Monday would be held, and apologies for any suffering my mother had gone through for a most regrettable mistake.

15   I think my mother's English almost had an effect on limiting my possibilities in life as well. Sociologists and linguists probably will tell you that a person's developing language skills are more influenced by peers. But I do think that the language spoken in the family, especially in immigrant families which are more insular, plays a large role in shaping the language of the child. And I believe that it affected my results on achievement tests, IQ tests, and the SAT. While my English skills were never judged as poor, compared to math, English could not be considered my strong suit. In grade school I did moderately well, getting perhaps B's, sometimes B-pluses, in English and scoring perhaps in the sixtieth or seventieth percentile on

achievement tests. But those scores were not good enough to override the opinion that my true abilities lay in math and science, because in those areas I achieved A's and scored in the ninetieth percentile or higher.

This was understandable. Math is precise; there is only one correct answer. 16 Whereas, for me at least, the answers on English tests were always a judgment call, a matter of opinion and personal experience. Those tests were constructed around items like fill-in-the-blank sentence completion, such as, "Even though Tom was _____, Mary thought he was _____." And the correct answer always seemed to be the most bland combinations of thoughts, for example, "Even though Tom was shy, Mary thought he was charming," with the grammatical structure "even though" limiting the correct answer to some sort of semantic opposites, so you wouldn't get answers like, "Even though Tom was foolish, Mary thought he was ridiculous." Well, according to my mother, there were very few limitations as to what Tom could have been and what Mary might have thought of him. So I never did well on tests like that.

The same was true with word analogies, pairs of words in which you were sup- 17 posed to find some sort of logical, semantic relationship—for example, "*Sunset* is to *nightfall* as _____ is to _____." And here you would be presented with a list of four possible pairs, one of which showed the same kind of relationship: *red* is to *stoplight, bus* is to *arrival, chills* is to *fever, yawn* is to *boring*. Well, I could never think that way. I knew what the tests were asking, but I could not block out of my mind the images already created by the first pair, "*sunset* is to *nightfall*"—and I would see a burst of colors against a darkening sky, the moon rising, the lowering of a curtain of stars. And all the other pairs of words—red, bus, stoplight, boring—just threw up a mass of confusing images, making it impossible for me to sort out something as logical as saying: "A sunset precedes nightfall" is the same as "a chill precedes a fever." The only way I would have gotten that answer right would have been to imagine an associative situation, for example, my being disobedient and staying out past sunset, catching a chill at night, which turns into feverish pneumonia as punishment, which indeed did happen to me.

I have been thinking about all this lately, about my mother's English, about 18 achievement tests. Because lately I've been asked, as a writer, why there are not more Asian Americans represented in American literature. Why are there few Asian Americans enrolled in creative writing programs? Why do so many Chinese students go into engineering? Well, these are broad sociological questions I can't begin to answer. But I have noticed in surveys—in fact, just last week—that Asian students, as a whole, always do significantly better on math achievement tests than in English. And this makes me think that there are other Asian-American students whose English spoken in the home might also be described as "broken" or "limited." And perhaps they also have teachers who are steering them away from writing and into math and science, which is what happened to me.

19   Fortunately, I happen to be rebellious in nature and enjoy the challenge of disproving assumptions made about me. I became an English major my first year in college, after being enrolled as pre-med. I started writing nonfiction as a freelancer the week after I was told by my former boss that writing was my worst skill and I should hone my talents toward account management.

20   But it wasn't until 1985 that I finally began to write fiction. And at first I wrote using what I thought to be wittily crafted sentences, sentences that would finally prove I had mastery over the English language. Here's an example from the first draft of a story that later made its way into *The Joy Luck Club,* but without this line: "That was my mental quandary in its nascent state." A terrible line, which I can barely pronounce.

21   Fortunately, for reasons I won't get into today, I later decided I should envision a reader for the stories I would write. And the reader I decided upon was my mother, because these were stories about mothers. So with this reader in mind—and in fact she did read my early drafts—I began to write stories using all the Englishes I grew up with: the English I spoke to my mother, which for lack of a better term might be described as "simple"; the English she used with me, which for lack of a better term might be described as "broken"; my translation of her Chinese, which could certainly be described as "watered down"; and what I imagined to be her translation of her Chinese if she could speak in perfect English, her internal language, and for that I sought to preserve the essence, but neither an English nor a Chinese structure. I wanted to capture what language ability tests can never reveal: her intent, her passion, her imagery, the rhythms of her speech and the nature of her thoughts.

22   Apart from what any critic had to say about my writing, I knew I had succeeded where it counted when my mother finished reading my book and gave me her verdict: "So easy to read."

Classification and Division

THREE TYPES OF RESISTANCE TO OPPRESSION

Martin Luther King Jr.

Martyred civil rights leader Martin Luther King Jr.'s, prose reflects the rich heritage of Southern preaching. "Three Types of Resistance to Oppression" draws on the oral tradition in its simple classification of major points.

Oppressed people deal with their oppression in three characteristic ways. One way is acquiescence: the oppressed resign themselves to their doom. They tacitly adjust themselves to oppression, and thereby become conditioned to it. In every movement toward freedom some of the oppressed prefer to remain oppressed. Almost 2800 years ago Moses set out to lead the children of Israel from the slavery of Egypt to the freedom of the promised land. He soon discovered that slaves do not always welcome their deliverers. They become accustomed to being slaves. They would rather bear those ills they have, as Shakespeare pointed out, than flee to others that they know not of. They prefer the "fleshpots of Egypt" to the ordeals of emancipation.

There is such a thing as the freedom of exhaustion. Some people are so worn down by the yoke of oppression that they give up. A few years ago in the slum areas of Atlanta, a Negro guitarist used to sing almost daily: "Ben down so long that down don't bother me." This is the type of negative freedom and resignation that often engulfs the life of the oppressed.

But this is not the way out. To accept passively an unjust system is to cooperate with that system; thereby the oppressed become as evil as the oppressor. Noncooperation with evil is as much a moral obligation as is cooperation with good. The oppressed must never allow the conscience of the oppressor to slumber. Religion reminds every man that he is his brother's keeper. To accept injustice or segregation passively is to say to the oppressor that his actions are morally right. It is a way of allowing his conscience to fall asleep. At this moment the oppressed fails to be his brother's keeper. So acquiescence—while often the easier way—is not the moral way. It is the way of the coward. The Negro cannot win the respect of his oppressor by acquiescing; he merely increases the oppressor's arrogance and contempt. Acquiescence is interpreted as proof of the Negro's inferiority. The Negro cannot win the respect of the white people of the South or the peoples of the world if he is willing to sell the future of his children for his personal and immediate comfort and safety.

4   A second way that oppressed people sometimes deal with oppression is to resort to physical violence and corroding hatred. Violence often brings about momentary results. Nations have frequently won their independence in battle. But in spite of temporary victories, violence never brings permanent peace. It solves no social problem; it merely creates new and more complicated ones.

5   Violence as a way of achieving racial justice is both impractical and immoral. It is impractical because it is a descending spiral ending in destruction for all. The old law of an eye for an eye leaves everybody blind. It is immoral because it seeks to humiliate the opponent rather than win his understanding; it seeks to annihilate rather than to convert. Violence is immoral because it thrives on hatred rather than love. It destroys community and makes brotherhood impossible. It leaves society in monologue rather than dialogue. Violence ends by defeating itself. It creates bitterness in the survivors and brutality in the destroyers. A voice echoes through time saying to every potential Peter, "Put up your sword." History is cluttered with the wreckage of nations that failed to follow this command.

6   If the American Negro and other victims of oppression succumb to the temptation of using violence in the struggle for freedom, future generations will be the recipients of a desolate night of bitterness, and our chief legacy to them will be an endless reign of meaningless chaos. Violence is not the way.

7   The third way open to oppressed people in their quest for freedom is the way of nonviolent resistance. Like the synthesis in Hegelian philosophy, the principle of nonviolent resistance seeks to reconcile the truths of two opposites—acquiescence and violence—while avoiding the extremes and immoralities of both. The nonviolent resister agrees with the person who acquiesces that one should not be physically aggressive toward his opponent; but he balances the equation by agreeing with the person of violence that evil must be resisted. He avoids the nonresistance of the former and the violent resistance of the latter. With nonviolent resistance, no individual or group need submit to any wrong, nor need anyone resort to violence in order to right a wrong.

8   It seems to me that this is the method that must guide the actions of the Negro in the present crisis in race relations. Through nonviolent resistance the Negro will be able to rise to the noble height of opposing the unjust system while loving the perpetrators of the system. The Negro must work passionately and unrelentingly for full stature as a citizen, but he must not use inferior methods to gain it. He must never come to terms with falsehood, malice, hate, or destruction.

9   Nonviolent resistance makes it possible for the Negro to remain in the South and struggle for his rights. The Negro's problem will not be solved by running away. He cannot listen to the glib suggestion of those who would urge him to migrate en masse to other sections of the country. By grasping his great opportunity in the South he can make a lasting contribution to the moral strength of the nation and set a sublime example of courage for generations yet unborn.

By nonviolent resistance, the Negro can also enlist all men of good will in his   10
struggle for equality. The problem is not a purely racial one, with Negroes set against
whites. In the end, it is not a struggle between people at all, but a tension between
justice and injustice. Nonviolent resistance is not aimed against oppressors but
against oppression. Under its banner consciences, not racial groups, are enlisted.

If the Negro is to achieve the goal of integration, he must organize himself   11
into a militant and nonviolent mass movement. All three elements are indispens-
able. The movement for equality and justice can only be a success if it has both a
mass and militant character; the barriers to be overcome require both. Nonviolence
is an imperative in order to bring about ultimate community.

A mass movement of militant quality that is not at the same time committed to   12
nonviolence tends to generate conflict, which in turn breeds anarchy. The support of
the participants and the sympathy of the uncommitted are both inhibited by the
threat that bloodshed will engulf the community. This reaction in turn encourages
the opposition to threaten and resort to force. When, however, the mass movement
repudiates violence while moving resolutely toward its goal, its opponents are revealed
as the instigators and practitioners of violence if it occurs. Then public support is mag-
netically attracted to the advocates of nonviolence, while those who employ violence
are literally disarmed by overwhelming sentiment against their stand.

WHAT FRIENDS ARE FOR

Phillip Lopate

Phillip Lopate is an acclaimed essayist who has won Guggenheim and National Endowment for the Arts fellowships. He edited a collection representing his specialty, The Art of the Personal Essay *(1994). "What Friends Are For" classifies the types of friendships people seek and develop in contemporary society as well as the reasons why we need them.*

1   Is there anything left to say about friendship after so many great essayists have picked over the bones of the subject? Aristotle and Cicero, Seneca and Montaigne, Francis Bacon and Samuel Johnson, William Hazlitt, Ralph Waldo Emerson, and Charles Lamb have all taken their cracks at it.

2   Friendship has been called "love without wings." On the other hand, the Stoic definition of love ("Love is the attempt to form a friendship inspired by beauty") seems to suggest that friendship came first. Certainly a case can be made that the buildup of affection and the yearning for more intimacy, without the release of sexual activity, keeps friends in a state of sweet-sorrowful itchiness that has the romantic quality of a love affair. We know that a falling-out between two old friends can leave a deeper and more perplexing hurt than the ending of a love affair, perhaps because we are more pessimistic about the affair's endurance from the start.

3   Our first attempted friendships are within the family. It is here we practice the techniques of listening sympathetically and proving that we can be trusted, and learn the sort of kindness we can expect in return.

4   There is something tainted about these family friendships, however. My sister, in her insecure adolescent phase, told me, "You love me because I'm related to you, but if you were to meet me for the first time at a party, you'd think I was a jerk and not worth being your friend." She had me in a bind: I had no way of testing her hypothesis. I should have argued that even if our bond was not freely chosen, our decision to work on it had been. Still, we are quick to dismiss the partiality of our family members when they tell us we are talented, cute, or lovable; we must go out into the world and seduce others.

5   It is just a few short years from the promiscuity of the sandbox to the tormented, possessive feelings of a fifth grader who has just learned that his best and only friend is playing at another classmate's house after school. There may be worse betrayals in store, but probably none is more influential than the sudden fickleness of an elementary school friend who has dropped us for someone more popular after all our careful, patient wooing. Often we lose no time inflicting the same betrayal on someone else, just to ensure that we have got the victimization dynamic right.

What makes friendships in childhood and adolescence so poignant is that we   6
need the chosen comrade to be everything in order to rescue us from the gothic in-
wardness of family life. Even if we are lucky enough to have several companions,
there must be a Best Friend.

I clung to the romance of the Best Friend all through high school, college, and   7
beyond, until my circle of university friends began to disperse. At that point, in my
mid-20s, I also acted out the dark, competitive side of friendship that can exist between two young men fighting for a place in life and love by doing the one unforgiv-
able thing: sleeping with my best friend's girl. I was baffled at first that there was no
way to repair the damage. I lost this friendship forever, and came away from that de-
bacle much more aware of the amount of injury that friendship can and cannot sustain. Perhaps I needed to prove to myself that friendship was not an all-permissive
resilient bond, like a mother's love, but something quite fragile. Precisely because best
friendship promotes such a merging of identities, such seeming boundarylessness,
the first major transgression of trust can cause the injured party to feel he is fighting
for his violated soul against his darkest enemy. There is not much room to maneuver
in a best friendship between unlimited intimacy and unlimited mistrust.

Still, it was not until the age of 30 that I reluctantly abandoned the best friend   8
expectation and took up a more pluralistic model. At present, I cherish a dozen friends
for their unique personalities, without asking that any one be my soul-twin. Whether
this alteration constitutes a movement toward maturity or toward cowardly pragmatism is not for me to say. It may be that, in refusing to depend so much on any one
friend, I am opting for self-protection over intimacy. Or it may be that, as we advance
into middle age, the life problem becomes less that of establishing a tight dyadic bond
and more one of making our way in a broader world, "society." Indeed, since Americans have so indistinct a notion of society, we often try to put a network of friendships in its place.

If a certain intensity is lost in the pluralistic model of friendship, there is also   9
the gain of being able to experience all of one's potential, half-buried selves, through
witnessing all the spectacle of the multiple fates of our friends. As it happens, the harem
of friends, so tantalizing a notion, often translates into feeling pulled in a dozen different directions, with the guilty sense of having disappointed everyone a little. It is also
a risky, contrived enterprise to try to make one's friends behave in a friendly manner
toward each other. If the effort fails, one feels obliged to mediate; if it succeeds too
well, one is jealous.

Whether friendship is intrinsically singular and exclusive or plural and demo-   10
cratic is a question that has vexed many commentators. Aristotle distinguished three
types of friendship: "friendship based on utility," such as businessmen cultivating each
other for benefit; "friendship based on pleasure," like young people interested in
partying; and "perfect friendship." The first two categories Aristotle calls "qualified
and superficial friendships," because they are founded on circumstances that could

easily change. The last, which is based on admiration for another's good character, is more permanent, but also rarer, because good men "are few." Cicero, who wrote perhaps the best treatise on friendship, also insisted that what brings true friends together is "a mutual belief in each other's goodness." This insistence on virtue as a precondition for true friendship may strike us as impossibly demanding: Who, after all, feels himself good nowadays? And yet, if I am honest, I must admit that the friendships of mine that have lasted longest have been with those whose integrity, or humanity, or strength to bear their troubles I continue to admire. Conversely, when I lost respect for someone, however winning he or she otherwise remained, the friendship petered away almost immediately. "Remove respect from friendship," said Cicero, "and you have taken away the most splendid ornament it possesses."

11   Friendship is a long conversation. I suppose I could imagine a nonverbal friendship revolving around shared physical work or sport, but for me, good talk is the point of the thing. Indeed, the ability to generate conversation by the hour is the most promising indication, during the uncertain early stages, that a possible friendship will take hold. In the first few conversations there may be an exaggeration of agreement, as both parties angle for adhesive surfaces. But later on, trust builds through the courage to assert disagreement, through the tactful acceptance that differences of opinion will have to remain.

12   Some view like-mindedness as both the precondition and the product of friendship. Myself, I distrust it. I have one friend who keeps assuming that we see the world eye-to-eye. She is intent on enrolling us in a flattering aristocracy of taste, on the short "we" list against the ignorant "they." Sometimes I do not have the strength to fight her need for consensus with my own stubborn disbelief in the existence of any such inner circle of privileged, cultivated sensibility. Perhaps I have too much invested in a view of myself as idiosyncratic to be eager to join any coterie, even a coterie of two. What attracts me to friends' conversation is the give and take, not necessarily that we come out at the same point.

13   "Our tastes and aims and views were identical—and that is where the essence of a friendship must always lie," wrote Cicero. To some extent, perhaps, but then the convergence must be natural, not, as Emerson put it, "a mush of concession. Better be a nettle in the side of your friend than his echo."

14   Friendship is a school for character, allowing us the chance to study, in great detail and over time, temperaments very different from our own. These charming quirks, these contradictions, these nobilities, these blind spots of our friends we track not out of disinterested curiosity: We must have this information before knowing how far we may relax our guard, how much we may rely on them in crises. The learning curve of friendship involves, to no small extent, filling out this picture of the other's limitations and making peace with the results. Each time I hit up against a friend's inflexibility I am relieved as well as disappointed: I can begin to predict, and arm myself in advance against repeated bruises. I have one friend who is always

late, so I bring a book along when I am to meet her. I give her a manuscript to read and she promises to look at it over the weekend. I prepare for a month-long wait.

Though it is often said that with a true friend there is no need to hold any- 15 thing back ("A friend is a person with whom I may be sincere. Before him I may think aloud," wrote Emerson), I have never found this to be entirely the case. Certain words may be too cruel if they are spoken at the wrong moment—or may fall on deaf ears, for any number of reasons. I also find with all my friends, as they must with me, that some initial resistance, restlessness, some psychic weather must be overcome before that tender ideal attentiveness may be called forth.

I have a good friend, Charlie, who is often very distracted whenever we first 16 get together. If we are sitting in a café he will look around constantly for the waiter, or be distracted by a pretty woman or the restaurant's cat. It would be foolish for me to broach an important subject at such moments, so I resign myself to waiting the half hour or however long it takes until his jumpiness subsides. Or else I draw this pattern grumpily to his attention. Once he has settled down, however, I can tell Charlie virtually anything, and he me. But the candor cannot be rushed. It must be built up to with the verbal equivalent of limbering exercises.

The friendship scene—a flow of shared confidences, recognitions, humor, ad- 17 vice, speculation, even wisdom—is one of the key elements of modern friendships. Compared to the rest of life, this ability to lavish one's best energies on an activity utterly divorced from the profit motive and free from the routines of domination and inequality that affect most relations (including, perhaps, the selfsame friendship at other times) seems idyllic. The friendship scene is by its nature not an everyday occurrence. It represents the pinnacle, the fruit of the friendship, potentially ever present but not always arrived at. Both friends' dim yet self-conscious awareness that they are wandering conversationally toward a goal that they have previously accomplished but that may elude them this time around creates a tension, an obligation to communicate as sincerely as possible, like actors in an improvisation exercise struggling to shape their baggy material into some climactic form. This very pressure to achieve "quality" communication may induce a sort of inauthentic epiphany, not unlike what sometimes happens in the last 10 minutes of a psychotherapy session. But a truly achieved friendship scene can be among the best experiences life has to offer.

Contemporary urban life, with its tight schedules and crowded appointment 18 books, has helped to shape modern friendship into something requiring a good deal of intentionality and pursuit. You phone a friend and make a date a week or more in advance; then you set aside an evening, as if for a tryst, during which to squeeze in all your news and advice, confession and opinion. Such intimate compression may add a romantic note to modern friendships, but it also places a strain on the meeting to yield a high quality of meaning and satisfaction, closer to art than life. If I see busy or out-of-town friends only once every six months, we must not only catch up on our lives but also convince ourselves within the allotted two hours together that we still share a special affinity, an inner track to each other's psyches, or the next meeting may be put off for years. Surely there must be another, saner rhythm of friendship in rural areas—or maybe not? I think about "the good old days" when friends would go on walking tours through England together, when Edith Wharton would bundle poor Henry James into her motorcar and they'd drive to the south of France for a month. I'm not sure my friendships could sustain the strain of travel for weeks at a time, and the truth of the matter is that I've gotten used to this urban arrangement of serial friendship "dates," where the pleasure of the rendezvous is enhanced by the knowledge that it will only last, at most, six hours. If the two of us don't happen to mesh that day (always a possibility)—well, it's only a few hours. And if it should go beautifully, one needs an escape hatch from exaltation as well as disenchantment. I am capable of only so much intense, exciting communication before I start to fade; I come to these encounters equipped with a six-hour oxygen tank. Is this an evolutionary pattern of modern friendship, or just a personal limitation?

19   Perhaps because I conceive of the modern friendship scene as a somewhat theatrical enterprise, a one-act play, I tend to be very much affected by the "set." A restaurant, a museum, a walk in the park through the zoo, even accompanying a friend on shopping errands— I prefer public turf where the stimulation of the city can play a backdrop to our dialogue, feeding it with details when inspiration flags.

20   I have a number of *chez moi* friends who always invite me to come to their homes while evading offers to visit me. What they view as hospitality I see as a need to control the mise-en-scène of friendship. I am expected to fit in where they are most comfortable, while they play lord of the manor, distracted by the props of decor, the pool, the unexpected phone call, the swirl of children, animals, and neighbors. Indeed, *chez moi* friends often tend to keep a sort of open house, so that in going over to see them—for a tête-à-tête, I had assumed—I will suddenly find their other friends and neighbors, whom they have also invited, dropping in all afternoon. There are only so many Sundays I care to spend hanging out with a friend's entourage before I become impatient for a private audience.

21   Married friends who own their own homes are apt to try to draw me into their domestic fold, whereas single people are often more sensitive about establishing a discreet space for the friendship to occur. Perhaps the married assume that a bachelor like me is desperate for home cooking and a little family life. I have noticed that it is not an easy matter to pry a married friend away from mate and milieu. For married people, especially those with children, the home often becomes the wellspring of all their nurturing feelings, and the single friend is invited to partake in the general flow. Maybe there is also a certain tendency on their part to kill two birds with one stone: They don't see enough of their spouse and kids, and they figure they can visit with you at the same time.

From my standpoint, friendship is a jealous goddess. Whenever a friend of mine marries, I have to fight to overcome the feeling that I am being "replaced" by the spouse. I don't mind sharing a friend with his or her family milieu—in fact I like it, up to a point—but eventually I must get the friend alone, or else, as a bachelor at a distinct power disadvantage, I risk becoming a mere spectator of familial rituals instead of a key player in the drama of friendship. 22

A person who lives alone usually has more energy to give to friendship. The danger is investing too much emotional energy in one's friends. When a single person is going through a romantic dry spell, he or she often tries to extract the missing passion from a circle of friends. This works only up to a point: The frayed nerves of protracted celibacy can lead to hypersensitive imaginings of slights and rejections, and one's platonic friends seem to come particularly into the line of fire. 23

Today, with the partial decline of the nuclear family and the search for alternatives to it, we also see attempts to substitute the friendship web for intergenerational family life. Since psychoanalysis has alerted us to regard the family as a mine field of unrequited love, manipulation, and ambivalence, it is only natural that people may look to friendship as a more supportive ground for relation. But in our longing for an unequivocally positive bond, we should beware of sentimentalizing friendship, as saccharine "buddy" movies and certain feminist novels do, and of neutering its problematic aspects. Besides, friendship can never substitute for the true meaning of family: If nothing else, it will never be able to duplicate the family's wild capacity for concentrating neurosis. 24

In short, friends can't be your family, they can't be your lovers, they can't be your psychiatrists. But they can be your friends, which is plenty. 25

When I think about the qualities that characterize the best friendships I've known, I can identify five: rapport, affection, need, habit, and forgiveness. Rapport and affection can only take you so far; they may leave you at the formal, outer gate of goodwill, which is still not friendship. A persistent need for the other's company, for the person's interest, approval, opinion, will get you inside the gates, especially when it is reciprocated. In the end, however, there are no substitutes for habit and forgiveness. A friendship may travel for years on cozy habit. But it is a melancholy fact that unless you are a saint you are bound to offend every friend deeply at least once in the course of time. The friends I have kept the longest are those who forgave me time and again for wronging them unintentionally, intentionally, or by the plain catastrophe of my personality. There can be no friendship without forgiveness. 26

DOUBLESPEAK

William Lutz

A professor of English at Rutgers University, William Lutz has long spoken out against the "conscious use of language as a weapon or tool by those in power." This selection, from his book Doublespeak *(1989), classifies evasive language into four recognizable types.*

1   There are no potholes in the streets of Tucson, Arizona, just "pavement deficiencies." The Reagan Administration didn't propose any new taxes, just "revenue enhancement" through new "user's fees." Those aren't bums on the street, just "nongoal oriented members of society." There are no more poor people, just "fiscal underachievers." There was no robbery of an automatic teller machine, just an "unauthorized withdrawal." The patient didn't die because of medical malpractice, it was just a "diagnostic misadventure of a high magnitude." The U.S. Army doesn't kill the enemy anymore, it just "services the target." And the doublespeak goes on.

2   Doublespeak is language that pretends to communicate but really doesn't. It is language that makes the bad seem good, the negative appear positive, the unpleasant appear attractive or at least tolerable. Doublespeak is language that avoids or shifts responsibility, language that is at variance with its real or purported meaning. It is language that conceals or prevents thought; rather than extending thought, doublespeak limits it.

3   Doublespeak is not a matter of subjects and verbs agreeing; it is a matter of words and facts agreeing. Basic to doublespeak is incongruity, the incongruity between what is said or left unsaid, and what really is. It is the incongruity between the word and the referent, between seem and be, between the essential function of language—communication—and what doublespeak does—mislead, distort, deceive, inflate, circumvent, obfuscate.

How to Spot Doublespeak

4   How can you spot doublespeak? Most of the time you will recognize doublespeak when you see or hear it. But, if you have any doubts, you can identify doublespeak just by answering these questions: Who is saying what to whom, under what conditions and circumstances, with what intent, and with what results? Answering these questions will usually help you identify as doublespeak language that appears to be legitimate or that at first glance doesn't even appear to be doublespeak.

First Kind of Doublespeak

5   There are at least four kinds of doublespeak. The first is the euphemism, an inoffensive or positive word or phrase used to avoid a harsh, unpleasant, or distasteful reality. But a euphemism can also be a tactful word or phrase which avoids directly

mentioning a painful reality, or it can be an expression used out of concern for the feelings of someone else, or to avoid directly discussing a topic subject to a social or cultural taboo.

When you use a euphemism because of your sensitivity for someone's feelings 6 or out of concern for a recognized social or cultural taboo, it is not doublespeak. For example, you express your condolences that someone has "passed away" because you do not want to say to a grieving person, "I'm sorry your father is dead." When you use the euphemism "passed away," no one is misled. Moreover, the euphemism functions here not just to protect the feelings of another person, but to communicate also your concern for that person's feelings during a period of mourning. When you excuse yourself to go to the "rest room," or you mention that someone is "sleeping with" or "involved with" someone else, you do not mislead anyone about your meaning, but you do respect the social taboos about discussing bodily functions and sex in direct terms. You also indicate your sensitivity to the feelings of your audience, which is usually considered a mark of courtesy and good manners.

However, when a euphemism is used to mislead or deceive, it becomes dou- 7 blespeak. For example, in 1984 the U.S. State Department announced that it would no longer use the word "killing" in its annual report on the status of human rights in countries around the world. Instead, it would use the phrase "unlawful or arbitrary deprivation of life," which the department claimed was more accurate. Its real purpose for using this phrase was simply to avoid discussing the embarrassing situation of government-sanctioned killings in countries that are supported by the United States and have been certified by the United States as respecting the human rights of their citizens. This use of a euphemism constitutes doublespeak, since it is designed to mislead, to cover up the unpleasant. Its real intent is at variance with its apparent intent. It is language designed to alter our perception of reality.

The Pentagon, too, avoids discussing unpleasant realities when it refers to 8 bombs and artillery shells that fall on civilian targets as "incontinent ordnance." And in 1977 the Pentagon tried to slip funding for the neutron bomb unnoticed into an appropriations bill by calling it a "radiation enhancement device."

Second Kind of Doublespeak

A second kind of doublespeak is jargon, the specialized language of a trade, profes- 9 sion, or similar group, such as that used by doctors, lawyers, engineers, educators, or car mechanics. Jargon can serve an important and useful function. Within a group, jargon functions as a kind of verbal shorthand that allows members of the group to communicate with each other clearly, efficiently, and quickly. Indeed, it is a mark of membership in the group to be able to use and understand the group's jargon.

But jargon, like the euphemism, can also be doublespeak. It can be—and often 10 is—pretentious, obscure, and esoteric terminology used to give an air of profundity, authority, and prestige to speakers and their subject matter. Jargon as doublespeak often makes the simple appear complex, the ordinary profound, the obvious insightful. In this sense it is used not to express but impress. With such doublespeak, the act of smelling something becomes "organoleptic analysis," glass becomes "fused silicate," a crack in a metal support beam becomes a "discontinuity," conservative economic policies become "distributionally conservative notions."

11   Lawyers, for example, speak of an "involuntary conversion" of property when discussing the loss or destruction of property through theft, accident, or condemnation. If your house burns down or if your car is stolen, you have suffered an involuntary conversion of your property. When used by lawyers in a legal situation, such jargon is a legitimate use of language, since lawyers can be expected to understand the term.

12   However, when a member of a specialized group uses its jargon to communicate with a person outside the group, and uses it knowing that the nonmember does not understand such language, then there is doublespeak. For example, on May 9, 1978, a National Airlines 727 airplane crashed while attempting to land at the Pensacola, Florida, airport. Three of the fifty-two passengers aboard the airplane were killed. As a result of the crash, National made an after-tax insurance benefit of $1.7 million, or an extra 18¢ a share dividend for its stockholders. Now National Airlines had two problems: It did not want to talk about one of its airplanes crashing, and it had to account for the $1.7 million when it issued its annual report to its stockholders. National solved the problem by inserting a footnote in its annual report which explained that the $1.7 million income was due to "the involuntary conversion of a 727." National thus acknowledged the crash of its airplane and the subsequent profit it made from the crash, without once mentioning the accident or the deaths. However, because airline officials knew that most stockholders in the company, and indeed most of the general public, were not familiar with legal jargon, the use of such jargon constituted doublespeak.

Third Kind of Doublespeak

13   A third kind of doublespeak is gobbledygook or bureaucratese. Basically, such doublespeak is simply a matter of piling on words, of overwhelming the audience with words, the bigger the words and the longer the sentences the better. Alan Greenspan, then chair of President Nixon's Council of Economic Advisors, was quoted in the *Philadelphia Inquirer* in 1974 as having testified before a Senate committee that "It is a tricky problem to find the particular calibration in timing that would be appropriate to stem the acceleration in risk premiums created by falling incomes without prematurely aborting the decline in the inflation-generated risk premiums."

14   Nor has Mr. Greenspan's language changed since then. Speaking to the meeting of the Economic Club of New York in 1988, Mr. Greenspan, now Federal Reserve chair, said, "I guess I should warn you, if I turn out to be particularly clear, you've probably misunderstood what I've said." Mr. Greenspan's doublespeak doesn't seem to have held back his career.

Sometimes gobbledygook may sound impressive, but when the quote is later   15
examined in print it doesn't even make sense. During the 1988 presidential campaign, vice-presidential candidate Senator Dan Quayle explained the need for a
strategic-defense initiative by saying, "Why wouldn't an enhanced deterrent, a more
stable peace, a better prospect to denying the ones who enter conflict in the first
place to have a reduction of offensive systems and an introduction to defensive capability? I believe this is the route the country will eventually go."

The investigation into the Challenger disaster in 1986 revealed the doublespeak   16
of gobbledygook and bureaucratese used by too many involved in the shuttle program. When Jesse Moore, NASA's associate administrator, was asked if the performance of the shuttle program had improved with each launch or if it had remained
the same, he answered, "I think our performance in terms of the liftoff performance
and in terms of the orbital performance, we knew more about the envelope we were
operating under, and we have been pretty accurately staying in that. And so I would
say the performance has not by design drastically improved. I think we have been able
to characterize the performance more as a function of our launch experience as opposed to it improving as a function of time." While this language may appear to be
jargon, a close look will reveal that it is really just gobbledygook laced with jargon. But
you really have to wonder if Mr. Moore had any idea what he was saying.

Fourth Kind of Doublespeak

The fourth kind of doublespeak is inflated language that is designed to make the   17
ordinary seem extraordinary; to make everyday things seem impressive; to give an
air of importance to people, situations, or things that would not normally be considered important; to make the simple seem complex. Often this kind of doublespeak isn't hard to spot, and it is usually pretty funny. While car mechanics may be
called "automotive internists," elevator operators members of the "vertical transportation corps," used cars "pre-owned" or "experienced cars," and black-and-white
television sets described as having "non-multicolor capability," you really aren't misled all that much by such language.

However, you may have trouble figuring out that, when Chrysler "initiates a   18
career alternative enhancement program," it is really laying off five thousand workers; or that "negative patient care outcome" means the patient died; or that "rapid
oxidation" means a fire in a nuclear power plant.

The doublespeak of inflated language can have serious consequences. In Pen-   19
tagon doublespeak, "pre-emptive counterattack" means that American forces attacked first; "engaged the enemy on all sides" means American troops were
ambushed; "backloading of augmentation personnel" means a retreat by American
troops. In the doublespeak of the military, the 1983 invasion of Grenada was conducted not by the U.S. Army, Navy, Air Force, and Marines, but by the "Caribbean
Peace Keeping Forces." But then, according to the Pentagon, it wasn't an invasion,
it was a "predawn vertical insertion."

NEW SUPERSTITIONS FOR OLD

Margaret Mead

Margaret Mead was a famous American anthropologist whose field expeditions to other cultures in the twenties and thirties resulted in well-known books such as Sex and Temperament in Three Primitive Societies *(1935). In the essay we reprint here, Mead analyzes the functions of superstitions.*

1   Once in a while there is a day when everything seems to run smoothly and even the riskiest venture comes out exactly right. You exclaim, "This is my lucky day!" Then as an afterthought you say, "Knock on wood!" Of course, you do not really believe that knocking on wood will ward off danger. Still, boasting about your own good luck gives you a slightly uneasy feeling—and you carry out the little protective ritual. If someone challenged you at that moment, you would probably say, "Oh, that's nothing. Just an old superstition."

2   But when you come to think about it, what is superstition?

3   In the contemporary world most people treat old folk beliefs as superstitions—the belief, for instance, that there are lucky and unlucky days or numbers, that future events can be read from omens, that there are protective charms or that what happens can be influenced by casting spells. We have excluded magic from our current world view, for we know that natural events have natural causes.

4   In a religious context, where truths cannot be demonstrated, we accept them as a matter of faith. Superstitions, however, belong to the category of beliefs, practices and ways of thinking that have been discarded because they are inconsistent with scientific knowledge. It is easy to say that other people are superstitious because they believe what we regard to be untrue. "Superstition" used in that sense is a derogatory term for the beliefs of other people that we do not share. But there is more to it than that. For superstitions lead a kind of half life in a twilight world where, sometimes, we partly suspend our disbelief and act as if magic worked.

5   Actually, almost every day, even in the most sophisticated home, something is likely to happen that evokes the memory of some old folk belief. The salt spills. A knife falls to the floor. Your nose tickles. Then perhaps, with a slightly embarrassed smile, the person who spilled the salt tosses a pinch over his left shoulder. Or someone recites the old rhyme, "Knife falls, gentleman calls." Or as you rub your nose you think, That means a letter. I wonder who's writing? No one takes these small responses very seriously or gives them more than a passing thought. Sometimes people will preface one of these ritual acts—walking around instead of under a ladder or hastily closing an umbrella that has been opened inside a house—with such remarks as "I remember my great-aunt used to . . ." or "Germans used to say you ought

not . . ." And then, having placed the belief at some distance away in time or space, they carry out the ritual.

Everyone also remembers a few of the observances of childhood—wishing on the first star; looking at the new moon over the right shoulder; avoiding the cracks in the sidewalk on the way to school while chanting, "Step on a crack, break your mother's back"; wishing on white horses, on loads of hay, on covered bridges, on red cars; saying quickly, "Bread-and-butter" when a post or a tree separated you from the friend you were walking with. The adult may not actually recite the formula "Star light, star bright . . . " and may not quite turn to look at the new moon, but his mood is tempered by a little of the old thrill that came when the observance was still freighted with magic.

Superstition can also be used with another meaning. When I discuss the religious beliefs of other peoples, especially primitive peoples, I am often asked, "Do they really have a religion, or is it all just superstition?" The point of contrast here is not between a scientific and a magical view of the world but between the clear, theologically defensible religious beliefs of members of civilized societies and what we regard as the false and childish views of the heathen who "bow down to wood and stone." Within the civilized religions, however, where membership includes believers who are educated and urbane and others who are ignorant and simple, one always finds traditions and practices that the more sophisticated will dismiss offhand as "just superstition" but that guide the steps of those who live by older ways. Mostly these are very ancient beliefs, some handed on from one religion to another and carried from country to country around the world.

Very commonly, people associate superstition with the past, with very old ways of thinking that have been supplanted by modern knowledge. But new superstitions are continually coming into being and flourishing in our society. Listening to mothers in the park in the 1930's, one heard them say, "Now, don't you run out into the sun, or Polio will get you." In the 1940's elderly people explained to one another in tones of resignation, "It was the Virus that got him down." And every year the cosmetics industry offers us new magic—cures for baldness, lotions that will give every woman radiant skin, hair coloring that will restore to the middle-aged the charm and romance of youth—results that are promised if we will just follow the simple directions. Families and individuals also have their cherished, private superstitions. You must leave by the back door when you are going on a journey, or you must wear a green dress when you are taking an examination. It is a kind of joke, of course, but it makes you feel safe.

These old half-beliefs and new half-beliefs reflect the keenness of our wish to have something come true or to prevent something bad from happening. We do not always recognize new superstitions for what they are, and we still follow the old ones because someone's faith long ago matches our contemporary hopes and fears. In the past people "knew" that a black cat crossing one's path was a bad omen, and they turned back home. Today we are fearful of taking a journey and would give anything to turn back—and then we notice a black cat running across the road in front of us.

10   Child psychologists recognize the value of the toy a child holds in his hand at bedtime. It is different from his thumb, with which he can close himself in from the rest of the world, and it is different from the real world, to which he is learning to relate himself. Psychologists call these toys—these furry animals and old, cozy baby blankets—"transitional objects"; that is, objects that help the child move back and forth between the exactions of everyday life and the world of wish and dream.

11   Superstitions have some of the qualities of these transitional objects. They help people pass between the areas of life where what happens has to be accepted without proof and the areas where sequences of events are explicable in terms of cause and effect, based on knowledge. Bacteria and viruses that cause sickness have been identified; the cause of symptoms can be diagnosed and a rational course of treatment prescribed. Magical charms no longer are needed to treat the sick; modern medicine has brought the whole sequence of events into the secular world. But people often act as if this change had not taken place. Laymen still treat germs as if they were invisible, malign spirits, and physicians sometimes prescribe antibiotics as if they were magic substances.

12   Over time, more and more of life has become subject to the controls of knowledge. However, this is never a one-way process. Scientific investigation is continually increasing our knowledge. But if we are to make good use of this knowledge, we must not only rid our minds of old, superseded beliefs and fragments of magical practice, but also recognize new superstitions for what they are. Both are generated by our wishes, our fears and our feeling of helplessness in difficult situations.

13   Civilized peoples are not alone in having grasped the idea of superstitions— beliefs and practices that are superseded but that still may evoke the different worlds in which we live—the sacred, the secular and the scientific. They allow us to keep a private world also, where, smiling a little, we can banish danger with a gesture and summon luck with a rhyme, make the sun shine in spite of storm clouds, force the stranger to do our bidding, keep an enemy at bay and straighten the paths of those we love.

Comparison and Contrast

A FABLE FOR TOMORROW

Rachel Carson

Known for her influential book Silent Spring *(1962), Rachel Carson is often regarded as the founder of the modern environmental movement. In "A Fable for Tomorrow," she draws a chilling contrast between a healthy community and one that has been ecologically devastated.*

There was once a town in the heart of America where all life seemed to live in harmony with its surroundings. The town lay in the midst of a checkerboard of prosperous farms, with fields of grain and hillsides of orchards where, in spring, white clouds of bloom drifted above the green fields. In autumn, oak and maple and birch set up a blaze of color that flamed and flickered across a backdrop of pines. Then foxes barked in the hills and deer silently crossed the fields, half hidden in the mists of the fall mornings.

Along the roads, laurel, viburnum and alder, great ferns and wildflowers delighted the traveler's eye through much of the year. Even in winter the roadsides were places of beauty, where countless birds came to feed on the berries and on the seed heads of the dried weeds rising above the snow. The countryside was, in fact, famous for the abundance and variety of its bird life, and when the flood of migrants was pouring through in spring and fall people traveled from great distances to observe them. Others came to fish the streams, which flowed clear and cold out of the hills and contained shady pools where trout lay. So it had been from the days many years ago when the first settlers raised their houses, sank their wells, and built their barns.

Then a strange blight crept over the area and everything began to change. Some evil spell had settled on the community: mysterious maladies swept the flocks of chickens; the cattle and sheep sickened and died. Everywhere was a shadow of death. The farmers spoke of much illness among their families. In the town the doctors had become more and more puzzled by new kinds of sickness appearing among their patients. There had been several sudden and unexplained deaths not only among adults but even among children, who would be stricken suddenly while at play and die within a few hours.

There was a strange stillness. The birds, for example—where had they gone? Many people spoke of them, puzzled and disturbed. The feeding stations in the backyards were deserted. The few birds seen anywhere were moribund; they trembled violently and could not fly. It was a spring without voices. On the mornings that had once throbbed with the dawn chorus of robins, catbirds, doves, jays, wrens, and scores of other bird voices there was now no sound; only silence lay over the fields and woods and marsh.

5   On the farms the hens brooded, but no chicks hatched. The farmers complained that they were unable to raise any pigs—the litters were small and the young survived only a few days. The apple trees were coming into bloom but no bees droned among the blossoms, so there was no pollination and there would be no fruit.

6   The roadsides, once so attractive, were now lined with browned and withered vegetation as though swept by fire. These, too, were silent, deserted by all living things. Even the streams were now lifeless. Anglers no longer visited them, for all the fish had died.

7   In the gutters under the eaves and between the shingles of the roofs, a white granular powder still showed a few patches; some weeks before it had fallen like snow upon the roofs and the lawns, the fields and streams.

8   No witchcraft, no enemy action had silenced the rebirth of new life in this stricken world. The people had done it themselves.

9   This town does not actually exist, but it might easily have a thousand counterparts in America or elsewhere in the world. I know of no community that has experienced all the misfortunes I describe. Yet every one of these disasters has actually happened somewhere, and many real communities have already suffered a substantial number of them. A grim specter has crept upon us almost unnoticed, and this imagined tragedy may easily become a stark reality we all shall know.

GLITTERING ALICE AND SAD ELEANOR

Richard Cohen

Richard Cohen, a reporter for the Washington Post, *is a political journalist who has written a book-length account of the resignation in disgrace of U.S. Vice President Spiro Agnew* (A Heartbeat Away, *1974). His interest in personality and politics is evident in the column we reprint here.*

1   It is one of those coincidences of history that Alice Roosevelt Longworth, daughter of the grand and unforgettable Teddy and wife of the totally forgettable Nicholas, died the very same week two more books were published about her cousin, Eleanor. The two hated each other—at least Alice hated Eleanor—thinking probably that they had little in common but a family name. They had something else: They were prisoners of their looks.

2   Alice, of course, was radiant and pretty—daughter of a president, a Washington debutante, a standard of style and grace, the one who gave the color Alice Blue to the nation as surely as her father gave his name to a certain kind of stuffed toy bear.

3   She married in the White House, took the speaker of the House of Representatives for her husband, and stayed pretty much at the center of things Washingtonian for something like 70 years. She was, as they say, formidable.

4   Eleanor, on the other hand, was homely. She had a voice pitched at the level of chalk on a blackboard, and the teeth of a beaver. She was awkward in both speech and manner and when she talked—when she rose to speak—the experience was both painful to her and her audience. She had a husband, but there is reason to believe that she was unloved by him. There is about Eleanor Roosevelt an aura of aching sadness, yet in her own way she, too, was formidable. She certainly endures.

5   It is interesting to consider how their looks—the way they looked to the world—shaped these two women. It is interesting because in some ways they were so similar. They were both Roosevelts—one of the Oyster Bay branch, the other of the Hyde Park—both well-off, both of the aristocracy, and both manifestly bright.

6   Eleanor's intelligence proclaimed itself. She threw herself into causes. She spoke for people who had no spokesperson and she spoke well. She championed the poor, the black, women and other minorities. She campaigned and lectured and gave speeches and she did this with such intensity and such effect that it is not too much to say that before her death she was either a goddess or a witch to most Americans.

7   I am partial to the goddess side, thinking that the worst you can call a person is not "do-gooder" but rather "do-nothinger." That is something you could never call Eleanor Roosevelt.

8   As for Alice, she showed her intelligence in her wit. It was she who said, "The secret of eternal youth is arrested development," and who commented on Wendell Willkie after he received the presidential nomination: "He sprang from the grass roots of the country clubs of America."

9   Her most admired remark, the one about Thomas Dewey looking like the "bridegroom on a wedding cake," was not hers at all. The reason we know is that she admitted it. She borrowed it, popularized it, but did not invent it.

10   No matter. She invented enough so that Washington adored her and presidents more or less routinely elbowed themselves to her side so that they could hear what she had to say.

11   Yet with Alice, there it stopped. She was what she was, and what she was was beautiful. She did more or less what was expected of pretty girls. She was perfect just being—just being Alice and being pretty—and in the America of both her youth and her maturity there was nothing better than to be rich and pretty and well-married.

12   That she was also intelligent was almost besides the point, like the gilding on a lily. And while she later became cherished for her wit, it was not because she could use it for any purpose, but because it was like her beauty itself: something of a jewel. She was the perfect appurtenance, the one men wanted seated next to them.

13   With Eleanor, the story is different. Her looks were not her strong suit and so she had to declare herself in another way—by intellect, character, indomitability. She did this well, found causes, gave purpose to her life and left this earth with the certainty that she had mattered.

14   The conventional view is to see Eleanor as sad and Alice as glittering. To an extent, I'm sure, that's true. But in reading the obituaries, in reading how Alice cruelly imitated Eleanor and mocked her good causes, you get the sense that Alice herself realized that something ironic had happened, that she had somehow become trapped by her own good looks, by her perfection, by her wit—that she had become the eternal debutante, frozen in time. Eleanor was actually doing something.

15   So now Eleanor and Alice are dead. One led a sad life, the other a glittering one. But one suspects that as the books came out on Eleanor, Alice realized the tables had turned. There is something sad about being an ugly duckling, but there is something sadder yet about being the belle of the ball after the music has stopped, the guests have gone home and the rest of the world has gone to work.

THAT LEAN AND HUNGRY LOOK

Suzanne Britt

Suzanne Britt, who teaches English at Meredith College in Raleigh, North Carolina, has also worked as a journalist. "That Lean and Hungry Look" takes an amusing look at the differences between "fat" people and "thin" people and will give the reluctant jogger ample reason to retire the Reeboks.

Caesar was right. Thin people need watching. I've been watching them for most of my adult life, and I don't like what I see. When these narrow fellows spring at me, I quiver to my toes. Thin people come in all personalities, most of them menacing. You've got your "together" thin person, your mechanical thin person, your condescending thin person, your tsk-tsk thin person, your efficiency-expert thin person. All of them are dangerous. 1

In the first place, thin people aren't fun. They don't know how to goof off, at least in the best, fat sense of the word. They've always got to be adoing. Give them a coffee break, and they'll jog around the block. Supply them with a quiet evening at home, and they'll fix the screen door and lick S&H green stamps. They say things like "there aren't enough hours in the day." Fat people never say that. Fat people think the day is too damn long already. 2

Thin people make me tired. They've got speedy little metabolisms that cause them to bustle briskly. They're forever rubbing their bony hands together and eying new problems to "tackle." I like to surround myself with sluggish, inert, easygoing fat people, the kind who believe that if you clean it up today, it'll just get dirty again tomorrow. 3

Some people say the business about the jolly fat person is a myth, that all of us chubbies are neurotic, sick, sad people. I disagree. Fat people may not be chortling all day long, but they're a hell of a lot *nicer* than the wizened and shriveled. Thin people turn surly, mean and hard at a young age because they never learn the value of a hot-fudge sundae for easing tension. Thin people don't like gooey soft things because they themselves are neither gooey nor soft. They are crunchy and dull, like carrots. They go straight to the heart of the matter while fat people let things stay all blurry and hazy and vague, the way things actually are. Thin people want to face the truth. Fat people know there is no truth. One of my thin friends is always staring at complex, unsolvable problems and saying, "The key thing is . . ." Fat people never say that. They know there isn't any such thing as the key thing about anything. 4

Thin people believe in logic. Fat people see all sides. The sides fat people see are rounded blobs, usually gray, always nebulous and truly not worth worrying about. But the thin person persists. "If you consume more calories than you burn," says 5 one of my thin friends, "you will gain weight. It's that simple." Fat people always grin when they hear statements like that. They know better.

6   Fat people realize that life is illogical and unfair. They know very well that God is not in his heaven and all is not right with the world. If God was up there, fat people could have two doughnuts and a big orange drink anytime they wanted it.

7   Thin people have a long list of logical things they are always spouting off to me. They hold up one finger at a time as they reel off these things, so I won't lose track. They speak slowly as if to a young child. The list is long and full of holes. It contains tidbits like "get a grip on yourself," "cigarettes kill," "cholesterol clogs," "fit as a fiddle," "ducks in a row," "organize" and "sound fiscal management." Phrases like that.

8   They think these 2,000-point plans lead to happiness. Fat people know happiness is elusive at best and even if they could get the kind thin people talk about, they wouldn't want it. Wisely, fat people see that such programs are too dull, too hard, too off the mark. They are never better than a whole cheesecake.

9   Fat people know all about the mystery of life. They are the ones acquainted with the night, with luck, with fate, with playing it by ear. One thin person I know once suggested that we arrange all the parts of a jigsaw puzzle into groups according to size, shape and color. He figured this would cut the time needed to complete the puzzle by at least 50 per cent. I said I wouldn't do it. One, I like to muddle through. Two, what good would it do to finish early? Three, the jigsaw puzzle isn't the important thing. The important thing is the fun of four people (one thin person included) sitting around a card table, working a jigsaw puzzle. My thin friend had no use for my list. Instead of joining us, he went outside and mulched the boxwoods. The three remaining fat people finished the puzzle and made chocolate, double-fudge brownies to celebrate.

10   The main problem with thin people is they oppress. Their good intentions, bony torsos, tight ships, neat corners, cerebral machinations and pat solutions loom like dark clouds over the loose, comfortable, spread-out, soft world of the fat. Long after fat people have removed their coats and shoes and put their feet up on the coffee table, thin people are still sitting on the edge of the sofa, looking neat as a pin, discussing rutabagas. Fat people are heavily into fits of laughter, slapping their thighs and whooping it up, while thin people are still politely waiting for the punch line.

11   Thin people are downers. They like math and morality and reasoned evaluation of the limitations of human beings. They have their skinny little acts together. They expound, prognose, probe and prick.

12   Fat people are convivial. They will like you even if you're irregular and have acne. They will come up with a good reason why you never wrote the great American novel. They will cry in your beer with you. They will put your name in the pot. They will let you off the hook. Fat people will gab, giggle, guffaw, gallumph, gyrate and gossip. They are generous, giving and gallant. They are gluttonous and goodly and great. What you want when you're down is soft and jiggly, not muscled and stable. Fat people know this. Fat people have plenty of room. Fat people will take you in.

ARE WOMEN WIMPS?

Carol Tavris

Carol Tavris is a social psychologist who lectures and writes, frequently from a feminist perspective. This selection is an excerpt from her book The Mismeasure of Woman *(1992), which emphasizes the similarities between women and men.*

"Man the Killer" and "Woman the Peacemaker" are symbols of two potentials   1
in human nature. By focusing on the men in power who make war (and the men in armies who fight), we overlook the women who support and endorse war, making it possible. By focusing on male violence, we overlook the men who promote pacifism and negotiation. By regarding aggressiveness as an entrenched and exclusively male quality, and pacifism as an inherent feminine quality, we overlook the ways in which societies in turmoil create dangerous, violent men, and we conveniently forget that most of the greatest pacifists and reformers in history have been men. Archetypes are not blueprints; flesh-and-blood men and women conform to them in only the most general of ways.

As political scientist Jean Bethke Elshtain has showed in *Women and War,* through-   2
out history women have been just as militant in wartime as men. Women have always participated in wars, in whatever ways their societies permitted: as combatants, as defenders, as laborers in the work force to produce war materials, as supporters of their warrior husbands and sons. Women have been all too willing to join in the glorification of nation above family, and to find honor in playing the "Spartan Mother" (the woman, nameless to history, who lost five sons in battle and gave thanks to the gods that Sparta won). A Spartan Mother in World War II, Aletta Sullivan, became a "Gold Star Mother" five times over after all five of her sons were killed when their ship was sunk off Guadalcanal. Was Mrs. Sullivan angry at the Navy, which incredibly stationed all of her sons on one ship? Did she call for an end to war? Now is a good time, she said to a crowd of shipworkers who had turned out to honor her, "to keep your chin up."

The persistence of Spartan Mothers, along with the weight of evidence of his-   3
tory and psychology, gives the lie to the sentimental yet appealing idea that because women give birth they are more inclined to oppose the destruction that accompanies warfare. " 'Mother' got drafted into propaganda service over and over, in all warring nations," observes Elshtain. She cites the "blood-curdling patriotism" of an English woman in World War I, who wrote a letter to the *London Morning Post* and signed it only "A Little Mother":

> [We] mothers of the British race . . . play the most important part in the
> history of the world, for it is we who "mother the men" who have to up-

hold the honour and traditions not only of our Empire but of the whole civilized world. . . . We women, who demand to be heard, will tolerate no such cry as Peace! Peace! where there is no peace.

4   Women have revealed their patriotic fervor not only by sending their sons to battle, but also, over the centuries, by being actively involved in warfare themselves as soldiers, resistance fighters, and terrorists. In the first century B.C., Plutarch described barbarians

> whose fierce women charged with swords and axes, and fell upon their opponents uttering a hideous outcry. . . . When summoned to surrender, they killed their children, slaughtered one another, or hanged themselves to trees.

5   In the Second World War, upward of one million Soviet women served in combat as snipers, machinegunners, artillery women, and tank women; they flew in three women's air regiments on bombing missions. Nadya Popova, a bomber pilot, recounted her experiences as matter-of-factly as any male pilot would: "War requires the ability to kill." Marisa Masu, an Italian Resistance fighter in World War II, described feelings that are no different from those of most male soldiers:

> At that time it was clear that each Nazi I killed, each bomb I helped to explode, shortened the length of the war and saved the lives of all women and children. . . . I never asked myself if the soldier or SS man I killed had a wife or children. I never thought about it.

6   We think of war as a male activity and value, but war has always given even noncombatant women an escape from domestic confinement—the exhilaration of a public identity and a chance to play a heroic role, usually denied them in their private lives. In American history, the Civil War was a major springboard for women's advancement into men's spheres, and the World Wars of the twentieth century had an even more liberating effect for many women: wars earned them the vote, got them into the arena of politics, got them better jobs, and vindicated the importance of their labor on the home front. Black women in World War II moved into higher-paying factory jobs.

7   Without understanding what war accomplishes for women, in emotional excitement, expanded opportunities, and tangible freedoms (and likewise what thrills and terrors war offers men), we perpetuate mythic notions that men love war and women loathe it. This notion infuses most of the current debates about whether women should be allowed in combat. Proponents on both sides tend to base their arguments on women's *nature*—whether women are or are not as able as men

to fight, whether combat does or does not destroy their femininity, and so on. This debate deflects attention from the question that really matters, namely, "What do women gain or lose by this decision?" Currently, women in the military lose money by not being allowed directly in combat, although, as we learned in the Persian Gulf War, they are at as great a risk of death by working in support services; they lose status and prestige; and they lose political clout. Military experience, especially in combat, is still an asset for those who run for high office (except for Ronald Reagan, who merely believed he had served in the Army).

Quite apart from what men and women do in wartime, bellicose and genocidal attitudes are by no means a male preserve. The same propaganda and ideology that motivate male members of a society ensnare its female citizens too. Iranian women joined Iranian men in chanting Death to America; British women joined British men to support a war with Argentina over the Falkland Islands; German women joined German men to support Hitler's dreams of world conquest; American women have joined American men in supporting virtually every one of our invasions, "police actions," and wars, most recently in the Persian Gulf. Women, for all their reputed empathic skills, have been as willing and able as men to regard the enemy as beasts or demons to be exterminated rather than as fellow human beings.

Thus, a Milwaukee woman, endorsing use of the atomic bomb at Hiroshima, wrote to her newspaper: "When one sets out to destroy vermin, does one try to leave a few alive in the nest? Certainly not!" Women have supported the Ku Klux Klan and its bloody outrages every bit as much as their men did; women didn't light the fires, perhaps, but they sewed the costumes that the cross-burners wore. In the late 1970s, David Duke (then Grand Wizard of the Knights of the KKK, now posing as a mainstream Republican) allowed women to become actual members, so Klanswomen today can attend den meetings and ritual cross burnings along with men—which they do. Across the country, women are organizing their own "white power" and "Aryan women's" groups, and they constitute upwards of a third of the *active* membership of hate groups such as skinheads, neo-Nazis, and "Christian Identity" sects.

None of this means that at any given moment in society, men and women will be precisely alike in their attitudes and values. Much has been made in recent years of the American gender gap in support for militarism. For instance, after Iraq invaded Kuwait in August 1990, a survey conducted by the Public Agenda Foundation reported that "support for launching a massive counterattack or an all-out war is 25% lower among women (35%) than among men (60%)." Similarly, two thirds of American men but "only" half of American women supported the U.S. invasion of Grenada, and, before the political revolution in Eastern Europe, more men than women said the United States should be "more forceful" with the Russians even if it leads to war.

What is behind this gender gap? Certainly, as historian Ruth Rosen points out, women "do not suffer from the dreaded 'wimp factor.' If they support peace, their womanhood is not endangered." On this point, I entirely agree. But I disagree with the second reason Rosen offers for the gender gap, the one most commonly heard: "As primary care-givers, women learn early to nurture life rather than destroy it." How I wish this assertion were true, but regrettably I see little evidence for it in the case of war. Men and women do not differ in their willingness to go to war, an enterprise that tends to destroy life. They merely differ in the reasons that would make them willing to go to war.

12   Psychologist Ofer Zur closely examined opinion polls and surveys that have been conducted in the last forty years, and he noticed a curious bias in the phrasing of questions. For example, one Roper Poll asked respondents "Would you be willing to fight . . . in case a foreign power tried to seize land in Central America?" Standing tall lest they be mistaken for wimps, men were far more likely than women to say yes. So, on polls like these, men consistently appear to be more violent and militaristic than women. However, when women are asked whether they would endorse a war for reasons that reflect other motives—such as saving the lives of loved ones or promoting group cohesion—women turn out to be more violent and militaristic than men. In Zur's research, women agreed more often than men did with statements such as "Any country which violates the right of innocent children should be invaded." Oh, good. Not only will that rationale keep the United States busy invading dozens of countries for the next century, it offers the government just the propaganda it wants to close the gender gap.

13   The point is that gender gaps widen or narrow with changing times, motives, and political circumstances, and they cannot be accounted for by an intrinsic female pacifism. Feminists who hoped the gender gap would lead to the defeat of Ronald Reagan and George Bush have learned that ideology and economics override gender in the voting booth.

14   The archetypes of Man as Just Warrior and Woman as Beautiful Soul are complimentary to both sexes. But they are ultimately untrue, defied by a more complex reality that includes ample illustrations of female bellicosity and male pacifism and self-sacrifice. It is time to sing of "arms and the woman": to recognize that women are the unindicted co-conspirators in the making of war.

Cause-and-Effect Analysis

HONEY, I WARPED THE KIDS

Carl M. Cannon

A journalist, Carl M. Cannon has worked for several newspapers and is now a reporter for the Baltimore Sun. *This article is the result of his reviewing research about television viewing and violence.*

Tim Robbins and Susan Sarandon implore the nation to treat Haitians with AIDS more humanely. Robert Redford works for the environment. Harry Belafonte marches against the death penalty. Actors and producers seem to be constantly speaking out for noble causes far removed from their lives. But in the one area over which they have control—the excessive violence in the entertainment industry—Hollywood activists remain silent.   1

The first congressional hearings on the effects of TV violence took place in 1954. Although television was still relatively new, its extraordinary marketing power was already evident. The tube was teaching Americans what to buy and how to act, not only in advertisements, but in dramatic shows, too.   2

Everybody from Hollywood producers to Madison Avenue ad men would boast about this power—and seek to use it on dual tracks: to make money and to remake society along better lines.   3

Because it seemed ludicrous to assert that there was only one area—the depiction of violence—where television did not influence behavior, the TV industry came up with this theory: Watching violence is cathartic. A violent person might be sated by watching a murder.   4

The notion intrigued social scientists, and by 1956 they were studying it in earnest. Unfortunately, watching violence turned out to be anything but cathartic.   5

In the 1956 study, one dozen 4-year-olds watched a "Woody Woodpecker" cartoon that was full of violent images. Twelve other preschoolers watched "Little Red Hen," a peaceful cartoon. Afterward, the children who watched "Woody Woodpecker" were more likely to hit other children, verbally accost their classmates, break toys, be disruptive, and engage in destructive behavior during free play.   6

For the next 30 years, researchers in all walks of the social sciences studied the question of whether television causes violence. The results have been stunningly conclusive.   7

8   "There is more published research on this topic than on almost any other social issue of our time," University of Kansas Professor Aletha C. Huston, chair of the
American Psychological Association's Task Force on Television and Society, told
Congress in 1988. "Virtually all independent scholars agree that there is evidence
that television can cause aggressive behavior."

9   There have been some 3,000 studies of this issue—85 of them major research
efforts—and they all say the same thing. Of the 85 major studies, the only one that
failed to find a causal relationship between TV violence and actual violence was paid
for by NBC. When the study was subsequently reviewed by three independent social
scientists, all three concluded that it actually did demonstrate a causal relationship.

10   Some highlights from the history of TV violence research:

11   • In 1973, when a town in mountainous western Canada was wired for TV sig-
     nals, University of British Columbia researchers observed first- and second-
     graders. Within two years, the incidence of hitting, biting, and shoving
     increased 160 percent.

12   • Two Chicago doctors, Leonard Eron and Rowell Heusmann, followed the
     viewing habits of a group of children for 22 years. They found that watch-
     ing violence on television is the single best predictor of violent or aggressive
     behavior later in life, ahead of such commonly accepted factors as parents'
     behavior, poverty, and race.

13   "Television violence affects youngsters of all ages, of both genders, at
     all socioeconomic levels and all levels of intelligence," they told Congress in
     1992. "The effect is not limited to children who are already disposed to
     being aggressive and is not restricted to this country."

14   • In 1988, researchers Daniel G. Linz and Edward Donnerstein of the University
     of California, Santa Barbara, and Steven Penrod of the University of Wiscon-
     sin studied the effects on young men of horror movies and "slasher" films.

15   They found that depictions of violence, not sex, are what desensitizes
     people. They divided male students into four groups. One group watched
     no movies, a second watched nonviolent X-rated movies, a third watched
     teenage sexual-innuendo movies, and a fourth watched the slasher films
     Texas Chainsaw Massacre, Friday the 13th, Part 2, Maniac, and *Toolbox Murders.*

16   All the young men were placed on a mock jury panel and asked a se-
     ries of questions designed to measure their empathy for an alleged female
     rape victim. Those in the fourth group measured lowest in empathy for the
     specific victim in the experiment—and for rape victims in general.

17   The anecdotal evidence is often more compelling than the scientific studies.
Ask any homicide cop from London to Los Angeles to Bangkok if TV violence in-
duces real-life violence and listen carefully to the cynical, knowing laugh.

Ask David McCarthy, police chief in Greenfield, Massachusetts, why 19-year-old Mark Branch killed himself after stabbing an 18-year-old female college student to death. When cops searched his room they found 90 horror movies, as well as a machete and a goalie mask like those used by Jason, the grisly star of *Friday the 13th*. 18

Or ask Sergeant John O'Malley of the New York Police Department about a 9-year-old boy who sprayed a Bronx office building with gunfire. The boy explained to the astonished sergeant how he learned to load his Uzi-like firearm: "I watch a lot of TV." 19

Numerous groups have called, over the years, for curbing TV violence: the National Commission on the Causes and Prevention of Violence (1969), the U.S. Surgeon General (1972), the National Institute of Mental Health (1982), and the American Psychological Association (1992) among them. 20

During that time, cable television and movie rentals have made violence more readily available while at the same time pushing the envelope for network television. But even leaving aside cable and movie rentals, a study of TV programming from 1967 to 1989 showed only small ups and downs in violence, with the violent acts moving from one time slot to another but the overall violence rate remaining pretty steady—and pretty similar from network to network. 21

"The percent of prime-time programs using violence remains more than seven out of ten, as it has been for the entire 22-year period," researchers George Gerbner of the University of Pennsylvania Annenberg School of Communication and Nancy Signorielli of the University of Delaware wrote in 1990. For the past 22 years, they found, adults and children have been entertained by about 16 violent acts, including two murders, in each evening's prime-time programming. 22

They also discovered that the rate of violence in children's programs is three times the rate in prime-time shows. By the age of 18, the average American child has witnessed at least 18,000 simulated murders on television. 23

But all of the scientific studies and reports, all of the wisdom of cops and grief of parents have run up against Congress' quite proper fear of censorship. For years, Democratic Congressman Peter Rodino of New Jersey chaired the House Judiciary Committee and looked at calls for some form of censorship with a jaundiced eye. At a hearing five years ago, Rodino told witnesses that Congress must be a "protector of commerce." 24

"Well, we have children that we need to protect," replied Frank M. Palumbo, a pediatrician at Georgetown University Hospital and a consultant to the American Academy of Pediatrics. "What we have here is a toxic substance in the environment that is harmful to children." 25

Arnold Fege of the national PTA added, "Clearly, this committee would not protect teachers who taught violence to children. Yet why would we condone children being exposed to a steady diet of TV violence year after year?" 26

THE COMPANY MAN

Ellen Goodman

Ellen Goodman, a Pulitzer Prize–winning journalist, has been with the Boston Globe *since 1967 and is the author of the widely syndicated column "At Large." The following column, "The Company Man," describes the lifelong and far-reaching effects—and the final futility —of workaholism.*

1   He worked himself to death, finally and precisely, at 3:00 A.M. Sunday morning.

2   The obituary didn't say that, of course. It said that he died of a coronary thrombosis—I think that was it—but everyone among his friends and acquaintances knew it instantly. He was a perfect Type A, a workaholic, a classic, they said to each other and shook their heads—and thought for five or ten minutes about the way they lived.

3   This man who worked himself to death finally and precisely at 3:00 A.M. Sunday morning—on his day off—was fifty-one years old and a vice-president. He was, however, one of six vice-presidents, and one of three who might conceivably—if the president died or retired soon enough—have moved to the top spot. Phil knew that.

4   He worked six days a week, five of them until eight or nine at night, during a time when his own company had begun the four-day week for everyone but the executives. He worked like the Important People. He had no outside "extracurricular interests," unless, of course, you think about a monthly golf game that way. To Phil, it was work. He always ate egg salad sandwiches at his desk. He was, of course, overweight, by 20 or 25 pounds. He thought it was okay, though, because he didn't smoke.

5   On Saturdays, Phil wore a sports jacket to the office instead of a suit, because it was the weekend.

6   He had a lot of people working for him, maybe sixty, and most of them liked him most of the time. Three of them will be seriously considered for his job. The obituary didn't mention that.

7   But it did list his "survivors" quite accurately. He is survived by his wife, Helen, forty-eight years old, a good woman of no particular marketable skills, who worked in an office before marrying and mothering. She had, according to her daughter, given up trying to compete with his work years ago, when the children were small. A company friend said, "I know how much you will miss him." And she answered, "I already have."

8   "Missing him all these years," she must have given up part of herself which had cared too much for the man. She would be "well taken care of."

His "dearly beloved" eldest of the "dearly beloved" children is a hard-working   9
executive in a manufacturing firm down South. In the day and a half before the
funeral, he went around the neighborhood researching his father, asking the neighbors what he was like. They were embarrassed.

His second child is a girl, who is twenty-four and newly married. She lives near   10
her mother and they are close, but whenever she was alone with her father, in a car
driving somewhere, they had nothing to say to each other.

The youngest is twenty, a boy, a high-school graduate who has spent the last   11
couple of years, like a lot of his friends, doing enough odd jobs to stay in grass and
food. He was the one who tried to grab at his father, and tried to mean enough to
him to keep the man at home. He was his father's favorite. Over the last two years,
Phil stayed up nights worrying about the boy.

The boy once said, "My father and I only board here."   12

At the funeral, the sixty-year-old company president told the forty-eight-year-   13
old widow that the fifty-one-year-old deceased had meant much to the company and
would be missed and would be hard to replace. The widow didn't look him in the
eye. She was afraid he would read her bitterness and, after all, she would need him
to straighten out the finances—the stock options and all that.

Phil was overweight and nervous and worked too hard. If he wasn't at the   14
office, he was worried about it. Phil was a Type A, a heart-attack natural. You could
have picked him out in a minute from a lineup.

So when he finally worked himself to death, at precisely 3:00 A.M. Sunday   15
morning, no one was really surprised.

By 5:00 P.M. the afternoon of the funeral, the company president had begun,   16
discreetly of course, with care and taste, to make inquiries about his replacement.
One of three men. He asked around: "Who's been working the hardest?"

THE STORY OF Z

Elizabeth Rapoport

Elizabeth Rapoport's work as a senior editor at Times Books/Random House probably explains her understanding of overwork. In this amusing essay, Rapoport describes how sleep has become an object of desire.

1   I've figured out the dirty little secret of women's fantasy lives. And it's got nothing to do with thumbing through "Herotica" or fondling Brad Pitt's backside or soaking in a penthouse Jacuzzi with Richard Gere. Sleep has become the sex of the 90's.

2   Sleep is replacing sex as that obscure object of desire that inhabits our daydreams—if we still have time for daydreams. When I indulge in an out-of-body experience during a particularly dull meeting, my richest, deepest, most rewarding fantasies aren't erotic. They're about checking out for hours and hours of glorious, uninterrupted sack time. I'm not mentally undressing my dishy seatmate on the commuter train; I'm wondering whether he'd take offense if I catnap on his shoulder until we get to Hartsdale. My idea of a phone sex line is 1-800-M-A-T-T-R-E-S.

3   Arlie Hochschild interviewed dozens of working mothers for her book *The Second Shift: Working Parents and the Revolution at Home.* Time and again, they talked about sleep the way starving people talk about food. But this problem is not reserved to working mothers. Far from it. I read a column a few months back about the chronic sleep deficit that's sweeping the country. Something like 80 percent of Americans are seriously sleep-deprived. (Or maybe it was that 80 percent have lower back pain, or 80 percent think Heather Locklear needs to touch up those roots. I nodded off somewhere in there.) Experts estimate that chronic sleeplessness costs the nation as much as $70 billion annually in lost productivity, accidents and medical bills. There was some maxim that if you fall asleep within five minutes of lights out, you can count yourself among the seriously sleep-deficient. (Wait, there are people who can stay awake for five minutes?)

4   I don't need Faith Popcorn or Gallup for confirmation. I know a trend when I'm living it. My friends and colleagues concur. Sarah says she would rather lay her head on a pillow than anywhere else. Maria says none of her friends want to fool around on the weekend; they just want to recover from the week (oh God, not another recovery movement). Barb claims that no one she knows is having sex—unless they're on some procreational full-court press to get those babies in before the buzzer sounds.

5   In fact, the only person to whom I expounded my sleep-as-sex theory who just didn't get it was a single, unencumbered, 20-something guy I work with. As I rambled on during one of my brief moments of clarity (the decaffeinated life is definitely not worth living), he rolled his eyes and said, "Sounds like all you need is a

good nap." Which sounded suspiciously like a guy saying that all I needed was a good roll in the hay. Which proves my point exactly.

Obviously, for working parents, small children are the big problem. I guess I should have had an inkling of the trouble ahead when I read a *Parents* magazine survey a few months after our first child was born. In response to the question, "How do you feel about sex after the baby?" one new mom answered, "Fine, just don't wake me." 6

I just edited this wonderful new book by a physician whose sex therapy clinic has successfully treated thousands of couples. The doctor confirms that fatigue is a big problem in people's sex lives. But when I pressed her for some solutions, I couldn't help but feel a tad disappointed. She explained that we go through these R.E.M. cycles several times a night, one every 90 minutes or so, at which time we become aroused — only we're not aware of it because we're out like a light. She recommends you set your alarm to go off 90 minutes after you fall asleep. The idea is, when you wake up you'll be in one of your sexy R.E.M. cycles, so you'll be in the mood. Yeah, you'll get me up after those precious 90 minutes when you pry my cold, dead fingers from around the pillow. 7

The women's magazines are certainly no help. *Cosmo* has yet to publish articles for the Exhausted Generation. How about "Douse His Candle: 15 Ways to Rev Up Your Z's" or "I Was the Office Narcomaniac"? And how long before the Surgeon General realizes that sleep is the ultimate safe sex? 8

I do see hope on the horizon. Two months ago my husband and I took our first real vacation—three days and two nights—away from our two small children. On our last pre-child vacation, we embarked on an exotic trip abroad with complicated transportation nexuses and an intricate itinerary. This time around, we didn't even bother picking a destination. Our only goal was so modest it was almost pathetic: to go to sleep at night and wake up whenever we happened to wake up—not when a tiny voice shouted "Uppies! Uppies!" in one of our ears. 9

The first morning we made it to 7:13. The second morning we lasted until almost 8:00. And I was a new woman. For the first time in memory, whenever I closed my eyes, they didn't pine to stay closed. I felt energized, alive . . . sexy! We were, in all modesty, animals. Two days after we returned, however, the inevitable exhaustion crept back in. We're looking forward to re-creating that connubial bliss soon— perhaps when the kids are in their surly, narcotized teenage years. In the meantime, my husband and I comfort ourselves that this too shall pass; we know that one day our lust for sleep will recede and truly smutty thoughts will regain their rightful pride of place in our fantasy lives. 10

Who knows? Perhaps that day will come sooner than you think, darling. There I'll be, draped in that low-cut black nightgown you bought me on our honeymoon in Florence, my hair back-lit by flickering candles, my limbs still moist from a fragrant tub, awaiting the caress of the massage oil that warms at your touch. 11

But for now, wake me and you're a dead man. 12

SEXUAL BIGOTRY

Roger Rosenblatt

Formerly a columnist and editor-at-large for Life *magazine, Roger Rosen-blatt is now a contributing editor for* Vanity Fair *and a columnist for* Family Circle. *In "Sexual Bigotry," he shows how even endearments can be used as tools to assert dominance.*

1   The reason people are having so much trouble identifying sexual harassment these days is that the offense has less to do with sex than gender. Ever since Professor Anita Hill accused Supreme Court nominee Judge Clarence Thomas of lewd and overbearing conduct toward her, the country has been trying to determine the difference between innocent fun and genuine pain.

2   But the pain felt by a woman who suffers indignities from men in a place of work rarely has anything to do with the men's sexual desires. The pain is experienced because women are made to feel inferior—inferior intellectually, emotionally, professionally—in a situation where they have every right to feel equal. They are not so much sex objects as targets of bigotry.

3   Now, bigotry, between sexes, unlike bigotry between races, is fraught with a lot of biological tension that can make it seem something other than it is. And sex often does involve the deliberate exertion of leverage or power.

4   But when some guy calls a female colleague "honey" and does nothing else suggestive, I think it's a stretch to assume that "honey" is a sign of his wanting to roll in the hay. When the word is dropped into, say, a professional disagreement, or a competition of views, however, it has the edge of an attack.

5   "That's all well and good, honey, but if you had as much experience with these things as I . . ."

6   In that sort of case, which is far more common than a man's making a pass, the term of endearment is actually a term of derision, of purposeful belittling. Not very subtly, the male in the office wants to tell the female: "OK. You've got a big, responsible job now. But this is still a man's world, *honey,* and I'm going to try and make you feel as uncomfortable in it as I possibly can."

7   The movie *Tootsie* brought out this kind of sexual bigotry as well as anything. Dustin Hoffman, passing as a woman, and playing an actress in a soap opera, chews out "her" director, played by Dabney Coleman (America's favorite male chauvinist pig), when Coleman uses the supposedly affectionate nickname of Tootsie. Coleman isn't interested in squeezing Tootsie's body but in squeezing her mind. He wants to make her feel she does not belong, or that she exists at his sufferance.

8   That, I think, is the real and brutal motive behind most sexual harassment—to keep a woman in her "place" whenever she emerges into a "man's place."

These recent years have been kind of hard on the old boys' network. (I know, 9
I'm an old boy myself.) In the 1990s men are finally beginning to realize that the
women's movement has moved; it has happened. With the economy requiring two
wage earners in a family, and the general enlightenment that follows a right idea,
nothing is going to make it *un*-happen.

Some men take the news well, some grudgingly, some angrily. Some take it an- 10
grily who only appear to take it well.

These are the ones you often find leering like Red Riding Hood's wolf over 11
the watercooler or reaching out to make a pinch. They don't want sex, they want
dominance. They want to set back the office clock to when those desks and name-
plates were all theirs.

We have seen this type of bigotry before, of course, but it was in the South be- 12
fore the 1960s, at swimming pools and lunch counters, when American blacks were
told they were not Americans.

And we saw it at the start of the century, when American Irish, Slavs, Jews, Ital- 13
ians, and others were told they were not Americans either: "Irish need not apply."
American Hispanics are told the same thing today, as are American Asians and
American Indians, and American homosexuals and the American handicapped.

With civil rights laws in place, bigots have nowhere to turn except toward lesser 14
forms of tyranny. The matter often lies in intention. Most male bigots intend to
bring women down, all right—not in the bed, in the whole society. They hope to in-
jure a woman's self-esteem by bringing her low. It is one sure way such men can
think better of themselves.

Like conventional bigots, too, they will treat the targets of their bigotry as in- 15
ferior because of fear. Usually men who behave badly toward women co-workers are
afraid of them, afraid that women will show them up as less capable or that the
women will band together in a sorority as clannish and exclusionary as men's clubs.
You wouldn't want *that*.

Many observers feel that the gray area in the harassment issue lies where a 16
woman misinterprets a man's intentions. I think that is so. Many men, myself sor-
rowfully included, are bumblers when it comes to knowing what's cute and what's
rude or worse.

But I also think that the misinterpretation of intentions is far more likely when 17
it comes to sexual desires than when it comes to bigotry.

No law can prove it, but the heart knows when it is being assaulted as some- 18
thing less, not worthy, not human. The man who does anything—anything at all—
to intentionally make a woman feel not human is no different from the coward
Klansman hiding his hatred under a sheet. He's not making love, he's making war.

BLACK MEN AND PUBLIC SPACE

Brent Staples

After earning a doctorate in psychology at the University of Chicago, Brent Staples became a reporter for the Chicago Sun Times; *he later accepted a position with the* New York Times, *where he is now an assistant editor. In the following well-known essay, Staples examines the fear and hostility that a black man's presence can sometimes arouse.*

1   My first victim was a woman—white, well dressed, probably in her early twenties. I came upon her late one evening on a deserted street in Hyde Park, a relatively affluent neighborhood in an otherwise mean, impoverished section of Chicago. As I swung onto the avenue behind her, there seemed to be a discreet, uninflammatory distance between us. Not so. She cast back a worried glance. To her, the youngish black man—a broad six feet two inches with a beard and billowing hair, both hands shoved into the pockets of a bulky military jacket—seemed menacingly close. After a few more quick glimpses, she picked up her pace and was soon running in earnest. Within seconds she disappeared into a cross street.

2   That was more than a decade ago. I was twenty-two years old, a graduate student newly arrived at the University of Chicago. It was in the echo of that terrified woman's footfalls that I first began to know the unwieldy inheritance I'd come into—the ability to alter public space in ugly ways. It was clear that she thought herself the quarry of a mugger, a rapist, or worse. Suffering a bout of insomnia, however, I was stalking sleep, not defenseless wayfarers. As a softy who is scarcely able to take a knife to a raw chicken—let alone hold one to a person's throat—I was surprised, embarrassed, and dismayed all at once. Her flight made me feel like an accomplice in tyranny. It also made it clear that I was indistinguishable from the muggers who occasionally seeped into the area from the surrounding ghetto. That first encounter, and those that followed, signified that a vast, unnerving gulf lay between nighttime pedestrians—particularly women—and me. And I soon gathered that being perceived as dangerous is a hazard in itself. I only needed to turn a corner into a dicey situation, or crowd some frightened, armed person in a foyer somewhere, or make an errant move after being pulled over by a policeman. Where fear and weapons meet—and they often do in urban America—there is always the possibility of death.

3   In that first year, my first away from my hometown, I was to become thoroughly familiar with the language of fear. At dark, shadowy intersections, I could cross in front of a car stopped at a traffic light and elicit the *thunk, thunk, thunk, thunk* of the driver—black, white, male, or female—hammering down the door locks. On less traveled streets after dark, I grew accustomed to but never comfortable with people crossing to the other side of the street rather than pass me. Then there were the

standard unpleasantries with policemen, doormen, bouncers, cabdrivers, and others whose business it is to screen out troublesome individuals *before* there is any nastiness.

I moved to New York nearly two years ago and I have remained an avid night walker. In central Manhattan, the near-constant crowd cover minimizes tense one-on-one street encounters. Elsewhere—in SoHo, for example, where sidewalks are narrow and tightly spaced buildings shut out the sky—things can get very taut indeed.   4

After dark, on the warrenlike streets of Brooklyn where I live, I often see women who fear the worst from me. They seem to have set their faces on neutral, and with their purse straps strung across their chests bandolier-style, they forge ahead as though bracing themselves against being tackled. I understand, of course, that the danger they perceive is not a hallucination. Women are particularly vulnerable to street violence, and young black males are drastically overrepresented among the perpetrators of that violence. Yet these truths are no solace against the kind of alienation that comes of being ever the suspect, a fearsome entity with whom pedestrians avoid making eye contact.   5

It is not altogether clear to me how I reached the ripe old age of twenty-two without being conscious of the lethality nighttime pedestrians attributed to me. Perhaps it was because in Chester, Pennsylvania, the small, angry industrial town where I came of age in the 1960s, I was scarcely noticeable against a backdrop of gang warfare, street knifings, and murders. I grew up one of the good boys, had perhaps a half-dozen fistfights. In retrospect, my shyness of combat has clear sources.   6

As a boy, I saw countless tough guys locked away; I have since buried several, too. They were babies, really—a teenage cousin, a brother of twenty-two, a childhood friend in his mid-twenties—all gone down in episodes of bravado played out in the streets. I came to doubt the virtues of intimidation early on. I chose, perhaps unconsciously, to remain a shadow—timid, but a survivor.   7

The fearsomeness mistakenly attributed to me in public places often has a perilous flavor. The most frightening of these confusions occurred in the late 1970s and early 1980s, when I worked as a journalist in Chicago. One day, rushing into the office of a magazine I was writing for with a deadline story in hand, I was mistaken for a burglar. The office manager called security and, with an ad hoc posse, pursued me through the labyrinthine halls, nearly to my editor's door. I had no way of proving who I was. I could only move briskly toward the company of someone who knew me.   8

Another time I was on assignment for a local paper and killing time before an interview. I entered a jewelry store on the city's affluent Near North Side. The proprietor excused herself and returned with an enormous red Doberman pinscher straining at the end of a leash. She stood, the dog extended toward me, silent to my questions, her eyes bulging nearly out of her head. I took a cursory look around, nodded, and bade her good night.   9

Relatively speaking, however, I never fared as badly as another black male journalist. He went to nearby Waukegan, Illinois, a couple of summers ago to work on   10 a story about a murderer who was born there. Mistaking the reporter for the killer, police officers hauled him from his car at gunpoint and but for his press credentials would probably have tried to book him. Such episodes are not uncommon. Black men trade tales like this all the time.

11   Over the years, I learned to smother the rage I felt at so often being taken for a criminal. Not to do so would surely have led to madness. I now take precautions to make myself less threatening. I move about with care, particularly late in the evening. I give a wide berth to nervous people on subway platforms during the wee hours, particularly when I have exchanged business clothes for jeans. If I happen to be entering a building behind some people who appear skittish, I may walk by, letting them clear the lobby before I return, so as not to seem to be following them. I have been calm and extremely congenial on those rare occasions when I've been pulled over by the police.

12   And on late-evening constitutionals I employ what has proved to be an excellent tension-reducing measure: I whistle melodies from Beethoven and Vivaldi and the more popular classical composers. Even steely New Yorkers hunching toward nighttime destinations seem to relax, and occasionally they even join in the tune. Virtually everybody seems to sense that a mugger wouldn't be warbling bright, sunny selections from Vivaldi's *Four Seasons*. It is my equivalent of the cowbell that hikers wear when they know they are in bear country.

CAMPUS RACISM 101

Nikki Giovanni

Nikki Giovanni is usually associated with the outpouring of Black writing in the 1960s and 1970s, a movement in which her poetry was prominent. She is a popular public reader of her works. This selection is from her book of essays Racism 101.

There is a bumper sticker that reads: TOO BAD IGNORANCE ISN'T PAINFUL. I like   1
that. But ignorance is. We just seldom attribute the pain to it or even recognize it when we see it. Like the postcard on my corkboard. It shows a young man in a very hip jacket smoking a cigarette. In the background is a high school with the American flag waving. The caption says: "Too cool for school. Yet too stupid for the real world." Out of the mouth of the young man is a bubble enclosing the words "Maybe I'll start a band." There could be a postcard showing a jock in a uniform saying, "I don't need school. I'm going to the NFL or NBA." Or one showing a young man or woman studying and a group of young people saying, "So you want to be white." Or something equally demeaning. We need to quit it.

I am a professor of English at Virginia Tech. I've been here for four years,   2
though for only two years with academic rank. I am tenured, which means I have a teaching position for life, a rarity on a predominantly white campus. Whether from malice or ignorance, people who think I should be at a predominantly Black institution will ask, "Why are you at Tech?" Because it's here. And so are Black students. But even if Black students weren't here, it's painfully obvious that this nation and this world cannot allow white students to go through higher education without interacting with Blacks in authoritative positions. It is equally clear that predominantly Black colleges cannot accommodate the numbers of Black students who want and need an education.

Is it difficult to attend a predominantly white college? Compared with what?   3
Being passed over for promotion because you lack credentials? Being turned down for jobs because you are not college-educated? Joining the armed forces or going to jail because you cannot find an alternative to the streets? Let's have a little perspective here. Where can you go and what can you do that frees you from interacting with the white American mentality? You're going to interact; the only question

is, will you be in some control of yourself and your actions, or will you be controlled by others? I'm going to recommend self-control.

4   What's the difference between prison and college? They both prescribe your behavior for a given period of time. They both allow you to read books and develop your writing. They both give you time alone to think and time with your peers to talk about issues. But four years of prison doesn't give you a passport to greater opportunities. Most likely that time only gives you greater knowledge of how to get back in. Four years of college gives you an opportunity not only to lift yourself but to serve your people effectively. What's the difference when you are called nigger in college from when you are called nigger in prison? In college you can, though I admit with effort, follow procedures to have those students who called you nigger kicked out or suspended. You can bring issues to public attention without risking your life. But mostly, college is and always has been the future. We, neither less nor more than other people, need knowledge. There are discomforts attached to attending predominantly white colleges, though no more so than living in a racist world. Here are some rules to follow that may help:

5   *Go to class.* No matter how you feel. No matter how you think the professor feels about you. It's important to have a consistent presence in the classroom. If nothing else, the professor will know you care enough and are serious enough to be there.

6   *Meet your professors.* Extend your hand (give a firm handshake) and tell them your name. Ask them what you need to do to make an A. You may never make an A, but you have put them on notice that you are serious about getting good grades.

7   *Do assignments on time.* Typed or computer-generated. You have the syllabus. Follow it, and turn those papers in. If for some reason you can't complete an assignment on time, let your professor know before it is due and work out a new due date—then meet it.

8   *Go back to see your professor.* Tell him or her your name again. If an assignment received less than an A, ask why, and find out what you need to do to improve the next assignment.

9   Yes, your professor is busy. So are you. So are your parents who are working to pay or help with your tuition. Ask early what you need to do if you feel you are starting to get into academic trouble. Do not wait until you are failing.

10   *Understand that there will be professors who do not like you;* there may even be professors who are racist or sexist or both. You must discriminate among your professors to see who will give you the help you need. You may not simply say, "They are all against me." They aren't. They mostly don't care. Since you are the one who wants to be educated, find the people who want to help.

11   *Don't defeat yourself.* Cultivate your friends. Know your enemies. You cannot undo hundreds of years of prejudicial thinking. Think for yourself and speak up.

Raise your hand in class. Say what you believe no matter how awkward you may think it sounds. You will improve in your articulation and confidence.

Participate in some campus activity. Join the newspaper staff. Run for office, join 　12 a dorm council. Do something that involves you on campus. You are going to be there for four years, so let your presence be known, if not felt.

You will inevitably run into some white classmates who are troubling because 　13 they often say stupid things, ask stupid questions—and expect an answer. Here are some comebacks to some of the most common inquiries and comments:

Q: What's it like to grow up in a ghetto? 　14
A: I don't know.

Q (from the teacher): Can you give us the Black perspective on Toni Morrison, 　15 Huck Finn, slavery, Martin Luther King, Jr., and others?
A: I can give you *my* perspective. (Do not take the burden of 22 million people on your shoulders. Remind everyone that you are an individual, and don't speak for the race or any other individual within it.)

Q: Why do all the Black people sit together in the dining hall? 　16
A: Why do all the white students sit together?

Q: Why should there be an African-American studies course? 　17
A: Because white Americans have not adequately studied the contributions of Africans and African-Americans. Both Black and white students need to know our total common history.

Q: Why are there so many scholarships for "minority" students? 　18
A: Because they wouldn't give my great-grandparents their forty acres and the mule.

Q: How can whites understand Black history, culture, literature, and so forth? 　19
A: The same way we understand white history, culture, literature, and so forth. That is why we're in school: to learn.

Q: Should whites take African-American studies courses? 　20
A: Of course. We take white-studies courses, though the universities don't call them that.

Comment: When I see groups of Black people on campus, it's really intimidating. 　21
Comeback: I understand what you mean. I'm frightened when I see white students congregating.

Comment: It's not fair. It's easier for you guys to get into college than for other 　22 people.
Comeback: If it's so easy, why aren't there more of us?

23   **Comment:** It's not our fault that America is the way it is.
Comeback: It's not our fault, either, but both of us have a responsibility to make changes.

24   It's really very simple. Educational progress is a national concern; education is a private one. Your job is not to educate white people; it is to obtain an education. If you take the racial world on your shoulders, you will not get the job done. Deal with yourself as an individual worthy of respect, and make everyone else deal with you the same way. College is a little like playing grown-up. Practice what you want to be. You have been telling your parents you are grown. Now is your chance to act like it.

THE RISE OF TEENAGE GAMBLING

Ricardo Chavira

*A freelance journalist, Ricardo Chavira has contributed to a number of
journals and magazines. In the following article, which appeared in the
February 25, 1991, issue of* Time *magazine, Chavira uses examples,
statistics, and cause-and-effect reasoning to develop his argument about the
problem of teenage gambling.*

Amid the throngs of gamblers in Atlantic City, Debra Kim Cohen stood out. A   1
former beauty queen, she dropped thousands of dollars at blackjack tables. Casino
managers acknowledged her lavish patronage by plying her with the perks commonly accorded VIP customers: free limo rides, meals, even rooms. Cohen, after all,
was a high roller. It apparently did not disturb casino officials that she was also a
teenager and—at 17—four years shy of New Jersey's legal gambling age.

Finally, Kim's father, Atlantic City detective Leonard Cohen, complained to   2
authorities. Kim was subsequently barred from casinos. But by then the damage had
been done. "She was an addicted gambler," Cohen says of his daughter. Moreover,
Kim had squandered all her money, including funds set aside for college. Officials
at the five casinos where she gambled claimed that her case was an anomaly.

On the contrary, Kim's sad case is only too common. Gambling researchers   3
say that of the estimated 8 million compulsive gamblers in America, fully 1 million
are teenagers. Unlike Kim, most live far from casinos, so they favor sports betting,
card playing and lotteries. Once bitten by the gambling bug, many later move on
to casinos and racetrack betting. "We have always seen compulsive gambling as a problem of older people," says Jean Falzon, executive director of the National Council on
Problem Gambling, based in New York City. "Now we are finding that adolescent
compulsive gambling is far more pervasive than we had thought."

Just 10 years ago, teenage gambling did not register even a blip on the roster   4
of social ills. Today gambling counselors say an average of 7% of their case loads involve teenagers. New studies indicate that teenage vulnerability to compulsive gambling hits every economic stratum and ethnic group. After surveying 2,700 high
school students in four states, California psychologist Durand Jacobs concluded that
students are 2½ times as likely as adults to become problem gamblers. In another
study, Henry Lesieur, a sociologist at St. John's University in New York, found eight
times as many gambling addicts among college students as among adults.

Experts agree that casual gambling, in which participants wager small sums, is   5
not necessarily bad. Compulsive betting, however, almost always involves destructive
behavior. Last fall police in Pennsauken, N.J., arrested a teenage boy on suspicion
of burglary. The youth said he stole items worth $10,000 to support his gambling

habit. Bryan, a 17-year-old from Cumberland, N.J., recently sought help after he was unable to pay back $4,000 he owed a sports bookmaker. Greg from Philadelphia says he began placing weekly $200 bets with bookies during his sophomore year in college. "Pretty soon it got to the point that I owed $5,000," he says. "The bookies threatened me. One said he would cut off my mother's legs if I didn't pay." Still Greg continued to gamble. Now 23, he was recently fired from his job after his employer caught him embezzling.

6   Why does gambling fever run so high among teens? Researchers point to the legitimization of gambling in America, noting that it is possible to place a legal bet in every state except Utah and Hawaii. Moreover, ticket vendors rarely ask to see proof of age, despite lottery laws in 33 states and the District of Columbia requiring that customers be at least 18 years old. "You have state governments promoting lotteries," says Valerie Lorenz, director of the National Center for Pathological Gambling, based in Baltimore. "The message they're conveying is that gambling is not a vice but a normal form of entertainment." Researchers also point to unstable families, low self-esteem and a societal obsession with money. "At the casinos you feel very important," says Rich of Bethesda, Md., a young recovering addict. "When you're spending money at the tables, they give you free drinks and call you Mister."

7   Efforts to combat teen problem gambling are still fairly modest. Few states offer educational programs that warn young people about the addictive nature of gambling; treatment programs designed for youths are virtually nonexistent. In Minnesota, where a study found that more than 6% of all youths between 15 and 18 are problem gamblers, $200,000 of the expected income from the state's new lottery will go toward a youth-education campaign. That may prove to be small solace. Betty George, who heads the Minnesota Council on Compulsive Gambling, warns that the lottery and other anticipated legalized gambling activities are likely to spur youth gambling.

8   Security guards at casinos in Atlantic City and Nevada have been instructed to be on the alert for minors. But it is a daunting task. Each month some 29,000 underage patrons are stopped at the door or ejected from the floors of Atlantic City casinos. "We can rationally assume that if we stop 29,000, then a few hundred manage to get through," says Steven Perskie, chairman of New Jersey's Casino Control Commission. Commission officials say they may raise the fines imposed on casinos that allow customers under 21 to gamble.

9   Counselors fear that little will change until society begins to view teenage gambling with the same alarm directed at drug and alcohol abuse. "Public understanding of gambling is where our understanding of alcoholism was some 40 or 50 years ago," says psychologist Jacobs. "Unless we wake up soon to gambling's dark side, we're going to have a whole new generation lost to this addiction."

IGNORANCE IS NOT BLISS

Eric Marcus

Eric Marcus is a widely published journalist and an associate producer for
Good Morning, America. *He frequently writes about gay and lesbian life,*
as he does in this "My Turn" column from Newsweek.

Sam Nunn didn't need to hold Senate hearings to come up with his "don't ask,   1
don't tell" solution for handling gays in the military. If he'd asked me, I could have
told him this was exactly the policy some of my relatives suggested years ago when I
informed them that I planned to tell my grandmother that I was gay. They said,
"She's old, it'll kill her. You'll destroy her image of you. If she doesn't ask, why tell?"

"Don't ask, don't tell" made a lot of sense to these relatives because it sounded   2
like an easy solution. For them, it was. If I didn't say anything to my grandmother,
they wouldn't have to deal with her upset over the truth about her grandson. But
for me, "not telling" was an exhausting nightmare, because it meant withholding
everything that could possibly give me away and living in fear of being found out.
At the same time, I didn't want to cause Grandma pain by telling her I was gay, so I
was easily persuaded to continue the charade.

If I hadn't been close to my grandmother, or saw her once a year, hiding the   3
truth would have been relatively easy. But we'd had a special relationship since she
cared for me as a child when my mother was ill, and we visited often, so lying to her
was especially difficult.

I started hiding the truth from everyone in 1965, when I had my first crush.   4
That was in second grade and his name was Hugh. No one told me, but I knew I
shouldn't tell anyone about it, not even Hugh. I don't know how I knew that liking
another boy was something to hide, but I did, so I kept it a secret.

I fell in love for the first time when I was 17. It was a wondrous experience,   5
but I didn't dare tell anyone, especially my family, because telling them about Bob
would have given me away. I couldn't explain to them that for the first time in my
life I felt like a normal human being.

By the time I was an adult, I'd stopped lying to my immediate family, with the   6
exception of my grandmother, and told them that I was gay. I was a second-rate liar
so I was lucky that Grandma was the only person in my life around whom I had to
be something I wasn't. I can't imagine what it's like for gays and lesbians in the military to hide the truth from the men and women with whom they serve. The fear of
exposure must be extraordinary, especially because exposure would mean the end
of their careers. For me, the only risk was losing Grandma's love.

Hiding the truth from her grew ever more challenging in the years that fol-   7
lowed. I couldn't tell her about the man I then shared my life with. I couldn't talk
about my friends who had AIDS because she would have wondered why I knew so

many ill men. I couldn't tell her that I volunteered for a gay peer-counseling center. I couldn't talk to her about the political issues that most interested me because she would have wondered why I had such passionate feelings about gay rights. Eventually I couldn't even tell her about all of my work, because some of my writing was on gay issues. In the end, all we had left to talk about was the weather.

8   If being gay were only what I did behind closed doors, there would have been plenty of my life left over to share with my grandmother. But my life as a gay man isn't something that takes place only in the privacy of my bedroom. It affects who my friends are, whom I choose to share my life with, the work I do, the organizations I belong to, the magazines I read, where I vacation and what I talk about. I know it's the same for heterosexuals because their sexual orientation affects everything, from a choice of senior-prom date and the finger on which they wear their wedding band to the birth announcements they send and every emotion they feel.

9   So the reality of the "don't ask, don't tell" solution for dealing with my grandmother and for dealing with gays in the military means having to lie about or hide almost every aspect of your life. It's not nearly as simple as just not saying, "I'm gay."

10   After years of "protecting" my grandmother I decided it was time to stop lying. In the worst case, I figured she might reject me, although that seemed unlikely. But whatever the outcome, I could not pretend anymore. Some might think that was selfish on my part, but I'd had enough of the "don't tell" policy, which had forced me into a life of deceit. I also hoped that by telling her the truth, we could build a relationship based on honesty, a possibility that was worth the risk.

11   The actual telling was far less terrifying than all the anticipation. While my grandmother cried plenty, my family was wrong, because the truth didn't kill her. In the five years since, Grandma and I have talked a lot about the realities of my life and the lives of my gay and lesbian friends. She's read many articles and a few books, including mine. She's surprised us by how quickly she's set aside her myths and misconceptions.

12   Grandma and I are far closer than we ever were. Last fall we even spent a week together in Paris for her birthday. And these days, we have plenty to talk about, including the gays in the military issue.

13   A few months ago, Grandma traveled with me to Lafayette College, Pa., where I was invited to give a speech on the history of the gay civil-rights movement. After my talk, several students took us to dinner. As I conversed with the young women across the table from me, I overheard my grandmother talking to the student sitting next to her. She told him he was right to tell his parents he was gay, that with time and his help they would adjust. She said, "Don't underestimate their ability to change."

14   I wish Sam Nunn had called my grandmother to testify before his Senate committee. He and the other senators, as well as Defense Secretary Les Aspin and the president, could do far worse than listen to her advice.

SEX, KIDS, AND THE SLUT LOOK

Joy Overbeck

Joy Overbeck is a freelance writer living in Denver, Colorado. She was moved to write this essay for Newsweek's *"My Turn" column when angered by a look at girls' fashions.*

The other day my 10-year-old daughter and I breached the prurient wilds of the Junior Fashion Department. Nothing in what she sneeringly calls the "little kid" department seems to fit anymore. She's tall for her age and at that awkward fashion stage between Little Red Riding Hood and Amy Fisher. She patrolled the racks, hunting the preteen imperative—a pair of leg-strangling white tights culminating in several inches of white lace. Everywhere were see-through dresses made out of little-flower-print fabric, lacy leggings, transparent tops and miniature bustiers for females unlikely to own busts. Many were garments that Cher would have rejected as far too obvious.

Lace leggings? When I went to grade school, you were sent home if you wore even normal pants. The closest we got to leggings were our Pillsbury Doughboy snow pants, mummy-padding we pulled on under our dresses and clumped around in as we braved the frigid blasts of winter. Today's high-school girls have long dressed like street-corner pros; but since when did elementary school become a Frederick's of Hollywood showroom?

Grousing that her dumb clothes compromised her popularity, the offspring had herded me to fashion's outer limits. She appeared to be the only 10-year-old in the area; the rest were 14 or so, unaccompanied by their mothers. She pranced up, holding out a hanger on which dangled a crocheted skirt the size of a personals ad and a top whose deep V-neck yawned like the jaws of hell.

"Isn't this great! I want this!" she yodeled, sunshine beaming from her sweet face once more. "You're 10 years old," I said. "Shhh," she hissed, whipping her head around in frantic oh-God-did-anybody-hear mode. Then she accused me of not wanting her to grow up. She's 10 years old and the kid talks like a radio shrink.

It's not really that I want her to be a little girl forever. It's just that it would be nice if she were a child during her childhood. Instead, she's been bathed in the fantasy of bodies and beauty that marinates our entire culture. The result is an insidious form of premature sexual awakening that is stealing our kids' youth.

Meredith was 8 and we were in the car, singing along to some heartbroken musical lament on the radio, when she said, "Mom, why is everything in the world about sex?" I laughed and asked where she got that idea. But then, listening as she knowledgeably recited examples from music, movies, MTV and advertising, it hit me that she was right. The message of our popular culture for any observant 8-year-old is: *sex rules*. Otherwise, why would it deserve all this air time, all this agony and ecstasy, all this breathless attention?

7   Kids pick up on the sexual laser focus of our society, then mimic what they see as the ruling adult craze, adding their own bizarre kid twist. Recently, I read that the authors of "The Janus Report on Sexual Behavior" were shocked to find how many had sex at 10, 11 and 12. Too young to know how to handle it, kids mix sex with the brutal competitiveness they learn in the two worlds they know best: sports and the streets. Sex is grafted onto their *real* consuming passion—to be the most radical dude or dudette in their crowd. Peer pressure—what I'm seeing now in my 10-year-old's wardrobe angst—takes over. The result is competitive sex: California gangs vying for the record in number of girls bedded; teenage boys raping girls my daughter's age in a heartless sexual all-star game where all that counts is the points you rack up. In Colorado Springs, not far from where I live, gangs are demanding that kids as young as 10 have sex as a form of initiation. It's the old "chicken" game in "Rebel Without a Cause," played with young bodies instead of cars.

8   The adult reaction to all of this is outrage. But why should we be shocked? Children learn by example. Sex is omnipresent. What do we expect when we allow fashion designers to dress us, grown women, in garments so sheer that any passing stranger can see us nearly naked for the price of a casual glance?

9   Or look at Madonna on the cover of *Vanity Fair* wearing only a pink inner tube and hair done up in cutesy '50s pigtails. Here's a 34-year-old heroine to little girls— the core of her fandom is about 14—posing as innocent jailbait. Inside, she romps on a playground in baby-doll nighties, toying with big, stuffed duckies and polar bears. This is a blatant child molester's fantasy-in-the-flesh. Does kiddie porn encourage sex crimes against children? Who cares!

10   Rudimentary good sense must tell us that sexualizing children not only sullies their early years, but also exposes them to real danger from human predators. What our culture needs is a little reality check: in an era when sexual violence against children is heartbreakingly common—a recent study estimates that about one quarter of women have been victims of childhood sexual abuse—anything that eroticizes our children is irresponsible, at best.

11   It's up to adults to explode the kids-are-sexy equation. Our kids need us to give them their childhood back. But this summer, the eroticization of our girl children proceeds apace. The crop tops! The tight little spandex shorts! (Our moms wore them under their clothes and called them girdles.) My daughter's right, everybody struts her stuff. I've seen 5-year-old Pretty Babies.

12   As for me, I don't care anymore if my kid has a hissy fit in the junior department. She's not wearing the Slut Look. Let her rant that I'm a hopelessly pathological mom who wants to keep her in pacifiers and pinafores forever. Let her do amateur psychoanalysis on me in public until my ears fry—I've shaken the guilt heebie-jeebies and drawn the line. So you can put those white lace spandex leggings back on the rack, young lady.

Index

Note: Words in italics denote word usage.

535

"Honey, I Warped the Kids,"
 Cannon, Carl M., 513–515
Hopefully, 408
"How to Write a Personal Letter,"
 Keillor, Garrison, 470–471
Human voice, writing in, 279–281
Hung/hanged, 408–409
Hyphens, 351, 362–363

Ideas
 arranging, for classification and
  division writing, 85
 for cause-and-effect analysis,
  128–130
 for comparison writing, 112–113
 for contrast writing, 112–113
 development, in paragraphs,
  235–237
 explanation of, example writing
  for, 61
 main, in précis, 175–176
 unified, in paragraph, 230
Idioms, 293, 363–364
"Ignorance Is Not Bliss," Marcus,
 Eric, 531–532
Illusion/allusion, 398
Illustrations. *See also* Example writing
 for concept clarification, 61–62
 for explanation of ideas, 61
 in fleshing out paragraph,
  236–237
 function of, 60
 to support claims/judgments,
  62–63
 thinking critical about, 60–63
Imaginative description, 32–36
Imply/infer/deduce, 404–405
Incubating, in exploration of topic
 material, 19
Indentation, hanging, 192, 219
Independent clauses, 253, 309, 340
 changing to dependent clauses,
  387–388
 separation of, 344–345
Indirect object, 306
Induction, in introduction to
 narrative essay, 41
Inductive organization, for
 persuasive writing, 145
Infer/deduce/imply, 404–405
Infinitive phrase, 255, 307
Informal tone, for process writing,
 53
Informal usage, 396
Informal writing, 286–287, 288
Information

in introduction to persuasive
 writing, 149–150
 as purpose, 5–6
Informative research paper, topics
 for, 167
Infotrac, 169–170
"In Groups, We Shrink from
 Loner's Heroics," Tavris,
 Carol, 68–70
In/into/in to/in two, 409
Insert mode, for word processor,
 426
Interjection. *See* Exclamation point
Interrupters, 339, 351
Interviewing, 18
Intransitive verbs, 303
Introductions
 for cause-and-effect analysis,
  126–127
 for classification writing, 89–91
 for comparison writing, 106–108
 composition of, 243–247
 for contrast writing, 106–108
 for definition writing, 74–75
 for division writing, 89–91
 for narrative essay, 41–42
 for persuasive writing, 149–151
 for process writing, 56
 of quotations, 181–182
Introductory words, comma usage
 for, 341
Invention, 13–19
 asking questions for, 15
 brainstorming for, 15–17
 freewriting for, 17–18
 incubating for, 19
 interviewing for, 18
 journal keeping for, 14–15
 posing problems for, 15
 scanning and reading for, 18–19
Ironic tone, 289
Irregardless, 409
Issue dodging, 366–367
Is when/is where, 409
It, as expletive, 358
Italics, 392–393
Its/it's, 410

Jargon, 283, 353
Job application letter
 general principles for, 444–445
 opening for, 445–446
 presenting qualifications in, 446
 writing to specific person, 445
Journal
 article, from electronic source

in reference list, 223
 in Works Cited list, 199
 articles in reference list, 222, 223
 keeping, 13–15
 Works Cited list for, 196
Judgments, supporting, example
 writing for, 62–63

Keillor, Garrison, "How to Write a
 Personal Letter," 470–471
Kimmel, Michael S., and Martin P.
 Levine, "AIDS: A Real Man's
 Disease," 77–79
Kind of/sort of, 410
King, Martin Luther, Jr., "Three
 Types of Resistance to
 Oppression," 487–489
Krents, Harold, "Darkness at
 Noon," 461–462

Lamott, Anne, "Shitty First
 Drafts," 478–481
Language
 colloquial, 284, 287, 288, 354,
  396
 formal, 354, 396
 gender-inclusive, 296–301
 unclear, avoidance of, 281–283
Latter/former, 407
Lay/lie, 410–411
Lead/led, 411
Leave/let, 411
Lecture, in Works Cited list, 198
Lecture notes, 438–439
Led/lead, 411
Lend/loan, 411
Length of essay, 83
Less/fewer, 406
Let/leave, 411
Letters
 job application, 444–446
 published, in Works Cited list, 197
 unpublished, in Works Cited list,
  197
Levine, Martin P., and Michael S.
 Kimmel, "AIDS: A Real
 Man's Disease," 77–79
Liable/likely, 412
Library use, for research paper,
 168–171
Lie/lay, 410–411
Like/as, 411–412
Likely/liable, 412
Limits of reason, recognition of,
 141
Line of reasoning, 138